A Rendezvous Reader

Alfred Jacob Miller, *The Thirsty Trapper* (37.1940.26).

A Rendezvous Reader

Tall, Tangled, and, True Tales of the Mountain Men, 1805-1850

Edited by

James H. Maguire
Peter Wild
and Donald A. Barclay

University of Utah Press
Salt Lake City

Library of Congress Cataloging-in-Publication Data

A rendezvous reader : tall, tangled, and true tales of the mountain
   men, 1805–1850 / edited by James H. Maguire, Peter Wild, and Donald
   A. Barclay.
      p.   cm.
   Includes bibliographical references (p.   ) and index.
   ISBN 0-87480-538-4 (alk. paper).—ISBN 0-87480-539-2 (pbk. :
alk. paper)
    1. Frontier and pioneer life—West (U.S.)—Sources.   2. Fur trade—
West (U.S.)—History—19th century—Sources.   3. West (U.S.)—
History—To 1848—Sources.   4. West (U.S.)—History—1848–1860—
Sources.   5. Fur traders—West (U.S.)—Biography.   6. Trappers—
West (U.S.)—Biography.   7. Fur traders' writings, American.
8. Trappers' writings, American.   I. Maguire, James H.   II. Wild,
Peter, 1940–   .   III.   Barclay, Donald A.
F596.R77   1997
978'.02—dc21   97-10969

Contents

Section III
Trappers and Their Trade

Section IV
Mountain Women

Section V
Famous Trappers

Section VI
Rendezvous

Section VII
Critics of the Fur Trade

Section VIII
Indians

Section IX
Animals

Section XII
Farewell to the Mountain-Man Life

Alfred Jacob Miller, *Trappers* (37.1940.29).

Acknowledgments

I would like to thank the Boise State University Library, my Boise State University English Department colleagues, my wife (Betty), my children (Emily and Stephen), my mother-in-law (Kathleen Keller), and my mother (Margaret Maguire).

—James H. Maguire

I want to thank my colleagues at New Mexico State University Library, Ellen Drewes of Las Cruces, my parents and sisters in Idaho, and especially my understanding wife, Darcie.

—Donald A. Barclay

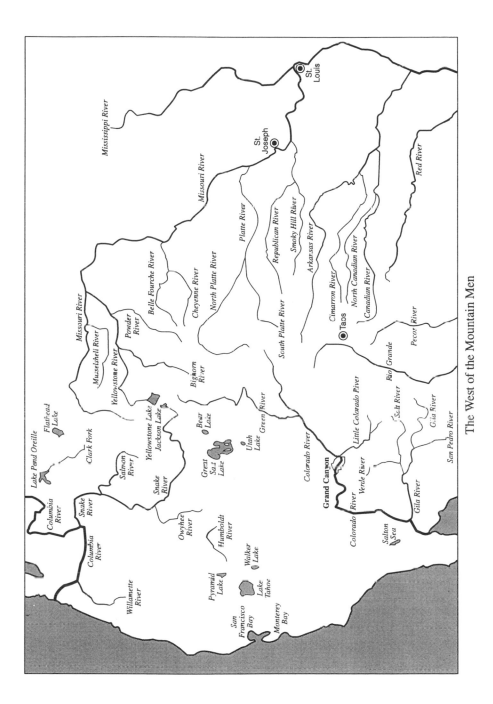

The West of the Mountain Men

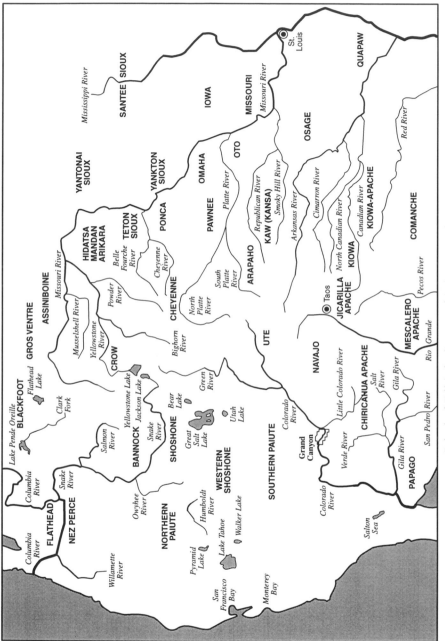

Principal Tribes in Contact with the Mountain Men

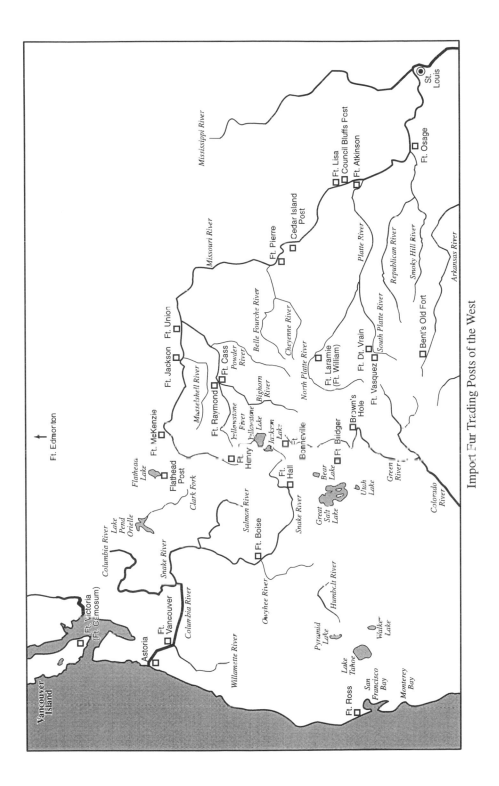

Import Fur Trading Posts of the West

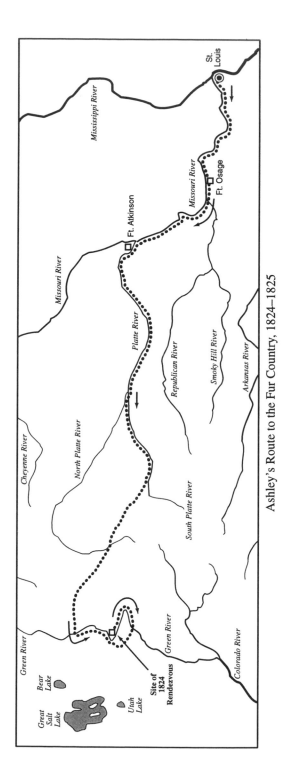

Ashley's Route to the Fur Country, 1824–1825

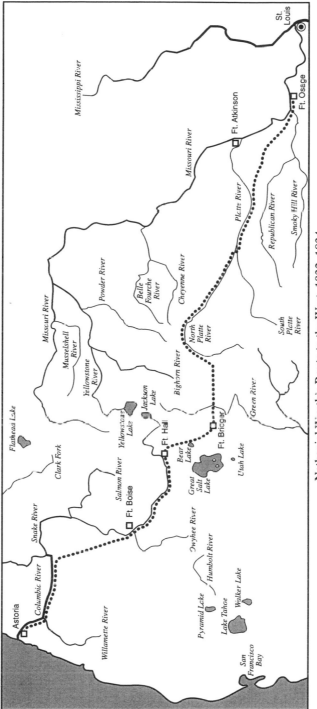

Nathaniel Wyeth's Route to the West, 1832–1834

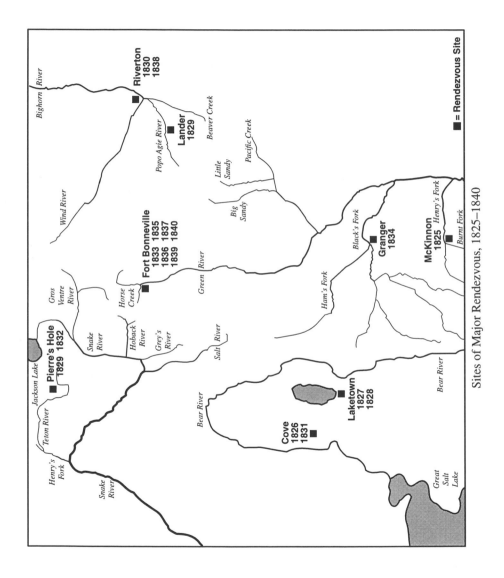

Sites of Major Rendezvous, 1825–1840

■ = Rendezvous Site

Riverton
1830
1838

Lander
1829

Fort Bonneville
1833 1835
1836 1837
1839 1840

Granger
1834

McKinnon
1825

Pierre's Hole
1829 1832

Laketown
1827
1828

Cove
1826 1831

Bighorn River

Beaver Creek

Popo Agie River

Pacific Creek

Little
Sandy

Wind River

Big
Sandy

Black's Fork

Henry's Fork

Burnt Fork

Green River

Gros
Ventre
River

Horse
Creek

Ham's Fork

Snake
River

Hoback
River

Grey's
River

Salt River

Jackson Lake

Teton River

Henry's
Fork

Snake
River

Bear River

Bear River

Great
Salt
Lake

Introduction

"Hurraw for us beavers!"
—John L. Hatcher, mountain man

The early plans for Mount Rushmore called for mountain men. Called for blasting heroic likenesses of Kit Carson, Jim Bridger, and John Colter into the solid mountain granite of South Dakota.

Hurraw for us beavers, indeed.

After (or perhaps before) you have read the narratives contained in this book, you might find yourself "hurrawing" because the boosters of Mount Rushmore shelved their original plans. After all, the mountain men's own narratives show that many of them were, at times, awfully brutal to deserve immortalization on the side of a mountain. Brutal to the environment, to the natives, and to each other.

But that is only one side of their story. And when you finish this book, you may find yourself thinking that, if any human face deserves to be on Mount Rushmore, it should be the face of a mountain man. For their narratives, spun from the most unique, most American experiences of a nation moving westward, tell of things great as well as brutal: A trapper returns from the dead. Hunters feast on buffalo intestines served on a dirty blanket. A missionary woman is astounded by the violence and vulgarity of the trappers' rendezvous.

The most famous mountain man of all, Kit Carson, is astounded in a different way: While attempting the rescue of a tortured woman, Carson finds himself described in the torn pages of a dime novel. His legend is being written even as he lives out the events that create it.

The writers of the narratives collected in this volume are a mixed lot. Trappers, flimflammers, adventuring European nobles, upward-gazing eastern missionaries, and just plain rascals. Some are hacks who never unsheathed a Green River knife, heated scribblers trying to transport themselves and their readers from crowded eastern cities into a world of happy mountain illusions. Others are more analytical sorts,

1

cooler heads who told (mostly) the truth—a truth, we might add, often so fascinating it easily stands on its own.

In bringing together these writers, we have created a book that is neither a history nor a treatise on the fur trade. Rather, it is a celebration of facts and fantasies so tightly interwoven that even the most dedicated scholars of the mountain man can't always distinguish the two. For our purposes, the distinction between fact and fantasy is unimportant. Simply turn to the first selection, a fabulous account of a trapper's visit to a "putrified forest," and allow yourself to be launched into a swirling world of delights. If at any time you feel you must try to unweave the facts from the fantasy, the bibliography includes many first-rate histories of the fur trade.

Of these histories, the general reader cannot do better than Bernard De Voto's *Across the Wide Missouri* (1947). Besides masterfully telling the story of the fur trade, *Across the Wide Missouri* includes De Voto's "Chronology of the Mountain Fur Trade." This listing of dates and events is helpful for understanding the economic rhythms of the mountain fur trade, which, like any modern business, was marked by the creation of new companies; the merger, sale, or bankruptcy of old ones; and the activities of individual entrepreneurs (commonly known in the fur trade as "free trappers").

To summarize De Voto's chronology, events begin with the Lewis and Clark expedition, which from 1804 to 1806 crossed the West to the mouth of the Columbia and then returned. Even as the expedition approached the settlements in Missouri, one of the men with Lewis and Clark, John Colter, headed back to the mountains with a party of trappers. A year later, in 1807, Manuel Lisa hired Colter and others to build a fur-trading fort at the mouth of the Big Horn River. In 1809 Lisa formed a partnership with William Clark, Pierre Chouteau, Sr., and Andrew Henry to found the Missouri Fur Company. They soon encountered competition from John Jacob Astor's Pacific Fur Company, which sent expeditions overland and by sea in 1811. Additional competition came from two British concerns: the Hudson's Bay Company and the Northwest Company, which were forced by a command of Parliament to merge in 1821.

In 1822 General William H. Ashley formed a partnership with Andrew Henry and advertised for a party of men to build a post at the mouth of the Yellowstone River. During the next several years, parts of the West were closed by Indian resistance, but determined trappers such as Jedediah Smith, Jim Bridger, and Etienne Provost explored the Snake River country and the region around the Great Salt Lake. Henry retired from the partnership in 1824, but Ashley held on. After pioneering the Platte route to the mountains and holding the first mountain rendezvous (an annual gathering of traders and trappers) on Henry's Fork of the Green River in 1825, Ashley sold the company to Jedediah Smith, Dave Jackson, and William Sublette in 1826. During the next three years, while Jedediah Smith crossed the Great Basin to California and, on a second trip, went into Oregon, the Astor trust grew to include the American Fur Company and the Columbia Fur Company. In 1830 Smith, Jackson, and Sublette sold their firm to employees, who renamed it the Rocky Mountain Fur Company. A year later, after Jedediah Smith had entered the Santa Fe trade, he was killed in a fight with Comanches at the Cimarron Crossing.

In 1832, Captain Benjamin Bonneville and Nathaniel J. Wyeth journeyed west, and Bonneville constructed a fort in western Wyoming which he named after himself. During that same year, the artist George Catlin ascended the Missouri. The following year, Captain William Drummond Stewart, a British nobleman, went west; he would make a second visit in 1837, this time accompanied by the American artist Alfred Jacob Miller. Wyeth had gone back east in 1833; when he returned to the West in 1834, he brought with him a Methodist missionary party and built Fort Hall in what is now southern Idaho. Economic evolution continued at a dizzying pace, as exemplified in De Voto's terse summary of just one business event of 1834:

> The RMF Company dissolves, being succeeded by a partnership of Fitzpatrick, Bridger, and Milton Sublette. The partnership gives up the old alliance with Sublette & Campbell and makes a contract with the American Fur Company and is presently absorbed. (De Voto 1947, 389)

In 1835 and 1836, parties of missionaries led by Samuel Parker, Marcus Whitman, and Henry Spalding passed through the fur country and witnessed the mountain rendezvous. Had they passed through a mere seven years later, there would have been no rendezvous to witness. So brief was the reign of the mountain man.

History can be as preposterous as chronologies can be exact. Behind the bright image of the hard-living, hard-drinking mountain man seizing *joie* from the day as best he could in the vastness of the Rocky Mountains—before a grizzly bear mauled him or an Indian lifted his scalp—lay one simple, embarrassing fact: a fashion fad. During the first part of the nineteenth century, the fad for beaver hats swept up every civilized, status-conscious gentleman in the cities of Europe and the United States. This fad created a demand for beaver that sent men trekking across the North American continent, risking life and limb to tap the living treasure trove of skins from the fat, broad-tailed rodents populating the pristine Rocky Mountains.

It took fewer than thirty years to trap out the treasure. The beaver's numbers were so depleted by the 1840s that the few left hardly were worth pursuing. In 1843—one year after the last rendezvous—the first wagons began passing over the Oregon Trail. In 1846 the infamous Donner party headed west; and the Mormons followed in 1847. After gold was discovered in California in 1848, it seemed like half the world was flooding into the West. By the 1850s a change in fashion from beaver hats to silk top hats led to a sharp decline in demand for what few pelts could still be trapped. Old trappers became scouts for government expeditions, for the army, and for wagon trains headed west. After the wagon trains reached Oregon or California, the trapper-scouts often stayed on and settled into respectability. Some trapping continued even after the Civil War, but by the time the first transcontinental railroad was completed in 1869 conditions had changed so much that the mountain-man way of life was kept alive only by hermits, eccentrics, and, in our day, history buffs who try to relive the past in order to understand it.

The boom-and-bust fate of the mountain man would be played out time and again in the West, most notably by the cowboy, the miner, and the logger. Yet between the rock of diminishing resources and the hard place of dependence on the whims of eastern markets, the mountain men lived out one of the most chromatic periods of American history. True, it involved only a few players—a handful, really, in relative terms. But those few led lives colorfully intense, spinning a whole mythology that continues to haunt far more civilized (and perhaps deprived) people.

We say "deprived" because to be young and full of hope, excitement whetted by dangers in the midst of natural abundance, is to live with a keen edge to one's soul. That's not to say that life in the mountains was easy. Want to catch a beaver? Then be prepared to spend hours wading in the freezing discomfort of gelid streams, ears alert for the sound of an enemy. Suffer a flesh wound? Cauterize it with a gun barrel heated red-hot. Run out of food during a long desert trek to better beaver grounds? Eat your moccasins. Unable to find water for day after bedeviling day? Sit down and die.

And to look at the situation in labor/management terms, many trappers were horribly exploited. Sure, some lived free and easy lives, but others owed their souls to the company store. That is, once a year they gathered at a foreordained place in the mountains to turn over their pelts to their employers. In return they got such necessities as powder and shot—and a line of credit that they often boozed and whored away in a few weeks of blazing debauchery. Whereupon the mountain man crawled back into the wilderness, head throbbing, to spend the next year working off his debt with savored memories as his companion and the glow of the next rendezvous twelve months hence the luring anticipation of his future. If, in the meantime, he wasn't shot, axed, trampled, frozen, drowned, or ripped apart to gratify some grizzly bear's daily protein quota. It was hard, hard going.

Yet consider the alternatives. In the first half of the nineteenth century people didn't have to worry much about "career choices." They didn't have many. If a mountain man had not been slithering through the willows on his belly while Blackfoot warriors sought his life as he sought theirs, he might be lugging stones day after day across some dreary New England field while his wife grew hardened by drudgery and his children died of diphtheria. Or he could have ended up in the *civilized* end of the fur business, working a seasonal job in some unwholesome hat manufactory where he risked the twin occupational menaces of consumption and mercury poisoning. As an alternative, those buffalo hump ribs roasting over a campfire while the stars swirled gaily above were the epitome of deliciousness.

In the pampered twentieth century, we cannot hope to recreate that deliciousness, only attempt to understand it. And if one way of understanding the past is to listen to the stories told by those who lived it, then we hope that the narratives that follow will give you that kind of understanding. Although many of the narratives contain elements of history, and although we have organized them into topical categories for the benefit of the historically minded, it is our intent to convey the *literary* experience of the fur trade rather than the historical experience. Because we want you to enjoy great storytelling with the fewest possible distractions, you will find each narrative accompanied by the briefest possible introduction. If you find your appetite whetted by what you read here, we hope that you will read some of the full narratives we have sampled to compile this anthology. (All the narratives we sampled are cited in full in the bibliography.)

More importantly, if we are the stories we tell—and if we tell the stories of those who came before us in the places where we live—then some part of us can assume the identity created by telling the tales of the mountain men. We hope that in reading these stories you will become part of them, will go beyond both the romance and the reality to discover the voices of the mountain men themselves as they told their stories around the campfires of a West that was vanishing fast, vanishing almost before the words they used to describe it were out of their mouths.

Note to the Reader: The selections used in this book have been gathered from a variety of sources. The editors have chosen to present them as they were published, including retaining original errors and inconsistencies in spelling, grammar, punctuation, and other matters. Editorial comments in the original printed form have been included and are presented here as they were found—that is, with square brackets or parentheses according to the original editors' decisions. In some cases, what may well be typographic errors also have been retained. The only editorial matter included within the texts for this book by this book's editors is identified by braces—{ }.

Tall Tales, Amazing Scenes, and Trickery of the Fur Trade

America's frontier provided the setting for much literature; and one of the richest and most American of those sources of literature was frontier humor. In the first half of the nineteenth century, the region known as the Old Southwest (Georgia, Mississippi, Alabama, Tennessee, Missouri, Louisiana, and Arkansas) gained considerable notoriety for its humor. M. Thomas Inge in *The Frontier Humorists* (1975) has identified the characteristics of this frontier humor: It is "masculine." It has elements of cruelty and scatology as well as a "streak of ribaldry of a frankness and outspokenness unmatched in the nineteenth century (except perhaps for Twain's *1601*)" (5). "Deserving of equal stress," Inge adds, "are its vitality, sturdy individualism, high spirits, and love of fun." Inge's description also fits the humor of the mountain men.

Like the Southern raconteurs (whose tales can be sampled in Hennig Cohen's anthology *Humor of the Old Southwest*), the mountain men used language that is earthy and racist. And like most occupational groups, they created their own jargon. Even the seemingly familiar words they used often have connotations that differ from those found in other regions. To learn more about this peculiar patois, read Richard C. Poulsen's *The Mountain Man Vernacular* (1985).

The trappers developed their jargon around the campfire, when there was little to do but tell stories. Some of them became master storytellers with national reputations. Jim Bridger's prowess as a humorous raconteur brought him considerable notice in the newspapers and books of his day, a body of writing summarized in Walter Blair

7

and Hamlin Hill, *America's Humor: From Poor Richard to Doonesbury* (1978).

Even if most mountain men never attained the fame that Bridger achieved as a storyteller, their narratives generally met with a favorable public reception. Still, we have to remember that it's not always easy to tell which mountain-man tales are true, which are embellished, which are stretched far beyond the facts, and which had their origin entirely in the teller's imagination. Some mountain men loved to play tricks on their comrades, on greenhorns, and on Indians, and telling tall tales is, simply, a kind of trick. Moreover, looking back on incidents such as battles between trappers and Indians, what was "true" probably depended on the teller's point of view and what he heard from others at the scene. Nor was there any one way to describe the western landscape, its strange wonders and its teeming wildlife. To a reader in the Boston or Philadelphia of the 1830s, any description of a mirage or a geyser or a place like the Grand Canyon might have seemed like a tall tale. A buffalo stampede or a grizzly bear attack needed no embellishment to sound almost preternatural. Although it's true, as Blair and other scholars have pointed out, that American humor, including that of the mountain men, has European antecedents, the mountain men and the West they roamed put a very distinctive gloss on the tales they told, humorous and otherwise.

1. The "Putrified Forest" of Black Harris

from George Frederick Ruxton, *Life in the Far West*

Step into a St. Louis restaurant in the 1830s and listen to the following conversation between a fashionable lady and a mountain man named Moses Harris (d. 1849), known to his fur-trapping companions as "Black Harris" because of his dark complexion, not because he was African American. One of his biographers, Jerome Peltier, thinks Harris was probably a member of William H. Ashley's first fur-trading journey up the Missouri in 1822. Harris definitely accompanied Ashley on his 1823 expedition. But Peltier says that "Black Harris was an enigma. Nothing is known of his beginnings, and various periods and phases of his life are mysteries." To see Peltier's full biographical sketch of Harris and to read detailed biographical accounts of other fur trappers and traders, consult the multivolume series *The Mountain Men and the Fur Trade of the Far West*, edited by LeRoy Reuben Hafen.

"Well, Mister Harris, I hear you're a great travler."

"Travler, marm," says Black Harris, "this niggur's no travler; I ar' a trapper, marm, a mountain-man, wagh!"

"Well, Mister Harris, trappers are great travlers, and you goes over a sight of ground in your perishinations, I'll be bound to say."

"A sight, marm, this coon's gone over, if that's the way your 'stick floats.' I've trapped beaver on Platte and Arkansa, and away up on Missoura and Yaller Stone; I've trapped on Columbia, on Lewis Fork, and Green River; I've trapped, marm, on Grand River and the Heely (Gila). I've fout the 'Blackfoot' (and d—d bad Injuns they arc); I've 'raised the hair' of more *than one* Apach, and made a Rapaho 'come' afore now; I've trapped in heav'n, in airth, and h—, and scalp my old head, marm, but I've seen a putrefied forest."

"La, Mister Harris, a what?"

"A putrefied forest, marm, as sure as my rifle's got hindsights, and *she* shoots center. I was out on the Black Hills, Bill Sublette knows the time—the year it rained fire—and everybody knows when that was. If thar wasn't cold doin's about that time, this child wouldn't say so. The snow was about fifty foot deep, and the bufler lay dead on the ground like bees after a beein'; not whar we was tho', for *thar* was no bufler, and no meat, and me and my band had been livin' on our mocassins (leastwise the parflesh), for six weeks; and poor doin's that feedin' is, marm, as you'll never know. One day we crossed a 'canon' and over a 'divide,' and got into a periara, whar was green grass, and green trees, and green leaves on the trees, and birds singing in the green leaves, and this in Febrary, wagh! Our animals was like to die when they see the green grass, and we all sung out, 'hurraw for summer doin's.'

" 'Hyar goes for meat,' says I, and I jest ups old Ginger at one of them singing birds, and down come the crittur elegant; its darned head spinning away from the body, but never stops singing, and when I takes up the meat, I finds it stone, wagh!

" 'Hyar's damp powder and no fire to dry it,' I says quite skeared.

" 'Fire be dogged,' says old Rube. 'Hyar's a hos as'll make fire come'; and with that he takes his axe and lets drive at a cottonwood. Schr-u-k—goes the axe agin the tree, and out comes a bit of the blade as big as my hand. We looks at the animals, and thar they stood shaking over the grass, which I'm doggone if it wasn't stone, too. Young Sublette comes up, and he'd been clerking down to the fort on Platte, so he know'd something. He looks and looks, and scrapes the tree with his butcher knife, and snaps the grass like pipe stems, and breaks the leaves a snappin' like Californy shells.

" 'What's all this, boy?' I asks.

" 'Putrefactions,' says he, looking smart, 'putrefactions, or I'm a niggur.' "

"La, Mister Harris," says the lady; "putrefactions, why, did the leaves, and the trees, and the grass smell badly?"

"Smell badly, marm," says Black Harris, "would a skunk stink if he was froze to stone? No, marm, this child didn't know what putrefactions was, and young Sublette's varsion wouldn't 'shine' nohow, so I chips a piece out of a tree and puts it in my trap-sack, and carries it in safe to Laramie. Well, old Captain Stewart (a clever man was that, though he was an Englishman), he comes along next spring, and a Dutch doctor chap was along too. I shows him the piece I chipped out of the tree, and he called it a putrefaction too; and so, marm, if that wasn't a putrefied peraira, what was it? For this hos doesn't know, and *he* knows 'fat cow' from 'poor bull,' anyhow."

2. A Mirage Near the Platte River

from William Marshall Anderson, *Rocky Mountain Journals of William Marshall Anderson*

Thanks to the western landscape and climate, mountain men sometimes saw strange sights. A mirage like the one that William Marshall Anderson (1807–1881) and his companions saw in 1834 can, however, easily be explained by reference to a physics textbook. The light is refracted by air having steep temperature gradients. Yet, as R. L. Gregory points out in "The Confounded Eye," such an illusion of perception is more than a mere error. Gregory says that such errors "may be experiences in their own right. They can illuminate reality. It is this power of illusion to illuminate which the artist somehow commands." In Anderson's diary, which historians Dale L. Morgan and Eleanor Towles Harris say is "one of the earliest documents of its kind," the description of the mirage makes our "unpoetic plains" mysterious and poetic.

May 22, 1834— We compute our march today at thirty miles. We shall probably cross the south fork of the Platte in the morning. Sublette thinks from the almost total disappearance of game, that Indians are near. Every man is now wide-awake and owl-like, his head and eyes turn in every direction. I am in luck. I have missed two buffalo today.

Oh, the mirage! the mirage! the waters of the plain! What a sight for a thirst-dying man. A terrible curse, and terribly expressed.

> May he at last, with lips of flame,
> On the parched desert, thirsting die;
> While lakes that shone in mockery nigh,
> Are fading off, untouched, untasted.

This was looked upon by stay-at-home philosophers, as the fancy touch of that [a] child of genius, but "truth is strange, stranger than fiction," even on the plains of America. Here, in our unpoetic deserts, the traveler sees large, clear and inviting lakes—rivers and rivulets, flashing and sparkling in the sun—beautiful groves, fern-covered rocks, and mountain shadows making the land cool for many a mile. I would not, for the wealth of Potosi, have one of these mock, delusive streams, spread out before me, if burning with fever and longing for a cool draught of good, cool water. After frequently admiring, and sometimes almost fearing this "Sah-rab," as it is called in Persia, I had an opportunity yesterday of comparing it with the waters of the Platte. Just before us, and at right angles with the river, ran a stream of almost equal magnitude, but much more clear and water-like than the muddy Platte. "Vive la bagatelle!" Before a thousand years roll by, I may feel no pride in these, my nightly scribblings. Perhaps, at some future time, I may turn up my wise, experienced nose, and say, what frothy nonsense! It may seem, and be, in fact, trifling; but whether trifling or not, it is pleasant trifling, so here goes "for some of that same."

3. Bighorn Horns Stuck High in the Pines

from Warren Angus Ferris, *Life in the Rocky Mountains*

In addition to mirages, mountain men saw unusual landmarks, some venerated by the Indians. One such unusual sight is described by Warren Angus Ferris (1810–1873) in the journal he kept to record his Rocky Mountain adventures from 1830 to 1836. Soon after his return to the east, he prepared the journal for publication, but the Philadelphia firm to which he sent the manuscript lacked the money to publish it at that time. Not until 1842 did episodes from Ferris's journal appear in the *Western Literary Messenger*, a periodical edited by Ferris's brother Charles.

On the east side of Bitter Root river, there is a singular curiosity, that I had not before observed, because it is situated under some rocky bluffs, almost impassable to horsemen, the proper road being on the west side of the river: it is the horn of an animal, called by hunters, the "Big-horn," but denominated by naturalists "Rocky Mountain Sheep;" of a very large size, of which two-thirds of its length from the upper end, is entombed in the body of a pine tree, so perfectly solid and firmly, that a heavy blow of an axe did not start it from its place.—The tree is unusually large and flourishing, and the horn in it some seven feet above the ground. It appears to be very ancient, and is gradually decomposing on the outside, which has assumed a reddish cast. The date of its existence has been lost in the lapse of ages, and even tradition is silent as to the origin of its remarkable situation. The oldest of Indians can give no other account of it, than that it was there precisely as at present, before their father's great grandfathers were born. They seldom pass it without leaving some trifling offering, as beads, shells, or other ornaments—tokens of their superstitious veneration for it. As high as they can reach, the bark of the tree is decorated with their trifles.

4. Drinking from a Dead Buffalo

from John Kirk Townsend, *Narrative of a Journey across the Rocky Mountains to the Columbia River*

Mountain men taxed the credulity of easterners not only with descriptions of unusual sights but also with accounts of survival under extreme conditions. John Kirk Townsend (1809–1851), a naturalist who accompanied Nathaniel J. Wyeth's 1834 expedition to the West, found one method of survival especially nauseating. Fortunately, Townsend survived the episode to announce his wildlife discoveries, including Townsend's warbler.

We were all suffering from excessive thirst, and so intolerable had it at length become, that Mr. Lee and myself proposed a gallop over to the Platte river, in order to appease it; but Richardson advised us not to, as he had just thought of a means of relieving us, which he immediately proceeded to put in practice. He tumbled our mangled buffalo over upon his side, and with his knife opened the body, so as to expose to view the great stomach, and still crawling and twisting entrails. The good missionary and myself stood gaping with astonishment, and no little loathing, as we saw our hunter plunge his knife into the distended paunch, from which gushed the green and gelatinous juices, and then insinuate his tin pan into the opening, and by depressing its edge, strain off the water which was mingled with its contents.

Richardson always valued himself upon his politeness, and the cup was therefore first offered to Mr. Lee and myself, but it is almost needless to say that we declined the proffer, and our features probably expressed the strong disgust which we felt, for our companion laughed heartily before he applied the cup to his own mouth. He then drank it to the dregs, smacking his lips, and drawing a long breath after it, with the satisfaction of a man taking his wine after dinner. Sansbury, the other hunter, was not slow in following the example set before him, and we, the audience, turned our backs upon the actors.

Before we left the spot, however, Richardson induced me to taste the blood which was still fluid in the heart, and immediately as it touched my lips, my burning thirst, aggravated by hunger, (for I had eaten nothing that day,) got the better of my abhorrence; I plunged my head into the reeking ventricles, and drank until forced to stop for breath. I felt somewhat ashamed of assimilating myself so nearly to the brutes, and turned my ensanguined countenance towards the missionary who stood by, but I saw no approval there: the good man was evidently attempting to control his risibility, and so I smiled to put him in countenance; the roar could no longer be restrained, and the missionary laughed until the tears rolled down his cheeks. I did not think, until afterwards, of the horrible ghastliness which must have characterized my smile at that particular moment.

When we arrived at the camp in the evening, and I enjoyed the luxury of a hearty draft of water, the effect upon my stomach was that of a powerful emetic: the blood was violently ejected without nausea, and I felt heartily glad to be rid of the disgusting encumbrance. I never drank blood from that day.

5. Joseph Walker's Tale of "Food" in Skin Bags

from John C. Frémont, *Report of the Exploring Expedition to the Rocky Mountains in the Years 1843–'44*

In 1842, the U. S. government sent west an exploring party that mapped the Oregon Trail through South Pass in Wyoming. John Charles Frémont (1813–1890) commanded the expedition, a post he gained with the help of his father-in-law, Senator Thomas Hart Benton of Missouri. Frémont employed some mountain men as guides and encountered others on the trail, and his report, published in 1843, includes some of their stories, among them Joseph Reddeford Walker's (1798–1876) tale of some strange food. For detailed studies of Frémont and Walker see Andrew F. Rolle's *John Charles Frémont: Character as Destiny* (1991), and Bil Gilbert's *Westering Man: The Life of Joseph Walker* (1983).

It was a handsome broad beach where we landed, behind which the hill, into which the island was gathered, rose somewhat abruptly; and a point of rock at one end enclosed it in a sheltering way; and as there was an abundance of driftwood along the shore, it offered us a pleasant encampment. We did not suffer our fragile boat to touch the sharp rocks; but, getting overboard, discharged the baggage, and, lifting it gently out of the water, carried it to the upper part of the beach, which was composed of very small fragments of rock.

Among the successive banks of the beach, formed by the action of the waves, our attention, as we approached the island, had been attracted by one 10 to 20 feet in breath, of a dark-brown color. Being more closely examined, this was found to be composed, to the depth of seven or eight, and twelve inches, entirely of the *larvae* of insects, or, in common language, of the skins of worms, about the size of a grain of oats, which had been washed up by the waters of the lake.

Alluding to this subject some months afterwards, when travelling through a more southern portion of this region, in company with Mr. Joseph Walker, an old hunter, I was informed by him, that, wandering with a party of men in a mountain country east of the great Californian range, he surprised a party of several Indian families encamped near a small salt lake, who abandoned their lodges at his approach, leaving everything behind them. Being in a starving condition, they were delighted to find in the abandoned lodges a number of skin bags, containing a quantity of what appeared to be fish, dried and pounded. On this they made a hearty supper; and were gathering around an abundant breakfast the next morning, when Mr. Walker discovered that it was with these, or a similar worm, that the bags had been filled. The stomachs of the stout trappers were not proof against their prejudices, and the repulsive food was suddenly rejected. Mr. Walker had further opportunities of seeing these worms used as an article of food; and I am inclined to think they are the same as those we saw, and appear to be a product of the salt lakes. It may be well to recall to your mind that

Mr. Walker was associated with Captain Bonneville in his expedition to the Rocky mountains; and has since that time remained in the country, generally residing in some one of the Snake villages, when not engaged in one of his numerous trapping expeditions, in which he is celebrated as one of the best and bravest leaders who have ever been in the country.

6. Red-Ant Bread

from Howard L. Conard, *"Uncle Dick" Wootton*

In matters of eating, other trappers experienced culinary culture shock remarkably similar to that of Joseph Walker and his party. Richens Lacy Wootton (1816–1893) describes just such an experience. Known as "Uncle Dick," Wootton came out west at the age of twenty and went to work for Charles Bent and Ceran St. Vrain's fur company. In 1838 he joined a party of older trappers who took him on a two-year hunt that covered much of the West, including parts of the Colorado River area. His later adventures included action in suppressing the Taos Rebellion of 1847, not to mention his construction (in 1866) and management (from 1866 until 1879) of a toll road over Raton Pass.

This reminds me of an amusing thing which happened when I was trapping on the Colorado River. There was a Yuma village near our camp, and one night some of the trappers went into the village and brought back with them, what they thought was some kind of bread. Without noticing it very particularly, they commenced eating, but it was not long before they discovered, that if they were eating bread, it was a different kind from any they had ever tasted before.

They made an examination of the stuff then, and found that what they had supposed were biscuits, were small cakes made of red ants, crushed together and dried in the sun.

7. A Band of Skunks Drives Off Some Trappers

from William Marshall Anderson, *Rocky Mountain Journals of William Marshall Anderson*

As we learn from Percy G. Adams's *Travelers and Travel Liars* (1962), his *Travel Literature and the Evolution of the Novel* (1983), and from Bruce Greenfield's *Narrating Discovery: The Romantic Explorer in American Literature, 1790–1855* (1992), travelers who kept journals such as those of William Marshall Anderson usually had a number of motives, not the least of which was eventual publication. Often, as in the next selection by traveler and mountain man Anderson, accounts that *might* be tall tales end up mixed in with a hodgepodge of different subjects.

August 27, 1834—and Wednesday—We are encamped quite early in the day, at a beautiful grove of mountain ash—I shall call it the ash-grove spring—This spot is on the south Side of the Platte in a deep cove, & bounded to the East & West by high perpendicular hills and immediately above the cedar bluff—The Pawnees have now & then, used this as a wintering place—To morrow we shall give general license to all disposed, to hunt the sullen buffalo—then we shall wend our way to sweet home—

August 28, 1834—Thursday. Counting this and its two predecessors fifty odd fat cows have fallen to silence the calls of our famelic stomachs—I have more than once heard the strange story which I am about to relate—I consider it corroborated sufficiently to bear the stamp of truth—A party of the Rocky mountain fur company, encamped on a branch of Black-foot river, was defeated and driven out of their tents by a small yet powerful foe, yes fifty well armed men, without a drop of blood, were compelled to take to an inglorious flight by fourteen pole cats Without sound of horn or beat of drum they marched over the field of action their tails aloft and waving like banners of victory—These comely, sweet scented gentlemen, unharming &

unharmed, surveyed the premises and retired—I suppose the worthy trappers, if challenged by the petty warriors,would have excused themselves in the same manner as a lion was reported to have done when a skunk threw down his gauntlet & dared him to the field—I will not fight, said the monarch of the woods, Why not? are you afraid? demanded the little brave—No—was the reply—but if we should contend, you alone would gain glory, if victorious, whereas, it would be known to my discredit for a month that I had been in the company of skun[k]s—It has been asserted by, or for Genl Ashley, that he was the first white discoverer of the great salt lake; in either case, he is to blame, as it is not the fact—The credit, if the accidental seeing of a spot is entitled to any credit, is due to Mr Provost of St. Louis—At all events it seems to be generally believed that Genl A. not only did not first find that remarkable inland sea, but, that he has not ever yet seen it—From the accounts of others, he gave a description of it— on which account it is sometimes called by his name—prompted by false glory he acquiesces in the reception of false honours—

8. Two Canadians Engage in an Eating Contest

from George Frederick Ruxton, *Adventures in Mexico and the Rocky Mountains*

The following description by George Frederick Ruxton (1821–1848) seems embellished by an imagination like that of Charles Dickens, Ruxton's fellow countryman. Ruxton came to the Rocky Mountains in 1846. His insightful but fictionalized account of his experiences among the trappers made him "not only the first, but also one of the most significant novelists of the fur trade," according to Neal Lambert, author of *George Frederick Ruxton* (1974).

Whether it is that the meat itself (which, by the way, is certainly the most delicious of flesh) is most easy of digestion, or whether the digestive organs of hunters are "ostrichified" by the severity of exercise, and the bracing, wholesome climate of the mountains and plains, it is a fact that most prodigious quantities of "fat cow" may be swallowed with the greatest impunity, and not the slightest inconvenience ever follows the mammoth feasts of the gourmands of the far west. The powers of the Canadian voyageurs and hunters in the consumption of meat strike the greenhorn with wonder and astonishment; and are only equalled by the gastronomical capabilities exhibited by Indian dogs, both following the same plan in their epicurean gorgings.

On slaughtering a fat cow, the hunter carefully lays by, as a tit-bit for himself, the "boudins" and medullary intestine, which are prepared by being inverted and partially cleaned (this, however, is not thought indispensable). The dépouillé or fleece, the short and delicious hump-rib and "tender loin," are then carefully stowed away, and with these the rough edge of the appetite is removed. But *the* course is, *par excellence*, the sundry yards of "boudin," which, lightly browned over the embers of the fire, slide down the well-lubricated throat of the hungry mountaineer, yard after yard disappearing in quick succession.

I once saw two Canadians* commence at either end of such a coil of grease, the mass lying between them on a dirty apishamore like the coil of a huge snake. As yard after yard glided glibly down their throats, and the serpent on the saddlecloth was dwindling from an anaconda to a moderate-sized rattlesnake, it became a great point with each of the feasters to hurry his operation, so as to gain a march upon his neighbour, and improve the opportunity by swallowing more than his just proportion; each, at the same time, exhorting the other, whatever he did, to feed fair, and every now and then, overcome by the unblushing attempts of his partner to bolt a vigorous mouthful, would suddenly jerk back his head, drawing out at the same moment, by the retreating motion, several yards of boudin from his neighbor's mouth and stomach (for the greasy viand required no mastication, and was bolted whole), and, snapping up himself the ravished portions, greedily swallowed them; to be in turn again withdrawn and subjected to a similar process by the other.

No animal requires so much killing as a buffalo. Unless shot through the lungs or spine, they invariably escape; and, even when thus mortally wounded, or even struck through the very heart, they will frequently run a considerable distance before falling to the ground, particularly if they see the hunter after the wound is given. If, however, he keeps himself concealed after firing, the animal will remain still, if

*The majority of the trappers and mountain-hunters are French Canadians and Saint-Louis French Creoles.

it does not immediately fall. It is a most painful sight to witness the dying struggles of the huge beast. The buffalo invariably evinces the greatest repugnance to lie down when mortally wounded, apparently conscious that, when once touching mother earth, there is no hope left him. A bull, shot through the heart or lungs, with blood streaming from his mouth, and protruding tongue, his eyes rolling, bloodshot, and glazed with death, braces himself on his legs, swaying from side to side, stamps impatiently at his growing weakness, or lifts his rugged and matted head and helplessly bellows out his conscious impotence. To the last, however, he endeavours to stand upright, and plants his limbs farther apart, but to no purpose. As the body rolls like a ship at sea, his head slowly turns from side to side, looking about, as it were, for the unseen and treacherous enemy who has brought him, the lord of the plains, to such a pass. Gouts of purple blood spurt from his mouth and nostrils, and gradually the failing limbs refuse longer to support the ponderous carcase; more heavily rolls the body from side to side, until suddenly, for a brief instant, it becomes rigid and still; a convulsive tremor seizes it, and, with a low, sobbing gasp, the huge animal falls over on his side, the limbs extended stark and stiff, and the mountain of flesh without life or motion.

9. Bucked into a Bunch of Prickly Pear

from Charles Larpenteur, *Forty Years a Fur Trader on the Upper Missouri*

Accidents that didn't kill or seriously injure mountain men sometimes made them laugh. Charles Larpenteur (1807–1872), author of the following selection, needed something to laugh about. Born in France, he came to the United States in 1818. At the 1833 rendezvous, he tended bar in the whiskey tent. After 1850, he tried to run fur-trading posts, but bad luck kept him from succeeding in business. Like many trappers and traders, he married an Indian woman. When she died, he married another, who also died before he did. His third wife, who apparently survived him, was white.

From this point to La Ramie's fort nothing took place worth mentioning except the overthrow of our long friend Marsh. It happened that, in traveling through a country thickly settled with prickly pears, bad luck would have it that a small particle of one accidentally found itself under the tail of his riding mule. The poor animal, finding itself so badly pricked, kicked and bucked at such a rate that our long friend was soon unsaddled, and thrown flat on his back in a large bunch of the prickly pears. Although he was over six feet in his stockings, the length of his limbs was not enough to reach out of the patch; and there he lay, begging for pity's sake of his comrades, as they passed by, to help him out of his prickly situation. But all he heard in reply to his entreaties was bursts of laughter throughout the company as they passed by, till he was relieved by Mr. Johnesse, who had charge of the rear. I could but pity the poor fellow, but, at the same time, his situation excited mirth. There he lay in a large bunch of prickly pears, stretched out as though he had been crucified. Poor Marsh! I shall remember him as long as I live.

10. Tricks of the Wily Old Le Blueux

from Thomas D. Bonner, *Life and Adventures of James P. Beckwourth*

Told straight or "stretched" a bit or expanded into full-blown tall tales, stories of the fur trappers' exploits often included an element of cunning or trickery. James P. Beckwourth (1800?–1866), one of the most famed of the mountain men, tells us how one of his comrades, "old Le Blueux," used his wits to outfox his foes. An African American, Beckwourth (or "Beckwith," as he was earlier called) joined William H. Ashley's 1824 expedition to the Rockies. The Crow Indians adopted Beckwourth into their tribe in 1828. His later colorful career took him to Florida for the Seminole wars, then to the Santa Fe Trail, the Mexican War, and the California and Colorado gold rushes. He was also at the Sand Creek Massacre in 1864. Bill Hotchkiss has depicted Beckwourth's life in a number of novels, among them *The Medicine Calf* (1981) and *Ammahabas* (1983).

A few days after our battle, one of our old trappers, named Le Blueux, who had spent twenty years in the mountains, came to me, and telling me he knew of a small stream full of beaver which ran into Lewis's

Fork, about thirty miles from camp, wished me to accompany him there. We being free trappers at that time, the chance of obtaining a pack or two of beaver was rather a powerful incentive. Gain being my object, I readily acceded to his proposal. We put out from camp during the night, and traveled up Lewis's Fork, leisurely discussing our prospects and confidently enumerating our unhatched chickens, when suddenly a large party of Indians came in sight in our rear.

The banks of the river we were traveling along were precipitous and rocky, and skirted with a thick bush. We entered the bush without a moment's hesitation, for the Indians advanced on us as soon as they had caught sight of us. Le Blueux had a small bell attached to his horse's neck, which he took off, and, creeping to a large bush, fastened it with the end of his lariat, and returned holding the other end in his hand. This stratagem caused the Indians to expend a great amount of powder and shot in their effort to kill the bell; for, of course, they supposed the bell indicated the position of ourselves. When they approached near enough to be seen through the bushes, we fired one gun at a time, always keeping the other loaded. When we fired the bell would ring, as if the horse was started by the close proximity of the gun, but the smoke would not rise in the right place. They continued to shoot at random into the bushes without injuring us or our faithful animals, who were close by us, but entirely concealed from the sight of the Indians. My companion filled his pipe and commenced smoking with as much sang froid as if he had been in camp.

"This is the last smoke I expect to have between here and camp," said he.

"What are we to do?" I inquired, not feeling our position very secure in a brush fort manned with a company of two, and beleaguered by scores of Black Foot warriors.

In an instant, before I had time to think, crack went his rifle, and down came an Indian, who, more bold than the rest, had approached too near to our garrison.

"Now," said Le Blueux, "bind your leggins and moccasins around your head."

I did so, while he obeyed the same order.

"Now follow me."

Wondering what bold project he was about to execute, I quietly obeyed him. He went noiselessly to the edge of the bluff, looked narrowly up and down the river, and then commenced to slide down the almost perpendicular bank, I closely following him. We safely reached the river, into which we dropped ourselves. We swam close under the bank for more than a mile, until they discovered us.

"Now," said my comrade, "strike across the stream in double quick time."

We soon reached the opposite bank, and found ourselves a good mile and a half ahead of the Indians. They commenced plunging into the river in pursuit, but they were too late. We ran across the open ground until we reached a mountain, where we could safely look back and laugh at our pursuers. We had lost our horses and guns, while they had sacrificed six or eight of their warriors, besides missing the two scalps they made so certain of getting hold of.

I had thought myself a pretty good match for the Indians, but I at once resigned all claims to merit. Le Blueux, in addition to all the acquired wiles of the Red Man, possessed his own superior art and cunning. He could be surrounded with no difficulties for which his inexhaustible brain could not devise some secure mode of escape.

11. A Trick Reveals the Cowardice of Some Eastern "Indian Fighters"

from Howard L. Conard, *"Uncle Dick" Wootton*

Mountain men tricked not only foes but also greenhorns, as "Uncle Dick" Wootton tells us in the selection that follows. The greenhorns in his account seem like that era's equivalents of today's thrill-seeking tourists, the kind who love to boast about their adventures.

That fall and winter I put in trading with the Indians and hunting about the fort, was a very prosperous one in a business way, and I scarcely had an adventure more thrilling than one which was a little out of the usual order, and very amusing. I was up at old Fort St. Vrain, something like forty miles north of Denver, and there was a party of fellows there, who had come out from St. Louis to see the wild west, and teach the "old timers" how to fight Indians. They were loud talkers, and almost every time they went out of the fort, would have a story of Indian killing to tell when they got back. Some of us had doubts about their ever having seen any real live fighting Indians, and one day we concluded to find out how they would act in case they had reason to think themselves in danger. We heard them talking about going out to gather wild cherries in a thicket some distance from the fort, and knowing that it was a good place for an Indian Ambuscade, I took a companion along with me, and rode out in advance of them to the thicket, where we secreted ourselves, after having picketed our horses where they would not be seen. The Eastern Indian slayers came along by and by, hitched their horses, laid down their guns, and then went into the thicket after the cherries. About the time they had gotten interested in their work, we commenced shooting off our pistols and yelling like Comanche Indians; and then you ought to have seen those Indian fighters run. They never fired a shot, and didn't even stop to pick up their guns, but made the best possible time in getting to the fort. When they got in they reported that they had been attacked by a large force of Indians; they had killed a good many of them and had only sought safety in flight, when they found that they could not contend against the overwhelming numbers of the savages. To account for the loss of their guns they said they had to swim the Platte River, and had been compelled to leave their weapons behind them.

My companion and I rode in shortly after they had finished the story of their thrilling adventure, and in a day or two the facts leaked out. Then those St. Louis braves wanted to go home, and they embraced the earliest opportunity afforded them of making a safe trip to the east.

12. John Colter's Flight from Blackfoot Indians

from **John Bradbury**, *Travels in the Interior of America*

The most legendary of the stories of mountain-man cunning and quick wit is the tale of John Colter's naked run for life. Colter (c. 1774–1813) was one of the members of the Lewis and Clark expedition. As the expedition was returning to the states, Manuel Lisa hired Colter to be a fur trapper and trader. Colter later worked for Pierre Menard and Andrew Henry. The next selection, a tale of Colter's famous escape, is from John Bradbury's *Travels in the Interior of America in the Years 1809, 1810, and*

1811 (1815). Bradbury (1768–1823) was born in Scotland. He became a naturalist and accompanied a fur-trading expedition financed by John Jacob Astor. Historian Roderick Nash says that when Bradbury's *Travels* was published it "became one of the most widely used sources of information about the American West" (Lamar, *Reader's Encyclopedia*, 118). In the twentieth century, Colter's ordeal was fictionalized in A. B. Guthrie, Jr.'s "Mountain Medicine," collected in *The Big It and Other Stories* (1960).

This man [John Colter] came to St. Louis in May, 1810, in a small canoe, from the head waters of the Missouri, a distance of three thousand miles, which he traversed in thirty days. I saw him on his arrival, and received from him an account of his adventures after he had separated from Lewis and Clarke's party: one of these, from its singularity, I shall relate. On the arrival of the party on the head waters of the Missouri, Colter, observing an appearance of abundance of beaver being there, he got permission to remain and hunt for some time, which he did in company with a man of the name of Dixon, who had traversed the immense tract of country from St. Louis to the head-waters of the Missouri alone. Soon after he separated from Dixon, and *trapped* in company with a hunter named Potts; and aware of the hostility of the Blackfeet Indians, one of whom had been killed by Lewis, they set their traps at night, and took them up early in the morning, remaining concealed during the day. They were examining their traps early one morning, in a creek about six miles from that branch of the Missouri called Jefferson's Fork, and were ascending in a canoe, when they suddenly heard a great noise, resembling the trampling of animals; but they could not ascertain the fact, as the high perpendicular banks on each side of the river impeded their view. Colter immediately pronounced it to be occasioned by Indians, and advised an instant retreat; but was accused of cowardice by Potts, who insisted that the noise was caused by buffaloes, and they proceeded on. In a few minutes afterwards their doubts were removed, by a party of Indians making their appearance on both sides of the creek, to the amount of five or six hundred, who beckoned them to come ashore. As retreat was now impossible, Colter turned the head of the canoe to the shore; and at the moment of its touching, an Indian seized the rifle belonging to Potts; but Colter, who is a remarkably strong man, immediately retook it, and handed it to Potts, who remained in the canoe, and on receiving it pushed off into the river. He had scarcely quitted the shore when an arrow was shot at him, and he cried out, *"Colter, I am wounded."*

Colter remonstrated with him on the folly of attempting to escape, and urged him to come ashore. Instead of complying, he instantly leveled his rifle at an Indian, and shot him dead on the spot. This conduct, situated as he was, may appear to have been an act of madness; but it was doubtless the effect of sudden, but sound reasoning; for if taken alive, he must have expected to be tortured to death, according to their custom. He was instantly pierced with arrows so numerous, that, to use the language of Colter, *"he was made a riddle of."* They now seized Colter, stripped him entirely naked, and began to consult on the manner in which he should be put to death. They were first inclined to set him up as a mark to shoot at; but the chief interfered, and seizing him by the shoulder, asked him if he could run fast? Colter, who had been some time amongst the Kee-kat-sa, or Crow Indians, had in a considerable degree acquired the Blackfoot language, and was also well acquainted with Indian customs. He knew that he had now to run for his life, with the dreadful odds of five or six hundred against him, and those armed Indians; therefore cunningly replied that he was a very bad runner, although he was considered by the hunters as remarkably swift. The chief now commanded the party to remain stationary, and led Colter out on the prairie three or four hundred yards, and released him, bidding him *to save himself if he could.* At that instant the horrid war whoop sounded in the ears of poor Colter, who, urged with the hope of preserving life, ran with a speed at which he was himself surprised. He proceeded towards the Jefferson Fork, having to traverse a plain six miles in breadth, abounding with the prickly pear on which he was every instant treading with his naked feet. He ran nearly half way across the plain before he ventured to look over his shoulder, when he perceived that the Indians were very much scattered, and that he had gained ground to a considerable distance from the main body, but one Indian, who carried a spear, was much before all the rest, and not more than a hundred yards from him. A faint gleam of hope now cheered the heart of Colter: he derived confidence from the belief that escape was within the bounds of possibility; but that confidence was nearly being fatal to him, for he exerted himself to such a degree, that the blood gushed from his nostrils, and soon almost covered the fore part of his body. He had now arrived within a mile of the river, when he distinctly heard the appalling sound of footsteps behind him, and every instant expected to feel the spear of his pursuer. Again he turned his head, and saw the savage not twenty yards from him. Determined if possible to avoid the expected blow, he suddenly stopped, turned round, and spread out his arms. The Indian, surprised by the suddenness of the action, and perhaps at the bloody appearance of Colter, also attempted to stop; but exhausted with running, he fell whilst endeavoring to throw his spear, which stuck in the ground, and broke in his hand. Colter instantly snatched up the pointed part, with which he pinned him to the earth, and then continued his flight. The foremost of the Indians, on arriving at the place, stopped till others came up to join them, when they set up a hideous yell. Every moment of this time was improved by Colter, who, although fainting and exhausted, succeeded in gaining the skirting of the cotton wood trees, on the borders of the fork, through which he ran, and plunged into the river. Fortunately for him, a little below this place there was an island, against the upper point of which a raft of drift timber had lodged. He dived under the raft, and after several efforts, got his head above water amongst the trunks of trees, covered over with smaller wood to the depth of several feet. Scarcely had he secured himself when the Indians arrived on the river, screeching and yelling, as Colter expressed it, "like so many devils." They were frequently on the raft during the day, and were seen through the chinks by Colter, who was congratulating himself on his escape, until the idea arose that they might set the raft on fire. In horrible suspense he remained until night, when hearing no more of the Indians, he dived from under the raft, and swam silently down the river to a considerable distance, when he landed, and traveled all night. Although happy in having escaped from the Indians, his situation was still dreadful: he was completely naked, under a burning sun; the soles of his feet were entirely filled with the thorns of the prickly pear; he was hungry, and had no means of killing game, although he saw abundance around him, and was at least seven days journey from Lisa's Fort, on the Bighorn branch of the Roche Jaune River. These were circumstances under which almost any man but an American hunter would have despaired. He arrived at the fort in seven days, having subsisted on a root much esteemed by the Indians of the Missouri, now known by naturalists as *psoralea esculenta*.

13, 14, and 15. Encounters with Grizzly Bears

Encounters with grizzly bears led to some of the most legendary stories of the mountain men. Hugh Glass (d. 1833) was a trapper who joined William H. Ashley's 1823 expedition and was wounded in a fight with the Arikara Indians. He recovered but then was mauled by a grizzly. The next two selections tell the story of his incredible survival. Glass lived and continued to trap until the winter of 1832–33, when the Arikara killed him, Edward Rose, and another trapper named Menard.

Our first account of Glass's ordeal is by Alfred Jacob Miller (1810–1874), a Baltimore-born painter who studied for a year at the Ecole des Beaux Arts in Paris. Miller was hired by Sir William Drummond Stewart to record in paintings scenes of his 1837 expedition along the Oregon Trail to Fort William.

George C. Yount (1794–1865), the author of the second and more detailed version of the Glass saga, was born in North Carolina and began fur trapping in New Mexico in about 1825. In 1828–29 he trapped northward, and Yount's Peak at the source of the Yellowstone River is named for him. After his trapping days, he became a rancher in California's Napa Valley.

The third selection, by Jacob Fowler (1764–1849), describes a grizzly attack on Lewis Dawson (d. 1821). Except for his violent death, we know little about Dawson. Fowler was born in Maryland, fought on the frontier at the end of the American Revolution, and served in the War of 1812. He kept a record of his exploration of the Arkansas River region in 1821, but his manuscript remained in the family archives until it was published in 1898.

13. The Grizzly Bear and Hugh Glass

from Alfred Jacob Miller, *The West of Alfred Jacob Miller*

The Indians have just driven the bear from his covert among some wild cherry bushes, which fruit is decidedly one of his weaknesses; of it he is remarkably fond. They are preparing to run him, giving him at the same time a wide berth, knowing very well the formidable qualities of the brute they have to deal with. As an arrow sometimes fails to pierce his body, owing to thick matted hair, they aim usually at the head, the most vulnerable part.

The great narratives at the camp fire are in connection with this animal;—one of the most singular was that of a man named Glass;—he with some companions on foot shot at a bear but only wounded him and now a chase commenced; he called to the others to run, and in doing so himself, tripped and fell;—by the time he arose and looked around, the beast confronted him. As he closed on him, G—— never losing his presence of mind discharged his pistol full into the body of the animal, at the same moment that the other fixed his claws deep into his flesh and rolled him to the ground. By the time his companions reached the spot, he was covered with blood, and the bear dead lying upon his body,—both appeared dead. The others pulled the bear from him, took his arms and returned to camp. Months elapsed;—the company was returning to the Fort;—they saw a man slowly approaching by the banks of the river, as he came nearer their eyes rested on a cadaverous figure with a head so disfigured as to be unknown. The astonishment of the party may be conceived when they heard a well-known voice call out, "Hallo! Bill! you thought I was 'gone under,' didn't you? hand over my horse and 'fixens.' I ain't dead yet by a cussed sight." It was the veritable Glass whom they left with the bear. In his recital he stated that after a time he recovered his senses & fed on the bear; as soon as he could gain strength sufficient, he took a supply of the meat with him, and on it and berries subsisted until he reached the Fort, a distance of 60 miles.

14. Another Account of Hugh Glass

from George C. Yount, *George C. Yount and His Chronicles of the West*

Among the numerous veteran Trappers, with whom Yount became acquainted, & was from time to time associated, was one by the name of Glass—In point of adventures dangers & narrow escapes & capacity for endurance, & the sufferings which befel him, this man was preeminent—He was bold, daring, reckless & excentric to a high degree; but was nevertheless a man of great talents & intellectual as well as bodily power—But his bravery was conspicuous beyond all his other qualities for the perilous life he led—

Glass first commenced life in the capacity of sailor; & after having followed the seas during several years, was captured by the desperate band of Pirates under the notorious Lafitte—The policy of this piratical champion was to allow all his captives to chose for themselves either to join & share his fortunes, & follow his lead, or submit to immediate death—Little time was allowed them to deliberate—

When the crew, of which Glass made a part learnt their conquerer's terms, he & one other instantly decided to become Pirates; & were hailed as good fellows, when they had taken the oath of allegiance, which was an awful one, & too horid to be written here—All went on well for a season, but the cruel murders to be perpetrated daily,—As they shuddered from their inmost souls & shrunk from those deeds of blood, it was impossible for them to conceil from their despotic lord the emotions of their hearts—

At length, as the piratical craft was lying secreted in one of the secluded friths of Texas, then a territory of Mexico, these two, Glass & his comrade were given to understand that they had been deemed unfit for the work of pirates & would, on the following day, be doomed to death—They therefore concluded to consult their own safety; & in the darkness of night, swam from the ship to the land & fled for life—This event proved the epoch of Glass's life; & from his own lips, Yount received the following history of his career, up to the time of his embarking for the upper waters of the Yellow Stone, on his last expedition, that in which terminated his eventful life—We shall afford the reader a hasty outline, which will make an episode of a few pages—

After leaving the piratical vessel, they wandered far back into the trackless wilderness, they knew not whither nor wherefore,—until they fell in among the people of the Pawnee nation, & were made their prisoners—After having travelled with the savages a few days, & the party having joined a more numerous band of their people, they came to a halt, & the preliminaries of the feat of burning them to the stake began—Tied to a tree they witnessed the whole scene—

One was to suffer at a time—Glass was reserved to suffer last, & therefore was compelled to stand by & witness the tortures of his comrade—An awful scene it surely was—His whole body, from head to foot having been stuck thick with splinters of pitch-pine, the faggots were lighted, & in the darkness of midnight, his spirit ascended in flames to Him who had given it being—

Now came his own final hour—And as two approached him to strip him of his apparel, the ruling Chief stood by to pierce his skin with the first splinter, which was deemed the royal privilege—Glass thrust his hand into his own bosom & drew from thence a large package of vermilian; an article which the savages value above all price—He gave the packet to the proud & haughty Brave, with an air of respect & affection & bowed his final farewell—The Chief opened & examined it, & then majestically stepped up to him, & cut the thongs with which he was bound, & taking him by the hand, with paternal regard & smiling delight, led him to his own wigwam. Then with soothing tenderness he lighted his pipe, & having smoked a few moments, in the presence of his numerous braves, he passed it to Glass, who also smoked a few whiffs & restored it to his liege lord—From that time he shared nothing but paternal & tender treatment—

With these Pawnees Glass roamed the wilderness in security many months, until they visited St. Louis; where he found means to escape from the Indians—Having resided in the City some eight or ten months, until Ashley sought him out & employed him to join a band of Thirty Trappers, which he had furnished & equipped to trap upon the Yellow Stone River under Maj. Henry—

Glass with this party of Trappers, ascended the Missouri, till they reached the territory of the Pickarees [Arickara]—These Indians had become troublesome, & a detachment of troops from Council Bluffs was out against them—Other friendly Indians had joined the whites & the Pickarees had been routed, & scattered far & near in the wilderness;—rendering it dangerous in the extreme, for the Trappers to thread their way towards their place of destination, to trap for furs—

As Maj. Henry pressed onwards towards the Yellow Stone, constrained to use great caution, he had struck a tributary of the Missouri & was following its channel, where the Buffalo & the Buffaloberries were found abundant & proved convenient for food— But the band must keep together, as they were liable, at any moment, to be assailed, by the Pickarees in ambush—He accordingly selected two distinguished hunters, one of which was Allen, of Mohave notoriety, & a bosom friend of Yount's to precede the party, from a half a mile to a mile, in order to kill meat for food—

Glass, as was usual, could not be kept, in obedience to orders, with the band, but persevered to thread his way alone through the bushes & chapparel—As the two hunters were wending their way, up the River, Allen discovered Glass dodging along in the forest alone; & said to his companion, "there look at that fellow, Glass; see him foolishly exposing his life—I wish some Grizzly Bear would pounce upon him & teach him a lesson of obedience to orders, & to keep in his place—He is ever off, scouting in the bushes & exposing his life & himself to dangers"—

Glass disappeared in the chapperel, & within half an hour his screams were heard—The two hunters hastened to his relief & discovered a huge Grizy Bear, with two Cubs—The monster had seized him, torn the flesh from the lower part of the body, & from the lower limbs—He also had his neck shockingly torn, even to the degree that an aperture appeared to have been made into the windpipe, & his breath to exude at the side of his neck—It is not probable however that any aperture was made into the windpipe—Blood flowed freely, but fortunately no bone was broken—& his hands & arms were not disabled—

The whole party were soon there, the monster & her cubs were slain, & the victim cared for in the best degree possible, under existing circumstances—A convenient hand litter was perpared & the sufferer carried by his humane fellow-trappers from day to day—He retained all his faculties but those of speech & locomotion—Too feeble to walk, or help himself at all, his comrads every moment waited his death— Day by day they ministered to his wants, & no one counted it any hardship—

Among those rude & rough trappers of the wilderness, fellow feeling & devotion to each others wants is a remarkable & universal feature or characteristic—It is admirable & worthy the imitation of even the highest grade of civilized men—We have remarked it at ever[y] step in the investigation, which, in preparing this work, has devolved on us—

After having thus carried Glass during six days, it became necessary for the party to croud their journey, as the season for trapping was fast transpiring—Maj. Henry therefore offered four hundred Dolls to any two of his men, who would volunteer to remain until he should die, decently bury him & then press on their way to overtake the main body—One man & boy volunteered to remain—They did so, & the party urged forward towards the Yellow Stone—

The two waited several days, & he still lived—No change was apparent,—They dressed his wounds daily, & fed & nourished him with water from the spring & such light food as he could swallow—Still he was speechless but could use his hands—Both his lower limbs were quite disabled—As he lay by the spring, Buffaloberries hung in clusters & in great profusion over him & around his bed, which was made soft with dry leaves & two blankets—

Quite discouraged & impatient for his death, as there remained no hope of his recovery, the two resolved to leave him there to die alone in the wilderness—They took from him his knife, camp kettle & Rifle, laid him smoothely on his blankets, & left him thus to die a lingering death, or be torn in pieces by the ferocious wild beasts & to be seen no more till they should meet him at the dread tribunal of eternal judgment—

"He could hear their every word, but could not speak nor move his body—His arms he could use—& he stretched them out imploringly, but in vain—They departed & silence reigned around him—Oppressed with grief & his hard fate, he soon became delirious—Visions of benevolent beings appeared, Around him were numerous friendly faces, smiling encouragement & exhorting him not to despond, & assuring him that all would be well at last—He declared to Yount that he was never alone, by day or by night—

He could reach the water & take it to his mouth in the hollow of his hand, & could pluck the berries from the bushes to eat as he might need—One morning, after several weeks, he found by his side a huge Rattlesnake—With a small stone he slew the reptile, jambed off its head & cast it from him—Having laid the dead serpant by his side he jambed off small parts from time to time, & bruised it thoroughly & moistened it with water from the spring & made of it a grateful food on which he fed from day to day—

At length the wolves came & took from under him his Blankets, & having dragged them some distance, tore them in pieces—, Thus he was left solely on his bed of leaves—In this condition he must have lain many weeks how many he could never tell—Meantime the two, the man & boy, false to their trust, came up with Maj. Henry & the party, & reported that Glass had died & they had decently buried his remains, & brot his effects with them, his gun, knife & Camp kettle, & received the promised reward for their fidelity, Four Hundred Dollars—

After a long period, his strength began to revive, & he crawled a few rods, & laid himself down again during several days—Then again he resumed his journey, every day increasing his distance some rods—after many long & tedious days, & even weeks—he found himself upon his feet & began to walk—Soon he could travel nearly a mile in a day This distance he even increased daily more & more—Thus covered with wounds, which would frequently bleed, & require much attention, he urged his journey through a howling wilderness, a distance of more than Two Hundred miles, to the nearest trading post—

Often by the way he would find the decaying carcases of Buffalos, which, wounded by the hunter, or some more powerful animal, had died—From these he gained nourishing food, by pounding out the marrow from the bones, & eating it seasoned with Buffaloberries & moistened with limped water from the brooks & springs—With sharp stones he would dig from the earth nourishing roots, which he had learned to discriminate while sojourning with the Paunees—

At this trading post [Fort Kiowa] he passed the winter, as Autumn had worn away, & the cold season had overtaken him there—During the bracing season of winter, his strength was rapidly restored—As the following spring opened [actually in October], he found himself again a well man, & able to resume his journey to rejoin Maj Henry & his band of trappers—Fortunately as he was about to depart, an express party arrived, on its way to carry orders to Maj. Henry, at his post on the Yellow Stone, & Glass joined this party [under Antoine Langevin] to accompany them to Henry's Fort—[He again missed death by a miracle, at the hands of the Rees.]

This journey was to Glass no more than a season of pastime & pleasure—Days, weeks & even months of journying were as nothing, after the scenes of the previous Summer & Autumn—He knew no fatigue but after a day's travel, could leap and frolic, like the young fawn—On reaching Maj Henry's encampment, the reader can better imagine than the writer describe the scene as he rode up to his old party of fellow trappers—One without, on seeing Glass ride up ran in to report to Maj H. & the rest that Glass had arrived [in December 1823]—

Impossible! Glass had been dead and buried more than a year & one of those who buried his remains was present—But Glass entered, told his story & recapitulated his wrongs & sufferings & asked for his Camp kettle & his Rifle—The Major replied by bringing the *recreant boy* before him—His Camp kettle was there, but the false & dastardly man had gone with Glass's Rifle to Council Bluffs—To the boy Glass addressed himself after the following manner— "Go, my boy—I leave you to the punishment of your own conscience & your God—If they forgive you, then be happy—I have nothing to say to you—but, dont forget thereafter that truth & fidelity are too valuable to be trifled with"—

15. Lewis Dawson in a Grizzly's Jaws

from Jacob Fowler, *The Journal of Jacob Fowler*

We Seen a Branch Puting in from the South Side Which We Sopose to be Pikes first forke and make for it—Crossed and Camped in a grove of Bushes and timber about two miles up it from the River We maid Eleven miles West this day—We Stoped Heare about one oclock and Sent back for one Hors that Was not able to keep up—We Heare found some grapes among the brush—While Some Ware Hunting and others Cooking Some picking grapes a gun Was fyered off and the Cry of a White Bare Was Raised We Ware all armed in an Instent and Each man Run His own Cors to look for the desperet anemel—the Brush in Which We Camped Contained from 10 to 20 acors Into Which the Bare Head [bear had] Run for Shelter find[ing] Him Self Surrounded on all Sides—threw this Conl glann With four others atemted to Run But the Bare being In their Way and lay Close in the brush undiscovered till the Ware With in a few feet of it—When it Sprung up and Caught Lewis doson and Pulled Him down in an Instent Conl glanns gun mised fyer or He Wold Have Releved the man But a large Slut Which belongs to the Party atacted the Bare With such fury that it left the man and persued Her a few steps in Which time the man got up and Run a few steps but Was overtaken by the bare When the Conl maid a second atempt to shoot but His [gun] mised fyer again and the

Slut as before Releved the man Who Run as before—but Was Son again in the grasp of the Bare Who Semed Intent on His distruction— the Conl again Run Close up and as before His gun Wold not go off the Slut makeing an other atack and Releveing the man—the Conl now be Came alarmed lest the Bare Wold pusue Him and Run up Stooping tree—and after Him the Wounded man and Was followed by the Bare and thus the Ware all three up one tree—but a tree standing in Rich [reach] the Conl steped on that and let the man and Bare pas till the Bare Caught Him [Dawson] by one leg and drew Him back wards down the tree. While this Was doing the Conl Sharpened His flint Primed His gun and Shot the Bare down While pulling the man by the leg be fore any of the party arived to Releve Him—but the Bare Soon Rose again but Was Shot by several other [men] Wo Head [who had] got up to the place of action—it Is to be Remarked that the other three men With Him Run off—and the Brush Was so thick that those on the out Side Ware Som time geting threw—

I Was my Self down the Crick below the brush and Heard the dredfull Screems of man in the Clutches of the Bare—the yelping of the Slut and the Hollowing of the men to Run in Run in the man Will be killed and noing the distance So grate that I Cold not get there in time to Save the man So that it Is much Easeer to Emagen my feellings than discribe them but before I got to the place of action the Bare Was killed and [I] met the Wounded man with Robert Fowler and one or two more asisting Him to Camp Where His Wounds Ware Exam- ined—it appeers His Head Was In the Bares mouth at least twice—and that When the monster give the Crush that Was to mash the mans Head it being two large for the Span of His mouth the Head Sliped out only the teeth Cutting the Skin to the bone Where Ever the tuched it—so that the Skin of the Head Was Cut from about the Ears to the top in Several derections—all of Which Wounds Ware Sewed up as Well as Cold be don by men In our Situation Haveing no Surgen nor Surgical Instruments—the man Still Retained His under Standing but Said I am killed that I Heard my Skull Brake—but We Ware Willing to beleve He Was mistaken—as He Spoke Chearfully on the Subgect till In the after noon of the second day When He began to be Restless and Some What delereous—and on examining a Hole in the upper part of His Wright temple Which We beleved only Skin deep We found the Brains Workeing out—We then Soposed that He did Heare His Scull Brake He lived till a little before day on the third day after being Wounded—all Which time We lay at Camp and Buried Him as Well as our meens Would admit Emedetely after the fattal axcident and

Haveing done all We Cold for the Wounded man We turned our aten-
tion [to] the Bare and found Him a large fatt anemel We Skined Him
but found the Smell of a polcat so Strong that We Cold not Eat the
meat—on examening His mouth We found that three of His teeth
Ware broken off near the gums Which We Sopose Was the Caus of His
not killing the man at the first Bite—and the one not Broke to be the
Caus of the Hole in the Right [temple] Which killed the man at last—
the Hunters killed two deer Cased the Skins for Baggs We dryed out
the Bares oil and Caryed it with us the Skin Was all so taken Care of—

16. The Recovery of Brain-Injured August Claymore

from Howard L. Conard, *"Uncle Dick" Wootton*

In his books for general readers, neurologist Oliver Sacks gives many
examples of at least partial recovery from brain injury. However, there
are few nineteenth-century examples of such recoveries, which makes the
following account all the more extraordinary because it happened on an
1838–39 hunt in the middle of a wilderness, hundreds of miles from any
doctor. Of August Claymore, we know only what Wootton tells us in his
selection and the fact that he posed for a photograph that appears in
"Uncle Dick" Wootton with the caption "Claymore, The Last of the Old
Trappers."

It was while we were trapping on the Green River, that August
Claymore, the oldest trapper in the mountains, who was a member of
our party met with an adventure which we all supposed would end his
life, but which he lived to tell of not many years ago, when he was the
only man in the country who still followed trapping as a business. He
fell in one day with a party of Snake Indians, and some way or other
they got into a quarrel, the result of which was that the Indians attacked him with their war clubs, and beat him until they thought he
was dead. Some of the trappers came upon them before they had taken
the old fellow's scalp, but his skull had been crushed, the brain had
been lacerated and a portion of it destroyed. We held a sort of trapper's

consultation and decided that we would have to bury Claymore before we broke camp. Strangely enough, however, he got well, and used to tell about his living to wear out the suit of clothes that one of the trappers donated for a burial suit.

17. "Old Charlefou" Tries an Epic Jump

from Howard L. Conard, *"Uncle Dick" Wootton*

The principal actor in the next selection, "Old Charlefou," is not listed in the index of the eleven-volume biographical series *The Mountain Men and the Fur Trade of the Far West*. "Uncle Dick" Wootton says that Charlefou was a French trapper who "had been inclined to think that the redskins should be shown rather more consideration than we usually gave them." After the incident Wootton describes (which happened on the same 1838–39 hunt when Claymore's brain was injured), Charlefou became an Indian hater. Wootton says that the Frenchman became so bigoted and hateful that when he later sat on a jury in Taos and slept through the trial, he voted to hang the Indian defendant anyway because "if he ain't guilty now he will be."

"Old Charlefou," as we always called the Frenchman who lost our calendar, had the worst luck of anybody in the party, who got back alive, with the exception of Claymore.

While we were up in Eastern Washington, he was out several miles from camp one day when a band of Blackfeet Indians got after him. He was riding a fine Nez Perces horse and kept so far ahead of the Indians that he was out of reach of their arrows. It was a race for life, but he was gaining on his pursuers and had begun to feel sure of reaching the camp safely, when he saw only a few feet in front of him one of those deep fissures in the earth which are characteristic of the Great Plateau. He dare not stop, and if he had turned either to the right or left, the Indians would have gained so much on him that he could hardly have escaped being captured or killed.

He put spurs to his horse and undertook to do what it seemed was the only thing for him to do under the circumstances, and that was to make his horse leap across the chasm.

The horse made a noble effort to carry out his master's plan of escape, but the distance across the breach was too great and horse and rider went to the bottom together. Charlefou had both legs broken and the horse was instantly killed.

The Indians came up and looked down into the gorge but as neither man nor horse showed any signs of life, and there was no way of getting down to where they were, without going to a good deal of trouble, they were left without being molested.

We started out to hunt Charlefou when he did not return to camp as usual, but did not find him for nearly a day after he had met with the accident.

He knew that we would make an effort to learn what had become of him, but feared that any signal which he might give, to notify us of his whereabouts would bring back the murderous Blackfeet. Finally, however, he made up his mind that he must take the chance of being discovered by the Indians, if he was to be found by his friends. He fired a few shots from his rifle, of which we fortunately heard the report, and after a great deal of hard work we succeeded in rescuing him from his perilous position.

There were no surgeons within five hundred miles of us that we knew of, so we had to set the broken bones ourselves. Then we made a litter out of poles, which we placed on two pack animals, and in this way we carried him from place to place for nearly two months.

18. William Craig Tricks Joe Walker

from Thom J. Beall, "Recollections of William Craig"

William Craig (1809–1869), who tells us about a practical joke he played on Joseph R. Walker, was born in West Virginia. Perhaps as early as 1825, Craig ran away from home to join the fur trade in St. Louis. He took part in the Battle of Pierre's Hole in 1832 and, after going with Walker's brigade to California, he settled in Brown's Hole in 1836, helping Joe Meek and Robert Newell to build Fort Davey Crockett. After Craig married a Nez Percé woman in 1838, he led Rev. Harvey Clark's missionary party to Fort Hall in 1839 and then went on to Lapwai, where his wife's father, Chief James, lived. In the aftermath of the Whitman Massacre,

Craig saved the Rev. Henry Harmon Spalding and his family. Idaho's Craig Mountains and the town of Craigmont are named after him.

Lewiston Morning Tribune, Sunday, March 3, 1918

At one time Craig in his reminiscent mood told me that in the year 1832 or 1833 a party of mountaineers were organized on Green River, now in Wyoming, for the purpose ostensibly of trapping for furs on the waters flowing from the Sierra Nevada mountains into the Pacific ocean. In fact the object was to steal horses from the Spaniards residing in California. In this party was Joe Walker, the head man; Joe Meek, Joe Gale, Bill Williams, Mark Head, Bob Mitchel, Alex Godey, Antoine Janise, William Craig and some others.

When ever they camped on a stream where the water would admit they usually stripped at their tepees or lodges and proceeded to the stream to take a plunge.

Now Craig tells this story: "The waters of the Humbolt river are of a milky cast, not clear, so one afternoon while camped on the said stream and being the first to strip, I started for the swimming hole and was just about to plunge in when I got a hunch that things were not as they should be and I had better investigate before taking a dive. I did so and found the water was about a foot and a half deep and the mud four, this condition being in the eddy. So I waded to where there was a current and found the water a little more than waist deep, no mud and good smooth bottom. In looking towards the camp I espied Joe Walker coming and he was jumping like a buck deer, and when he arrived at the brink he says to me: 'How is it?' 'Joe,' I replied, 'it is just splendid.' With that he plunged head-first into that four and a half feet of blue mud.

"Fearing trouble and not being interested in the subsequent proceedings, I made myself scarce by hiding in the brush on the opposite side and in so doing I ran into some rosebrier bushes and scratched myself some, but I was so full of laughter I did not mind that. I peeped through the bushes just in time to see him extricate himself from the mud. He then washed the mud off as well as he could, returned to the tepee, put on his clothes, shot his rifle off, cleaned it, then reloaded it and hollered at me and said: 'Now show yourself and I'll drop a piece of lead into you,' which I failed to do as I did not want to be encumbered with any extra weight especially at that time. I was compelled to remain in hiding nearly the whole afternoon. Before sundown I was told to come into camp and get my supper and leave, that I could not travel any further with that party.

"I was very glad of the permit for it was rather monotonous out there in the brush with nothing but a blanket around me and nobody to talk to and my pipe in camp. I soon dressed myself and then it was time to chew. Our company was divided into messes and each mess was provided with a dressed buffalo hide. It was spread on the ground and the grub placed upon it. When supper was announced we sat down. I sat opposite to Walker and in looking at him I discovered some of that blue mud of the Humbolt on each side of his nose and just below his eyelids, and I could not help laughing. He addressed me in an abrupt manner and said: 'What the h—l are you laughing at.' I told him that gentlemen generally washed before eating. With that the others observed the mud and they too roared with laughter in which Walker joined, but he threatened if ever I played another such trick on him he would kill me as sure as my name was Craig."

This place on the Humbolt river was ever afterward called by the mountain men, "Walker's Plunge," or "Hole."

19. Dead Man's Hand . . . and Everything Else

from Frances Fuller Victor, *River of the West*

Joseph L. Meek (1810–1875) told Frances Fuller Victor (1826–1902) about his life as a mountain man, and she transcribed his narrative and published it under the title *River of the West* (1870). Born in Virginia, Meek hired on as a trapper with William Sublette in 1829, the year of the incident he describes in the following selection. Meek went on to have an adventurous and perilous career as a trapper, joining Walker's 1833 expedition to California, hunting with Kit Carson in Blackfoot Indian country, fighting a grizzly bear, and marrying the daughter of a Nez Percé chief. Meek and Robert Newell guided a wagon train to Oregon in 1840, and Meek and his Indian wife and family settled on a farm in the Willamette Valley. Frances Fuller Victor had been a writer for many years before she met Meek. Her *Poems of Sentiment and Imagination* (co-authored with her sister) was published in 1851; the Beadle dime-novel series brought out two of her narratives about life in Nebraska; and her "Florence Fane" columns appeared in *The Golden Era* during 1863–64. She is the subject of Jim Martin's *A Bit of a Blue: The Life and Work of Frances Fuller Victor* (1992).

One of the free trapper's special delights was to take in hand the raw recruits, to gorge their wonder with his boastful tales, and to amuse himself with shocking his pupil's civilized notions of propriety. Joe Meek did not escape this sort of "breaking in;" and if it should appear in the course of this narrative that he proved an apt scholar, it will but illustrate a truth—that high spirits and fine talents tempt the tempter to win them over to his ranks. But Joe was not won over all at once. He beheld the beautiful spectacle of the encampment as it has been described, giving life and enchantment to the summer landscape, changed into a scene of the wildest carousal, going from bad to worse, until from harmless noise and bluster it came to fighting and loss of life. At this first rendezvous he was shocked to behold the revolting exhibition of four trappers playing at a game of cards with the dead body of a comrade for a card-table! Such was the indifference to all the natural and ordinary emotions which these veterans of the wilderness cultivated in themselves, and inculcated in those who came under their influence. Scenes like this at first had the effect to bring feelings of home-sickness, while it inspired by contrast a sort of penitential and religious feeling also. According to Meek's account of those early days in the mountains, he said some secret prayers, and shed some secret tears. But this did not last long. The force of example, and especially the force of ridicule, is very potent with the young; nor are we quite free from their influence later in life.

20 and 21. Indian Humor on the Frontier

Cultural clashes on the frontier sometimes led to situations that seemed funny to someone in one or more of the cultural groups involved. The following two selections give examples of such humor. For an informative and entertaining discussion of Indian humor see Vine Deloria, Jr., *Custer Died for Your Sins* (1969).

20. White Man Who Scalps Himself

from Howard L. Conard, *"Uncle Dick" Wootton*

I remember a funny thing that happened there that winter, and I laugh yet when I think of it. We had some visitors at the fort who were from St. Louis and were friends of Bent and St. Vrain.

Among them was the most comical fellow I ever knew, whom we called "Belzy" Dodd. I don't know what his first name really was, but "Belzy" was what we called him.

His head was as bald as a billiard ball, and by the way, we had the first billiard table brought to Colorado, at the fort that winter.

Dodd wore a wig, and one day when there were a number of Indians hanging about, he concluded to have a bit of fun with them.

He walked around, eyeing the Indians savagely for some time, and finally, dashing in among them, he gave a series of war whoops which discounted the Comanche yells, and pulling off his wig, he threw it down at the feet of the astonished and terror stricken red men.

The Indians thought the fellow had jerked off his own scalp, and not one of them waited to see what would happen next. They left the fort running like scared jack rabbits, and after that none of them could be induced to come near Dodd.

They named him "the-white-man-who-scalps-himself," and I think he could have traveled across the plains alone with perfect safety.

21. Indians Joke with Glasses

from Jacob Fowler, *The Journal of Jacob Fowler*

29th nov 1821

the Snow Has Intirely disappeered and the ground dry as dust—
the Remainder of the War partey Have all Returned

on our Way up the River before our arivel at the Indeans Camp I
broke one of the glasses out of my Specks—and on puting them on
one day I soon felt the Hand of an Indean grasp them from my face
He maid off as fast as poseble I gave up the Specks for lost but Head
no moad of Replaceing them—In a Short time I Heard great Shouting
and laffing and looking to See What Was the Caus I discovered the
Indean that Head taken my Specks Leading an other With the Specks
on His face the felow Was Led up to me and I was shoon that He Head
but on Eye—and that the Specks Wold Sute Him better [than] me as
the Head but one glass Heare Eanded the Joack the Returned the
Specks in much good Humor amongst all the Ware present

22 and 23. Bizarre Events on the Frontier

Paul Kane (1810–1871) and John Brown (1817–1899), the authors of
the next two selections, recount events so bizarre that they seem like tall
tales. Born in Ireland and brought by his family to Canada at the age of
eight, Kane went to the United States in 1836 and spent the years from
1841 to 1845 in Europe. A painter, he was called "the pioneer of Canada's western artists," and he traveled throughout the Canadian West in
1845 and from 1846 to 1848.

Brown, a native of Massachusetts, was said to have fought with Sam
Houston at the Battle of San Jacinto in 1836. Brown hunted and trapped
throughout the Rocky Mountains for over a decade. In 1845, in Taos, he

married Louisa Sandoval, who had been married to Jim Beckwourth. Brown settled with his family in southern Colorado, but he joined the gold rush to California in 1849. In 1861, he and his partners started a ferry across the Colorado River at Fort Mojave. Since the American Society for Psychical Research was founded in 1885, two years before Brown's narrative was published, we surmise that his memories of his psychic experiences are confabulations evoked by his contemporaries' strong interest in psychic phenomena. The fact is that such phenomena have never stood the test of scientific proof, as Victor J. Stenger explains in his *Physics and Psychics* (1990). Howard Kerr's *Mediums, and Spirit-Rappers, and Roaring Radicals* (1972) discusses the nineteenth century's fascination with spiritualism.

22. A Scots Bagpiper Astonishes Some Indians

from Paul Kane, *Paul Kane's Frontier*

Oct. 9th.—The track still continued bad, and we saw no game; so that our time passed very monotonously, as we had to keep pace with the loaded horses. A Highlander of the name of Colin Frazer had joined our party. He was on his way to a small post, of which he had the charge, at the head of the Athabasca River, in the Rocky Mountains, where he had resided for the last eleven years. He had been brought to the country by Sir George Simpson, in the capacity of his piper, at the time when he explored Frazer's River, and made an extensive voyage through country hitherto little known, and among Indians who had seen few or no white men. He carried the pipes with him, dressed in his Highland costume; and when stopping at forts, or wherever he found Indians, the bagpipes were put in requisition, much to the astonishment of the natives, who supposed him to be a relation of the Great Spirit, having, of course, never beheld so extraordinary a looking man, or such a musical instrument, which astonished them as much as the sound produced. One of the Indians asked him to intercede with the Great Spirit for him; but Frazer remarked, the petitioner little thought how limited his influence was in that quarter.

23. John Brown Foresees Indians Coming

from John Brown, *Mediumistic Experiences of John Brown*

Our little party of six had completed their labor for the day by setting our traps, and had retired about two miles, and had scarcely lain down to rest, when some one, unseen by me, removed the robe, with which I was covered, then took me by the arm, pulled and shook me, telling me, at the same time, to get up and go away from there, and be quick, that all would be killed if we remained. Thus it continued till at last I got up, told the men what I had heard and felt. Fisher, one of our men, also stated that he had been treated the same way and advised all to leave; we soon had our horses saddled and went about one mile out in the desert, where we slept soundly. In the morning we retraced our steps to the little valley we had so abruptly left, and there, where we had lain down, was the trail made by a war party of Blackfoot Indians, who had passed in the night, without distinguishing our sign from that of elk, deer, etc. Had we stayed there, all would have been killed before we could rise to our feet. In all candor let me ask who was it that saved our lives by moving us from under the tomahawk of the savage Blackfoot?

24. John L. Hatcher's Visit to Hell

from Lewis H. Garrard, *Wah-to-Yah and the Taos Trail*

We end this section as we began it, with a selection that shows a mountain man's imaginative powers at a comic apex. The mountain man in this case, John L. Hatcher (c. 1812–c. 1898), was born in Virginia and became an employee at Bent's Old Fort on the Arkansas River in 1835. Hatcher hunted for various parties; and in 1853, along with Kit Carson, Lucien

Maxwell, and thirty other men, he drove a herd of sheep from New Mexico to California. In 1859 he settled in California's Sonoma Valley, but eight years later he sold out and moved to Oregon.

Lewis H. Garrard (1829–1887), the transcriber of Hatcher's tale, was the seventeen-year-old son of a wealthy Philadelphia family when he headed west along the Santa Fe Trail in 1846, looking for fun and adventure. Garrard's *Wah-to-Yah and the Taos Trail* (1850), from which the following selection is taken, recounts his adventures in the West. For a more detailed discussion of Garrard and his book see Edward Halsey Foster, *Josiah Gregg and Lewis H. Garrard* (1977).

"Hatch, old hos! hyar's the coon as would like to hear of the time you seed the old gentleman. You's the one as savys all 'bout them diggin's."

"Well, Louy, sence you ask it, and as Garmon's aguardiente *is* good, I don't care ef I *do* tell that yarn; but it's mity long."

"What one is that?" asked Garmon.

"Why, the old beaver says as how he was in hell once—eh, Hatch?"

"Sartain! this old hos wasn't any whar else—wagh!" replied Hatcher to Louy's doubting remark; "an' I tellee, it's me *kin* tell the yarn."

He kept the pipe in his mouth, the stem hard held between the teeth, using his hands and knife to cut from a solid plug of "Missouri manufactured" a fresh pipe of strong tobacco. His eyes were fast fixed on an imaginary object in the yellow-pine blaze, and his face indicated a concentration of thought to call back important items for the forthcoming incongruous story, attractive by reason of its improbability—interesting in the manner of delivery.

"*Well!*" taking a puff at his pipe to keep in fire, "it's me as had been to Fort William (Bent's Fort) to get powder, Galena, an' a few contraptions, one beginning of robe season. I stuck around, waitin' for my possibles, which Holt was fixin' for me. Only a small train was from the States, an' goods were high—two plews a plug for bacca, three fur powder, an' so on. Jim Finch, as went under on the 'Divide,' told me thar was lots of beaver on the Purgatoire. Nobody knowed it; they think the creek's cleared. At the kanyon, three suns from the fort, I sot my traps. I was by myself; fur you know beaver's not to be trapped by two—they're shy as a coyote as runs round camp to snaw a rope, or steal an apishamore. I'll be darned if ten Injuns didn't come screechin' rite onter me. I cached—*I did*—an' the niggurs made for the prairie with my animals. I tellee, this hos was fawché (mad); but he kept dark fur an hour. I heerd a trampin' in the bushes, an' in breaks my little gray mule. Thinks I, them Rapahoes aint smart; so I ties her to grass. But the Injuns had skeered the beaver, an' I stays in camp, eatin' parflêche and lariat. Now I 'gan to feel wolfish an' squeamish, an' somethin' was pullin' an' gnawin' at my innards, like a wolf in a trap. Jest then an idee struck me, that I'd been hyar afore, tradin' liquor to the Yutes.

"I looked round fur sign, and hurraw fur the mountains, if I didn't find the câche. An' now, if this hos hasn't kissed the rock as was pecked with his butcherknife to mark the place, he's ongrateful. Maybe the gravel wasn't scratched up from that câche *some!* an' *me*, as would have given my traps fur '*old bull*,' rolled in the arwardenty—wagh!

"I was weaker an' a goat in the spring; but when the Touse was opened, I fell back, an' let it run in. In four swallers I 'cluded to pull up stakes fur the headwaters of Purgatoire for meat. I roped old Blue, tied on my traps, an' left.

"It used to be the best place in the mountains fur meat—me an' Bill Williams *has* made it *come*—but nothin' was in sight. Things looked mity strange, an' I wanted to make back track; 'but,' sez I, 'hyar I ar, an' doesn't turn, surely.'

"The bushes was scorched an' curled, an' the cedar was like fire had been put to it. The big brown rocks was covered with black smoke, an' the little drink in the bottom of the kanyon was dried up. We was now most under the old twin peaks of Wah-to-yah; the cold snow on top looked mity cool an' refreshin'.

"Somethin' was wrong; I must be shovin' backards, an' that afore long, or I'll go under; an' I jerked the rein, but I'll be doggone—an' it's true as there's meat a runnin'—Blue kept goin' forrad. I laid back, an' cussed an' kicked till I *saw blood*, sartain; an' I put out my hand fur my knife to kill the beast, but the Green River {knife} wouldn't come. I tellee some onvisible sperit had a paw thar, an' it's me as says it—bad 'medicine' it was that trappin' time.

"Loosin' my pistol—the one traded at 'Big Horn,' from Suckeree Tomblow, time I lost my Yute squaw—an' primin' my rifle, I swore to keep rite on; fur, after stayin' ten year, that's past, in these mountains, to be fooled this way wasn't the game fur me, no how.

"Well, we—I say 'we,' fur Blue *was* some—good as a man any day; I could talk to her, an' she'd turn her head as ef she onderstood me. Mules *are* knowin' critters—next thing to human. At a sharp corner, Blue snorted, an' turned her head, but couldn't go back. Thar, in front, was a level kanyon, with walls of black an' brown an' gray stone, an' stumps of burnt pinyon hung down ready to fall onter us; an', as we passed, the rocks and trees shook an' grated an' creaked. All at oncet Blue tucked tail, backed her ears, bowed her neck, an' hinnied rite out, a raring onto her hind legs, a pawin' an' snickerin'. This hos doesn't see the cute of them notions; he's fur examinin', so I goes to jump off, to lam the fool; but I was stuck tight as ef tar was to the saddle. I took my gun—that ar iron," (pointing to his rifle, leaning against a tree), "an' pops Blue over the head, but she squealed an' dodged, all the time pawin'; but 'twasn't no use, an' I says, 'You didn't cost moren two blankets when you was traded from the Yutes, an two blankets aint worth moren six plews at Fort William, which comes to *dos pesos* a pair, you consarned ugly picter—darn you, anyhow!' Jest then I heerd a laffin'. I looks up, an' two black critters—they wasn't human, sure, fur they had tails an' red coats (Injun cloth, like that traded to the Navyhoes), edged with shiny white stuff, an' brass buttons.

"They kem forrad an' made two low bows. I felt fur my scalp knive (fur I thought they was 'proachin' to take me), but I couldn't use it—they were so *darned* polite.

"One of the devils said, with a grin an' bow, 'Good mornin', Mr. Hatcher?'

" 'H——!' sez I, 'how do you know me? I swar *this* hos never saw you afore.'

" 'Oh! we've expected you a long time,' said the other, 'and we are quite happy to see you—we've known you ever since your arrival in the mountains.'

"I was gittin' sorter scared. I wanted a drop of arwerdenty mity bad, but the bottle was gone, an' I looked at them in astonishment, an' said—'the devil!'

" 'Hush!' screamed one, 'you must not say that here—keep still, you will see him presently.'

"I felt streaked, an' cold sweat broke out all over me. I tried to say my prayers, as I used to at home when they made me turn in at night—

"Now I lay me down to sleep—
"Lan'lord fill the flowin' bowl.

"P'shaw! I'm off agin, I can't say it; but if this child *could* have got off his animal, he'd tuk 'har,' and gone the trail fur Purgatoire.

"All this time the long-tailed devils was leadin' my animal (an' me on top of her, the biggest fool dug out) up the same kanyon. The rocks on the sides was pecked as smooth as a beaverplew, rubbed with the grain, an' the ground was covered with bits of cedar, like a cavyard of mules had been nippin' an' scatterin' 'em about. Overhead it was roofed; leastwise it was dark in thar, an' only a little light come through holes in the rock. I thought I knew whar we was, an' eeched awfully to talk, but I sot still an' didn't ax questions.

"Presently we were stopped by a dead wall—no opening anywhar. When the devils turned from me, I jerked my head around quick, but thar was no place to get out—the wall had growed up ahind us too. I was mad, an' I wasn't mad nuther; fur I expected the time had come fur this child to go under. So I let my head fall onter my breast, an' I pulled the old wool hat over my eyes, an' thought for the last, of the beaver I had trapped, an' the buffler as had took my G'lena pills in thar livers, an' the 'poker' an' 'euker' I'd played to rendevoo an' Fort William. I felt cumfortable as eatin' 'fat cow' to think I hadn't cheated any one.

"All at once the kanyon got bright as day. I looked up, an' thar was a room with lights, an' people talkin' an' laffin', an' fiddles a screechin'. Dad, an' the preacher to Wapakonnetta, told me the fiddle was the Devil's invention; I believe it now.

"The little feller as had hold of my animal, squeaked out—'Get off your mule, Mr. Hatcher!'

" 'Get off!' sez I, for I was mad as a bull pecked with Camanche lances, fur his disturbin' me, 'get off? I have been trying to, ever sence I came in this infernal hole.'

" 'You can do so now. Be quick, for the company is waitin',' sez he, piert-like.

"They all stopped talkin' an' were lookin' rite at me. I felt riled. 'Darn your company. I've got to lose my scalp anyhow, an' no difference to me how soon—but to obleege ye'—so I slid off as easy as ef I'd never been stuck.

"A hunchback boy, with little gray eyes way in his head, took old Blue away. I might never see her agin, an' I shouted—'poor Blue! goodbye Blue!'

"The young devil snickered; I turned around mity starn—'stop your laffin' you hellcat—ef I am alone, I can take you,' an' I grabs fur my knife to wade into his liver; but it was gone—gun, bulletpouch, an' pistol—like mules in a stampede.

"I stepped forrad with a big feller, with har frizzled out like an old buffler's just afore sheddin' time; an' the people jawin' worse 'an a cavyard of parokeets, stopped, while Frizzly shouted—

"'Mr. Hatcher, formerly of Wapakonnetta, latterly of the Rocky Mountains!'

"*Well*, thar I stood. Things was mity strange, an' every darned niggur on 'em looked so pleased like. To show 'em manners, I said—'How are ye!' an' I went to bow, but chaw my last 'bacca ef I could, my breeches was so tight—the heat way back in the kanyon had shrunk them. They were too polite to notice it, an' I felt fur my knife to rip the doggone things, but recollecting the scalptaker was stolen, I straightens up, an' bows my head. A kind-lookin' smallish old gentleman, with a black coat and briches, an' a bright, cute face, an' gold spectacles, walks up an' pressed my hand softly—

"'How do you do, my dear friend? I have long expected you. You cannot imagine the pleasure it gives me to meet you at home. I have watched your peregrinations in the busy, tiresome world, with much interest. Sit down, sit down; take a chair,' an' he handed me one.

"I squared myself on it, but a ten-pronged buck wasn't done sucking, when I last sot on a cheer, an' I squirmed awhile, oneasy as a gut-shot coyote. I jumps up, an' tells the old gentleman them sort of 'state fixins,' didn't suit this beaver, an' he prefers the floor. I sets cross-legged like in camp as easy as eatin' *boudin*. I reached for my pipe—a feller's so used to it—but the devils in the kanyon had câched *it* too.

"'You wish to smoke, Mr. Hatcher?—we will have cigars. Here!' he called to an imp near him, 'some cigars.'

"They was brought on a waiter, size of my bulletbag. I empties 'em in my hat, for good cigars ain't to be picked up on the peraira every day, but lookin' at the old man, I saw somethin' was wrong. To be polite, I ought to have taken but one.

"'I beg pardon,' says I, scratchin' my old scalp, 'this hos didn't think—he's been so long in the mountains, he forgets civilized doins,' an' I shoves the hat to him.

"'Never mind,' says he, wavin' his hand, an' smilin' faintly, 'get others,' speakin' to the boy aside him.

"The old gentleman took one, and touched his finger to the end of my cigar—it smoked as ef fire had beens sot to it.

"'Wagh! the devil!' screams I, drawin' back.

"'The same!' chimed in he, biting off the little eend of his'n, an' bowin' an' spittin' it out—'the same, sir.'

"'The same! what?'

"'Why—the Devil.'

"'H——! this ain't the holler tree for this coon—I'll be makin' "medicin";' so I offers my cigar to the sky, an' to the earth, like Injun.

" 'You must not do that *here*—out upon such superstition,' says he, sharplike.

" 'Why?'

" 'Don't ask so many questions—come with me,' risin' to his feet, an' walkin' off slow, a blowin' his cigar smoke, over his shoulder in a long line, an' I gets along side of him, 'I want to show you my establishment—did not expect to find this down here, eh?'

"My briches was stiff with the allfired heat in the kanyon, an' my friend seein' it, said, 'Your breeches are tight; allow me to place my hand on them.'

"He rubbed his fingers up an' down once, an' by beaver, they got as soft as when I traded them from the Pi Yutes on the Heely (you mind, Louy, my Yute squaw; old Cutlips, her bos, came with us far as Sangry Christy goldmine. *She's* the squaw that dressed them skins).

"I now felt as brave as a buffler in spring. The old man was so clever, an' I walked 'longside like a 'quaintance. We stopped afore a stone door, an' it opened without touchin'.

" 'Hyar's damp powder, an' no fire to dry it,' shouts I, stoppin'.

" 'What's the matter—do you not wish to perambulate through my possessions?'

" 'This hos doesn't savy what the "human" for prerambulate is; but I'll walk plum to the hottest fire in your settlement, if that's all you mean.'

"The place was hot, an' smelt bad of brimstone; but the darned screechin' *took* me. I walks up to t'other eend of the 'lodge,' an' steal my mule, if thar wasn't Jake Beloo, as trapped with me to Brown's Hole! A lot of hellcats was a pullin' at his ears, an' a jumpin' on his shoulders, a swingin' themselves to the ground by his long har. Some was runnin' hot irons in him, but when we came up, they went off in a corner a laffin' and talkin' like wildcats' gibberish on a cold night.

"Poor Jake! he came to the bar, lookin' like a sick buffler in the eye. The bones stuck through the skin, an' his har was matted an' long—all over jest like a blind bull, an' white blisters spotted him, with water runnin' out of 'em. 'Hatch, old feller! *you* here, too?—how are ye?' says he, in a faint-like voice, staggerin' an' catchin' on to the bar fur support—'I'm sorry to see you *here*, what did you'—he raised his eyes to the old man standin' ahind me, who gave him *such* a look: he went howlin' an' foamin' at the mouth to the fur eend of the den, an' fell down, rollin' over the damp stones. The devils, who was chucklin' by a furnis, whar was irons a heatin', approached easy, an' run one into his back. I jumped at 'em and hollered, 'You owdacious little hellpups, let him alone; ef my sculptaker was hyar, I'd make buzzard feed of your meat, an' *parflêche* of your dogskins,' but they squeaked out to 'go to the devil.'

" 'Wagh!' says I, 'ef I *ain't* pretty close to his lodge, I'm a niggur!'

"The old gentleman speaks up, 'take care of yourself, Mr. Hatcher,' in a mity soft, kind voice; an' he smiled so calm an' devilish—it nigh on froze me. I thought ef the ground would open with a yairthquake, an' take me in, I'd be much obleeged any how. Thinks I—you saint-forsaken, infernal hell-chief, how I'd like to stick my knife in your withered old breadbasket.

" 'Ah! my dear fellow, no use in tryin'—that is a *decided* impossibility'—I jumped ten feet. I swar, a 'medicine' man couldn't a heerd me, for my lips didn't move; an' how *he* knew is moren this hos *kin* tell.

" 'Evil communications corrupt good manners. But I see your nervous equilibrium is destroyed—come with me.'

"At t'other side, the old gentleman told me to reach down for a brass knob. I thought a trick was goin' to be played on me, an' I dodged.

" 'Do not be afraid; turn it when you pull—steady there—that's it'—it came, an' a door, too. He walked in. I followed while the door shut of itself.

" 'Mity good hinges!' sez I, 'don't make a noise, an' go shut without slammin' an' cussen' 'em.'

" 'Yes—yes! some of my own importation; no! they were made here.'

"It was dark at first, but when the other door opened, thar was too much light. In another room was a table in the middle, with two bottles, an' little glasses like them to the Saint Louy drink houses, only prettier. A soft, thick carpet was on the floor—an' a square glass lamp hung from the ceiling. I sat cross-legged on the floor, an' he on a sofy, his feet cocked on a cheer, an' his tail quoiled under him, cumfortable as traders in a lodge. He hollered somethin' I couldn't make out, an' in comes two, black, crooked-shank devils, with a round bench on one leg, an' a glass with cigars in it. They *vamosed*, an' the old coon inviting me to take a cigar, helps himself, an' rared his head back, while I sorter lays on the floor, an' we smoked an' talked.

"We was speakin' of the size of the apple Eve ate, an' I said thar were none but crabapples until we grafted them, but he replied, thar *was* good fruit until the flood. Then Noah was so hurried to git the yelaphants, pinchin bugs, an' sich varment aboard, he furgot good appleseed, until the water got knee-deep; so he jumps out, gathers a lot of sour crabs, crams 'em in his pockets, an' Shem pulled him with a rope in the ark agin.

"I got ahead of him several times, an' he sez—'Do you *really* believe the preachers, with their smooth faces, upturned eyes, and whining cant?'

" 'Sartainly I do! cause they're mity kind and good to the poor.'

" 'Why I had no idea you were so ignorant—I assuredly expected more from so sensible a man as you!'

" 'Now, look'ee hyar, this child isn't used to be abused to his own face—I—I tell 'ee it's mity hard to choke down—ef it ain't, sculp me!'

" 'Keep quiet, my young friend, suffer not your temper to gain the mastery; let patience have its perfect work. I beg your pardon sincerely—and so you believe the Bible, and permit the benighted preachers to gull you unsparingly. Come now! what is the reason you imagine faith in the Bible is the work to take you to Heaven?'

" 'Well, don't *crowd* me an' I'll think a little—why, it's the oldest history anyhow: so they told me at home. I used to read it myself, old hos—this child did. It tells how the first man an' his squaw got hyar, an' the buffler, an' antelope, an' beaver, an' hosses too. An' when I see it on the table, somethin' ahind my ribs thumps out: "look, John, thar's a book you must be mighty respectful to," an' *somehow*, I believe it's moren human, an' I tell 'ee, its agin natur to believe otherwise, wagh!'

"Another thing, the old gentleman mentioned, I thought was pretty much the fact. When he said he fooled Eve, an' *walked* about, I said it was a *snake* what deceived the ole 'oman.

" 'Nonsense! snake indeed! I can satisfactorily account for that— but why think you so?'

" 'Because the big Bibles, with picters, has a snake quoiled in an appletree, pokin' out his tongue at Adam's squaw.'

" 'P'shaw! the early inhabitants were so angry to think that Satan could deceive their first mother, and entail so much misery on them, that, at a meeting to which the principal men attended, they agreed to call me a serpent, because a serpent can insinuate himself so easily. When Moses compiled the different narratives of the earlier times, in his five books, he wrote it so too. It is typical, merely, of the wiles of the devil—my humble self'—an' the old coon bowed, 'and an error, it seems, into which the whole world, since Moses, have irretrievably fallen. But have we not been sitting long enough? Take a fresh cigar, an' we will walk. That's Purgatory where your quondam friend, Jake

Beloo, is. He will remain there a while longer, and, if you desire it, can go, though it cost much exertion to entice him here, and then only, after he drank hard.'

" 'I wish you would, sir. Jake's as good a companyero as ever trapped beaver, or gnawed poor bull in spring, an' he treated his squaw as ef she was a white woman.'

" 'For your sake, I will; we may see others of your acquaintance before leaving this,' sez he, sorter queer-like, as if to say—'no doubt of it.'

"The door of the room we had been talkin' in, shut of its own accord. We stopped, an' he touchin' a spring in the wall, a trapdoor flew open, showin' a flight of steps. He went first, cautioning me not to slip on the dark sta'ars; but I shouted 'not to mind me, but thankee for tellin' it though.'

"We went down, an' down, an' down, till I 'gan to think the old cuss was goin' to get *me* safe, too, so I sung out—'Hello! which way; we must be mity nigh under Wah-to-yah, we've been goin' on so long?'

" 'Yes!' sez he, much astonished, 'we're just under the twins. Why, turn and twist you ever so much, you loose not your reckoning.'

" 'Not by a long chalk! this child had his bringin' up to Wapakon-netta, an' that's a fact.'

"From the bottom we went on in a dampish, dark sort of a passage, gloomily lit up, with one candle. The grease was runnin' down the block as had an augerhole bored in it for a candlestick, an' the long snuff to the eend was red, an' the blaze clung to it, as ef it hated to part company, an' turned black, an' smoked at the p'int in mournin'. The cold chills shook me, an' the old gentleman kept so still, the echo of my feet rolled back so hollow an' solemn. I wanted liquor mity bad—mity bad.

"Thar was noise smothered-like, an' some poor feller would cry out worse 'an Camanches chargin'. A door opened, and the old gentle-man touchin' me on the back, I went in, an' he followed. It flew to, an' though I turned rite round, to look fur 'sign' to 'scape, ef the place got too hot, I couldn't find it.

" 'Wa-agh!' sez I.

" 'What now, are you dissatisfied?'

" 'Oh, no! I was just lookin' to see what sort of a lodge you have.'

" 'I understand you perfectly, sir—be not afraid.'

"My eyes were blinded in the light, but rubbin' 'em, I saw two big snakes comin' at me, thar yaller an' bloodshot eyes shinin' awfully, an' thar big red tongues dartin' back an' forad, like a painter's paw, when he slaps it on a deer, an' thar wide jaws open, showin' long, slim, white fangs. On my right, four ugly animals jumped at me, an' rattled ther chains—I *swar*, ther heads were bigger an' a buffler's in summer. The snakes hissed an' showed thar teeth, an' lashed thar tails, an' the dogs howled, an' growled, an' charged, an' the light from the furnis flashed out brighter an' brighter; an' above me, an' around me, a hundred devils yelled, an' laffed, an' swore, an' spit, an' snapped ther bony fingers in my face, an' leaped up to the ceiling into the black, long spiderwebs, an' rode on the spiders bigger an' a powderhorn, an' jumped off onter my head. Then they all formed in line, an' marched, an' hooted, an' yelled: an' when the snakes jined the percession, the devils leaped on thar backs an' rode. Then some smaller ones rocked up an' down on springin' boards, an' when the snakes kem opposite, darted way up in the room an' dived down in their mouths, screechin' like so many Pawnees for sculps. When the snakes was in front of us, the little devils came to the eend of the snakes' tongues, laffin', an' dancin', an' singin' like eediuts. Then the big dogs jumped clean over us, growlin' louder 'an a cavyard of grisly b'ar, an' the devils holdin' on to thar tails, flopped over my head, screamin'—'we've got you— we've got you at last!'

"I couldn't stand it no longer, an' shuttin' my eyes, I yelled rite out, an' groaned.

" 'Be not alarmed,' and my friend drew his fingers along my head an' back, an' pulled a little narrow, black flask from his pocket with— 'take some of this.'

"I swallered a few drops. It tasted sweetish an' bitterish—I don't exactly *savy* how, but soon as it *was* down, I jumped up five times an' yelled—'out of the way, you little ones, an' let me ride;' an' after runnin' long side, and climbin' up his slimy scales, I got straddle of a big snake, who turned his head around, blowin' his hot, sickenin' breath in my face. I waved my old wool hat, an' kickin' him in a fast run, sung out to the little devils to git up behind, an' off we all started, screechin' 'Hooraw fur Hell!' The old gentleman rolled over an' bent himself double with laffin', till he putty nigh choked. We kept goin' faster an' faster till I got on to my feet (though the scales were mity slippery) an' danced Injun, an' whooped louder than 'em all.

"All at once, the old gentleman stopped laffin', pulled his specta- cles down on his nose an' said—'Mr. Hatcher, we had better go now,' an' then he spoke somethin' I couldn't make out, an' the animals all stood still; I slid off, an' the little hellcats a pinchin' my ears, an' pullin' my beard, went off squeakin'. Then they all formed in a halfmoon afore us—the snakes on ther tails, with heads way up to the black cobwebby roof; the dogs rared on thar hindfeet, an' the little devils hangin' every whar. Then they all roared, an' hissed, an' screeched seven times, an' wheelin' off, disappeared, just as the light went out, leaving us in the dark.

" 'Mr. Hatcher,' sez the old gentleman agin, movin' off, 'you will please amuse yourself until I return;' but seein' me look wild, 'you have seen too much of me to feel alarmed for your own safety. Take this imp fur a guide, an' if he is impertinent, *put him through*; and, for fear the exhibitions may overcome your nerves, imbibe a portion of this cordial,' which I did, an' everything danced afore my eyes, an' I wasn't a bit scairt.

"I started fur a red light as came through the crack of a door, a stumblin' over a three-legged stool, an' pitchin' my last cigar stump to one of the dogs, chained to the wall, who ketched it in his mouth. When the door was opened by my guide, I saw a big blaze like a peraira on fire—red and gloomy; an' big black smoke was curlin', an' twistin', an' shootin', an' spreadin', and the flames a licking the walls, goin' up to a pint, and breakin' in to a wide blaze, with white an' green ends. Thar was bells a tollin', an' chains a clinkin', an' mad howls an' screams; but the old gentleman's 'medicine' made me feel as independent as a trapper with his animals feedin' round him, two pack of beaver in camp, with traps sot fur more.

"Close to the hot place, was a lot of merry devils laffin' an' shoutin' with an old pack of greasy cards—it minded me of them we played with to rendezvoo—shufflin' 'em to 'Devil's Dream,' an' 'Money Musk;' then they 'ud deal in slow time, with 'Dead March in Saul,' whistlin' as solemn as medicine men. Then they broke out of a sudden with 'Paddy O'Rafferty,' which made this hos move about in his moccasins so lively, one of them as was playin', looked up an' sed—'Mr. Hatcher, won't you take a hand—make way, boys, fur the gentleman.'

"Down I sot amongst 'em, but stepped on the little feller's tail, who had been leadin' the Irish jig. He hollered till I got off it—'Owch! but it's on my tail ye are!'

" 'Pardon,' sez I, 'but you're an Irishman!'

" 'No, indeed; I'm a hellimp, he! he! who-oop! I'm a hellimp,' an' he laffed, and pulled my beard, an' screeched till the rest threatened to choke him ef he didn't stop.

" 'What's trumps?' sez I, 'an' whose deal?'

" 'Here is my place,' sez one, 'I'm tired playin'; take a horn,' handin' me a black bottle, 'the game's poker, an' it's your deal next—

there's a bigger game of poker on hand,' an' pickin' up an iron rod heatin' in the fire, he pinched a miserable burnin' feller ahind the bars, who cussed him, an' run way in the blaze outen reach.

"I thought I was *great* at poker by the way I took the plews an' traps from the boys to rendezvoo, but hyar the slick devils beat me without half tryin'. When they slapped down a bully pair, they 'ud screech an' laff worse 'an fellers on a spree. Sez one—'Mr. Hatcher, I reckon you're a hos at poker away to your country, but you can't shine down here—you are nowhar'. That feller lookin' at us through the bars, was a preacher up to the world. When we first got him, he was *all-fired* hot and thirsty. We would dip our fingers in water, an' let it run in his mouth, to get him to teach us the best tricks—he's a trump—he would stand an' stamp the hot coals, and dance up and down, while he told us his experience. Whoopee! how we would laugh! He has delivered two *long* sermons of a Sunday, and played poker at night on fip antes, with the deacons, for the money bagged that day; and, when he was in debt, he exhorted the congregation to give more fur the poor heathen in a foreign land, a dying and losing their souls for the want of a little money to send 'em a gospel preacher—that the poor heathen 'ud be damned to eternal fire ef they *didn't* make up the dough. The gentleman as showed you around—Old Sate, we call him—had his eye on the preacher for a long time. When we got him, we had a barrel of liquor, and carried him around on our shoulders, until tired of the fun, and then threw him in the furnace yonder. We call him "Poke," for that was his favorite game. Oh, Poke!' shouted my friend, 'come here; thar's a gentleman wishes you—we'll give you five drops of water, an' that's more than your old skin's worth.'

"He came close, an' though his face was poor, an' all scratched, an' his har swinged mity nigh off, 'make meat' of this child if it wasn't old Cormon as used to preach to the Wapakonnetta settlement! Many a time this coon's har's stood on eend, when he preached about t'other world. He came close, an' I could see the chains tied on his wrists, whar they had worn to the bone, showin' the raw meat, an' dried and runnin' blood. He looked a darned sight worse an' ef Camanches had skulped him.

" 'Hello! old coon,' sez I, 'we're both in that awful place you talked so much about, but I ain't so bad off as you, yet. This young gentleman,' pointin' to the devil who told me of his doins—'this young gentleman has been tellin' me how you took the money you made us throw in on Sunday.'

" 'Yes,' sez he, 'ef I had only acted as I told others to do, I would not have been here scorching for ever and ever—water! water! John, my son, fur my sake, a little water.'

"Just then a little rascal stuck a hot iron in him, an' off he ran in the flames, caching on the cool side of a big chunk of fire, a lookin' at us fur water; but I cared no more fur him than the Pawnee, whose topknot was tucked in my belt, fur stealin' my cavyard to the Coon Creeks; an' I sez—

" 'This hos doesn't give a *cuss* fur you; you're a sneakin' hypercrite; you deserve all you've got an' more too—an', lookee hyar, old boy, it's me as says so.'

"I strayed off a piece, pretendin' to get cool; but this coon 'gan to git *scairt*, an' that's a fact, fur the devils carried Cormon till they got tired of him; 'an',' sez I to myself, 'an' *haint* they been doin' me the same way? I'll *cache*—I will—fur I'm not overly good, specially since I came to the mountains. Wagh! but this beaver must be movin' fur deep water, if that's the way your stick floats' (a floating stick attached to the chain marks the spot of the submerged beavertrap).

"Well now, this child felt sorter queer, so he santers 'long slowly, till he saw an open place in the rock; not mindin' the imps who was drinkin' away like trappers on a bust. It was so dark thar, I felt my way mity still (fur I was afraid they 'ud be after me); I got almost to a streak of light, when thar was sich a rumpus back in the cave as give me the trimbles. Doors was slammin', dogs growlin' an' rattlin' thar chains, an' the devils a screamin'. They come a chargin'. The snakes was hissin' sharp an' wiry; the beasts howled out long an' mournful; an' thunder rolled up overhead, an' the imps was yellin' an' screechin' like mad.

" 'It's time to break fur timber, sure,' and I run as ef a wounded buffler was raisin' my shirt with his horns. The place was damp, an' in the narrow rock, lizards an' vipers an' copperheads jumped out at me, an' clum on my legs, but I stompt an' shook 'em off. Owls, too, flopped thar wings in my face, an' hooted at me, an' fire blazed out, an' lit the place up, an' brimstone smoke came nigh on chokin' me. Lookin' back, the whole cavyard of hell was comin', an' devils on devils, nothin' but devils, filled the hole.

"I threw down my hat to run faster, an' then jerked off my old blanket, but still they was gainin'. I made one jump clean out of my moccasins. The big snake in front was closer an' closer, with his head drawed back to strike; then a helldog raked up nearly long side, pantin' an' blowin' with the slobber runnin' outen his mouth, an' a lot of devils hangin' on to him, was cussin' me an' screechin'. I strained every jint, but no use, they still gained—not fast—but gainin' they was. I jumped an' swore, an' leaned down, an' flung out my hands, but the dogs was nearer every time, an' the horrid yellin' an' hissin' way back, grew louder an' louder. At last, a prayer mother used to make me say, I hadn't thought of fur twenty year or more, came rite afore me clear as a powderhorn. I kept runnin' an' sayin' it, an' the niggurs held back a little. I gained some on them—Wagh! I stopped repeatin', to get breath, an' the foremost dog made such a lunge at me, I forgot it. Turnin' up my eyes, thar was the old gentleman lookin' at me, an' keepin' alongside, without walkin'. His face warn't more than two feet off, an' his eyes was fixed steady, an' calm an' devilish. I screamed rite out. I shut my eyes but he was thar too. I howled an' spit an' hit at it, but couldn't git the darned face away. A dog ketched hold of my shirt with his fangs, an' two devils, jumpin' on me, caught me by the throat, a tryin' to choke me. While I was pullin' 'em off, I fell down, with about thirty-five of the infernal things, an' the dogs, an' the slimy snakes a top of me, a mashin' an' taren' me. I bit big pieces out of them, an' bit an' bit agin, an' scratched an' gouged. When I was most give out, I heerd the Pawnee skulp yell, an' use my rifle fur a pokin' stick, ef in didn't charge a party of the best boys in the mountains. *They* slayed the devils right an' left, an' sot 'em runnin' like goats, but this hos was so weak fightin', he fainted away. When I come to, we was on the Purgatoire, just whar I found the liquor, an' my companyeros was slappin' thar wet hats in my face, to bring me to. Round whar I was layin', the grass was pulled up an' the ground dug with my knife, and the bottle, cached when I traded with the Yutes, was smashed to flinders 'gainst a tree.

" 'Why, what on airth, Hatcher, have ye bin doin' hyar? You was a kickin' an' taren' up the grass, an' yellin' as ef yer "har" was taken. Why, old hos, this coon don't savy them hifelutin' notions, he doesn't!'

" 'The devils from hell was after me,' sez I mity gruff, 'this hos has seen moren ever he wants to agin.'

"They tried to git me outen the notion, but I swar, an' I'll stick to it, this child saw a heap more of the all-fired place than he wants to agin; an' ef it aint fact, he doesn't know 'fat cow' from 'poor bull'— Wagh!

So ended Hatcher's tale of Wah-to-yah, or what the mountaineer saw when he had the *mania potu.*

Heading for the Mountains

Young men who heard or read tales by some of the mountain men and yearned to emulate them could find newspaper advertisements announcing jobs for those who wanted to become fur trappers. Most of those who responded to such calls came to St. Louis; then, after securing employment, traveled on to Independence to await the departure of the fur company's westward-bound party. But prospective trappers could go to many other jumping-off points. If they signed on with the Hudson's Bay Company, they might head to the Rockies from points in Canada. Other would-be mountain men might follow the Santa Fe Trail or leave Fort Smith, Arkansas, for a southern route. Some might take a ship from Boston or New York to sail around the Horn, later stopping in the Sandwich Islands (Hawaii) before going on to Oregon. Whatever their point of departure, they usually traveled along routes traced by Indians and by the earliest explorers and trappers. Some journeyed by boat up the Missouri River. Others took what would later be known as the Oregon Trail. Printed maps were few and sparsely detailed, so most veterans of the fur trade relied on the maps they carried in their heads, adding features each time they took a new route or heard the tale of someone else who had.

The time it took to get from the settlements to the mountains varied, of course. Distances now covered by airplanes in minutes and by cars in hours could take days or weeks for trappers on horses or mules. We know from William Marshall Anderson's journal that the Sublette party of 1834 took from 1 May to 7 June to travel from Independence, Missouri, to Independence Rock in present-day Wyoming. A trip up the Missouri could take several months. Travel across mountains and deserts naturally took longer than a trek over a similar distance on the plains or along a river, all else being equal (though it seldom was). Rain, snow, hail, wind—all could slow a caravan to a crawl. And buffalo—sometimes miles of them—could hamper forward progress for days.

Once across the plains or off shipboard, the novice trapper and his party might arrive at a fort or post built by a fur company or, in some cases, by an independent trapper. Some of these establishments lasted barely a season or two, and some received new names when they changed hands. The following list includes only some of the main fur trade forts, the dates when they were built, and their locations.

1795—Fort Edmonton (Alberta); built by the Hudson's Bay Company (HBC) near the present site of Edmonton.

1802—Cedar Island Post (South Dakota); built by Regis Louisel near the junction of the White and Missouri rivers.

1807—Fort Raymond (Montana); built by Manuel Lisa at the confluence of the Bighorn and Yellowstone rivers.

1809—Council Bluffs Post (Iowa); built by the Missouri Fur Company.

1809—Kullyspell House (Idaho); built by David Thompson near Lake Pend Oreille.

1810—Fort Henry (Montana); built by Andrew Henry and John Colter between the Jefferson and Madison rivers.

1811—Astoria (Oregon); built by John Jacob Astor's Pacific Fur Company (later run by the HBC) at the mouth of the Columbia River.

1812—Fort Ross (California); built by the Russian-American Company on the coast north of San Francisco.

1812—Fort Lisa (Iowa); built by Manuel Lisa at the Council Bluffs.

1817—Fort Pierre (South Dakota); built across the Missouri from present-day Pierre.

1824—Fort Vancouver (Washington); built by the HBC on the site of present-day Vancouver, Washington.

1829—Fort Union (Montana); built by Kenneth Mackenzie

on the north bank of the Missouri River five miles above the mouth of the Yellowstone.

1832—Fort Bonneville (Wyoming); built by Benjamin L. E. Bonneville five miles north of Horse Creek on the Green River.

1832—Fort Cass (Wyoming); built by the American Fur Company near the mouth of the Bighorn River.

1833—Bent's Old Fort [also called Fort William] (Colorado); built by Charles Bent and Ceran St. Vrain twelve miles upstream from the confluence of the Purgatoire and Arkansas rivers on the north bank of the Arkansas.

1833—Fort Jackson (Montana); built by Francois A. Chardon near the mouth of Milk River.

1834—Fort Laramie [originally called Fort William] (Wyoming); built by William Sublette and Robert Campbell at the junction of the Laramie and North Platte rivers.

1834—Fort Hall (Idaho); built by Nathaniel J. Wyeth on the Snake River above the mouth of the Portneuf; sold to the HBC in 1837.

1834—Fort Boise (Idaho); built by Thomas McKay, an independent operator associated with the HBC, just north of the site of John Reid's short-lived fort built in 1813 at the confluence of the Snake and Boise rivers.

1835—Fort Vasquez (Colorado); built by Louis Vasquez on the South Platte River near present-day Denver. Within two or three years after the erection of Fort Vasquez, competing forts Lupton, Jackson, and St. Vrain were built nearby.

Late 1830s—Brown's Hole [now Brown's Park] (Colorado), a short-lived post called "Fort Misery" by the trappers; built on the Green River near what is now the Colorado-Utah border.

1843—Fort Camosum [later renamed Fort Victoria] (British Columbia); built by the HBC on the site of present-day Victoria.

1843—Fort Bridger (Wyoming); built by James Bridger and Louis Vasquez on Black Fork of the Green River.

More information on the forts can be found in David J. Wishart, *The Fur Trade of the American West, 1807–1840* (1992).

After the greenhorn trapper's party had passed one or more forts, it might head to that season's rendezvous site. (In Section VI, "Rendezvous," we include a list of those sites.) Veteran trappers might lead a party to favorite gathering spots such as North Park, South Park, and Brown's Hole in present-day Colorado, or Pierre's Hole in present-day Idaho, or Jackson's Hole in present-day Wyoming. Trappers who went west on the Santa Fe Trail might stop at Taos and Santa Fe before going on to trap in the mountains.

During the weeks of travel, the greenhorns listened to seasoned mountain men recount their adventures, and in the process the beginners learned much about the fur trade and about the mechanics of setting traps and skinning beaver. And when they saw the mountains for the first time, many of those young men thought they had come to a new Garden of Eden.

25. Ashley's Newspaper Ad for 100 Men

from William H. Ashley, *The West of William H. Ashley*

In 1821 William H. Ashley (1778–1838) and Andrew Henry (1775?–1833) formed a partnership in the fur trade. The following selection is an ad they placed the following year in a St. Louis newspaper. In 1822, and for several years thereafter, Ashley led expeditions up the Missouri River and, in 1824, over South Pass. In 1825 he descended the Green River and met a party of trappers led by Etienne Provost from Taos. After 1826 Ashley resumed his business affairs in St. Louis and never returned to the mountains, although he acted as supplier, banker, and sales agent for William L. Sublette and his partners, Jedediah Smith and David Jackson. In 1831 Ashley won election to the U.S. House of Representatives, where he served until his death from pneumonia in 1838.

Missouri Gazette & Public Advertiser,
TO
Enterprising Young Men

   The subscriber wishes to engage ONE HUNDRED MEN, to ascend the river Missouri to its source, there to be employed for one, two or three years—For particulars, enquire of Major Andrew Henry, near the Lead Mines, in the County of Washington, (who will ascend with, and command the party) or to the subscriber at St. Louis.

                                                    Wm. H. Ashley

February 13, 1822.

26. Mixed Motives for Becoming a Mountain Man

from Warren Ferris, *Life in the Rocky Mountains*

As he expressed them, Warren Ferris's motives for becoming a mountain man in 1830 sound somewhat like the opening paragraph of Herman Melville's *Moby-Dick*, in which Ishmael gives his reasons for going whaling. (Melville scholars do not, however, include Ferris in the list of authors whose work Melville had read.)

Westward! Ho! It is the sixteenth of the second month, A. D. 1830, and I have joined a trapping, trading, hunting expedition to the Rocky Mountains. *Why*, I scarcely know, for the motives that induced me to this step were of a mixed complexion,—something like the pepper and salt population of this city of St. Louis. Curiosity, a love of wild adventure, and perhaps also a hope of profit,—for times *are* hard, and my best coat has a sort of sheepish hang-dog hesitation to encounter fashionable folk—combined to make me look upon the project with an eye of favour. The party consists of some thirty men, mostly Canadians; but a few there are, like myself, from various parts of the Union. Each has some plausible excuse for joining, and the aggregate of disinterestedness would delight the most ghostly saint in the Roman calendar. Engage for money! no, not they;—health, and the strong desire of seeing strange lands, of beholding nature in the savage grandeur of her primeval state,—these are the only arguments that *could* have persuaded such independent and high-minded young fellows to adventure with the American Fur Company in a trip to the mountain wilds of the great west. But they are active, vigorous, resolute, daring, and such are the kind of men the service requires. The Company have no reason to be dissatisfied, nor have they. Everything *promises* well. No doubt there will be two fortunes apiece for us. Westward! Ho!

27 and 28. Manners Along the Trail.

As the painter Alfred Jacob Miller tells us in the first of the following two selections, tempers sometimes frayed on the journey west, so the leader of a fur-trapping party had to know how to discipline his men when fights broke out. A fixed routine, like the one described by John Ball in the second selection, probably helped to maintain order. Ball (1794–1884), a native of New Hampshire, accompanied Nathaniel J. Wyeth's party in 1832; but, after the 1833 rendezvous, Ball joined a party of Rocky Mountain Fur Company trappers led by Milton Sublette and Henry Fraeb.

27. Fighting in Camp

from Alfred Jacob Miller, *The West of Alfred Jacob Miller*

Caravan *en route*
The government of a band of this kind is somewhat despotic, being composed of a heterogeneous mass of people from all sections, free and comp^y trappers, traders, half-breeds, and Indians. Our leader was admirably calculated for it, as he understood well the management of unruly spirits. He had served under Wellington in the Peninsular Campaigns, and at the battle of Waterloo,—indeed seemed to be in a measure composed of the same iron that formed the "Great Duke" himself.

It was amusing to see how he managed belligerents. Two men in camp one day commenced fighting. It was reported to him, and he said, "Let them alone":—finally, one was dreadfully beaten and put *hors de combat*. On this being reported, he sent for the vanquished, who presented himself in sorry plight. "You have been fighting and are whipped,"—"*Oui, mon Capitan*,"—"By Jove! I am heartily glad to hear it," quoth the Captain, "I am certain you have nothing to boast of, Go." He then sent for the conqueror, who approached his presence with a jaunty impudent look. "You have whipped Louis?" "*C'est vrai*," whereupon the Captain told him, if he heard of his boasting of it, in any manner, he would dismount him and make him walk for a week. This was cold comfort for our hero, who expected to be congratulated, but the efficacy of the treatment was most effectual;—no more fighting took place in the camp. To whip a man and then not be permitted to brag of it was not what they bargained for.

28. The Mode of Encampment

from John Ball, *John Ball . . . Autobiography*

Now came a march of day after day up this North Platte of great sameness. The main band keeping straight on the way, when the buffalo were not met with crossing our tracks. A few of the best hunters, each with two horses, one to ride and another on which to pack the meats, would leave the band and range the country back, kill and dress the animal and bring the meat to our night's encampment.

And I should have before described our mode of encamping. Mr. Sublette leading the band, always selected the ground, having reference in doing so to water, always encamping on the river or other stream, to feed for horses and the safety of the place for defense in case of an attack, which he seemed to rather expect. And if such place was reached by that time, he usually ordered "halt" by the middle of the afternoon, so as to give the horses time to feed and make full preparation for night. The horses were unpacked and men or messes arranged in a manner to leave a large hollow square, the stream forming one side. And then the horses were immediately hoppled, four feet tied together, and turned out of camp and a guard placed beyond them, to keep them from straying too far or drive them in if attacked. Then about sundown he would cry out "ketch up, ketch up" always repeating his order. Then each man would bring in the horses he had charge of, keep them still hoppled and tie them to short stakes carried with us, driven close into the ground, giving each one as much room as could be without interfering with others, so that they could feed also during the night. Then a guard, changed every three hours, sat for the night. As soon as light in the morning the order would be "turn out, turn out." And all would rise from their earthly beds, turn the horses out to bite, get a hearty breakfast, then the horses were saddled and packed and formed in line and the order given to "march." And as a reward for their expedition, the first ready took their place nearest to the commandant. In the middle of the day a stop was made, the horses unpacked to rest them, but not turned out, and a lunch taken by the men, if wished, of meat already cooked, and in half an hour pack up and march on.

29. Buffalo Covering the Prairie

from Warren Angus Ferris, *Life in the Rocky Mountains*

Descriptions like the following give us some idea of the awe some novice mountain men felt when they first saw buffalo by the thousands covering miles of prairie and plains. To learn more about the bison see Larry Barsness, *Heads, Hides, and Horns: The Compleat Buffalo Book* (1985). Section IX of *Rendezvous Reader*, "Animals," includes additional selections on buffalo and references to bison studies.

On the fourteenth, hurrah, boys! we saw a buffalo; a solitary, stately old chap, who did not wait an invitation to dinner, but toddled off with his tail in the air. We saw on the sixteenth a small herd of ten or twelve, and had the luck to kill one of them. It was a patriarchal fellow, poor and tough, but what of that? we had a roast presently, and champed the gristle with a zest. Hunger is said to be a capital sauce, and if so our meal was well seasoned, for we had been living for some days on boiled corn alone, and had the grace to thank heaven for meat of *any* quality. Our hunters killed also several antelopes, but they were equally poor, and on the whole we rather preferred the balance of the buffalo for supper. People soon learn to be dainty, when they have a choice of viands. Next day, oh, there they were, thousands and thousands of them! Far as the eye could reach the prairie was literally covered, and not only covered but crowded with them. In very sooth it was a gallant show; a vast expanse of moving, plunging, rolling, rushing life—a literal sea of dark forms, with still pools, sweeping currents, and heaving billows, and all the grades of movement from calm repose to wild agitation. The air was filled with dust and bellowings, the prairie was alive with animation,—I never realized before the majesty and power of the mighty tides of life that heave and surge in all great gatherings of human or brute creation. The scene had here a wild sublimity of aspect, that charmed the eye with a spell of power, while the natural sympathy of life with life made the pulse bound and almost madden with excitement. Jove but it was glorious! and the next day too, the dense masses pressed on in such vast numbers, that we were compelled to halt, and let them pass to avoid being overrun by them in a literal sense. On the following day also, the number seemed if possible more countless than before, surpassing even the prairie-blackening accounts of those who had been here before us, and whose strange tales it had been our wont to believe the natural extravagance of a mere travellers' turn for romancing, but they must have been true, for such a scene as this our language wants words to describe, much less to exaggerate. On, on, still on, the black masses come and thicken—an ebless deluge of life is moving and swelling around us!

30 and 31. Forts of the Fur Trade

The next two selections describe two of the most important forts of the fur trade. In 1837, Alfred Jacob Miller not only did a painting of Fort Laramie, he also described it in writing. "Bent's Fort" can refer to any of the three forts that the Bent brothers built in southeastern Colorado from the 1830s to 1853. The brothers included Charles (1799–1847), George (1814–1847), Robert (1816–1841), and William (1809–1869). For detailed studies see David Lavender, *Bent's Fort* (1954), and Jackson W. Moore, *Bent's Old Fort: An Archeological Study* (1973).

Thomas Jefferson Farnham (1804–1848), author of the selection about Bent's Fort, won an election to become captain of a party of nineteen that he led west from Independence, Missouri, in 1839. He returned to his home in Peoria in 1840, but in 1846 or 1847 he moved west permanently, settling in San Francisco, where he practiced law until his death.

30. The Interior of Fort Laramie

from Alfred Jacob Miller, *The West of Alfred Jacob Miller*

The view is from the great entrance looking West, and embraces more than half the Court, or area. When this space is filled with Indians and Traders—as it is at slated periods, the scene is lively and interesting They gather here from all quarters. From the Gila at the South, the Red River at the North, and the Columbia River West, each has its quota and representatives. Siouxs, Bannocks, Mandans, Crows, Snakes, Pend-Orielles, Nez Percés, Cheyennes, and Delawares,—all except the Blackfeet, who are *bête noirs* and considered *de trop*. As a contrast, there are Canadian Trappers, free and otherwise, Half breeds, Kentuckians, Missourians, and Down Easters. A Saturnalia is held the first day and some excesses committed. But after this trading goes briskly forward.

There was a cannon or two sleeping in the towers over the two main entrances,—the Indians having an aversion to their being wakened, entertaining a superstitious reverence for them. They are intended to keep the peace. This fort was built by Robert Campbell who named it Fort William in honor of his friend and partner Wm. Sublette. These gentlemen were the earliest pioneers after Mess^ors Lewis and Clarke, and had many battles with the Indians. Once, in an encounter with the Blackfeet, they made their wills in true soldier-like fashion as they rode along, appointing each the executor of the other. We had almost daily intercourse with Sublette, Campbell, and Gov. Clarke in St. Louis, before we started. Capt. Lewis had at that time deceased. In an encounter with the Blackfeet Mr. Sublette received a poisoned ball, from which he never recovered. I have heard that he ultimately died from it.

31. Bent's Fort

from **Thomas Jefferson Farnham**, *Travels in the Great Western Prairies*

Fort William, or Bent's Fort, on the north side of the Arkansas, eighty miles north by east from Taos in the Mexican dominions, and about one hundred and sixty miles from the mountains, was erected by gentlemen owners in 1832, for purposes of trade with the Spaniards of Santa Fe and Taos, and the Eutaw, Cheyenne and Cumanche Indians. It is in the form of a parallelogram, the northern and southern sides of which are about a hundred and fifty feet, and the eastern and western a hundred feet in length. The walls are six or seven feet in thickness at the base, and seventeen or eighteen feet in height. The fort is entered through a large gateway on the eastern side, in which swing a pair of immense plank doors. At the north-west and south-east corners stand two cylindrical bastions, about ten feet in diameter and thirty feet in height.

These are properly perforated for the use of cannon and small arms; and command the fort and the plains around it. The interior area is divided into two parts. The one and the larger of them occupies the north-eastern portion. It is nearly a square. A range of two story houses, the well, and the blacksmith's shop are on the north side; on the west and south are ranges of one-story houses; on the east the blacksmith's shop, the gate and the outer wall. This is the place of business. Here the owners and their servants have their sleeping and cooking apartments, and here are the storehouses. In this area the Indians in the season of trade gather in large numbers and barter, and trade, and buy, under the guardianship of the carronades of the bastions loaded with grape, and looking upon them. From this area a passage leads between the eastern outer wall and the one-story houses, to the caral or cavy-yard, which occupies the remainder of the space within the walls. This is the place for the horses, mules, &c., to repose in safety from Indian depredations at night. Beyond the caral to the west and adjoining the wall, is the waggon-house. It is strongly built, and large enough to shelter twelve or fifteen of those large vehicles which are used in conveying the peltries to St. Louis, and goods thence to the post. The long drought of summer renders it necessary to protect them from the sun.

The walls of the fort, its bastions and houses, are constructed of adobies or unburnt bricks, cemented together with a mortar of clay. The lower floors of the building are made of clay, a little moistened and beaten hard with large wooden mallets; the upper floors of the two-story houses and the roofs of all are made in the same way and of the same material, and are supported by heavy transverse timbers covered with brush. The tops of the houses being flat and gravelled, furnish a fine promenade in the moonlight evenings of that charming climate. The number of men employed in the business of this establishment is supposed to be about sixty. Fifteen or twenty of them in charge of one of the owners, are employed in taking to market the buffalo robes, &c., which are gathered at the fort, and in bringing back with them new stocks of goods for future purchases. Another party is employed in hunting buffalo meat in the neighbouring plains; and another in guarding the animals while they cut their daily food on the banks of the river. Others, under command of an experienced trader, goes into some distant Indian camp to trade. One or more of the owners, and one or another of these parties which chances to be at the post, defend it and trade, keep the books of the company, &c. Each of these parties encounters dangers and hardships, from which persons within the borders of civilization would shrink.

The country in which the fort is situated is in a manner the common field of several tribes, unfriendly alike to one another and the whites. The Eutaws and Cheyennes of the mountains near Santa Fe, and the Pawnees of the great Platte, come to the Upper Arkansas to meet the buffalo in their annual migrations to the north; and on the trail of these animals follow up the Cumanches. And thus in the months of June, August, and September, there are in the neighbourhood of these traders from fifteen to twenty thousand savages ready and panting for plunder and blood. If they engage in battling out old causes of contention among themselves, the Messrs. Bents feel comparatively safe in their solitary fortress. But if they spare each other's property and lives, they occasion great anxieties at Fort William; every hour of day and night is pregnant with danger. These untameable savages may drive beyond reach the buffalo on which the garrison subsists; may begirt the fort with their legions, and cut off supplies; may prevent them from feeding their animals upon the plains; may bring upon them starvation and the gnawing their own flesh at the door of death! All these are expectations, which as yet the ignorance alone of the

Indians as to the weakness of the post, prevents from becoming realities. But at what moment some chieftain or white desperado may give them the requisite knowledge, is an uncertainty which occasions at Fort William many well-grounded fears for life and property.

Instances of the daring intrepidity of the Cumanches which occurred just before and after my arrival here, will serve to show the hazards and dangers of which I have spoken. About the middle of June, 1839, a band of sixty of them, under cover of night, crossed the river, and concealed themselves among the bushes growing thickly on the bank near the place where the animals of the establishment feed during the day. No sentinel being on duty at the time, their presence was unobserved; and when morning came the Mexican horseguard mounted his horse, and with the noise and shoutings usual with that class of servants when so employed, drove his charge out of the fort, and riding rapidly from side to side of the rear of the band, urged them on, and soon had them nibbling the short dry grass in a little vale within grape-shot distance of the guns of the bastions. It is customary for a guard of animals about these trading-posts to take his station beyond his charge; and if they stray from each other, or attempt to stroll too far, to drive them together, and thus keep them in the best possible situation to be hurried hastily to the caral, should the Indians, or other evil persons, swoop down upon them. As there is constant danger of this, his horse is held by a long rope and grazes around him, that he may be mounted quickly, at the first alarm, for a retreat within the walls. The faithful guard at Bent's, on the morning of the disaster I am relating, had dismounted after driving out his animals, and sat upon the ground, watching with the greatest fidelity for every call of duty, when these fifty or sixty Indians sprang from their hiding places, ran upon the animals, yelling horribly, and attempted to drive them across the river. The guard, however, nothing daunted, mounted quickly, and drove his horse at full speed among them. The mules and horses hearing his voice amidst the frightning yells of the savages, immediately started at a lively pace for the fort; but the Indians were on all sides, and bewildered them. The guard still pressed them onward, and called for help; and on they rushed, despite the efforts of the Indians to the contrary. The battlements were covered with men. They shouted encouragement to the brave guard—"Onward! onward!" and the injunction was obeyed. He spurred his horse to his greatest speed from side to side, and whipped the hindermost of the band with his leading rope. He had saved every animal; he was within twenty yards of the open gate; he fell; three arrows from the bows of the Cumanches had cloven his heart. Relieved of him, the lords of the quiver gathered their prey, and drove them to the borders of Texas, without injury to life or limb. I saw this faithful guard's grave. He had been buried a few days. The wolves had been digging into it.

32. Independence Rock, the Trappers' Post Office

from William Marshall Anderson, Rocky Mountain Journals

Independence Rock, described in the next selection, is now one of Wyoming's state historical sites. Off Wyoming State Highway 220, not far from the Sweetwater River, Independence Rock lies only a long day's walk from the continental divide.

June 7, 1834—Jack Frost, how do you do? I am like "John Anderson, my Jo," with his frosty pow. My head is whiter than usual this morning. The ground is covered [for a half inch] with a white robe, all around a lake, which is about three hundred yards long by one hundred wide, and the exudation forms a fringe of one half mile, extending every way from the water's edge. The trappers call this "Glauber Salts Lake" [I have no means to test it. It has a sudden purgative effect.] It seems that luxuries, necessaries, and apothecary stuff are spread all over the earth, as well for the irrational as for the rational creature. And here comes in the salt weed. It is a short, withered looking plant, with small leaves, which are strongly saline, as if they had been steeped in brine. In the fall of the year, wild horses and buffalo are very fond of it and it is said that in the winter the meat of all browsing animals is naturally and sufficiently seasoned by it.

We have breakfasted this morning at the base of Rock Independence [a very large and uncommon looking rock]. There are few places better known or more interesting to the mountaineer than this huge boulder. Here they look for and often obtain information of intense interest to them. On the side of the rock names, dates and messages, written in buffalo-grease and powder, are read and re-read with as much eagerness as if they were letters in detail from long absent friends. Besides being a place of advertisement, or kind of trappers' post office, it possesses a reputation and a fame peculiar to itself. It is a large, egg-shaped mass of granite, entirely separate and apart from all other hills, or ranges of hills [upon a dead level plain]. One mile in circumference, and about six or seven hundred feet high, without a particle of vegetation, and with no change known but the varying sparkles of mica which are seen by the light of the sun by day and the moon by night. Some years ago, a party of buffalo killers and beaver skinners celebrated here our national jubilee on the great Fourth of July. What noise, what roar of powder and pomp of patriotism surrounded and echoed from this eternal monument my informant did not say, nor can I imagine. I shall suppose the immortal Declaration was talked over, Washington toasted, and Rock Independence baptised into the old confederacy. [In silence I laid upon my back gazing upon its grey granite sides—I breathed the prayer, that my country's *Union* & Independence might be co-existent with that Rock.]

June 8, 1834—[We are all on the qui vive for the red men—We have discovered no fresh signs, but this is the region of their dark doings, and we might as well, both watch and pray.] We are now in a very dangerous region, and our motto is, or should be, "watch and pray". There is a great deal of the first done, I know, and very little of the latter, I suspect.

Oh, lovely beyond all loveliness is the setting sun, gilding the snow-capped peaks of the Seets-ca-dee! But hold! scribbler! leave something in your inkstand! I must, indeed, for having exhausted all my superlatives, unless I resort to pure invention, I have nothing to add to the description of the Black Hill view. In apology for that night's overflow, I have this to say: I had never been more than fifty miles from home, was on very high ground, and had been reading Phillips' speeches for twenty days. Seets-ca-dee is called by some Mount of the Winds, but means, in the Crow language, Prairie Cock. They call Green River Seets-ca-dee Azh-ee, or Prairie Cock River.

33 and 34. Trappers at a Rendezvous

In the next two selections, Alfred Jacob Miller tells what happened after trappers reached a rendezvous. For more about Miller, see Miller's own *Braves and Buffalo: Plains Indian Life in 1837* (1973), and Karen Reynolds and William Johnston, *Alfred Jacob Miller: Artist on the Oregon Trail* (1982).

33. Trappers

from Alfred Jacob Miller, *The West of Alfred Jacob Miller*

The trappers may be said to lead the van in the march of civilization,—from the Canadas in the North to California in the South;—from the Mississippi East to the Pacific West; every river and mountain stream, in all probability, have been at one time or another visited and inspected by them. Adventurous, hardy, and self-reliant,—always exposed to constant danger from hostile Indians, and extremes of hunger and cold,—they penetrate the wilderness in all directions in pursuit of their calling.

Harris (nicknamed Black) told us at the camp fire that he carried expresses for the Fur Company from the Western side of the Rocky Mountains to Fort Laramie for years:—he said the journeys were made alone, and his plan was to ride all night, and cache or hide himself during the day;—he carried with him a supply of dried meat so as to avoid making fires, which would have infallibly betrayed him. On being asked if he had not felt lonesome sometimes on these solitary excursions?—he laughed as if it was a good joke—"never knew in his life what it was to feel lonesome, or low spirited." The trappers in the sketch are *en repose*, the peculiar caps on their heads are made by themselves, to replace felt hats, long since worn out or lost,—their fringed shirts, "leggings," moccasins &c., are made by the Indian women, and sewed throughout with sinew instead of thread, which they do not possess.

34. Trappers Starting on a Beaver Hunt

from Alfred Jacob Miller, *The West of Alfred Jacob Miller*

Trappers are divided into three classes,—the hired, the free, and the trapper "on his own hook." After the Saturnalia which continues for 3 days at the rendezvous where they take their fill of eating & drinking, they then commence seriously their preparation for departure. On starting for the hunt the trapper fits himself out with full equipment. In addition to his animals he procures 5 or 6 traps (usually carried in a trap-sack), ammunition, a few pounds of tobacco, a supply of moccasins, a wallet called a "possible sack," gun, bowie knife, and sometimes a tomahawk.

Over his left shoulder and under his right arm hang his buffalo powderhorn, a bullet pouch in which he carries balls, flint, and steel, with other knickknacks.

Bound round his waist is a belt, in which is stuck his knife in a sheath of Buffalo hide, made fast to the belt by a chain or guard of some kind, and on his breast a pipe holder, usually a *gage d'amour* in the shape of a heart, worked in porcupine quills by some dusky charmer. Encircled with danger, they wander far and near in pursuit of "sign" of beaver. Ever on the alert, a turned leaf, grass pressed down, or the uneasiness of his animals, are signs palpable to him of proximity to an Indian foe, and places him on his guard.

With these precautions, he generally outwits the wily savage under equal advantages. Their motives of action have been happily described by the poet,—

> *Let him who crawls enamoured of decay,*
> *Cling to his couch, and sicken years away,*
> *Heave his thick breast and shake his palsied head,—*
> *Ours,—the fresh turf and not the feverish bed.*

35. How to Trap Beaver

from Robert Campbell, *A Narrative*

Once in the mountains, most beginning fur trappers probably received on-the-job training, but some of them might have read about the tricks of the trade in the many mountain-man narratives published during the period. Here, for example, is some how-to advice from Robert Campbell (1804–1879), who was born in Ireland, joined Ashley's 1825 expedition, fought at the Battle of Pierre's Hole (1832), and helped William Sublette build Fort Laramie in 1834. After 1835, Campbell became a St. Louis merchant and died one of the wealthiest men in Missouri. For more information about the paraphernalia Campbell mentions, see O. P. Russell, *Firearms, Traps, and Tools of the Mountain Man* (1967).

We remained in Cache valley only a couple of weeks, long enough to complete the traffic with the trappers.

After we left Cache valley, Jackson and Sublette met us on Bear river. Ashley then sold out his interest in the fur trade, to Smith, his partner, and to Jackson and Sublette, the new firm being known as Smith, Jackson & Sublette.

We now had buffalo meat in great plenty.

In fact we found the buffalo in great numbers at the head of Grand Island, after Ashley joined us.

It was their grand crossing place in their annual migratory tramps from the Arkansa to the Forks of the Missouri.

They have been there until within four or five years (1870).

While engaged in preparations for trapping the beaver, I will mention some peculiar traits of that sagacious animal. The beaver has a little bag under the tail, or more properly an oil sac near the anus.

The trapper takes this castoreum from this sac, and uses it as bait, it having served the beaver, by providing the where-with to oil himself.

While constructing their dams, some are seen bringing sticks and bushes for the purpose, while others dive to the bottom of the stream and bring up mud to plaster the sticks and bushes of the structure.

They are seen near these dams and at their "lodges" on the banks of the stream, where they ooze out this castoreum, which is understood to be a signal to other beavers. The trappers set their traps at these places. This castoreum, some of the old hunters use in this way. They take a piece of willow, strip off the bark and wash it, so as to leave no scent, as the beaver's sense of smell is exquisite, and then put castoreum on it.

The willow is attached to the trap and floats over it, when the beaver attracted to the smell approaches and is caught. The animal flounders about until drowned, but if he gets on the bank, with the trap, he has been known to bite off his feet to regain his liberty.

The trappers generally set out from camp with eight traps each. When they moved camp they cached what provisions were not necessary for the hunt, as dependence was made on game.

Arriving at good hunting ground a stop was made of some two or three days in a place, or even for one day.

They then set their traps for three or four miles up and down the stream. These trappers consisted mostly of men hired in St. Louis for eighteen months. Then there were what were called free hunters, who lived entirely on what they killed. We seldom had any bread.

When the supplies were brought up in the Summer, about two pounds of bread each, for one hundred men were brought in for the feast, made once a year,—and only then did they have bread.

Flour cost one dollar for a pint cupfull.

The trappers would make a feast of batter fried in melted buffalo tallow—a sort of fritter and call their friends around to partake.

Each man brought his pan and his knife, and very little liquor would be sold out—except to the old trappers. The single men among the trappers would mess half a dozen together. The air was pure and perfectly healthy. Every man, on-going to the cities would come back after spending his earnings. It was a bold, dashing life.

From this part of the country they could not carry buffalo skins away, owing to the cost of land transportation.

After the formation of the Company, the partners, Smith, Sublette and Jackson divided up the country between them.

Smith took a party of fifteen or twenty men, and started to go below Salt Lake, where he suffered from want of water.

Eventually they got down on the Colorado river and fell in with a band of the Mohaves.

In crossing the river, part of the men got over, leaving ten on the other side, when the Mohaves, to the number of thirty began to maneuver about in a hostile manner, Smith and the balance of the men with him attacked and killed four out of the thirty. Isaac Gallraith, a powerful man, died from his wounds, subsequently, on the Arkansas, about fifty miles from Bent's fort.

They then went to California. Smith and Turner came back poor and joined us the next Summer, (1827) at Sweet Water Lake, which empties into Bear Lake, where the rendezvous of Smith, Jackson and Sublette was then established.

When Smith left for Colorado, Jackson and Sublette with myself ascended the Snake river and tributaries near the Three Tetons and hunted along to the forks of the Missouri, following the Gallatin, and trapped along across the headwaters of the Columbia.

(1827) We then came back and wintered in Cache valley, and got our goods which we had cached the season before.

36 and 37. Romanticizing the Mountains

In the first of the following two selections, Maryland-born Thomas James (1782–1847) expresses the view of many eastern trappers when they first saw the mountains. The second selection, a poem by Warren Angus Ferris, shows that some mountain men tried their own hand at verse, even if their efforts seldom rose above the level of doggerel. For studies of others who saw the region as an area of surpassing beauty see William H. Goetzmann and William N. Goetzmann, *The West of the Imagination* (1986) and Chris Bruce, *Myth of the West* (1990). For more about the West's early verse, see Tom Trusky, "Western Poetry, 1850–1950" (1987).

36. A Rocky Mountain "Garden of Eden"

from Thomas James, *Three Years Among the Indians and Mexicans*

On the third day we issued from very high and desolate mountains on both sides of us, whose tops are covered with snow throughout the year, and came upon a scene of beauty and magnificence combined, unequalled by any other view of nature that I ever beheld. It really realized all my conceptions of the Garden of Eden. In the west the peaks and pinnacles of the Rocky Mountains shone resplendent in the sun. The snow on their tops sent back a beautiful reflection of the rays of the morning sun. From the sides of the dividing ridge between the waters of the Missouri and Columbia there sloped gradually down to the bank of the river we were on, a plain, then covered with every variety of wild animals peculiar to this region, while on the east another plain arose by a very gradual ascent and extended as far as the eye could reach. These and the mountain sides were dark with buffaloes, elk, deer, moose, wild goats, and wild sheep; some grazing, some lying down under the trees, and all enjoying a perfect millennium of peace and quiet. On the margin the swans, geese, and pelicans cropped the grass or floated on the surface of the water. The cottonwood trees seemed to have been planted by the hand of man on the bank of the river to shade our way, and the pines and cedars waved their tall, majestic heads along the base and on the sides of the mountains.

The whole landscape was that of the most splendid English park. The stillness, beauty, and loveliness of this scene struck us all with indescribable emotions. We rested on the oars and enjoyed the whole view in silent astonishment and admiration. Nature seemed to have rested here, after creating the wild mountains and chasms among which we had voyaged for two days. Dougherty, as if inspired by the scene with the spirit of poetry and song, broke forth in one of Burns' noblest lyrics, which found a deep echo in our hearts.

37. Poem: "Mountain Scenery"

from Warren Angus Ferris, *Life in the Rocky Mountains*

MOUNTAIN SCENERY

Where dark blue mountains towering rise
Whose craggy summits cleave the skies
Whose sides are decked with giant pines
With branch and encircling vines

There thund'ring torrents bounding far
From rock to rock dissolve in air
Or larger streams with lion rage
Burst through the barriers that encage

And sweeping onward to the plain
Deposit ruins and again
Proceed: but mask what force subdued
Their whirlwind terror now not rude

No longer they with fury hurl
Rocks from their beds in Eddies whirl
Tall pines, nor yet with deaf'ning roar
Assail the echoing mountains hoar

But milder than the summer breeze
Flow gently winding through the trees
Or smoothly flow and softly glide
Through woodless plains and valleys wide

Trappers and Their Trade

In Richard White's essay on "Animals and Enterprise" in *The Oxford History of the American West* (1994), he writes: "At the height of the beaver trade in 1832, the Missouri and Rocky Mountain systems deployed perhaps one thousand trappers, the Hudson's Bay Company provided another six hundred, and a smaller number of free trappers worked out of Taos." Many trappers remained in the mountains year after year, some because they wanted to, many because they had to in order to pay the company for indebtedness resulting from sprees at rendezvous and from outfitting charges. Probably, then, the total number of mountain men engaged in the fur trade during the first half of the nineteenth century didn't exceed fifteen or twenty thousand, not more than the number of participants at some of the twentieth century's simulated rendezvous.

Thanks to the 292 biographical sketches included in *The Mountain Men and the Fur Trade of the Far West*, edited by LeRoy R. Hafen, scholars can compare the men who actually participated in the fur trade with the fur trappers of popular myth. William R. Swagerty, whose 1980 statistical analysis of the Hafen series biographical studies is the basis for his "Marriage and Settlement Patterns of Rocky Mountain Trappers and Traders," cautions that "one must be wary of the stereotyping and compartmentalizing of the mountain men which has characterized writing on the subject since the 1830s." In the introduction to Section IV, "Mountain Women," we will have more to say about Swagerty's findings. As Howard R. Lamar points out in *The Trader on the American Frontier: Myth's Victim* (1977), one reason for the stereotyping of mountain men is that late-nineteenth-century reporters interviewed surviving trappers and traders and reached conclusions on the basis of those interviews; but there were three generations of mountain men (the first born around 1775, the second around 1798–1800, and the third around 1812–1816), and the reporters talked only with members of the last generation.

Lamar also reports the conclusion of Harvey L. Carter and Marcia C. Spencer that "60 percent of the fur traders in the Rocky Mountains were of French, French-Canadian, or French-Indian descent." Spaniards had also been engaged in trading furs in the Southwest since at least the eighteenth century, and many of the fur traders were of Hispanic descent. As our introductions to selections have already indicated, a number of mountain men were born in the British Isles and went westward in stages or in one long journey. Other trappers were born in Maryland, Virginia, North Carolina, or Kentucky and came to Missouri when their families settled there. Swagerty says that "one out of every hundred trappers and traders was an Indian," but mountain men "of African descent were almost unknown in the trade, with the exceptions of James Beckwourth and Edward Rose." Some Kanakas, natives of the Hawaiian Islands, headed east to the Rockies after first coming on ship to Astoria in the Oregon country.

A few mountain men such as Robert Campbell grew rich, went back east, and lived past the age of seventy. Some, like Tim Goodale, uneasy in the gold-rush towns and cities and among the advancing waves of farmers and ranchers, moved to remote areas in the northern Rockies where they could live out their days with their Indian wives in the wilderness style they had come to love. John Brown and other trappers joined the California gold rush and either settled in the Golden State or went on to other gold rushes. Wagon trains of pioneers hired many other mountain men, who guided the trains to Oregon or California and then settled there with the pioneers. Finally, a number of trappers and traders died on the job. In *Jedediah Smith and the Opening of the West* (1953), Dale L. Morgan includes information about deaths among employees of Ashley, Smith, Jackson, and Sublette: in a company that employed from 80 to 180 employees per year, the total number of dead from 1823 to 1829 was 94 (343–45).

Such statistics, generalizations, and analyses can answer questions about the history and sociology of the fur trade, but the selections that follow bring to life much that lies behind those dry details and numbers. The mountain men tell us what they did, how they did it, what perils they faced, and what disappointments and rewards awaited them.

38. Division of Labor among Mountain Men

from William Thomas Hamilton, *My Sixty Years on the Plains*

William Thomas Hamilton (1822–1908) tells how "trappers divided the work." Born in the Cheviot Hills near the English-Scottish border, Hamilton came to the United States in 1825 and eventually settled in St. Louis. In 1842 he was suffering from poor health, and since his father thought that a trip on a fur-trapping expedition might be salubrious, he purchased for his son a partnership with "Old Bill" Williams and George Perkins. Their party trapped until 1845, but Hamilton stayed in the West, trapping in the Big Horns and the Arkansas River area. He joined the gold rush to California in 1849 and settled there. After his wife and child died in childbirth in 1851, Hamilton joined trapper friends in fighting California Indians. He knew Indian sign language so well that he was called "Master of the Signs." He spent his last years in Montana.

The reader may be interested in knowing just how a company of twenty trappers divided the work in the business of collecting furs among hostile Indians.

In the first place, everything was held in common, which means that the value of all furs trapped was equally divided. All the men could not trap, for a picket had to be constantly on duty. A guard remained with the horses during the day. During the night the horses were corralled. One man had to take care of camp, and generally two men acted as skinners and caretakers of all the furs brought in. The remainder set traps, and all kept a sharp lookout for Indians. No shooting was allowed while setting traps, as a shot signified Indians, at which signal all were on the alert.

A general rule that was followed by all mountain men was to strap stay-chains or trace-chains to the horses' fetlocks. It was impossible for them to stampede with such a fixing. When trappers lost their horses they were obliged to go to some rendezvous and restock, as furs could not be collected without horses.

39 and 40. Making a Fur Cache

One of the most celebrated authors of his day, Washington Irving (1783–1859) gathered the materials for *Astoria* (1836) from fur-trade magnate John Jacob Astor and his employees and wrote the book in collaboration with his nephew Pierre Irving. Historian James P. Ronda says that "*Astoria* was and remains what Irving intended it to be: a compelling tale of romance and adventure." In addition to exciting narrative, some passages of *Astoria*, such as the first of the next two selections, offer reliable information about fur-trade practices such as making a cache. Mary Weatherspoon Bowden's *Washington Irving* (1981) gives an introduction to Irving's life and works. In the second selection, John C. Frémont tells why one particular group of trappers had to make a cache. For a fictionalized version of Frémont's life see David Nevin's 1983 novel, *Dream West*.

39. Making a Cache

from Washington Irving, *Astoria*

A cache is a term common among traders and hunters to designate a hiding place for provisions and effects. It is derived from the French word *cacher*, to conceal, and originated among the early colonists of Canada and Louisiana; but the secret depository which it designates was in use among the aboriginals long before the intrusion of the white men. It is, in fact, the only mode that migratory hordes have of preserving their valuables from robbery during their long absences from their villages or accustomed haunts, on hunting expeditions, or during the vicissitudes of war. The utmost skill and caution are required to render these places of concealment invisible to the lynx eye of an Indian. The first care is to seek out a proper situation, which is generally some dry low bank of clay on the margin of a water course. As soon as the precise spot is pitched upon, blankets, saddle cloths, and other coverings are spread over the surrounding grass and bushes, to prevent foot tracks, or any other derangement; and as few hands as possible are employed. A circle of about two feet in diameter is then nicely cut in the sod, which is carefully removed, with the loose soil immediately beneath it, and laid aside in a place where it will be safe from any thing that may change its appearance. The uncovered area is then digged perpendicularly to the depth of about three feet, and is then gradually widened so as to form a conical chamber six or seven feet deep. The whole of the earth displaced by this process, being of a different colour from that on the surface, is handed up in a vessel, and heaped into a skin or cloth, in which it is conveyed to the stream and thrown into the midst of the current, that it may be entirely carried off. Should the cache not be formed in the vicinity of a stream, the earth thus thrown up is carried to a distance and scattered in such manner as not to leave the minutest trace. The cave being formed, is well lined with dry grass, bark, sticks and poles, and occasionally a dried hide. The property intended to be hidden is then laid in, after having been well aired: a hide is spread over it, and dry grass, bark, brush and stones thrown in and trampled down until the pit is filled to the neck. The loose soil which had been put aside is then brought and rammed down firmly to prevent its caving in, and is frequently sprinkled with water to destroy the scent, lest the wolves and bears should be attracted to the place, and root up the concealed treasure. When the neck of the cache is nearly level with the surrounding surface, the sod is again fitted in with the utmost exactness and any bushes, stocks or stones that may have originally been about the spot, are restored to their former places. The blankets and other coverings are then removed from the surrounding herbage; all tracks are obliterated; the grass is gently raised by the hand to its natural position, and the minutest chip or straw is scrupulously gleaned up and thrown into the stream. After all is done the place is abandoned for the night, and, if all be right next morning, is not visited again, until there be a necessity for re opening the cache. Four men are sufficient in this way, to conceal the amount of three tons weight of merchandize in the course of two days. Nine caches were required to contain the goods and baggage which Mr. Hunt found it necessary to leave at this place.

40. Trappers Make a Cache

from John C. Frémont, *Report of the Exploring Expedition to the Rocky Mountains in the Years 1843–'44*

June 28.—We halted to noon at an open reach of the river, which occupies rather more than a fourth of the valley, here only about four miles broad. The camp had been disposed with the usual precaution, the horses grazing at a little distance attended by the guard, and we were all sitting quietly at our dinner on the grass, when suddenly we heard the startling cry "*du monde!*" In an instant, every man's weapon was in his hand, the horses were driven in, hobbled and picketed, and horsemen were galloping at full speed in the direction of the new comers, screaming and yelling with the wildest excitement. "Get ready, my lads!" said the leader of the approaching party to his men, when our wild-looking horsemen were discovered bearing down upon them; "*nous allons attraper des coups de baguette.*" They proved to be a small party of fourteen, under the charge of a man named John Lee, and, with their baggage and provisions strapped to their backs, were making their way on foot to the frontier. A brief account of their fortunes will give some idea of navigation in the Nebraska. Sixty days since, they had left the mouth of Laramie's fork, some three hundred miles above, in barges laden with the furs of the American Fur Company. They started with the annual flood, and, drawing but nine inches water, hoped to make a speedy and prosperous voyage to St. Louis; but, after a lapse of forty days, found themselves only one hundred and thirty miles from their point of departure. They came down rapidly as far as Scott's bluffs, where their difficulties began. Sometimes they came upon places where the water was spread over a great extent, and here they toiled from morning until night, endeavoring to drag their boat through the sands, making only two or three miles in as many days. Sometimes they would enter an arm of the river, where there appeared a fine channel, and, after descending prosperously for eight or ten miles, would come suddenly upon dry sands, and be compelled to return, dragging their boat for days against the rapid current; and at others, they came upon places where the water lay in holes, and, getting out to float off their boat, would fall into water up to their necks, and the next moment tumble over against a sandbar. Discouraged at length, and finding the Platte growing every day more shallow, they discharged the principal part of their cargoes one hundred and thirty miles below Fort Laramie, which they secured as well as possible, and, leaving a few men to guard them, attempted to continue their voyage, laden with some light furs and their personal baggage. After fifteen or twenty days more struggling in the sands, during which they made but one hundred and forty miles, they sunk their barges, made a cache of their remaining furs and property, in trees on the bank, and, packing on his back what each man could carry, had commenced, the day before we encountered them, their journey on foot to St. Louis.

41 and 42. Accidents in the Wilderness

Trappers often had to cope with accidents that, in a wilderness setting, became life-threatening. Physical hardships like those described by Warren Ferris in the following selection become a means of metaphysical exploration in the two mountain-man novels of Don Berry: *Trask* (1960) and *Moontrap* (1962). Then, Kit Carson (1809–1868), one of the most famous of the mountain men, explains how he and his companions responded to a medical emergency. There will be much more about Carson in Section V, "Famous Trappers."

41. Losing One's Clothes and Returning Naked to Camp

from Warren Angus Ferris, *Life in the Rocky Mountains*

On the 8th, I returned to camp, which had moved down and was now in a fertile bottom fifteen miles below the fort. Here we remained tranquilly, nothing worthy of record occurring until the evening of the 11th, when four of our trappers, who had been absent from camp some time, returned in a state of perfect nudity and most unparalleled misery. Their bodies were broiled by the heat of the sun to that degree, that the pain produced by coming in contact with our clothes was almost insupportable.

It seems that, four days previous, they prepared a raft for the purpose of crossing Lewis river; having before ascertained that it was not fordable, and when every arrangement was completed, they drove their horses, which swam over safely, and landed on the shore opposite. Stripping themselves for greater security, they pushed off into the stream. The velocity of the current, however, capsized their raft, on which their guns, traps, saddles, blankets, beavers and clothes were fastened, and carried the whole under an immense quantity of floating drift wood, beyond the possibility of recovery; and they only saved their lives by swimming, which they with difficulty accomplished, and faint, weary, and despairing, landed on the other side, reduced by this unfortunate accident to a condition the most miserable and hopeless.—A few moments reflection, while taking a little rest, convinced them that their only chance of saving their lives, lay in endeavoring to find and reach our camp, naked and entirely destitute of arms, provisions, and other necessaries as they then were. With scarcely a ray of hope to cheer them on their dreary task, they mounted their bare backed horses, and started in quest of us. The burning heat of the sun parched their skins, and they had nothing to shield them from his powerful rays; the freezing air of the night chilled and benumbed their unprotected bodies, and they had no covering to keep off the cold; the chill storms of rain and hail pelted mercilessly on them, and they could not escape the torture; the friction produced by riding without a saddle or any thing for a substitute, chaffed off the skin, and even flesh, and without any means of remedying the misfortune, or alleviating the pain, for they were prevented from walking by the stones and sharp thorns of the prickly pair [pear], which lacerated their feet. They were compelled, though the agony occasioned by it was intense, to continue their equestrian march, till amidst this accumulation of ills, they reached our camp; where by kind treatment, and emollient applications, their spirits were restored and their sufferings relieved. Add to the complications of woes above enumerated, the knawing pangs of hunger which the reader will infer, that they must have experienced in no slight degree, from the fact that they did not taste a morsel of food during those four ages of agony, and we have an aggregate of suffering hardly equalled in the history of human woe.

42. Mountain Surgery

from Kit Carson, *Kit Carson's Autobiography*

On the road, one of the party, Andrew Broadus, met with a serious accident. He was taking his rifle out of a wagon for the purpose of shooting a wolf and, in drawing it out, accidentally discharged it, receiving the contents in the right arm. We had no medical man with us, and he suffered greatly from the effects of the wound. His arm began to mortify and we all were aware that amputation was necessary. One of the party stated that he could do it. Broadus was prepared for any experiment that was considered of service to him. The doctor set to work and cut the flesh with a razor and sawed the bone with an old saw. The arteries being cut, to stop the bleeding, he heated a kingbolt from one of the wagons and burned the affected parts, and then applied a plaster of tar taken off the wheel of a wagon. The patient became perfectly well before our arrival in New Mexico.

43 and 44. The Lifestyle of Mountain Men

The mountain man's lifestyle contrasted sharply with that of his counterparts in settled areas back east. The contrast became a subject for many novelists. In "The Art of the Mountain Man Novel," David Stouck writes:

> As James K. Folsom has put it, the central question posed by the western novel is whether man is more blessed in a state of nature or in civilization. In the mountain man novel the answer would seem to be the primitive life. In none of these novels does the hero go back east to resume life with family and friends. He

cannot bear to give up his freedom, his love of adventure, or the beauty of the unspoiled wilderness.

Stouck and other critics of the Western American novel see the works of George Frederick Ruxton as the main source for many twentieth-century mountain-man novels. In the following selection, Ruxton expresses sentiments strikingly similar to those Stouck says are characteristic of the hero in the twentieth-century novels.

In the second selection, William Thomas Hamilton points out that some mountain men brought the best of civilization with them.

43. The Freedom and Loneliness of Mountain Life

from **George Frederick Ruxton**, *Adventures in Mexico and the Rocky Mountains*

When I turned my horse's head from Pike's Peak I quite regretted the abandonment of my mountain life, solitary as it was, and more than once thought of again taking the trail to the Bayou Salado, where I had enjoyed such good sport.

Apart from the feeling of loneliness which any one in my situation must naturally have experienced, surrounded by stupendous works of nature, which in all their solitary grandeur frowned upon me, and sinking into utter insignificance the miserable mortal who crept beneath their shadow; still there was something inexpressibly exhilarating in the sensation of positive freedom from all worldly care, and a consequent expansion of the sinews, as it were, of mind and body, which made me feel elastic as a ball of Indian rubber, and in a state of such perfect *insouciance* that no more dread of scalping Indians entered my mind than if I had been sitting in Broadway, in one of the windows of Astor House. A citizen of the world, I never found any difficulty in investing my resting-place, wherever it might be, with all the attributes of a home; and hailed, with delight equal to that which the artificial comforts of a civilized home would have caused, the, to me, domestic appearance of my hobbled animals, as they grazed around the camp, when I returned after a hard day's hunt. By the way, I may here remark that my *sporting* feeling underwent a great change when I was necessitated to follow and kill game for the support of life, and as a means of subsistence; and the slaughter of deer and buffalo no longer became *sport* when the object was to fill the larder, and the excitement of the hunt was occasioned by the alternative of a plentiful feast or a banyan; and, although ranking under the head of the most red-hot of sportsmen, I can safely acquit myself of ever wantonly destroying a deer or buffalo unless I was in need of meat; and such consideration for the feræ naturæ is common to all the mountaineers who look to game alone for their support. Although liable to an accusation of barbarism, I must confess that the very happiest moments of my life have been spent in the wilderness of the far West; and I never recall but with pleasure the remembrance of my solitary camp in the Bayou Salado, with no friend near me more faithful than my rifle, and no companions more sociable than my good horse and mules, or the attendant coyote which nightly serenaded us. With a plentiful supply of dry pine-logs on the fire, and its cheerful blaze streaming far up into the sky, illuminating the valley far and near, and exhibiting the animals, with well-filled bellies, standing contentedly at rest over their picket-pins, I would sit cross-legged enjoying the genial warmth, and, pipe in mouth, watch the blue smoke as it curled upwards, building castles in its vapoury wreaths, and, in the fantastic shapes it assumed, peopling the solitude with figures of those far away. Scarcely, however, did I ever wish to change such hours of freedom for all the luxuries of civilized life, and, unnatural and extraordinary as it may appear, yet such is the fascination of the life of the mountain hunter, that I believe not one instance could be adduced of even the most polished and civilized of men, who had once tasted the sweets of its attendant liberty and freedom from every worldly care, not regretting the moment when he exchanged it for the monotonous life of the settlements, nor sighing, and sighing again, once more to partake of its pleasures and allurements.

Nothing can be more social and cheering than the welcome blaze of the camp fire on a cold winter's night, and nothing more amusing or entertaining, if not instructive, than the rough conversation of the single-minded mountaineers, whose simple daily talk is all of exciting adventure, since their whole existence is spent in scenes of peril and privation; and consequently the narration of their every-day life is a tale of thrilling accidents and hair-breadth 'scapes, which, though simple matter-of-fact to them, appear a startling romance to those who are not acquainted with the nature of the lives led by these men, who, with the sky for a roof and their rifles to supply them with food and clothing, call no man lord or master, and are free as the game they follow.

A hunter's camp in the Rocky Mountains is quite a picture. He does not always take the trouble to build any shelter unless it is in the snow-season, when a couple of deerskins stretched over a willow frame shelter him from the storm. At other seasons he is content with a mere breakwind. Near at hand are two upright poles, with another supported on the top of these, on which is displayed, out of reach of hungry wolf or coyote, meat of every variety the mountains afford. Buffalo dépouillés, hams of deer and mountain-sheep, beaver-tails, &c., stock the larder. Under the shelter of the skins hang his powder-horn and bullet-pouch; while his rifle, carefully defended from the damp, is always within reach of his arm. Round the blazing fire the hunters congregate at night, and whilst cleaning their rifles, making or mending mocassins, or running bullets, spin long yarns of their hunting exploits, &c.

Some hunters, who have married Indian squaws, carry about with them the Indian lodge of buffalo-skins, which are stretched in a conical form round a frame of poles. Near the camp is always seen the "graining-block," a log of wood with the bark stripped and perfectly smooth, which is planted obliquely in the ground, and on which the hair is removed from the skins to prepare them for being dressed. There are also "stretching-frames," on which the skins are placed to undergo the process of dubbing, which is the removal of the flesh and fatty particles adhering to the skin, by means of the *dubber*, an instrument made of the stock of an elk's horn. The last process is the "smoking," which is effected by digging a round hole in the ground and lighting in it an armful of rotten wood or punk. Three sticks are then planted round the hole, and their tops brought together and tied. The skin is then placed on this frame, and all the holes by which the smoke might escape carefully stopped: in ten or twelve hours the skin is thoroughly smoked and ready for immediate use.

The camp is invariably made in a picturesque locality, for, like the Indian, the white hunter has ever an eye to the beautiful. The broken ground of the mountains, with their numerous tumbling and babbling rivulets, and groves and thickets of shrubs and timber, always afford shelter from the boisterous winds of winter, and abundance of fuel and water. Facing the rising sun the hunter invariably erects his shanty, with a wall of precipitous rock in rear to defend it from the gusts which often sweep down the gorges of the mountains. Round the camp his animals, well hobbled at night, feed within sight, for nothing does a hunter dread more than a visit from the horse-stealing Indians; and to be "afoot" is the acmé of his misery.

44. Mountain Men Were Great Readers

from William Thomas Hamilton, *My Sixty Years on the Plains*

I found the Scotchman and the Kentuckian well educated men. The latter presented me with a copy of Shakespeare and an ancient and modern history which he had in his pack.

We had an abundance of reading matter with us; old mountain men were all great readers. It was always amusing to me to hear people from the East speak of old mountaineers as semi-barbarians, when as a general rule they were the peers of the Easterners in general knowledge.

45 and 46. Troubles With Insects

For much of their time in the mountains, trappers had to endure the bites of mosquitoes and other insects. The first of the next two selections gives Robert Stuart's account of being bugged when he was headed overland toward the states in 1812. Stuart (1785–1848) was born in Scotland and emigrated to Canada in 1807. Three years later, he and his uncle David joined Astor's Pacific Fur Company and sailed on the *Tonquin* to Oregon. Returning overland in 1812, Stuart arrived in St. Louis in 1813. He moved to Detroit in 1834 and served as state treasurer of Michigan from 1840 to 1841. He also was Superintendent of Indian Affairs from 1841 to 1845.

John Work (c. 1792–1861), the author of the second selection, writes about the mosquitoes that tormented him on the Snake country expedition of 1830–31. A native of Ireland, Work was a fur trader for the Hudson's Bay Company for many years. In 1853 he and his family moved to Victoria, Vancouver Island, where he farmed and served in the provincial legislature until his death.

45. Mosquitoes, Flies, and Other Bugs

from Robert Stuart, *On the Oregon Trail*

Last night the musquitoes assailed us in innumerable host, and completely deprived our eyelids of their usual functions; even after the dew had fallen, these infernal pests still continued their music to our no small annoyance.—

Monday 17th—The Flies are [or] musquitoes tormented our horses greatly over night, causing them to ramble to a considerable distance, which made it late before they were collected and loaded—

Wednesday 19th—The excessive heat that has prevailed since we left wood pile Creek is very much diminished, and the suffocating, sultry nights have given place to agreeably cool ones, in consequence of which our musquitoe serenades are so irregular that it is only now and then we hear the song of a solitary warbler—The cause of this decrease in our nocturnal tormentors is owing to the nearly total disappearance of the river bottoms, for the hills are now in the neighborhood, and the declivities serve as its banks—our relief from torments has not been of long duration, for another nearly allied in blood to the former assail us most unmercifully, in innumerable *hordes*, for the greater part of the day—so that the sand Flies, these champions of light, may verily be paired with the imps of darkness—

46. Swamps and Mosquitoes Hinder Trapping

from John Work, *The Snake Country Expedition of 1830–1831*

Sundy 7. Fine warm weather. Marched 21 Miles S.S.W. along the W side of an extensive plain to near Ogden's river, the plain here is partially overflowed and become a swamp. We could scarcely find a spot to encamp, among the lodges the horses are nearly bogging, and to mend the matter we are like to be devoured by innumerable swarms of musquitoes, which do not allow us a moments tranquillity, and so torment the horses that notwithstanding their long day's march, they cannot feed. All hands are ahead of the camp with their traps but found the river so high, having overflowed its banks that they could not approach it except in chance places. three of the men set 9 traps which were all that could be put in the water. I much regret finding the river so high that it cannot be hunted, As the people's last reliance was upon the few beaver which they expected to take in it, in order to make up their hunt but more particularly for food. The most of them are becoming very scarce of provisions and they have now no other resource but to kill horses. Some of the people nearly devoured their horses crossing the swamp on their way to the camp. They saw a small herd of Antelopes in the plain but they could not be approached. A few wild fowl were killed, of which there are a good many in the swamp.

47 and 48. Culinary Delights in the Wilderness

As the next two selections indicate, mountain men learned to appreciate a new diet and cuisine, some of which they learned about from Indians who relied on native plants such as the camas for their subsistence. For more information about this important food plant see Dawn Stram Statham, *Camas and the Northern Shoshone: A Biogeographic and Socioeconomic Analysis* (1982).

47. How to Cook Camas Root

from Warren Angus Ferris, *Life in the Rocky Mountains*

During our journey, I witnessed the process of cooking "Kamas," a small root about the size of a crab apple, which abounds in many parts of this country, in the rich bottoms that border most of the streams and rivers. The mode of preparing this root, is almost identical with that by which the south sea Islanders cook their cannibal and swinish food, and the west Indians their plantain. The squaws, by whom all the avocations of domestic labour are performed, excavate round holes in the earth two feet deep, and three in diameter, which are then filled with dry wood and stones in alternate layers, and the fuel fired beneath. When the wood consumes the heated stones fall to the bottom, and are then covered with a layer of grass, upon which two or three bushels of kamas roots, according to the capacity of the whole, [hole] are placed, and covered with a layer of grass, and the whole coated over with earth, upon which a large fire is kept burning for fifteen hours. Time is then allowed for the kamas to cool, when the hole is opened, and if perfectly done, the roots which were before white, are now of a deep-black colour, not disagreeable to the taste, and having something the flavour of liquorice. Thus prepared, the kamas is both edible and nutritious, and forms no inconsiderable item of food with many of the Rocky Mountain tribes.

48. Good Eats—Boudins

from Thomas Jefferson Farnham, *Travels in the Great Western Prairies*

Saying this he seized the intestines of the buffalo, which had been properly cleaned for the purpose, turned them inside out, and as he proceeded stuffed them with strips of well salted and peppered tender loin. Our "*boudies*" thus made, were stuck upon sticks before the fire, and roasted till they were thoroughly cooked and brown. The sticks were then taken from their roasting position and stuck in position for eating; that is to say, each of us with as fine an appetite as ever blessed a New England boy at his grandsire's Thanksgiving dinner, seized a stick pit, stuck it in the earth near our couches, and sitting upon our haunches, ate our last course—the dessert of a mountain host's entertainment. These wilderness sausages would have gratified the appetite of those who had been deprived of meat a less time than we had been. The envelopes preserve the juices with which while cooking, the adhering fat, turned within, mingles and forms a gravy of the finest flavour.

49. Making a Serape from a Navajo Blanket

from William Thomas Hamilton, *My Sixty Years on the Plains*

As the next selection indicates, Navajo blankets had gained renown by the time of the mountain men. It's also clear that trappers could obtain a variety of goods from trade throughout the West.

Our party now started to get ready for the fall trapping season, which opened in the mountains on the 15th of September. Williams had to go to Santa Fe on business, but he promised to be back in the spring and organize a party for a two-years expedition.

He traded his mule, which was a good one, for a Navajo's blanket. The blankets are world-renowned. It is a question if any manufactured by civilized men are their equal. They are absolutely waterproof, and are made by the women entirely by hand. The colors are fast, and the secret of the art is known only to the Indians.

Williams presented me with his, and I kept it many years, making a serape of it. This is done by cutting a slit in the centre large enough for the head to go through, and it will keep one perfectly dry in wet weather.

50, 51, and 52. The Fur Trade as a Business Enterprise

The selections have shown that a life in the fur trade included beautiful scenery and exciting adventure. But fur trapping and trading were also parts of a business, as the following three selections make clear. Men like Nathaniel J. Wyeth (1802–1856) entered the fur trade to make money. Wyeth's first western business venture in 1832 failed and he returned empty-handed to his home in Boston, where he had run an ice company. On his way home, however, he contracted with Milton Sublette and Thomas Fitzpatrick to bring them supplies at the 1834 rendezvous. He did bring the supplies, but Fitzpatrick refused to buy. In competitive revenge, Wyeth built Fort Hall. When he returned to Boston in 1836, he sold the fort to the Hudson's Bay Company.

We must also stress that even though they were not businessmen like Wyeth, many trappers were sober, reliable, and industrious individuals. The Hudson's Bay Company employed such men for years, and their experience proved invaluable to the company. A case in point is John Work's remarkable retention of the details of fur-trapping history. For histories of the fur trade see Hiram Martin Chittenden, *The Fur Trade of the Far West* (1902); Paul C. Phillips, *The Fur Trade* (1961); and Peter Charles Newman's three-volume history of the Hudson's Bay Company, *Company of Adventurers* (1985).

50. Wyeth Asks Bonneville to Hunt

from Nathaniel J. Wyeth, *Correspondence and Journals of Captain Nathaniel J. Wyeth, 1831–1836*

To Captain Bonneville of Salmon River June 22d 1833.
Sir

I send you the following proposition for a mutual hunt in the country south of the Columbia river which I visited last autumn and winter. As to the prospect of Beaver there I will only say that I have no doubt of taking 300 skins fall and spring. As much sign as would give me this I have seen. I have little doubt much more might be found, but in that country a hunt cannot be made with horses alone, boats must be used. I have obtained some maps of the country beside my own observations in it, and I have little doubt but I can make my way through it without guides, who cannot be procured. As this country is distant an immediate answer is required. As it regards the mules [?] Horses would do but are by no means so good for grass in some places is very bad. If the number required is a very great objection 9 would do but goods enough to buy 3 more must be given in their stead. The men that are wanted must be good, peaceable and industrious, but need not be trappers. I would prefer good men who have not been more than one year in the country. In case of agreement being made you are to engage to deliver what letters I wish to send home, a boy about 13 years old and about 25 lbs. sundrys. The expenses of the boy in the States my brother in N. York will pay to whom he is to be delivered. The boy will have a mule to carry him. With so many animals as I have and so few men I cannot come to the forks and I think these Indians will go no further than where in your route to Green River you strike the plain of the Three Butes. There I hope to see you and in case you acceed to the proposal, with all the things required in it, this hunt to be for one year to meet you at your rendezvous of next year the furs to be equally divided between us and I to have the right to take mine at any time during the year yourself to have the right to send a man to see to your interests—

PROPOSITION.

To be furnished by Mr B.	To be furnished by Mr. Wyeth.
9 men, armed, clothed for the year with saddles & c	19 horses
12 mules	3 mules
9 skins dressed for making boats	20 traps
40 good traps	3 men with myself
1 doz files	2 doz knives
4 doz knives	1 Lodge
20 lbs tobacco	Cooking apparatus
200 lbs grease, if possible	vermillion.
3 bales Indian meat	fish Hooks a few sundrys.
	10 lbs powder and lead.
	14 pr. Horse shoes.

a few small tools

3 axes

12 pair Horse shoes (if you have them.)

4 pack saddles and Harness.

6 pair of lashes[?]

25$ for cost of sundrys

25 lbs. powder and lead with it.

4 pack saddles and Harness.

—said man to do duty the same as the other men and to have no other control than to secure your interest in the division of the skins. In case you are ready to make this arrangement you need make no doubt of my being ready to enter at once on it except that in the mean time I loose my animals.

You to have the liberty of sending a load of goods to pay off the men you furnish. All property at the risk of its owner, neither to be responsible for the debts of the othor.

Yrs &c.

[No signature.]

51. Mr. Mackenlie—Super Manager

from Paul Kane, *Paul Kane's Frontier*

The morning after our arrival the thermometer stood at 7° below zero. Such intense cold had not been felt by the oldest inhabitants of these regions. It had the effect of killing nearly all the cattle that had become acclimated, as they are never housed. The Columbia, too, was frozen over, an unprecedented circumstance, so that my travels were for a time interrupted. I was, however, very comfortably quartered at Mr. Mackenlie's residence, who amused me in the long winter evenings over a good fire by his interesting tales of Indian life, with which he was well conversant. I will relate a couple of his anecdotes.

While he was in charge of a fort in New Caledonia, which is situated south of the Columbia River, he had a carat of tobacco, or three pounds, stolen from him. It was all that he had at that time, and of course was a serious loss. Supposing it to have been taken by some of the Indians, who were trading in large numbers about the establishment at that time, he requested the chief to call a council of all the tribe, as he had something to say to them. On this they all assembled and squatted down, leaving an open space in the centre, into which he walked with his fowling piece; this he loaded with two balls in the presence of the assembly, after which he related the circumstance of his loss, and stated his belief that some one of the Indians then present had taken it. He then told them that he wished that every one present would place his mouth to the muzzle of the gun, and blow into it, assuring them that it would injure no one innocent of the theft; but, on the other hand, if the guilty party should attempt to do so, it would inevitably kill him. He himself set the example of blowing into the piece, standing muzzle upwards on the ground; the chief followed, as well as the whole tribe, with the exception of one man, who sat hanging down his head, and when called upon by the chief to follow the example of the rest refused, saying, that he would not tempt the Great Spirit, for that he had taken the tobacco, and would return it, which he accordingly did.

Whilst Mr. Mackenlie was in charge of Walla-Walla he exhibited an instance of great presence of mind under very trying circumstances. His clerk had a quarrel and fight with the son of the chief, whom he beat. The Indian thereupon collected a large party of the tribe, and rushed with them into the yard of the fort, and attempted to seize the offender for the purpose of taking his life. Mr. Mackenlie kept them off for some time, but finding he could do so no longer, he ordered one of the men to bring him out a keg of powder, the head of which he knocked in, and taking a flint and steel from his pocket, he stood over it as if about to ignite it, telling the Indians that if they did not immediately depart he would show them how a white chief could die and destroy his enemies. The Indians took the alarm, and fled through the gates, which he immediately barred against them, secretly sending the clerk the next day to another post out of their reach.

52. A Prodigious Memory of How Many Beaver Were Trapped Eleven Years Ago

from John Work, *The Snake Country Expedition of 1830–1831*

Tuesdy 5. Fine weather. Our course was this day West about 16 miles. The road pretty level but in places very stony, indeed the country particularly on the South side of the river very stony but level. 17 beaver were taken. We are now said to have reached the valley where beaver were expected to have been found numerous, yet there appears little prospects of our expectations being realized. A small party of hunters 11 years ago took 300 beaver in two short encampments about this place and then not cleanly hunted, and it is not known to have been hunted since. The hunters concur in opinion that beaver are very scarce at present, from what cause there is a great difference of opinion. Some think the scarcity is occasioned by a fire which overran the country here some years back, marks of which still remain. Others think that they have been destroyed by some distemper, besides which different other causes are assigned. Some destroying distemper is the most probable cause of their disappearance. There is no doubt they were formerly very numerous the banks of the river are in many places hollow by their old holes. There being little willows and only reeds many places along the bank their lodges are not numerous, but their holes in abundance everywhere. 17 Beaver were taken.

Wedy 6. Weather fine. Did not move camp today in order to allow the hunters to set their traps and examine the river. Some of the men went to a considerable distance down the river to where rocky dalls commence. no beaver marks worth mentioning to be seen, though this portion of the river is where we expected to find them most abundant. As nothing worth while is to be obtained it is unnecessary to proceed farther down the river we shall therefore return back upon our road tomorrow. 12 beaver were taken. Several of the people were sick from eating of the beaver. The river about here and indeed farther up is burdened with reeds, on the roots of which the beaver feed, but whether it is these or other roots that communicate the quality of sickening the people to their flesh it is not easy to say. hemlock is also found Along the river the roots of which they are said to eat indeed they may feed upon different other roots and plants which may escape the notice of the hunters. The leaves of the reeds particularly and some other plants are covered with a glutinous *saccarine* substance sweet to the taste, which adheres to everything that touches it, the clothes of the hunters who pass through the reeds are covered with it. The leaves are also covered generally on the under side with innumerable swarms of green insects somewhat in shape & size resembling lice. They are so thick that they are floating in clouds down the river.

53, 54, and 55. *Conflicts in the Fur Trade*

The business of fur trapping often led to conflicts among the trappers and between the trappers and the Indians. The three selections that follow give examples of how such conflicts arose and how they were dealt with.

Peter Skene Ogden (1794–1854), author of the first selection, was born in Quebec City, Canada, of American loyalist parents. He went to work for John Jacob Astor and then was employed by the North West Company. In 1824 he took charge of the Snake country fur brigade, and in 1828 he discovered the Humboldt River and explored its full length. He also went from Oregon through the Great Basin to the Colorado River. He later served as chief factor at Fort Vancouver from 1845 until 1852. Although Ogden refers to the Snake Indians as "villains," his common-law wife was an Indian.

For information about Paul Kane, author of the second selection, see the introduction to selections 22 and 23.

The author of the third selection is Job Francis Dye (1807–1883). A Kentuckian by birth, in 1830 he joined a trapping party that started out from Fort Smith, Arkansas, went to Pike's Peak, and wintered in Taos. In 1831, after going to California with Ewing Young's party, Dye trapped sea otter. He started a number of businesses, married a Mexican woman, and in 1839 applied for Mexican citizenship. He also played a part in the Bear Flag Revolt of 1846. Except for some years in the 1860s and early

1870s when he followed gold rushes to Idaho and northern Nevada, he remained in California until his death.

53. "Power Gives Right"

from Peter Skene Ogden, "The Peter Skene Ogden Journals"

Friday 25th.

Snow and storms continue, a terrible winter. A man who went in quest of lost traps arrived with reports of fearful distress of the Americans. Horses dead, caches rifled. I believe this as a trapper saw calico among the Snakes, traded from the Snakes of the Plains. The Americans are determined to proceed but find it is to no purpose these extravagant offers. They are making snowshoes themselves wh. they ought to have done 2 wks. ago. I cannot ascertain the motive of their journey south. I dread their returning with liquor. A small quantity would be most advantageous to them but the reverse to me. I know not their intentions but had I the same chance they have, long since I would have had a good stock of liquor here, and every beaver in the camp would be mine. If they succeed in reaching their camp they may bring 20 or 30 trappers here which would be most injurious to my spring hunt. As the party have now only 10 traps, no good can result to us if they succeed in reaching their depot and returning here. We have this in our favor; they have a mountain to cross, and before the snow melts can convey but little property from the depot as with horses they cannot reach here before April.

Saturday 26.

The Snakes have now about 400 guns obtained in war excursions against Blackfeet and from trappers they have killed and stolen caches. In the plunder of Reid's Fort, they secured 40. Still these villains are allowed to go unmolested. In any other part of the world, the guilty are punished in England a man is executed. Power gives the right. Here we have both power and right, but dare not punish the guilty. Were proper statements sent to England or to the Honuble Hudson's Bay Com. I am confident greater power would be granted to Indian traders; and surely they would not make an improper use of them. This is the plan the American gentlemen adopt with tribes on the Missouri; the Spanish also. The missionaries have done but little: and murders are no longer heard of among the Spaniards. Threats are of no avail among the Snakes.

54. Deserters

from Paul Kane, *Paul Kane's Frontier*

During the night, two of our Sandwich Islanders deserted. A boat was immediately unloaded, and sent back, with the view of intercepting them at the Cascades. They had received 10£. sterling each in goods as their outfit, and, in passing the Cascades, had hid their bags in the woods, and hoped to get back again to the coast with their booty. Their pursuers, however, discovered their track, and found the goods, though they did not find the men; but knowing they must be near the place, they got Tomaquin to look after them. The next morning, Tomaquin with three of his tribe, brought them in: each of the Indians, while paddling, carried his knife in his mouth, ready to strike should the Islanders make any resistance. It appeared that they had visited his camp in the night, on which he assembled his tribe and surrounded them; when the Islanders, thinking they were going to be killed, surrendered and begged for mercy. Tomaquin was rewarded with four blankets and four shirts. The next thing was to punish the deserters, and very little time was wasted in either finding a verdict or carrying it out. Our guide, a tall powerful Iroquois, took one of them, and Mr. Lewis seized the other, as they stepped from the canoe: the punishment consisted in simply knocking the men down, kicking them until they got up, and knocking them down again until they could not get up any more, when they finished them off with a few more kicks. Mr. Lewis, although a very powerful man, had only his left hand, a gun having exploded in his right, shattering it so dreadfully that he was obliged to have it cut off at the wrist; but the operation having been performed in the roughest backwood fashion, it often pained him, and the doctors wanted him to let them cut it off again, so as to make a good stump, but he would not let them. On this stump he usually wore a heavy wooden shield, but, luckily for the poor Islanders, it was not on when they landed, or, as he said himself, he might have killed them. The punishment of those men must of course appear savage and severe to persons in civilised life, but it is only treatment of this kind that will keep this sort of men in order; and desertion or insubordination, on journeys through the interior, is often attended by the most dangerous consequences to the whole party.

55. Murder

from Job Francis Dye *Recollections of a Pioneer, 1830–1852*

After feasting on bear-meat to our heart's content, we traveled on down the stream (Salt River) about three days, when Cambridge Green and James Anderson had a dispute, about setting their traps; each one claiming that the other had set his trap on pre-empted ground. Anderson had caught a beaver and brought it into camp, when Green complained to Capt. Young, that Anderson had infringed on forbidden ground, and caught his beaver. Captain Young said, "what makes you let him do it—if I could not prevent him any other way, I would shoot him." Green never replied to this foolish remark, spoken in levity, but buckled on his pistol and picked up his rifle; he then stepped to a large pine tree, and shot Anderson, killing him, as he was standing by our camp-fire, smoking his pipe. On being shot, Anderson raised his head and discovered Green coming out from behind the pine tree, with a pistol in his hand, and then he exclaimed, "You d——d rascal," at the same time starting for him, but after making two or three steps, he fell dead. We buried him under the tree where he fell. This was one of the most unpleasant incidents of our long and tedious expedition, so dangerous to life and limb.

We continued down the Jila [Gila] river until we came near the junction of the San Carlos. While in the canon, Capt. Young decided to send eleven men to trap through the canon. This proved a perilous expedition; the Indians pursued us day and night, shooting at us, stealing our traps and stealing or shooting our mules. One night, James Green being on guard, Santiago Cordero, a New Mexican from Taos, came passing by him in the dark; Green shot, and killed Cordero dead. Green was much mortified at the heart-rending event, and wept like a child.

56. Out of Baccy

from Robert Stuart, *On the Oregon Trail*

Robert Stuart gives an example of the way mountain men adapted or improvised when they ran out of supplies—in this case, tobacco.

Friday January 1st 1813—Was solely devoted to the gratification of our appetites: all work was suspended for the day, and we destroyed an immoderate quantity of Buffalo Tongues, Puddings, and the choicest of the meat—Our stock of Virginia weed being totally exhausted, Mr. McClellan's Tobacco Pouch was cut up and smoked as a substitute, in commemoration of the new year.—

57. Hardships for Riches— But Still Poor

from Nathaniel J. Wyeth, *Journals of Captain Nathaniel J. Wyeth, 1831–1836*

The many reasons for Nathaniel Wyeth's complaints, as he expresses them in the following selection, are detailed in Don Berry's *A Majority of Scoundrels: An Informal History of the Rocky Mountain Fur Company* (1961).

11th. Last night grew cold and set in for a hard snow storm with a gale of wind from the W.S.W. which continued without intermission until sunset today so we did not move camp the cracking of the falling trees and the howling of the blast was more grand than comfortable it makes two individuals feel their insignificance in the creation to be seated under a blankett with a fire in front and 3$^1/_2$ feet of snow about them and more coming and no telling when it will stop. tonight tis calm and nearly full moon it seems to shine with as much indifference as the storms blow and wether for weal or woe, we two poor wretches seem to be little considered in the matter. The thoughts that have run through my brain while I have been lying here in the snow would fill a volume and of such matter as was never put into one, my infancy, my youth, and its friends and faults, my manhoods troubled stream, its vagaries, its aloes mixed with the gall of bitterness and its results *viz* under a blankett hundreds perhaps thousands of miles from a friend, the Blast howling about, and smothered in snow, poor, in debt, doing nothing to get out of it, despised for a visionary, nearly naked, but there is one good thing plenty to eat health and heart.

Alfred Jacob Miller, *Hunting Elk among the Black Hills* (37.1940.3).

Alfred Jacob Miller, *Caravan "En Route"* (37.1940.51).

Alfred Jacob Miller, *Attack by Crow Indians* (37.1940.179).

Alfred Jacob Miller, *Breakfast at Sunrise* (37.1940.52).

Alfred Jacob Miller, *Escaping from Blackfeet* (37.1940.67).

Alfred Jacob Miller, *Trappers Starting for Beaver Hunt* (37.1940.1).

Alfred Jacob Miller, *Preparing for a Buffalo Hunt* (37.1940.2).

Alfred Jacob Miller, *Laramie's Fort* (37.1940.49).

Alfred Jacob Miller, *Large Encampment Near the Cut Rocks* (37.1940.110).

Alfred Jacob Miller, *Camp Fire, Preparing for the Evening Meal* (37.1940.4).

Alfred Jacob Miller, *The Grizzly Bear* (37.1940.125).

Alfred Jacob Miller, *Free Trappers in Trouble* (37.1940.163).

Mountain Women

In "Marriage and Settlement Patterns of Rocky Mountain Trappers and Traders," William R. Swagerty discusses his statistical analysis of the information in LeRoy Hafen's series *The Mountain Men and the Fur Trade of the Far West*. Studying not only the 292 biographical essays collected in the Hafen series but also twenty additional biographies, Swagerty found that

> most trappers had only one wife (1.45 average). By 1834 first marriage had taken place for the majority. Of 312 cases, 182, 58.3 percent, never married again. Some of these marriages occurred before the husband headed west. However, 106, or 38.9 percent, of 272 first marriages were with Indian women. Twenty men married mixed bloods, while forty-four (16.1 percent) wedded Anglo-Americans. Many French-American marriages (9.2 percent) were consummated before the men involved left the St. Louis area; however, only six of the forty-two known Canadians married other Canadians. Fifty-two trappers who frequented Santa Fe married Spanish-American women there or in Taos (19.1 percent of all first marriages and 67.7 percent of all who would eventually settle in the Taos region), while of those who went on to California, only one-half married daughters of the Californios.

Swagerty's analysis yielded many more statistics, including the fact that more than two-thirds of the mountain men's first marriages were with women who had not been married before. Also, most unmarried trappers found a wife within a year or two after reaching the mountains;

"the average marriage lasted fifteen years and produced three children"; and about a third of the trappers and traders married more than once, some three or four times.

Those statistics and others provided by Swagerty and other scholars answer some, but only some, of our questions about the relationships between women and mountain men. The selections in this section present some of the mountain men's stories about the women in their lives. We would have preferred to balance the men's views with samples of what the women thought and felt; unfortunately, except for Marie Dorion's sad story of the massacre of her husband and his party (included in Section VIII), we could find no published writings by any wives of the mountain men, although we have included an excerpt from the narrative of a daughter of a trapper. In the absence of other women's voices, we must emphasize that the lives of most nineteenth-century women were hard. All but rich women had to work hard, and most men looked upon women as inferior to men, except for women's supposedly superior emotional and spiritual capacity. Some husbands were kind, some were indifferent, some were brutes—and the mountain men probably varied little, if at all, from that general pattern. The most striking difference between mountaineers and the males in settled areas is that the former, following Indian custom, often literally bought their wives. But such purchases did not preclude love as a major motive for the marriage. And the narratives indicate that an informal system of divorce also seemed to be accepted by the trappers and traders.

To find out more about mountain-man marriages and about the children of such unions see Lewis O. Saum, *The Fur Trader and the Indian* (1965); Walter O'Meara, *Daughters of the Country: The Women of the Fur Traders and Mountain Men* (1968); Sylvia Van Kirk, *"Many Tender Ties": Women in Fur-Trade Society, 1670–1870* (1980); Juliet Thelma Pollard, "The Making of the Metis in the Pacific Northwest; Fur Trade Children: Race, Class, and Gender" (1990); and Nancy Shoemaker, *Negotiators of Change: Historical Perspectives on Native American Women* (1995).

58 and 59. Buying A Wife

The next two selections explain the process of buying a wife. Both accounts make clear that cultural relativism sometimes followed from the observation of cultural differences in social practices such as courtship and marriage. Since the time of Columbus's first voyage to the New World, cultural relativism had been, in fact, the result of much of the contact between Europeans and Native Americans. What distinguishes the mountain men from other European-American observers in this regard is that, in response to what they learned from native cultures, some of the trappers and traders significantly altered their own lifestyles.

58. The Trapper's Bride

from Alfred Jacob Miller, *The West of Alfred Jacob Miller*

The scene represents a Trapper taking a wife, or purchasing one. The prices varying in accordance with circumstances. He (the trapper) is seated with his friend, to the left of the sketch, his hand extended to his promised wife, supported by her father and accompanied by a chief, who holds the calumet, an article indispensable in all grand ceremonies. The price of acquisition, in this case, was $600 paid for in the legal tender of this region: viz: Guns, $100 each, Blankets $40 each, Red Flannel $20 pr. yard, Alcohol $64 pr. Gal., Tobacco, Beads &c. at corresponding rates.

A Free Trapper (white or half-breed), being ton or upper circle, is a most desirable match, but it is conceded that he is a ruined man after such an investment, the lady running into unheard of extravagancies. She wants a dress, horse, gorgeous saddle, trappings, and the deuce knows what beside. For this the poor devil trapper sells himself, body and soul, to the Fur Company for a number of years. He traps beaver, hunts the Buffalo and bear, Elk &c. The furs and robes of which the Company credit to his account.

59. Buying Wives

from Thomas Jefferson Farnham, *Travels in the Great Western Prairies*

These winters in Brown's hole are somewhat like winters among the mountains of New England, in the effects they produce on the rise and progress of the art of all arts—the art of love. For, as among the good old hills of my native clime, quiltings, and singing-schools, and evening dances, when the stars are shining brightly on the snow crust, do soften the heart of the mountain lad and lassie, and cause the sigh and blush to triumph over all the counsels of maiden aunts and fortune-tellers; so here in this beautiful valley, and in the skin lodge village of the Snakes, there are bright evenings, beaming stars, and mellow moons, and social circles for singing the wild ditties of their tribe, and for sewing with the sinews of the deer, their leggings, moccasins and buffalo robes, and for being bewitched with the tender passion.

The dance, too, enlivens the village. The musician chants the wild song, and marks the time by regular beatings with a stick upon a sounding board; and light heels, and sturdy frames, and buxom forms respond to his call. To these, and other gatherings, the young go, to see who are the fairest, and best, and most loved of the throng. Our friend Cupid goes there too. Yes, Cupid at an Indian dance! And there measuring bow and arrow with those who invented them, he often lays at his feet, I am told, the proudest hawk's feather that adorns the brow of Chief or Chiefess. For, on the morning after the dance, it not unfrequently happens that he of the beard is compelled, by force of certain uneasy sensations about the heart, to apply to some beardless one for the balm of sweet smiles for his relief.

He does not wait for the calm hour of a Sunday night. Nor does he delay putting the question by poetical allusions to the violet and firmament. No! Calm hour and the poetry of nature have no charms for him. He wants none of these. Our friend Cupid has cast an arrow into his heart, bearded with the stings of irresistible emotion; and he seeks that mischievous fair one, her alone who selected the arrow and the victim; her alone who was a "particeps criminis" in the loss of that great central organ of his life, called in the annals of Christian countries, "the heart." No! his course is vastly more philosophical and single-minded, (I mean no offence to my countrymen—none to you, ye Britons over the waters,) than the ginger-bread, sugar-candy courtships of Christian people. He first pays his addresses to his band of horses; selects the most beautiful and valuable of them all, and then goes with his chosen horse to the lodge of his chosen girl's father or mother, or if both these be dead, to the lodge of her eldest sister, ties the animal to the tent pole, and goes away. After his departure, the inmates of the lodge issue from it, and in due form examine the horse, and if it appears to be worth as much as the girl whom the owner seeks, an interview is had, the horse taken by the parents, or sister, as the case may be, and the lover takes the girl. A fair business transaction, you perceive, my readers—"a quid pro quo"—a compensation in kind.

The girl, received in exchange for the horse, becomes the absolute personal property of the enamoured jockey, subject to be re-sold whenever the state of the market and his own affection will allow. But if those, whose right it is to judge in the matter, are of opinion that the girl is worth more than the horse, another is brought; and if these are not enough, he of the beard may bring another, or get Cupid to shoot his heart in another direction.

There are many benefits in this mode of obtaining that description of legal chattels called a wife, over the mode usually adopted among us. As for example: by this mode there is a price given for a valuable article. Now to my apprehension, this is an improvement upon our plan; for it removes entirely from certain old daddies, the necessity of disposing of their daughters by gift, to certain worthless, portionless young men, who are merely virtuous, talented, honest and industrious; an evil of no small magnitude, as may be learned by inquiry in the proper quarter. But the Indian system of matrimony extirpates it. Wealth measures off affection and property by the peck, yard or dollar's worth, as circumstances require; and no young lady of real genuine property, respectability and standing, and family, will think of placing her affections upon a talented, virtuous and industrious, promising and prosperous coxcomb of poverty; nor, vice versâ, will a young man of these vulgar qualities have the unfathomable barefacedness to propose himself to a young lady of real genuine property respectability, property form, property face, property virtue, property modesty, and property intelligence.

No, bless the day! such impudence will cease to interfere with the legitimate pretensions of those who are able—while they declare their passion mighty, unalterable and pure—to place in the hands from which they receive the dear object of their property love, the last quoted price of the family stock.

60 and 61. Love and Loneliness—Matters of the Heart

Mountain-man musings on matters of the heart could sometimes be humorous, sometimes lugubrious, as in the following two selections.

60. A Scene on the "Big Sandy" River

from Alfred Jacob Miller, *The West of Alfred Jacob Miller*

The sketch may be said to represent a small slice of an Indian paradise;—Indian women, horses, a stream of water, shade trees, and the broad prairie to the right, on which at times may be seen countless herds of Buffalo, Elk, and deer.

The women look innocent enough, but some of the Trappers conceive them difficult studies. An experienced trapper giving his advice to a younger, who had been smitten by the charms of a dusky Venus, discoursed something in this wise,—"Look ye hyar now! I've raised the ha'r of more than one Camanche, and hunted and trapped a heap, Wagh! from Red River away up among the Britishers to Heely (Gila) in the Spanish Country, and from old Mis- sou- rye to the sea of Californey; b'ar and beaver sign are as plain to me as Chimley Rock on Platte, but darn my old heart if this child ever could shine in making out the sign lodged in a woman's breast." "Look ye sharp or you're a gone beaver, ye cus't green horn, I'll be dog gone if you ain't, Tiya! Wagh!!"

61. Loneliness

from Francois A. Chardon, *Chardon's Journal at Fort Clark 1834–1839*

Sunday 14th—Mild Beautiful Weather. The Indians went across the River in search of Cattle—but returned late in the Evening without haveing seen any—Extremely lonesome and low Spirited—I hardly know how to account for it, but I have always found Sunday to be the dullest and longest day in the week—that is—the Sundays spent in the Indian Country—I suppose it is because we are apt to contrast the scene with that of civilized life—when Kin and acquaintances all assemble at the sound of the *church going bell*—Although the solemn tolling of a church bell—never possessed much attraction for me, (only so far as Served to announce the time and place where bright eyes were to be seen.) But I could not help feeling this evening—(Whilst gazing round on this dreary, Savage waste,) That could I at this moment hear even the tinkling of a sheep bell—much less the Solemn toll of the church going bell, that the joyful Sound would repay Me for whole Months of privation. Alas, how little do we suspect during our halcyon days of Youth—Surrounded by all that can cheer our gloomy path through life, what Years of Sorrow are Yet in Store, But I will not repine for joys that is past and gone.

'For joys that is past let us never repine,
Nor grieve for the days of auld lang syne'

62. "Bourgeois W——r, & His Squaw"

from Alfred Jacob Miller, *The West of Alfred Jacob Miller*

The "Bourgeois W——r" mentioned in the next selection is probably Joseph R. Walker, the mountain man mentioned in Selection 5 who served as a guide for one of Frémont's expeditions. Walker also guided many emigrant wagon trains to California, where he spent his last years on a nephew's ranch. On July 8, 1845, an officer in the U. S. Dragoons, Philip St. George Cooke, wrote this description of Walker: "This afternoon Mr. Walker, whom we met at Independence Rock, and who is now on his way to California, visited our camp: he has picked up a small party at Fort Laramie; and wild-looking creatures they are—white and red. This man has abandoned civilization,—married a squaw or squaws, and prefers to pass his life wandering in these deserts carrying on, perhaps, an almost nominal business of hunting, trapping, and trading—but quite sufficient to the wants of a chief of savages. He is a man of much natural ability, and apparently of prowess and ready resource." (Anderson, 383)

The term "Bourgeois" is given in the mountains to one who has a body of trappers placed under his immediate command. Capt. W———r, being trustworthy and intelligent, received an appointment of this kind, and with his men had many battles with the Indians. A story was told us by the trappers of an exquisite revenge the Indians practiced on them. He had been victorious in a battle with a tribe, and the Indians, finding themselves worsted, proposed to bury the tomahawk and invited him to a feast and pipe smoking. Of course the worthy Captain was ready to make friends and smoke the pipe of peace, for no matter how hard you may pound in battle, you must of necessity receive some pounding in return, and the Captain felt sore from the loss of some of his men. The feast was plentiful, and our Capt. always with a good appetite enjoyed it, doing full justice to their hospitality, & after a hearty smoke, returned to his men,—but horror of horrors! in a short time they had let him know that he had partaken of a meal composed of his own men!* Only fancy his blasphemy, rage, and disgust. We thought of asking him the particulars of this matter, but prudence forbade. It was not complimentary to his usual acuteness—he had evidently been "taken in and done for."

The sketch exhibits a certain etiquette. The Squaw's station in travelling is at a considerable distance in the rear of her liege lord, and never at the side of him. W———r had the kindness to present the writer a dozen pair of moccasins worked by this squaw—richly embroidered on the instep with colored porcupine quills. He did him also the favor to have some Indian dances exhibited, that he might have an opportunity of seeing them—so he did not care to risk his friendship by questions touching his famous and recherche feast.

---

*It must not be inferred from this that the American Indians are essentially cannibals. Their purpose was revenge, which they would have at any price. *Coûte qui Coûte.*

63. A Shivaree

from Francois Chardon, *Chardon's Journal at Fort Clark 1834–1839*

In the popular mind, shivarees, although not unique to the Old West, nevertheless remain associated with it because of the depiction of a shivaree in Lynn Riggs's *Green Grow the Lilacs*, a 1931 folk play that Rodgers and Hammerstein used as the model for their 1943 musical, *Oklahoma!* As Riggs's play shows, violence sometimes spoiled the fun of a shivaree. The one Francois Chardon describes in the following selection at least passed without any deaths.

Saturday 27—Snow storm last Night, the prairies are all covered Put up two small equipments for the Rees and Gros Ventres, Set the Men to Make balls—Old Charboneau, an old Man of 80, took to himself and *others* a young Wife, a young Assinneboine of 14, a Prisoner that was taken in the fight of this summer, and bought by me of the Rees, the young Men of the Fort, and two *rees*, gave to the Old Man a splendid *Chàrivèree*, the Drums, pans, Kittles &c Beating; guns fireing &c. The Old gentleman gave a feast to the Men, and a glass of grog—and went to bed with his young wife, with the intention of doing his best—The two Indians who had never saw the like before, were under the apprehension that we were for Killing of them, and sneaked off—

64. Ready to Travel an Hour After Giving Birth

from Nathaniel J. Wyeth, *Correspondence and Journals of Captain Nathaniel J. Wyeth, 1831–1836*

After a frontier wedding and a shivaree, the bride and groom customarily set about starting a family, even though the offspring would arrive not only thousands of miles from a hospital but also hundreds of miles from any fort or post.

29th {July} We remained all day making meat with a hot sun this morning sent 3 men down the creek fishing they caught 21 Salmon Trout and returned at 10 this afternoon it rained hard and during the storm the squaw of one of the party was delivered of a Boy in the bushes wither she had retired for the purpose it[s] head was thickly covered with Black hair it was as white as is usual with the whites in less than an hour afterwards the squaw made her appearance in camp as well and able for a days travel as usual it continued raining all night and until 8 of the 30 on which acc. our march was defered for the day which was afterward fine and our meat dried well. 4 Beavers were caught from about 12 traps last night during the day one of the party saw an indian which must have been a Blackfoot as otherwise he would have come to camp yesterday and today we had Thunder & Hail as well as rain.

65. Two Good Horses for One Bad Wife

from Washington Irving, *The Adventures of Captain Bonneville*

Washington Irving wrote his narrative of Captain Benjamin Bonneville's adventures by consulting the captain's journal, which Bonneville had sold to him for a thousand dollars. Because the journal has not survived, we cannot know how much Irving altered what he found in it. We do know from comparing Irving's own journal with a version of it he published in *A Tour on the Prairies* (1835) that he romanticized and touched up the original by using a number of literary devices. Given that record, the following account of a sort of elopement is probably a more "literary" treatment than was the original journal entry. Readers interested in Irving's depiction of mountain men should consult Robert Edson Lee, *From West to East: Studies in the Literature of the American West* (1966); and Richard H. Cracroft, *Washington Irving: The Western Works* (1974).

Benjamin Louis Eulalie de Bonneville (1796–1878) was born near Paris to a father who was a radical journalist and a friend of Lafayette, Condorcet, and Thomas Paine. The Bonnevilles emigrated to the United States in 1803 when Napoleon rose to power. Bonneville graduated from West Point in 1815 and then served at various frontier army posts during the 1820s. In 1832 he led a force of 110 men to the Green River. During the three years he spent in the mountains, he built Fort Bonneville (known as "Fort Nonsense" to veteran trappers) and proved that loaded wagons could cross South Pass in Wyoming. Some have argued that Bonneville used his fur trade activities to disguise his *real* purpose for being in the West—to gather intelligence for the United States government. It is not known whether Bonneville was a spy; however, he later fought in the Mexican War and also served the Union in the recruiting service during the Civil War.

Matters were going on thus pleasantly and prosperously, in this motley community of white and red men, when, one morning, two stark free trappers, arrayed in the height of savage finery, and mounted on steeds as fine and as fiery as themselves, and all jingling with hawks' bells, came galloping, with whoop and halloo, into the camp.

They were fresh from the winter encampment of the American Fur Company, in the Green River valley; and had come to pay their old comrades of Captain Bonneville's company a visit. An idea may be formed from the scenes we have already given of conviviality in the wilderness, of the manner in which these game birds were received by those of their feather in the camp; what feasting; what revelling; what boasting; what bragging; what ranting and roaring, and racing and gambling, and squabbling and fighting, ensued among these boon companions. Captain Bonneville, it is true, maintained always a certain degree of law and order in his camp, and checked each fierce excess: but the trappers, in their seasons of idleness and relaxation, require a degree of license and indulgence, to repay them for the long privations, and almost incredible hardships of their periods of active service.

In the midst of all this feasting and frolicking, a freak of the tender passion intervened, and wrought a complete change in the scene. Among the Indian beauties in the camp of the Eutaws and Shoshonies, the free trappers discovered two, who had whilom figured as their squaws. These connexions frequently take place for a season; and sometimes, continue for years, if not perpetually; but are apt to be broken when the free trapper starts off, suddenly, on some distant and rough expedition.

In the present instance, these wild blades were anxious to regain their belles; nor were the latter loath once more to come under their protection. The free trapper combines, in the eye of an Indian girl, all that is dashing and heroic in a warrior of her own race, whose gait, and garb, and bravery he emulates, with all that is gallant and glorious in the white man. And then the indulgence with which he treats her; the finery in which he decks her out; the state in which she moves; the sway she enjoys over both his purse and person, instead of being the drudge and slave of an Indian husband: obliged to carry his pack, and build his lodge, and make his fire, and bear his cross humors and dry blows.—No; there is no comparison, in the eyes of an aspiring belle of the wilderness, between a free trapper and an Indian brave.

With respect to one of the parties, the matter was easily arranged. The beauty in question was a pert little Eutaw wench, that had been taken prisoner, in some war excursion, by a Shoshonie. She was readily ransomed for a few articles of trifling value; and forthwith figured about the camp in fine array, "with rings on her fingers, and bells on her toes," and a tossed up, coquettish air, that made her the envy, admiration, and abhorrence, of all the leathern-dressed, hard-working squaws of her acquaintance.

As to the other beauty, it was quite a different matter. She had become the wife of a Shoshonie brave. It is true, he had another wife, of older date than the one in question; who, therefore, took command in his household, and treated his new spouse as a slave: but the latter was the wife of his last fancy, his latest caprice; and was precious in his eyes. All attempt to bargain with him, therefore, was useless: the very proposition was repulsed with anger and disdain. The spirit of the trapper was roused; his pride was piqued as well as his passion. He endeavored to prevail upon his quondam mistress to elope with him. His horses were fleet; the winter nights were long and dark: before daylight, they would be beyond the reach of pursuit; and once at the encampment in Green River valley, they might set the whole band of Shoshonies at defiance.

The Indian girl listened and longed. Her heart yearned after the ease and splendor of condition of a trapper's bride, and throbbed to be freed from the capricious control of the premier squaw; but she dreaded the failure of the plan, and the fury of a Shoshonie husband. They parted; the Indian girl in tears, and the madcap trapper more mad than ever, with his thwarted passion.

Their interviews had, probably, been detected, and the jealousy of the Shoshonie brave aroused: a clamor of angry voices was heard in his lodge, with the sound of blows, and of female weeping and lamenting. At night, as the trapper lay tossing on his pallet, a soft voice whispered at the door of his lodge. His mistress stood trembling before him. She was ready to follow whithersoever he should lead.

In an instant, he was up and out. He had two prime horses, sure, and swift of foot, and of great wind. With stealthy quiet, they were brought up and saddled; and, in a few moments, he and his prize were careering over the snow, with which the whole country was covered. In the eagerness of escape, they had made no provision for their journey: days must elapse before they could reach their haven of safety, and mountains and prairies be traversed, wrapped in all the desolation of winter. For the present, however, they thought of nothing but flight; urging their horses forward over the dreary wastes, and fancying, in the howling of every blast, they heard the yell of the pursuer.

At early dawn, the Shoshonie became aware of his loss. Mounting his swiftest horse, he set off in hot pursuit. He soon found the trail of the fugitives, and spurred on in hopes of overtaking them. The winds, however, which swept the valley, had drifted the light snow into the prints made by the horses' hoofs. In a little while, he lost all trace of them, and was completely thrown out of the chase. He knew, however, the situation of the camp toward which they were bound, and a direct course through the mountains, by which he might arrive there sooner than the fugitives. Through the most rugged defiles, therefore, he urged his course by day and night, scarce pausing until he reached the camp. It was some time before the fugitives made their appearance. Six days, had they been traversing the wintry wilds. They came, haggard with hunger and fatigue, and their horses faltering under them. The first object that met their eyes, on entering the camp, was the Shoshonie brave. He rushed, knife in hand, to plunge it in the heart that had proved false to him. The trapper threw himself before the cowering form of his mistress, and, exhausted as he was, prepared for a deadly struggle. The Shoshonie paused. His habitual awe of the white man checked his arm; the trapper's friends crowded to the spot, and arrested him. A parley ensued. A kind of *crim. con.* adjudication took place; such as frequently occurs in civilized life. A couple of horses were declared to be a fair compensation for the loss of a woman who had previously lost her heart: with this, the Shoshonie brave was fain to pacify his passion. He returned to Captain Bonneville's camp, somewhat crest-fallen, it is true; but parried the officious condolements of his friends, by observing, that two good horses were very good pay for one bad wife.

66. A Trapper Tries to Mollify His Wife

from Nathaniel J. Wyeth, *Correspondence and Journals of Captain Nathaniel J. Wyeth, 1831–1836*

To learn more about the historical context of such documents as the letter that is our next selection, readers should consult not only the original published source but also two general-reference sources: *The Reader's Encyclopedia of the American West* (1977), edited by Howard R. Lamar; and *The Oxford History of the American West* (1994), edited by Clyde A. Milner, Carol A. O'Connor, and Martha A. Sandweiss.

St. Louis March 31st 1834

Dear wife (Cambridge)

Your fav. of 13th came to hand this morning and was very acceptable. I am glad to find you will take some care of the trees. Perhaps they will not grow for our use but some one will get the benefit and it will be pleasant to leave even such a memorial of our having once existed. It is true that Mr. Fitzpatric was robbed by the Crow Indians but I was in hopes that you would not hear of it. I knew it before I left Cambridge but did not wish to alarm you. I do not think there is much danger with so large party as I shall have.

Mr. Nuttall and Mr. Townsend another naturalist passed through this place to the rendezvous last week and their goods went by the vessell so there is no doubt of his going. The Missionarys came here this morning. Mr. Abbot is at the rendezvous taking care of the horses. Batiste and the Indian I have also sent up to the rendezvous. Batiste continues a pretty good boy. I shall think of your request for seeds and pretty stones while I am on my way out and certainly shall not forget my promise to send for you if there is any chance of doing so with propriety but you must not be too sanguine a thousand circumstances may prevent it altho I desire it much. I feel as much as you can do the lonesomeness of my way of life but you know the success of what I have undertaken is life itself to me and if I do fail in it they shall never say that it was for want of perseverance. But this is my last attempt and if I am not successfull I must come home and endeavour the best way I can to get a living and to pay my debts which will then be heavy. Still I am yet sanguine that I shall succeed. I will take good care of myself and perhaps the life which began in turmoil may yet end in quiet and peace and our sun go down from a clear sky. I should be desolate indeed if I thought that the residue of life was to be as unsettled as the past and I cannot but reproach myself that I have made you in some measure a widow while you ought to be enjoying yourself. I am afraid that you will brood over hopes that have been blasted by me who should have been with you to fulfil them and at hand in time of need to cherish and support. These things make me melancholy and I half believe I have got the Blues.

Jacob writes me that he is about getting married. The people from Galena all say that he is doing well. I hope so but cant. help doubting whether it is permanent.

Good bye My Dear wife and may God bless you.

N. J. Wyeth

67. Catherine McDonald's Narrative

from Winona Adams, "An Indian Girl's Story"

The following account is part of an Indian woman's recollection of a trapping trip to the mouth of the Colorado River taken around the year 1841. Her name was Catherine McDonald (c. 1827–c. 1891), and she was of mixed Indian and European blood. Catherine McDonald's story of Edenic innocence and infernal violence was first written down by her husband in 1875 but was not published until 1930, when Montana librarian Winona Adams edited it for *The Frontier*, a regional magazine. This narrative makes us wonder how many other stories of the fur trade lie forgotten in old issues of magazines, in archives, and in family papers.

In this camp I saw the tallest women ever I beheld. A half-aged woman talkative and clever at signs told me we were in the lands of a great chief. Soon we were visited by his two daughters accompanied by a stout Indian carrying a basket of fruits on his head. The two girls were of an equal height and both virgins that knew not man. They were a full fathom high, each of them erect and straight as larch trees. Their forelocks were cut straight above the eyebrows and the rest of their hair flowing down combed over their backs covered their knees. Their naked paps were prominent and firm as unripened cherries. Their feet of fine strong heels and long curved instep, but their toes were large, square and muscular, as they never wore a shoe. They were both entirely naked save for a short skirt they wore from the navel down to half a span above their knees. These skirts were twisted and wove out of the hair of the finest scalps which their father cut from the heads of his enemies. Their looks were solemn and inquiring, their walk easy and erect. They wore a tasteful collar of seed beads, red, black, white and green, around their necks and pendent fringes covered with the same beads from their ears to their collar-bones. The calves of their legs were not highly rounded, being so tall, but the hairs thereon were few and fine and their shinbones were clean edged and thin skinned. As they sat near me on the sand I offered each a handful of dried buffalo meat, at which they smiled gladness and thanks and ate only as became modest virgins to eat. I wondered how they were husbandless, but it was clear that few men could please them. The other woman told me they were often and ardently applied for, but they would not surrender their person to any man they yet saw. They loved and clung to one another as their fingers to their hands. Their faces were fairer than their bodies, as they always reclined and lay naked in the warm sands. I wondered how the common kidnapper, the sensual Spaniard, had not found them. But they were always on the watch, their country terrible and far, and their father was dreaded even by the Spaniards and as for them both they would surely die together happy sisters! White man, did ever you see a happy woman, be here and look at those two. Yet in their own wild innocence they too in their wilder country like the naked couple of your own garden trembled anon at the apprehension of some fiend.

This nation is of tall stature and very swift of foot. They had no firearms but every Indian had his bow in hand. They were powerfully built for foot endurance. The hairs on their limbs were long, their headlocks long and straight down. Every man had an eagle's feather that played tied to his scalp. They ran foot races of 10 to 20 miles and in those deep and warm sands often beat their horses.

From this camp we followed the river three days trapping it. The country had the same awful loneliness and desolation on its face. We came upon a bottom of dense underbrush that pulled some of our packs off of our horses. When least expecting it we debouched on a round plain entirely surrounded by that brush. Here we found Indians gardening and we camped by them and trapped. Four or five of our traps were stolen. The trappers were enraged. My father's traps were never touched; he often found an Indian guarding his traps. He used to give the Indians all the beaver meat he and I did not consume. At last the trappers resolved to make a day of revenge for their five traps and designed to attack the Indians in their own camp unawares. My father was invited to join in the bloody work, but he refused saying, "I did not come here to war but to catch fur. These Indians may know nothing about your traps. They may have been taken by some distant thieves. Why arm to murder these poor hospitable people? They have no arms but clubs and bows. Why do you take rifles? The poor people. Take clubs only, if you are brave men but I will not be with you. Your purpose for five old traps is cruel and bad." Early the next morning before breakfast the party took to their arms. There was one low little cliff which overlooked the Indian camp and the river. Behind the top of it unseen the riflemen lay. The first shot fired was at an old grey-headed savage who was quietly taking his breakfast facing the sun in the door of his little home. He was struck in the ball of the knee and as he sat the ball followed and shattered to pieces his thighbone. He fell backward and looked toward the cliff. His mates at first laughed seeing him fall, whereupon the old man with anguish in his face said, "Why laugh you at me? Look, they are killing us." They looked. The cry of alarm was out and high, and as the startled Indians stood out to learn and look more the riflemen fired. Yells of woe from men, women and children filled the place. The dead and wounded lay there. The active ran to the river. Men, women and children plunged in and swam, but they were picked off by these cruel marksmen. The women made every effort to swim and save their children. Women who had one or two children made by terrible labor a safe landing with them on the other side, but those who had three and four children could not get over and gradually sank with them, going faithful to the death to what was their only solace and delight in that lonely valley.

Watching the fire I noticed one woman just as she landed on the other side fall dead from a bullet that entered her back. Two men too I saw drop on the other side, hit there by our unerring game rifles. One of the men swam until he found bottom and as he walked out he was hit. He staggered, walked and fell dead. The other staggered from the river about 200 paces and fell dead. Sometimes the Indians dove and came up only with their mouths to breathe when these fatal rifles found their heads and they sank forever. The trappers after this work went into the deserted camp, pillaged everything they liked in it and killed the old Indian who was first hit in the knee. They then came back perfectly unconcerned and smoked and jested over the success of their revenge. I noticed that the French Canadians of the party did not join in this cruel affair of tears. In the avenging jesting over their infernal work they said that some of those long black rifles might have sharpened their sights with buttons of the red coats at New Orleans.

Famous Trappers

In "The Mountain Man as Western Hero: Kit Carson," a chapter in Henry Nash Smith's *Virgin Land* (1950), the author writes:

> The notion that men who ranged the wilderness had fled from the restraints of civilization—for better or worse, according to the social philosophy of the observer—had been greatly strengthened during the 1830's by the spectacular development of the Rocky Mountain fur trade. The fur trapper, or Mountain Man, was much more clearly uncivilized than Daniel Boone had been. The prime theater of his activities lay hundreds of miles distant from the frontier beyond the Great American Desert, and was not a region that invited agricultural settlement. He had adopted many more Indian ways than had the typical pioneers of the area east of the Mississippi. His costume, his speech, his outlook on life, often enough his Indian squaw, gave him a decidedly savage aspect. Yet the trappers dominated the exploration of the trans-Mississippi region, and the successor of Boone and Leatherstocking in the role of typical Wild Western hero was certain to be a mountain man. (88)

Smith says that Kit Carson was considered the embodiment of all that the mountain man as hero should be. Carson was "the best known mountain man," says Smith, because he figured so prominently in John C. Frémont's reports, which his wife, Jessie Benton Frémont, had skillfully edited.

Smith traces the process by which writers transmuted Carson's deeds and life into a form suitable for an American hero. We will have more to say about Carson and that process of transformation in the introduction to a number of selections by and about him. Although other trappers were not as well known as Carson, their deeds nevertheless earned them considerable fame. We have already noted the legendary feats of John Colter and Hugh Glass. Of the many trappers and traders included in Dan L. Thrapp's four-volume *Encyclopedia of Frontier Biography* (1988 and 1994) and of the 292 subjects of biographical studies in *The Mountain Men and the Fur Trade of the Far West* (the multivolume series edited by LeRoy R. Hafen), dozens achieved some kind of public notice.

Many other selections in other sections of this anthology could also be placed appropriately in this section. We have, however, selected for this section narratives by and about only seven of the mountain men: Jedediah Smith, Bill Williams, Pegleg Smith, Jim Beckwourth, "Old Gabe" Jim Bridger, Milton Sublette, and Kit Carson. Each of the stories by or about them illustrates some, if not most, of the qualities that made of the mountain man the new Western hero. Men who led such exciting and adventurous lives became irresistible subjects for biographers and novelists. The sad irony, which the mountain men themselves recognized, is that all they did—the trapping, the trading, the guiding of wagon trains—destroyed the very conditions that had made possible their adventurous lives and their rise to fame.

68. Jedediah Smith Faces Death from Thirst

from Jedediah Smith, *The Travels of Jedediah Smith*

A deeply religious and literate gentleman, Jedediah Strong Smith (1799–1831) earned a reputation as one of the most important of the mountain men because of his extended expeditions through vast unexplored areas of the West. Born in the state of New York of New England parents, he joined Ashley's 1822 expedition. After setting out with Ashley on his 1823 expedition, Smith was mauled by a grizzly. In 1825, Smith and Ashley became partners; and, the following year, Smith, David Jackson, and William L. Sublette bought out Ashley. In the late summer of 1826 Smith left Soda Springs in present-day Idaho on an expedition to the Southwest. The next selection is from the journal he kept on that journey. It tells of his return in late June of 1827, when he and his party crossed the desert in present-day Utah. Smith survived that desert crossing and went on to lead other fur-trapping parties. He escaped the massacre of most of his men in Oregon in 1828, but three years later some Comanches found him alone on the Cimarron River and killed him.

In *Jedediah Smith and the Opening of the West* (1964), historian Dale L. Morgan presents a detailed study of Smith's career in the fur trade. See also George R. Brooks's introduction to his edition of *The Southwest Expedition of Jedediah S. Smith* (1989). For accounts of other desert experiences see Peter Wild's anthology *The Desert Reader* (1991).

June 23d N E 35 Miles. Moving on in the morning I kept down the creek on which we had encamped until it was lost in a small Lake. We then filled our horns and continued on our course, passing some brackish as well as some verry salt springs and leaving on the north of the latter part of the days travel a considerable Salt Plain. Just before night I found water that was drinkable but continued on in hopes of find better and was obliged to encamp without any.

June 24th N E 40 Miles I started verry early in hopes of soon finding water. But ascending a high point of a hill I could discover nothing but sandy plains or dry Rocky hills with the Exception of a snowy mountain off to the N E at the distance of 50 or 60 Miles. When I came down I durst not tell my men of the desolate prospect ahead. but framed my story so as to discourage them as little as possible. I told them I saw something black at a distance near which no doubt we would find water. While I had been up on the one of the horses gave out and had been left a short distance behind. I sent the men back to take the best of his flesh for our supply was again nearly exhausted whilst I would push forward in search of water. I went on a short distance and waited until they came up. They were much discouraged with the gloomy prospect but I said all I could to enliven their hopes and told them in all probability we would soon find water. But the view ahead was almost hopeless. With our best exertion we pushed forward walking as we had been for a long time over the soft sand. That kind of traveling is verry tiresome to men in good health who can eat when and what they choose and drink as often as they desire. and to us worn down with hunger and fatigue and burning with thirst increased by the blazing sands it was almost insupportable. At about 4 O Clock we were obliged to stop on the side of a sand hill under the shade of a small Cedar. We dug holes in the sand and laid down in them for the purpose of cooling our heated bodies. After resting about an hour we resumed our wearysome journey and traveled until 10 O Clock at night when we laid down to take a little repose. Previous to this and a short time after sun down I saw several turtle doves and as I did not recollect of ever having seen them more than 2 or 3 miles from water I spent more than a hour in looking for water but it was in vain. Our sleep was not repose for tormented nature made us dream of things we had not and for the want of which it then seemed possible and even probable we might perish in the desert unheard of and unpitied. In those moments how trifling were all those things that hold such an absolute sway over the busy and the prosperous world. My dreams were not of Gold or ambitious honors but of my distant quiet home of murmuring brooks of cooling cascades. After a short rest we continued our march and traveled all night. The murmur of falling waters still sounding in our ears and the apprehension that we might never live to hear that sound in reality weighed heavily uppon us.

June 25th When morning came it saw us in the same unhappy situation pursuing our journey over the desolate waste now gleming in the sun and more insupportably tormenting than it had been during the night. At 10 O Clock Robert Evans laid down in the plain under the shade of a small cedar being able to proceed no further. The Mountain of which I have before spoken was apparently not far off and we left him and proceeded onward in the hope of finding water in time to return with some in season to save his life. After traveling about three Miles we came to the foot of the Mt and then to our inexpressible joy we found water. Goble plunged into it at once and I could hardly wait to bath my burning forehead before I was pouring it down regardless of the consequences. Just before we arrived at the spring I saw two indians traveling in the direction in which Evans was left and soon after the report of two guns was heard in quick succession. This considerably increased our apprehension for his safety but shortly after a smoke was seen back on the trail and I took a small kettle of water and some meat and going back found him safe. he had not seen the indians and had discharged his gun to direct me where he lay and for the same purpose had raised a smoke. He was indeed far gone being scarcely able to speak. When I came the first question he asked me was have you any water! I told him I had plenty and handed the kettle which would hold 6 or 7 quarts in which there was some meat mixed with the water. O says he why did you bring the meat and putting the kettle to his mouth he did not take it away untile he had drank all the water of which there was at least 4 or 5 quarts and then asked me why I had not brought more. This however revived him so much that he was able to go on to the spring. I cut the horse meat and spread it out to dry and determined to remain for the rest of the day that we might repose our wearied and emaciated bodies. I have at different times suffered all the extremes of hunger and thirst. Hard as it is to bear for succesive days the knawings of hunger yet it is light in comparison to the agony of burning thirst, and [o]n the other hand I have observed that a man reduced by hunger is some days in recovering his strength. A man equally reduced by thirst seems renovated almost instantaneneously. Hunger can be endured more than twice as long as thirst. To some it may appear surprising that a man who has been for several days without eating has a most incessant desire to drink and although he can drink but a little at a time yet he wants it much oftener than in ordinary circumstances. In the course of the day several indians showed themselves on the high points of the hills but would not come to my camp.

69. Bill Williams—The Old Man of the Mountains

from Mathew C. Field, *Prairie and Mountain Sketches*

Before he became a Rocky Mountain free trapper, William S. "Bill" Williams (1789–1849) had been an itinerant Baptist preacher and, from 1813 to 1825, a trapper and trader with the Osage Indians. In 1833, while a member of Joseph R. Walker's California expedition, Williams became one of the first European-Americans to see the Yosemite Valley. He later lived among the Utes and served as a guide on Frémont's third and fourth expeditions. While on that fourth expedition, he was killed by Ute Indians in revenge for attacks on them by American dragoons. For an extended account of his life see Alpheus Hoyt Favour, *Old Bill Williams, Mountain Man* (1936).

Mathew C. Field (1812–1844), author of this selection, began adult life as an actor. In 1839 he visited Bent's Fort and Taos, and he joined the 1843 Rocky Mountain excursion of Sir William Drummond Stewart. It was probably on the latter trip that he heard Bill Williams's fantastic tale.

SKETCH: THE OLD MAN OF THE MOUNTAINS
[September 8–14]
[New Orleans *Daily Picayune*, January 4, 1844]

The world should be made acquainted with some of the strange characters who have buried themselves away from civilization among the rocks of the West.

There is one whimsical old genius who is noted particularly among the trapper tribe as the prince of queer ones. He calls himself *William S. Williams, M.T.*, and he is most resolutely determined upon having the title initials "M.T." always affixed to his name. He is the oldest man in the mountains, having fully resolved to live and die there, and more droll anecdotes are told about him than would fill a pair of volumes of modern size. *M.T.* is meant to signify *Master Trapper*, and the old man has just seized upon the whim of insisting that this distinguishing mark shall on all occasions and under all circumstances be attached to his name. He chanced at one time to fall into a mortal quarrel with a Blackfeet Indian, and upon achieving advantage, he at once seized upon the red fellow's scalp-lock.

"Bill Williams!" shouted the Indian, whose knowledge of English consisted in the capacity of pronouncing this singular old white man's name.

"William S. Williams, *M.T.*, if you please," said the old man of the mountains, as he coolly darted the point of his knife around the scalp-lock and tore it off!

This extraordinary individual is now about fifty-five or sixty years of age, and he has lived more than half his life in the mountains. He declares that he never was anywhere else, but it is remembered that he was once a Methodist preacher in the States, and it is known that he is an educated man, with a critical knowledge of Greek and Latin. By his own words, he was "rolled out of a thunder storm in the mountains," for he found himself there and don't remember anything else. He is quite certain he is not human, and has a strong persuasion that he was "translated from the Great Bear, or some other luminous celestial animal, for some most particular and especial purpose that is meant to be made known to him hereafter."

He was never known to wear a hat, but once in the winter, finding his head cold, he shot a wolf, scalped the animal and drew the warm skin on to his own head! For all such eccentric things this old man is remarkable, but, perhaps, the singularity of his character may be better shown by relating an odd meeting he once had with a young fellow fresh from the States. Williams was camping alone when the young fellow encountered him.

"*Hum!*" said the old man in soliloquy, "here comes another enormous fool of a young rascal to crowd us here in the mountains! We shan't have an inch of elbow room left! 'Cook, old cake, cook!' " said he, addressing a lump of dough that he was turning over on the coals of his solitary fire with his naked toes, that protruded through his venerable moccasins. "Cook, old cake! here comes a white fool, and he's hungry of course. Now, you miserable young blockhead, do you know me?" said the old man to the stranger.

"I guess I do," said the boy, for he was a wandering sprig of Yankee land.

"You *guess*," replied the old eccentric, "you're a pretty sample of a scalp-lock to come here guessing! Had you nobody to keep you at home, that you must come strolling out here among bears and Blackfeet? How do you know me?"

"I reckon I guess."

"O, you're a big figure at mathematics! You had better get rid of your guessing and your reckoning if you want to live among the rocks. Take up that chunk of burnt dough there, and stuff it down your ravenous maw!"

"Thank you—I'm not hungry."

"Don't come here to tell lies, sir; we are honest men in the mountains, and you mustn't come here to contaminate us with your civilization. You *are* hungry, and you know it, and you must eat that cake; I've got another. Do you take me for an antediluvian not to share my dinner with you?"

"Aint you the man they call Bill Williams?" said the hungry lad, as he greedily devoured the cake.

"*What* do they call me?" roared Bill, with the growl of a wounded bear.

"William Williams, I think!" answered the young aspirant in the trapping trade, with a half frightened tone of subdued respect.

"William S. Williams, M.T., young buzzard's meat!" replied the master trapper, drawing himself up with the air of a Julius Caesar. "Look here, boy, do you see that *butte?* There's a hole in it, and that's where I put my bones."

"Bones!" said the boy, greatly bewildered at the words of the old man.

"Yes, *Wah!*" continued Bill, lifting his rifle and imitating a shot, "there's where I bury my dead; that's my bone-house!"

"Why you don't—"

"Don't tell me I don't," interrupted the old man, "or I'll don't you, knock me dead, if I don't! How would you like to sleep there tonight? Eat away, and don't be gaping at a natural christian like a born fool! I always stow away my white bones decently. Eat away, you stupid young blockhead, and stop staring. I dare say you call yourself a gentleman! Happy of your acquaintance. If you have done eating, just remember that you have dined with William S. Williams, M.T."

This odd encounter happened almost word for word as here set down, and it may give the reader a fair idea of one of the drollest beings that ever lived. Surly, abrupt and eccentric, the old fellow is yet noted for benevolence and stern honesty. He once took off his coat of deerskin, when it was almost the last remnant of apparel in his possession, and threw it over the shoulders of a poor, shivering squaw. He sleeps curled up by the camp-fire, with his head in the ashes, embracing an old rifle, that has been mended and mended again with "buffalo tug," until scarcely a particle of the original stock is left. He works hard, makes money, and gives everything away to others who may happen to be in distress. He once threatened to shoot an old friend who sent him a letter with an offer of assistance! Old William S. Williams, M.T., will accept of charity from no man breathing. Such a character is now pillowing his grey hairs among the snows of the west, and there he will live and die, while this rough sketch, no doubt, presents all the world will ever know of The Old Man of the Mountains!

70. How "Pegleg" Smith Got His Name

from George C. Yount, *George C. Yount and His Chronicles of the West*

The next narrative tells how Thomas "Pegleg" Smith (1797–1866) got his nickname. Born in Kentucky, Smith had worked on Mississippi River flatboats before he signed up in St. Louis with a caravan headed for Santa Fe in 1824. He trapped throughout the Southwest, and, in 1827, after hearing news that Indians had almost wiped out a party of French trappers a few days before, he, Milton Sublette, and thirty other trappers massacred more than a hundred Papago (now known as Tohono O'Odham) Indians, including men, women, and children. The incident that gave him his nickname took place in 1828. In the 1830s, Pegleg stole Indian children and sold them as slaves to Mexican traders. He later switched to stealing horses in California and selling them at Bent's Fort. Before he died, he married a number of Indian women, lived with them in northeastern Utah, and, pockets bulging with gold-bearing ore, told stories of a fabulous gold strike.

For more information about the necessary, albeit amateur, medical practices described in this selection and in Selection 42 see Robert F. Karolevitz, *Doctors of the Old West* (1967).

They went on to a winter camp, on Green River waters, probably in Brown's Hole, and there Tom lost his leg. The facts about this are confused; so many stories have been told. Pegleg himself is responsible for a few different versions, embellished no doubt during the stimulus of the bottle. We select here the parts of an early, little-known account that seem most plausible.

Tom was shot in a fair fight (or from ambush), by rifle fire (or by an arrow). The bullet (or the arrow) shattered both bones of his lower leg just below the ankle (or through the ankle, or just below the knee). Tom turned quickly to jump for his gun and collapsed short of it (or: "he raised his rifle to his shoulder and fired at the spot where his enemy lay hidden from sight" and killed him!).

He thought "a whole mountain had fell on my left foot, and before I knew it I was lyin' flat on my face bleedin' like a stuck pig. . . . I had a ball plump through my left ankle which smashed all the bones into splinters!

"They picked me up and made me as comfortable as they could, but that wasn't much. Arter we had a council what we should do . . . the leg would mortify . . . and I was a gone coon sure. The boys had a talk among themselves and then . . . [Milt Sublette] told me what they thought.

" 'Pete,' said he, 'there's one chance for ye—and only one. Ef we can get that mashed foot off of ye and rest here a few days till the worst pain is over we *may* get ye . . . [away] on horseback by goin' slow. Ef ye start as ye are, or ef you stay here as you are, you'll mortify and die, sure. We'll stay by ye, in course, but we can't doctor up such a leg as that, and it's a gonner anyhow, what say ye?'

" 'We larn to settle things quick out on the plains and I saw they was right . . . so I axed him ef he thought he *could* take it off.'

" 'Well,' said he, 'I seen it done once when I was huntin' with the Crow Injins and I think I can do it their fashion.'

" 'Go ahead, then,' said I, 'its my duty not to lose a chance.'

"There was no more talk about it, but they went to work to fix things at once. One of our huntin' knives was sharpened on a stone till it would cut a hair. Another one was notched along the edge with a hatchet, till it made a tol'able good saw, and the barrel of one of the Injin guns was put in a fire and kept red hot. When they got all this done they propped me up agin a tree and tied me fast so I couldn't move, and then they gave me about a pint of Old Bald Face to drink, I ain't very skeery now, nor was I then, but when they said the time had come I tell *you*, boys, I felt like a drawed skunk and no mistake. It was no use to go back though, so I grit my teeth and gave the signal.

"First they tied a strip o' green deer's hide around my leg above the knee, so tight it sunk into the flesh all around: I've got the mark of it now. Then [Milt] took the sharp knife and cut down to the bones just below the knee. I stood that pretty well for the leg was numb from the tight band round it. Then [someone] pulled down the bottom flesh and [Milt] took the sawknife and sawed off both bones. *That* was a teaser, but it was nothing to what was comin' for as [s]oon as the leg dropped, [someone] handed [Milt] the *red hot gunbarrel and he rubbed it over the stump till it fizzled and smoked worse nor a venison steak!*

"I just let one yell out o' me you could ha' heerd a mile, and then I don't remember anything more, for, though it may look sneakin', for the first time in my life I believe I fainted away. When I come to they'd got me bandaged up all right, with a birch bark poultice on the stump and a flask full o' water, with a hole punched in the bottom . . . so it kept drappin' on the stump . . . it was more than two weeks before they dared move me . . . travelin' slow all the time and liftin' me off the horse whenever I wanted to rest . . . I was nothin' but a skilliton and it was more than six months before I was my own man agin . . . that's the way I lost my leg, Colonel, and now let's liquor, for talkin's dry work."

It was said that Tom was taken to the Ute villages, where the squaws nursed him, chewing up roots and spitting them on the stump. Later when the severed bones worked loose, Milton Sublette and Tom managed to pull them out, using a bullet mold as forceps. Tom then whittled himself an oaken peg leg and strapped it on so that he could easily and rapidly remove it. It wasn't entirely a handicap as he found it handy to wield as a club in bar room "arguments." His name was "Pegleg" from then on and the Indians called him 'Wa-ke-to-co'—the man with one foot.

71 and 72. Incidents from the Life of James Beckwourth

Many mountain men adopted at least part of the lifestyle of Indians they encountered, and the Indians even adopted some trappers into their bands. The Crows, for example, made Jim Beckwourth one of them. His fame grew as a result of his experiences as a Crow and because of a meeting that Bernard DeVoto describes in *Across the Wide Missouri*:

In the early eighteen-fifties, a wandering journalist [Thomas D. Bonner] found Jim in California, beginning to be old, his mountain days behind him, and ghosted his reminiscences. The result, *The Life and Adventures of James P. Beckwourth*, is one of the gaudiest books in our literature and may well be the goriest: at least more Indians are killed in it than in any other book known to this student. Various writers have appraised it variously but, apart from yarns in which Jim unnecessarily quadruples his own daring, it is in the main trustworthy and is sometimes an indispensable witness to the events it deals with. (128)

The next two selections come from Beckwourth and Bonner's gaudy book and deal with events after Jim's adoption by the Crows in 1828. During his six years with the tribe, he married a number of Indian women.

71. Beckwourth Settles Down with the Crow Indians

from Thomas D. Bonner, *Life and Adventures of James P. Beckwourth*

While conversing to the extent of my abilities with my father in the evening, and affording him full information respecting the white people, their great cities, their numbers, their power, their opulence, he suddenly demanded of me if I wanted a wife; thinking, no doubt, that, if he got me married, I should lose all discontent, and forego any wish of returning to the whites.

I assented of course.

"Very well," said he, "you shall have a pretty wife and a good one."

Away he strode to the lodge of one of the greatest braves, and asked one of his daughters of him to bestow upon his son, who the chief must have heard was also a great brave. The consent of the parent was readily given. The name of my prospective father-in-law was Black-lodge. He had three very pretty daughters, whose names were Still-water, Black-fish, and Three roads.

Even the untutored daughters of the wild woods need a little time to prepare for such an important event, but long and tedious courtships are unknown among them.

The ensuing day the three daughters were brought to my father's lodge by their father, and I was requested to take my choice. "Still-water" was the eldest, and I liked her name; if it was emblematic of her disposition, she was the woman I should prefer. "Still-water," accordingly, was my choice. They were all superbly attired in garments which must have cost them months of labor, which garments the young women ever keep in readiness against such an interesting occasion as the present.

The acceptance of my wife was the completion of the ceremony, and I was again a married man, as sacredly in their eyes as if the Holy Christian Church had fastened the irrevocable knot upon us.

Among the Indians, the daughter receives no patrimony on her wedding-day, and her mother and father never pass a word with the son-in-law after—a custom religiously observed among them, though for what reason I never learned. The other relatives are under no such restraint.

My brothers made me a present of twenty as fine horses as any in the nation—all trained war-horses. I was also presented with all the arms and instruments requisite for an Indian campaign.

My wife's deportment coincided with her name; she would have reflected honor upon many a civilized household. She was affectionate, obedient, gentle, cheerful, and, apparently, quite happy. No domestic thunder-storms, no curtain-lectures ever disturbed the serenity of our connubial lodge. I speedily formed acquaintance with all my immediate neighbors, and the Morning Star (which was the name conferred upon me on my recognition as the lost son) was soon a companion to all the young warriors in the village. No power on earth could have shaken their faith in my positive identity with the lost son. Nature seemed to prompt the old woman to recognize me as her missing child, and all my new relatives placed implicit faith in the genuineness of her discovery. Greenwood had spoken it, "and his tongue was not crooked." What could I do under the circumstances? Even if I should deny my Crow origin, they would not believe me. How could I dash with an unwelcome and incredible explanation all the joy that had been manifested on my return—the cordial welcome, the rapturous embraces of those who hailed me as a son and a brother, the exuberant joy of the whole nation for the return of a long-lost Crow, who, stolen when a child, had returned in the strength of maturity, graced with the name of a great brave, and the generous strife I had occasioned in their endeavors to accord me the warmest welcome? I could not find it in my heart to undeceive these unsuspecting people and tear myself away from their untutored caresses.

Thus I commenced my Indian life with the Crows. I said to myself, "I can trap in their streams unmolested, and derive more profit under their protection than if among my own men, exposed incessantly to assassination and alarm." I therefore resolved to abide with them, to guard my secret, to do my best in their company, and in assisting them to subdue their enemies.

There was but one recollection troubled me, and that was my lonely one in St. Louis. My thoughts were constantly filled with her. I knew my affection was reciprocated, and that her fond heart beat alone for me; that my promise was undoubtingly confided in, and that prayers were daily offered for my safety, thus distant in the mountains, exposed to every peril. Repeatedly I would appoint a day for my return, but some unexpected event would occur and thrust my resolution aside. Still I hoped, for I had accumulated the means of wealth sufficient to render us comfortable through life; a fortunate return was all I awaited to consummate my ardent anticipation of happiness, and render me the most blessed of mortals.

Before proceeding farther with my Indian life, I will conduct the reader back to our camp the evening succeeding to my disappearance from Bridger. He was on the hill, crossing over to me as agreed upon, when he saw me in the hands of the Indians, being conducted to their village, which was also in sight. Seeing clearly that he could oppose no resistance to my captors, he made all speed to the camp, and communicated the painful news of my death. He had seen me in the charge of a whole host of Shi-ans, who were conducting me to camp, there to sacrifice me in the most improved manner their savage propensities could suggest, and then abandon themselves to a general rejoicing over the fall of a white man. With the few men he had in camp it was hopeless to attempt a rescue; for, judging by the size of the village, there must be a community of several thousand Indians. All were plunged in gloom. All pronounced my funeral eulogy; all my daring encounters were spoken of to my praise. My fortunate escapes, my repeated victories were applauded in memory of me; the loss of their best hunter, of their kind and ever-obliging friend, was deeply deplored by all.

"Alas! had it not been for that lamentable quarrel," they exclaimed, "he would still have been among us. Poor Jim! peace to his ashes!"

Bridger lamented that he had advised me to leave the camp, and again that he had separated from me at the Forks. "If we had kept together," he murmured, "his fate might have been prevented, for doubtless one of us would have seen the Indians in time to have escaped."

Thus, as I was afterward informed by some of the party, was my memory celebrated in that forlorn camp. Farther, having conceived a deep disgust at that vicinity, they moved their camp to the head waters of the Yellow Stone, leaving scores of beaver unmolested in the streams.

The faithful fellows little thought that, while they were lamenting my untimely fall, I was being hugged and kissed to death by a whole lodge full of near and dear Crow relatives, and that I was being welcomed with a public reception fully equal in intensity, though not in extravagance, to that accorded to the victor of Waterloo on his triumphal entry into Paris.

Bridger had never supposed that the Indians who he saw leading me away were Crows, he being ignorant that he was so near their territory. His impression was that these were Cheyennes, hence I was given up for dead and reported so to others. My death was communicated to the rendezvous when the fall hunt was over, and there was a general time of mourning in mountain style.

I say "mountain style" in contradistinction to the manner of civilized circles, because, with them, when the death of a comrade is deplored, his good deeds alone are celebrated; his evil ones are interred with his bones. Modern politics have introduced the custom of perpetuating all that is derogatory to a man's fair fame, and burying in deep oblivion all that was honorable and praiseworthy. Hence I say, Give me the mountaineer, despite all the opprobrium that is cast upon his name, for in him you have a man of chivalrous feeling, ready to divide his last morsel with his distressed fellow—ay, and to yield the last drop of his blood to defend the life of his friend.

72. Beckwourth Astonishes His Fellow Traders

from Thomas D. Bonner, *Life and Adventures of James P. Beckwourth*

It was now the fall of the year. I had been a Crow for many moons. It was time to repair to the trading-post to obtain what articles we needed. I determined to accompany the party, and at least attend to the sale of my own effects. What peltry I had was worth three thousand dollars in St. Louis, and I was solicitous to obtain something like an equivalent in exchange for it.

We proceeded to Fort Clarke, on the Missouri. I waited until the Indians had nearly completed their exchanges, speaking nothing but Crow language, dressed like a Crow, my hair as long as a Crow's, and myself as black as a crow. No one at the post doubted my being a Crow. Toward the conclusion of the business, one of my tribe inquired in his own language for "be-has-i-pe-hish-a." The clerk could not understand his want, and there was none of the article in sight for the Indian to point out. He at length called Kipp to see if he could divine the Indian's meaning.

I then said in English, "Gentlemen, that Indian wants scarlet cloth."

If a bomb-shell had exploded in the fort they could not have been more astonished.

"Ah," said one of them, "you speak English! Where did you learn it?"

"With the white man."

"How long were you with the whites?"

"More than twenty years."

"Where did you live with them?"

"In St. Louis."

"In St. Louis! in St. Louis! You have lived twenty years in St. Louis!"

Then they scanned me closely from head to foot, and Kipp said, "If you have lived twenty years in St. Louis, I'll swear you are no Crow."

"No, I am not."

"Then what may be your name?"

"My name in English is James Beckwourth."

"Good heavens! why I have heard your name mentioned a thousand times. You were supposed dead, and were so reported by Captain Sublet."

"I am not dead, as you see; I still move and breathe."

"This explains the mystery," he added, turning to the clerk, "of those beaver-skins being marked 'J.B.' Well, well! if you are not a strange mortal!"

All this conversation was unintelligible to my Crow brethren, who were evidently proud to see a Crow talk so fluently to the white man.

"Now," I said, "I have seen you transact your business without interposing with a word. You have cleared two or three thousand per cent. of your exchanges. I do not grudge it you. Were I in your place I should do the same. But I want a little more liberal treatment. I have toiled hard for what I have obtained, and I want the worth of my earnings."

I set my own price upon my property, and, to the great astonishment of my Indian brethren, I returned with as large a bale of goods as theirs would all together amount to. But, as I have said, an Indian is in no wise envious, and, instead of considering themselves unfairly used, they rejoiced at the white man's profusion to me, and supposed the overplus he had given me was an indemnity for the captivity they had held me in.

On our return I made various presents to all my wives, some of whom I did not see for months together, and to many other relatives. I had still a good stock to trade upon, and could exchange with my brethren at any rate I offered. They placed implicit confidence in my integrity, and a beaver-skin exchanged with me for one plug of tobacco contented them better than to have exchanged it for two with the white man.

I had the fairest opportunity for the acquisition of an immense fortune that ever was placed in man's way. By saying one word to the tribe I could have kept the white trader forever out of their territory, and thus have gained the monopoly of the trade of the entire nation for any term of years. That I am not now in possession of a fortune equal to that of an Astor or a Girard is solely the fault of my own indolence, and I do not to this moment see how I came to neglect the golden opportunity.

73. "Old Gabe"

from J. Lee Humfreville, *Twenty Years among Our Savage Indians*

The section on tall tales would have been just as appropriate for the following selection, but we have chosen to place it here because the teller is more famous than any one of his many tales. James "Jim" or "Old Gabe" Bridger (1804–1881) followed the early life pattern of many of his fellow trappers. He was born in Virginia, then moved near St. Louis, and joined Ashley on his 1822 expedition. In 1824 or early 1825 he may have been the first white man to see the Great Salt Lake. He trapped for the firm of Smith, Jackson, and Sublette; he then joined the Rocky Mountain Fur Company as a partner from 1830 until its dissolution in 1834. Almost legendary is the story of Bridger being wounded by an Indian arrow at the Battle of Pierre's Hole (1832) and then having the arrowhead lodged in his back until Dr. Marcus Whitman, the missionary, removed it in 1835. "Old Gabe" and Louis Vasquez formed a partnership and built Fort Bridger in southwestern Wyoming in 1843. Both before and after Bridger sold his share of the fort to the Mormons in 1853, he served as a guide. Among those he led were Capt. Howard Stansbury's expedition of 1850, Sir George Gore's hunting party of 1851, Col. Albert Sidney Johnston's army deployment in the so-called Mormon War of 1857–58, Capt. William V. Raynold's Yellowstone expedition of 1859–60, Capt. E. L. Berthoud's exploration of 1861, the Powder River expedition of 1865–66, and Grenville M. Dodge's Union Pacific Railroad survey of the late 1860s. Bridger married three Indian women; and, after each of them died, he sent his children to Missouri to be educated. In 1868 he moved to Westport, Missouri. Episodes of his career were fictionalized by dime novelist E. Z. C. Judson (writing as Ned Buntline), and Bernard DeVoto called Bridger "an atlas of the West." For a full biography see J. Cecil Alter, *James Bridger* (1925). J. Lee Humfreville, the author of this selection, was an army officer who served many years in the West.

Bridger was much sought after by emigrants crossing the plains, for his reputation as a guide and Indian fighter was well known. They would annoy him with all sorts of questions, which would often compel the old man to beat a retreat; yet he had a streak of humor, and would give them a ghost story every now and then. Some of these stories were unique. He had a quick and surprisingly vivid imagination, and he reeled off story after story with a spontaneity that was astonishing. He told these stories, too, with a solemn gravity that was intensely amusing. I know that I am largely indebted to him for often keeping up my spirits when they were at the lowest ebb. I always knew something good was coming when he began to tell a story, but I never dared to smile until the climax was reached, for that would have spoiled it all.

"Is there anything remarkable to be seen about here?" an inquisitive pilgrim asked him one day.

"W-a-l-l," he replied, in a peculiar drawling tone, which he generally assumed in telling stories, in order, I believe, to gain time to give his imagination fuller play, "There's a cur'ous mountain a few miles off'n the road, to the north of here, but the dogon'd trouble is you can't see the blamed thing."

"A mountain and can't see it—that's curious," interrupted the pilgrim. "How large is it?"

"Wall, I should say it's nigh onto three miles in circumference at the base, but its height is unknown," continued Bridger with imperturbable gravity.

"Is it so high you can't see the top of it?" inquired the puzzled traveler.

"That's what I say, stranger; you can't see the base of it either. Didn't you ever hear of Crystal Mountain?"

"I never did."

"Wall, I'll tell you what it is. It's a mountain of crystal rock, an' so clear that the most powerful field glasses can't see it, much less the naked eye. You'll wonder, p'r'aps, how a thing that can't be seen no how wus ever discovered. It came about in this way. You see, a lot of bones an' the carcasses of animals and birds wus found scattered all around the base. You see they ran or flew against this invisible rock and jest killed themselves dead. You kin feel the rock an' that's all. You can't see it. It's a good many miles high, for everlastin' quantities of birds' bones are jest piled up all around the base of it."

On another occasion he told one of these persistent questioners the story of a gold mine, which he said was not far from the Overland road.

"Why the gold's so plentiful," said Bridger, "that all that's necessary to secure it is to jest pick it up. Great nuggets of the purest gold are scattered all over the ground. There's no diggin' to be done, or rock crushin' machines an' siftin' required. You orter to stop over and fill your pockets; you'll find it mighty useful on your journey. Anybody who's in want of gold need only go there an' load himself."

"Do you mean to say that it is free to anybody?" asked the traveler.

"Free as the air we breathe," said Bridger.

"How can we get there?" one of the listening crowd ventured to inquire.

"*Hire, a buggy*—easiest thing in the world," answered Bridger.

The joke was that a buggy could not be had nearer than six hundred miles.

Another story of this strange and eccentric character:

"You must have had some curious adventures with, and hair-breadth escapes from, the Indians, during your long life among them," observed one of a party of a dozen or more, who had been relentlessly plying him with questions.

"Yes, I've had a few," he responded, reflectively, "and I never to my dyin' day shall forget one in perticlar."

The crowd manifested an eager desire to hear the story. I will not undertake to give his words, but no story was ever more graphically told, and no throng of listeners ever followed a story's detail with more intense interest. He was on horseback and alone. He had been suddenly surprised by a party of six Indians, and putting spurs to his horse sought to escape. The Indians, mounted on fleet ponies, quickly followed in pursuit. His only weapon was a six-shooter. The moment the leading Indian came within shooting distance, he turned in his saddle, and gave him a shot. His shot always meant a dead Indian. In this way he picked off five of the Indians, but the last one kept up the pursuit relentlessly and refused to be shaken off.

"We wus nearin' the edge of a deep and wide gorge," said Bridger. "No horse could leap over that awful chasm, an' a fall to the bottom meant sartin death. I turned my horse suddint an' the Injun was upon me. We both fired to-once, an' both horses wus killed. We now engaged in a han'-to-han' conflict with butcher knives. He wus a powerful Injun—tallest I ever see. It wus a long and fierce struggle. One moment I hed the best of it, an' the next the odds wus agin me. Finally————"

Here Bridger paused as if to get breath.

"How did it end?" at length asked one of his breathless listeners, anxiously.

"*The Injun killed me*," he replied with slow deliberation. The climax freed him from further questioning by that party.

While on a visit to St. Louis, one of his old mountaineer friends of the American Fur Company met him on the street, and greeting him, said: "Jim, what are you doing here?" With an oath he answered, "I'm trying to find my way out of these ———— cañons;" adding, "This is the meanest camp I ever struck in my life. I have met more'n a thousand men in the last hour, and nary one of 'em has asked me to come to his lodge and have something to eat."

When on a visit to Washington, he was introduced to the President. After staring at him in amazement for a few moments, Bridger turned to the member of Congress who had introduced him, and said, "Looks jest like any other man, don't he?" He had expected to see in the President a superhuman person, and he was much astonished to find that he looked very much like other people.

While his trading post flourished at Fort Bridger he was supposed to have a large amount of money in his possession. Some desperadoes entered his house one night for the purpose of robbing him. Bridger, awakening from his sleep, quickly said, "What are you lookin' for?" One of the desperadoes answered, "We are looking for your money." Bridger replied, "Wait jest a minute an' I'll git up and help you." This disconcerted the robbers, and knowing their man they concluded not to wait until he "got up," but quickly departed.

74. Milton Sublette Takes Back Furs from Spanish Authorities in Santa Fe

from Josiah Gregg, *Commerce of the Prairies* (1841)

Four of the five Sublette brothers—William Louis Sublette (1799–1845), Milton Green Sublette (1801–1837), Andrew Whitley Sublette (1808?–1853), and Solomon Perry Sublette (1816?–1857)—were involved in some capacity in the fur trade. Pinckney W. Sublette (1812?–1828), the fifth brother, was killed in Blackfoot country, where he had been taken for his health. William and Milton became the best known of the family, and stories of their exploits abound. The following selection is about one of Milton's daring acts. He had joined the Gila River expedition of Ewing Young in 1826, and he was a member of the Pratte–St. Vrain expedition into the northern Rockies in 1827–28. Called by one reporter the "Thunderbolt of the Rockies," Milton joined four partners in 1830 to found the Rocky Mountain Fur Company; at its dissolution in 1834 he continued in partnership with Thomas Fitzpatrick and Jim Bridger. Milton Sublette fought at the Battle of Pierre's Hole in 1832, and in that same year he married the Shoshone beauty Mountain Lamb. Also in 1832 he guided Nathaniel J. Wyeth through Blackfoot country to Oregon. A year later, he agreed to buy supplies from Wyeth at the next year's rendezvous, but when Wyeth showed up with the goods at the 1834 rendezvous, Sublette reneged on the agreement. In 1835 his left leg had to be amputated (probably because of bone cancer), and he died two years later at Fort Laramie.

The writer who tells the story about Sublette, Josiah Gregg (1806–1850), engaged in the New Mexico trade from 1831 to 1840. For information about Gregg see Paul Horgan's *Josiah Gregg and His Vision of the Early Far West* (1979).

Few men, perhaps, have done more to jeopard the interests of American traders, or to bring the American character itself into contempt, than Armijo, the present arbitrary governor of New Mexico. I am happy to say, however, that in the midst of his many oppressions, he was once at least obliged to "knock under" to one of those bold and daring spirits of the Rocky Mountains whom obstacles rather energize than subdue. This was about the year 1828, during Armijo's previous governorship. A law was then in existence which had been enacted by the general Congress prohibiting foreigners from trapping beaver in the Mexican territory, under penalty of confiscation, etc.; but as there were no native trappers in New Mexico, Gov. Baca and his successor (Narbona) thought it expedient to extend licenses to foreigners, in the name of citizens, upon condition of their taking a certain proportion of Mexicans to learn the art of trapping. In pursuance of this disposition, Gov. Narbona extended a license to one Ewing Young, who was accompanied by a Mr. Sublette, brother of Capt. Wm. Sublette, and almost equally celebrated for his mountain adventures. Previous to the return of this party from their trapping expedition, Armijo had succeeded Narbona in office, and they were informed that it was his intention to seize their furs. To prevent this, they deposited them at a neighboring village, where they were afterwards discovered, seized, and confiscated. The furs being damp, they were spread out in the sun before the *Guardia*, in Santa Fé, when Sublette, perceiving two packs of beaver which had been his own property, got by honest labor, instantly seized them and carried them away before the eyes of the whole garrison, and concealed both them and his own person in a house opposite. The entire military force was immediately put in requisition, and a general search made for the offender and his prize; but in vain: indeed, if the truth must be spoken, the troops seemed to have as little desire to find Sublette as the latter had of being found; for his character was too well known to leave any room for hope that his capture could be effected without a great deal of trouble. In the meanwhile, Armijo raved, and threatened the Americans for not ferreting out their countryman and delivering him over to justice. Failing to produce any impression by blustering, however, he caused a couple of cannons to be pointed at the house where the offender was supposed to be concealed, declaring at the same time that he would batter it down; but all to no purpose. Mr. Sublette finally conveyed his furs in safety to the frontier, and thence to the United States.

75-80. Adventures of Kit Carson

Biographies about Kit Carson (1809–1868) started to appear even before his death. DeWitt C. Peters's *The Life and Adventures of Kit Carson, The Nestor of the Rocky Mountains, from Facts Narrated by Himself* (1858) started a list followed by Charles Burdett's *Life of Kit Carson: The Great Western Hunter and Guide* (1862) and, after Carson's death, by John S. C. Abbott's *Christopher Carson, Familiarly Known as Kit Carson* (1873). Readers learned from these books that Carson was born in 1809 in Kentucky, moved with his family to Missouri in 1812, fled from an apprenticeship and joined a caravan bound for New Mexico in 1826, and accompanied trapper Ewing Young from 1828 to 1831 through southern Arizona to California and back to Arizona. As two of the following six selections indicate, Carson attended the 1835 rendezvous at the Green River. He first married an Arapaho woman, who died, and then a Cheyenne, who divorced him. He moved on to Bent's Fort, where he hunted during 1841–42. In 1842 John C. Frémont hired Carson as a guide, and Carson also served in that capacity on subsequent Frémont expeditions. In 1843 Carson married fifteen-year-old Josefa Jaramillo of Taos. During the Civil War, he served the Union as colonel of the First New Mexico Infantry and was breveted brigadier general after the battle of Valverde in February 1862. He joined military campaigns against the Navajo, the Mescalero Apache, and the Kiowa from 1862 to 1865.

The narrator of the first selection about Carson is Joe Meek, who told his story to Frances Fuller Victor. The third and fourth of the six Carson selections describe his famous duel at the 1835 rendezvous. Denis McLoughlin's *Wild and Woolly: An Encyclopedia of the Old West* (1975) includes this account of the duel:

> A bit of Arapaho fluff named Waa-Nibe (Singing Grass) had built up pressures in these men, and the tough talk developed into a duel on horseback. Shuman [Shunar], a red-bearded giant of a man whose jaws would have served as a bear trap, was confident

of victory, but after the flintlocks had thundered, he was to bite the dust completely unpressurized, while Carson lived to marry the girl. . . . A girl was born of the couple, and when Singing Grass died in 1842, Carson took the child to St. Louis to be educated. (79)

Samuel Parker (1779–1866), who gives the first of the following two accounts of the Carson-Shunar duel, came west as a missionary, and his journal provides a detailed, if very pious, account of all he saw on his journey.

The last selection consists of Carson's own telling of his attempt to rescue a captured woman and of finding a novel she had been reading—a novel about Carson. Henry Nash Smith says the novel was probably Charles Averill's *Kit Carson, the Prince of the Gold Hunters* (1849). (A chapter from this novel is included in Section XI of this reader.) In *The Dime Novel Western* (1978), Daryl Jones says that Averill's novel and Emerson Bennett's best-selling 1849 novel *The Prairie Flower*, in which Carson plays a minor role, inspired publishers of dime novels to include titles about Carson in their lists. Indeed, Jones adds, "From the early 1860s through the 1890s Carson appeared in more than seventy original tales and reprints written by a host of dime novelists." (58)

For twentieth-century studies of Carson see Edwin L. Sabin, *Kit Carson Days: 1809–1868* (1935); Harvey Lewis Carter, *Dear Old Kit: The Historical Christopher Carson* (1968); and Lawrence C. Kelly, *Navajo Roundup: Selected Correspondence of Kit Carson's Expedition Against the Navajo, 1863–1865* (1970).

75. Buffalo Hunting with the Nez Percé and Kit Carson

from Frances Fuller Victor, *River of the West*

"Thar war a lot of us trappers happened to be at a Nez Perce and Flathead village in the fall of '38, when they war agoin' to kill winter meat; and as their hunt lay in the direction we war going, we joined in. The old Nez Perce chief, *Kow-e-so-te* had command of the village, and we trappers had to obey him, too.

"We started off slow; nobody war allowed to go ahead of camp. In this manner we caused the buffalo to move on before us, but not to be alarmed. We war eight or ten days traveling from the Beaverhead to Missouri Lake, and by the time we got thar, the whole plain around the lake war crowded with buffalo, and it war a splendid sight!

"In the morning the old chief harangued the men of his village, and ordered us all to get ready for the surround. About nine o'clock every man war mounted, and we began to move.

"That war a sight to make a man's blood warm! A thousand men, all trained hunters, on horseback, carrying their guns, and with their horses painted in the height of Indians' fashion. We advanced until within about half a mile of the herd; then the chief ordered us to deploy to the right and left, until the wings of the column extended a long way, and advance again.

"By this time the buffalo war all moving, and we had come to within a hundred yards of them. *Kow-e-so-te* then gave us the word, and away we went, pell-mell. Heavens, what a charge! What a rushing and roaring—men shooting, buffalo bellowing and trampling until the earth shook under them!

"It war the work of half an hour to slay two thousand or may be three thousand animals. When the work was over, we took a view of the field. Here and there and everywhere, laid the slain buffalo. Occasionally a horse with a broken leg war seen; or a man with a broken arm; or maybe he had fared worse, and had a broken head.

"Now came out the women of the village to help us butcher and pack up the meat. It war a big job; but we war not long about it. By night the camp war full of meat, and everybody merry. Bridger's camp, which war passing that way, traded with the village for fifteen hundred buffalo tongues—the tongue being reckoned a choice part of the animal. And that's the way we helped the Nez Perces hunt buffalo."

"But when you were hunting for your own subsistence in camp, you sometimes went out in small parties?"

"Oh yes, it war the same thing on a smaller scale. One time Kit Carson and myself, and a little Frenchman, named Marteau, went to run buffalo on Powder River. When we came in sight of the band it war agreed that Kit and the Frenchman should do the running, and I should stay with the pack animals. The weather war very cold and I didn't like my part of the duty much.

"The Frenchman's horse couldn't run; so I lent him mine. Kit rode his own; not a good buffalo horse either. In running, my horse fell with the Frenchman, and nearly killed him. Kit, who couldn't make his horse catch, jumped off, and caught mine, and tried it again. This time he came up with the band, and killed four fat cows.

"When I came up with the pack-animals, I asked Kit how he came by my horse. He explained, and wanted to know if I had seen anything of Marteau: said my horse had fallen with him, and he thought killed him. 'You go over the other side of yon hill, and see,' said Kit.

" 'What'll I do with him if he is dead?' said I.

" 'Can't you pack him to camp?'

" 'Pack h——l' said I; 'I should rather pack a load of meat.'

" 'Waal,' said Kit, 'I'll butcher, if you'll go over and see, anyhow.'

"So I went over, and found the dead man leaning his head on his hand and groaning; for he war pretty bad hurt. I got him on his horse, though, after a while, and took him back to whar Kit war at work. We soon finished the butchering job, and started back to camp with our wounded Frenchman, and three loads of fat meat."

"You were not very compassionate toward each other, in the mountains?"

"That war not our business. We had no time for such things. Besides, live men war what we wanted; dead ones war of no account."

76. Carson Gets His Horses Back from Crows and Takes Revenge

from Kit Carson, *Kit Carson's Autobiography*

In January, 1833, a party of men who had been out hunting returned about dark. Their horses were very poor, having been fed during the winter on cottonwood bark, and they turned them out to gather such nourishment as they could find. That night a party of about fifty Crow Indians came to our camp and stole nine of the horses that were loose. In the morning we discovered sign of the Indians and twelve of us took the trail and traveled about forty miles. It was getting late. Our animals were fatigued for the snow was deep, and the passing of many herds of buffaloes during the day caused us a great deal of difficulty in keeping the trail. At length we saw a grove of timber at a distance of two or three miles. Taking into consideration the condition of our animals, we concluded to make for it and camp for the night. On our arrival, however, we saw fires about four miles ahead of us. We tied our animals to trees, and as soon as it became dark, took a circuitous route for the Indian camp.

We planned to come upon the Indians from the direction in which they were traveling. It took us some time to get close enough to the camp to discover their strength, as we had to crawl, and use all the means that we were aware of to elude detection. After maneuvering in this direction for some time, we came within about one hundred yards of their camp. The Indians were in two forts of about equal strength. They were dancing and singing, and passing the night jovially in honor of their robbery of the whites. We spied our horses, which were tied near the entrance of one of the forts. Let come what would, we were bound to get them. We remained concealed in the brush, suffering severely from the cold, until the Indians laid down to sleep.

When we thought they were all asleep, six of us crawled towards our animals, the rest remaining where they were as a reserve for us to fall back on in case we did not meet with success. We hid behind logs and crawled silently towards the fort, the snow being of great service to us for when crawling we were not liable to make any noise. We finally reached the horses, cut the ropes, and by throwing snow balls at them drove them to where our reserve was stationed. We then held a council, taking the views of each in regard to what had best be done. Some were in favor of retiring; having recovered their property and received no damage, they were willing to return to camp. Not so with those that had lost no animals. They wanted satisfaction for the trouble and hardships they had gone through while in pursuit of the thieves. Myself and two others were the only ones that had not lost horses and we were determined to have satisfaction, let the consequences be ever so fatal. The peace party could not get a convert to their side. Seeing us so determined to fight (there is always a brotherly affection existing among trappers and the side of danger is always their choice), it was not long before all agreed to join us in our perilous enterprise.

We started the horses that had been retaken to the place where we had tied our other animals, with three of our men acting as an escort. We then marched directly for the fort from which we had taken our horses. When we were within a few paces of it, a dog discovered us and began to bark. The Indians were alarmed and commenced to get up, when we opened a deadly fire, each ball taking its victim. We killed nearly every Indian in the fort. The few that remained were wounded and made their escape to the other fort, whose inmates commenced firing on us, but without any effect, since we kept concealed behind trees, firing only when we were sure of our object. It was now near day, and the Indians could see our force, which was so weak they concluded to charge on us. We received them calmly, and when they got very close fired on them, killing five, and the balance returned to their fort. After some deliberation among themselves, they finally made another attempt, which met with greater success. We had to retreat, but there was much timber in the vicinity, and we had but little difficulty in making our camp, where, being reinforced by the three men with the horses, we awaited the approach of the enemy. Since they did not attack us, we started for our main camp and arrived there in the evening. During our pursuit of the lost animals we suffered considerably, but in the success of recovering our horses and sending many a redskin to his long home, our sufferings were soon forgotten. We remained in our camp without any further molestation until spring, when we started for Laramie River on another trapping expedition.

77. Kit Carson Fights a Rival at Rendezvous

from Samuel Parker, *Journal of an Exploring Tour Beyond the Rocky Mountains*

A few days after our arrival at the place of rendezvous, and when all the mountain men had assembled, another day of indulgence was granted to them, in which all restraint was laid aside. These days are the climax of the hunter's happiness. I will relate an occurrence which took place near evening, as a specimen of mountain life. A hunter, who goes technically by the name of the great bully of the mountains, mounted his horse with a loaded rifle, and challenged any Frenchman, American, Spaniard, or Dutchman, to fight him in single combat. Kit Carson, an American, told him if he wished to die, he would accept the challenge. Shunar defied him—C. mounted his horse, and with a loaded pistol rushed into close contact, and both almost at the same instant fired. C.'s ball entered S's hand, came out at the wrist, and passed through the arm above the elbow. S.'s ball passed over the head of C. and while he went for another pistol, Shunar begged that his life might be spared. Such scenes, some times from passion, and some times for amusement, make the pastime of their wild and wandering life. They appear to have sought for a place where, as they would say, human nature is not oppressed by the tyranny of religion, and pleasure is not awed by the frown of virtue. The fruits are visible in all the varied forms to which human nature, without the restraints of civil government, and cultivated and polished society, may be supposed to yield. In the absence of all those motives, which they would feel in moral and religious society, refinement, pride, a sense of the worth of character, and even conscience, give place to unrestrained dissoluteness. Their toils and privations are so great, that they are not disposed to take upon themselves the labor of climbing up to the temple of science. And yet they are proficients in one study, the study of profuseness of language in their oaths and blasphemy. They disdain commonplace phrases which prevail among the impious vulgar in civilized countries, and have many set phrases, which they appear to have manufactured among themselves, which they have committed to memory, and which, in their imprecations, they bring into almost every sentence and on all occasions. By varying the tones of their voices, they make them expressive of joy, hope, grief, and anger. In their broils among themselves, which do not happen every day, they would not be ungenerous. They would see "fair play," and would "spare the last eye;" and would not tolerate murder, unless drunkenness or great provocation could be pleaded in extenuation of guilt.

Their demoralizing influence with the Indians has been lamentable, and they have imposed upon them, in all the ways that sinful propensities dictate. It is said they have sold them packs of cards at high prices, calling them the bible; and have told them, if they should refuse to give white men wives, God would be angry with them and punish them eternally: and on almost any occasion when their wishes have been resisted, they have threatened them with the wrath of god. If these things are true in many instances, yet from personal observation, I should believe, their more common mode of accomplishing their wishes has been by flattery and presents. The most of them squander away their wages in ornaments for their women and children.

78. A Rendezvous Duel

from Kit Carson, *Kit Carson's Autobiography*

There was a large Frenchman in the party of Captain Drips, an overbearing kind of man, and very strong. He made a practice of whipping every man that he was displeased with—and that was nearly all. One day, after he had beaten two or three men, he said he had no trouble to flog Frenchmen, and as for Americans, he would take a switch and switch them. I did not like such talk from any man, so I told him that I was the worst American in camp. There were many who could thrash him but for the fact that they were afraid, and that if he used such expressions any more, I would rip his guts.

He said nothing but started for his rifle, mounted his horse, and made his appearance in front of the camp. As soon as I saw this, I mounted my horse also, seized the first weapon I could get hold of, which was a pistol, and galloped up to him and demanded if I was the one he intended to shoot. Our horses were touching. He said no, drawing his gun at the same time so he could have a fair shot at me. I was prepared and allowed him to draw his gun. We both fired at the same time, and all present said that but one report was heard. I shot him through the arm and his ball passed my head, cutting my hair and the powder burning my eye, the muzzle of his gun being near my head when fired. During the remainder of our stay in camp we had no more bother with this French bully.

79. Kit Carson Saves Captain Frémont from an Icy River

from John C. Frémont, *Report of the Exploring Expedition to the Rocky Mountains in the Years 1843–'44*

February 23.—This was our most difficult day: we were forced off the ridges by the quantity of snow among the timber, and obliged to take to the mountain-sides, where, occasionally, rocks and a southern exposure afforded us a chance to scramble along. But these were steep, and slippery with snow and ice; and the tough evergreens of the mountain impeded our way, tore our skins, and exhausted our patience. Some of us had the misfortune to wear moccasins with *parflêche* soles, so slippery that we could not keep our feet, and generally crawled across the snow beds. Axes and mauls were necessary to-day, to make a road through the snow. Going ahead with Carson to reconnoiter the road, we reached in the afternoon the river which made the outlet of the lake. Carson sprang over, clear across a place where the stream was compressed among rocks, but the *parflêche* sole of my moccasin glanced from the icy rock, and precipitated me into the river. It was some few seconds before I could recover myself in the current, and Carson, thinking me hurt, jumped in after me, and we both had an icy bath. We tried to search awhile for my gun, which had been lost in the fall, but the cold drove us out; and, making a large fire on the bank after we had partially dried ourselves, we went back to meet the camp. We afterwards found that the gun had been slung under the ice which lined the banks of the creek.

80. On a Failed Rescue Carson Finds a Dime Novel

from Kit Carson, *Kit Carson's Autobiography*

In October, the train of a Mr. White was attacked by the Jicarilla Apache. White was killed, and his wife and child were taken prisoners. A party was organized in Taos, with Leroux and Fisher as guides, to rescue them. When they reached Rayado, I was also employed as a guide. We marched to the place where the depredation had been committed, and then followed the trail of the Indians. I was the first man to discover the camp where the murder had been perpetrated. The trunks of the unfortunate family had been broken open, the harnesses cut to pieces, and everything else that the Indians could not carry away with them had been destroyed. We tracked them for ten or twelve days over the most difficult trail that I have ever followed. Upon leaving their camps they would separate in small groups of two or three persons and travel in different directions, to meet again at some appointed place. In nearly every camp we found some of Mrs. White's clothing, and these discoveries spurred us to continue the pursuit with renewed energy.

We finally came in view of the Indian camp. I was in the advance, and at once started for it, calling to our men to come on. The commanding officer ordered a halt, however, and no one followed me. I was afterwards informed that Leroux, the principal guide, had advised the officer to halt us, as the Indians wished to have a parley. The latter, seeing that the troops did not intend to charge, commenced packing up in all haste. Just as the halt was ordered, the commanding officer was shot; the ball passed through his coat, his gauntlets that were in his pocket, and his shirt, stopping at the skin, and doing no other damage than making him a little sick at the stomach. The gauntlets had saved his life, sparing a gallant officer to the service of his country. As soon as he had recovered from the shock given him by the ball, he ordered the men to charge, but it was too late to save the captives. There was only one Indian left in the camp, who was promptly shot while he was running into the river in a vain effort to escape. At a distance of about 200 yards, the body of Mrs. White was found, still perfectly warm. She had been shot through the heart with an arrow not more than five minutes before. She evidently knew that some one was coming to her rescue. Although she did not see us, it was apparent that she was endeavoring to make her escape when she received the fatal shot.

I am certain that if the Indians had been charged immediately on our arrival, she would have been saved. They did not know of our approach, and as they were not paying any particular attention to her, perhaps she could have managed to run towards us, and if she had, the Indians would have been afraid to follow her. However, the treatment she had received from them was so brutal and horrible that she could not possibly have lived very long. Her death, I think, should never be regretted by her friends. She is surely far more happy in heaven, with her God, than among her friends on this earth.

I do not wish to be understood as attaching any blame to the officer in command of the expedition or to the principal guide. They acted as they thought best for the purpose of saving Mrs. White. We merely differed in opinion at the time, but I have no doubt that they now see that if my advice had been taken, her life might have been saved, for at least a short period.

We pursued the Indians for about six miles on a level prairie. We captured all their baggage and camp equipage, many of them running off without any of their clothing. We also took some of their animals. One warrior was killed, and two or three children were captured. We found a book in the camp, the first of the kind I had ever seen, in which I was represented as a great hero, slaying Indians by the hundred. I have often thought that Mrs. White must have read it, and knowing that I lived nearby, must have prayed for my appearance in order that she might be saved. I did come, but I lacked the power to persuade those that were in command over me to follow my plan for her rescue. They would not listen to me and they failed. I will say no more regarding this matter, nor attach any blame to any particular person, for I presume the consciences of those who were the cause of the tragedy have severely punished them ere this.

Rendezvous

On July 1, 1825, a group of about 120 trappers who had gathered on Henry's Fork, in what is now the state of Wyoming, took part in the first rendezvous. William Ashley, the organizer of this open-air business meeting, purchased the trappers' beaver pelts at prices ranging from $2.00 to $5.00 per pound. *Engagés* who had earlier signed contracts with Ashley got the lesser amount; free trappers, the greater. To the newly flush trappers Ashley sold tobacco at $2.00 or $3.00 per pound, knives at $2.50 each, lead at $1.00 per pound, and both coffee and sugar at $1.50 per pound.

As the cold, hard numbers suggest, rendezvous were, above all, occasions for business transactions. No lone trapper could afford the time and trouble of personally transporting his season's catch to St. Louis, some seventy-days' journey from the trapping grounds, so he sold his pelts to someone like William Ashley who had the means to get them to market. How much did it cost to transport a pelt to the nearest market? In 1826, when Ashley proposed to carry to St. Louis pelts belonging to Smith, Jackson, and Sublette, his rate was $1.12½ per pound—roughly a third of what a mountain man got for his pelts at the rendezvous site.

Once he had been credited for his furs, a trapper would then become a consumer, paying "mountain prices" that reflected both high transportation costs and the seller's monopoly. Mountain prices stung, and there was only one known remedy for that sting—alcohol. Unfortunately for the trappers, this remedy was also sold at mountain prices and had the sad side effect of loosening a trapper's purse strings to the point where the fur company often headed back to St. Louis in possession of a trapper's pay as well as his pelts.

In many ways the rendezvous is a perfect model of nineteenth-century laissez-faire capitalism. But to look at the rendezvous solely as a business occasion is to miss part of the story. Like a nineteenth-century version of modern-day Las Vegas, rendezvous was not just a place for sharp business types to separate suckers from their hard-earned wages. It was also a place for working stiffs to let down their hair, debauch, and forget about the aches and pains of their ordinary lives. Conspicuous consumption was one of the ways trappers let loose at rendezvous. Besides buying the items necessary to get through the next hunting season, trappers could blow their pelts on niceties like coffee, sugar, and new clothes. For the women, there were "frofraws" like bells, mirrors, and cloth. Because women were present, rendezvous are popularly thought of as times of sexual debauch, and, given what we know of human nature and of the freewheeling ways of trappers, there is undoubtedly some truth to this notion. But, on the other hand, many trappers had wives who accompanied them year round, so it wasn't as if trappers all went for months at a time without female companionship.

Drinking was, of course, a big part of rendezvous. Big because alcohol was a tool used by fur companies to virtually enslave trappers; big because liquor often wasn't available at other times of the year; and big because rendezvous was one of the few times when it was safe to get roaring drunk. Out on his own, a drunken trapper was completely vulnerable to the worst that the elements and his enemies could do; at rendezvous, a drunken trapper might wake up broke and hung over, but at least his hair would still be attached to that aching head of his. Just as widespread as drinking was gambling—on horse races, on shooting contests, and on various games of chance that could leave men and women, literally, without the clothes on their backs. Not surprisingly, the rendezvous mix of money, sex, alcohol, and gambling frequently led to fights that could involve fists, knives, firearms, or all of the above.

This is not to suggest that all the rendezvous entertainment involved vice. There was singing and dancing. There was the pleasure of meeting old friends and the pleasure of storytelling. There were athletic contests of all sorts. There were even church services and Bible reading. Tame stuff, perhaps, but part of rendezvous nonetheless.

It might be said that people today make too much of rendezvous. After all, there were only seventeen major gatherings, and rendezvous was not the only time that trappers got together. During the cold months, trappers would gather for companionship and protection in what they called "Winter Quarters." Still, it is the rendezvous that captures the imagination and, for many, remains the ultimate symbol of the fur trade.

A list of the major rendezvous:
Rendezvous Creek—1825 (Wyoming)
Willow Valley—1826 (Utah)
Sweet Lake—1827 (Utah)
Sweet Lake—1828 (Utah)
Popo Agie (Wyoming)—Pierre's Hole (Idaho)—1829
Wind River—1830 (Wyoming)
Willow Valley—1831 (Utah)
Pierre's Hole—1832 (Idaho)
Green River—1833 (Wyoming)
Ham's Fork—1834 (Wyoming)
Green River—1835 (Wyoming)
Green River—1836 (Wyoming)
Green River—1837 (Wyoming)
Wind River—1838 (Wyoming)
Green River—1839 (Wyoming)
Green River—1840 (Wyoming)

For those interested in learning more about the history of the rendezvous, Fred R. Gowans's *Rocky Mountain Rendezvous* (1985) is a good starting point.

81 and 82. Harmony at the Rendezvous

It is important to remember that, despite their conflicts, trappers and Indians often shared the same locations in peace. Rendezvous provided an opportunity for such harmonious gatherings, as Alfred Jacob Miller reminds us in the next two selections. To sample more literature of the American West—not only from the fur-trade era but also from later periods—see J. Golden Taylor's anthology *The Literature of the American West* (1971), and James C. Work's collection *Prose and Poetry of the American West* (1991).

81. Scene at Rendezvous

from Alfred Jacob Miller, *The West of Alfred Jacob Miller*

Scene at "Rendezvous"

> *These are the gardens of the desert,—these*
> *The unshorn fields, boundless & beautiful,*
> *For which the speech of England has no name*
> *—The "prairies"!*

A large body of Indians, Traders, and Trappers are here congregated, and the view seen from a bluff is pleasing and animated.

In the middle distance a race is being run, the horses in all cases running in a direct line and never in a circle as with us. The bets pending on the result are extraordinary in character and diversity, and the Indians are passionately fond of this species of gambling. If an Indian happens to lose all,—he will stake the dress he wears against 3 or 4 ounces of vermillion (worth here about $4 per oz.), and if you win can demand it at once, leaving him almost in the condition of

Adam before the fall. The Company's tent is besieged on such occasions. No matter who lose, they are sure to win.

Ball playing with bandys and other games are largely indulged in, and the Company make it a point to encourage the Indians in these sports to divert their minds from mischief. White Lodges ranging from 12 to 16 ft. in height are scattered at random over the plain and reach almost to the foot of the distant mountains.

82. Rendezvous

from Alfred Jacob Miller, *The West of Alfred Jacob Miller*

Rendezvous

The scene represented is the broad prairie; the whole plain is dotted with lodges and tents, with groups of Indians surrounding them;—In the river near the foreground Indians are bathing; to the left rises a bluff overlooking the plain whereon are stationed some Braves and Indian women. In the midst of them is Capt. Bridger in a full suit of steel armor. This gentleman was a famous mountain man, and we venture to say that no one has travelled here within the last 30 years without seeing or hearing of him. The suit of armor was imported from England and presented to Capt. B. by our commander;—it was a fac-simile of that worn by the English life-guards, and created a sensation when worn by him on stated occasions.

At this encampment we met the noted character "Mark-head" who received such grevious treatment from a bear (already noticed). A singular story of him was recounted here to us. About a year previous to making this journey, a leader of one of the bands lost some horses, and enraged at the circumstance, declared that he would give $500 for the scalp of the Indian who had purloined them. Markhead who was listening chose to take this literally, although it was meant in mere idle bravado. In a few days thereafter Markhead brought him the scalp of the veritable Indian, giving indubitable proofs of its being from the head of the delinquent, and demanded the fulfillment of the promise.

83 and 84. Trappers' Rendezvous in Canada

Artist Paul Kane shows in the next two selections that Canadian trappers came together to socialize much as did American trappers. Howard R. Lamar's *The Trader on the American Frontier* (1977) also describes frontier trading practices and refutes Hollywood stereotypes that depict the life of the trader as one of almost perpetual violence. Paul Kane himself is the subject of Bruce Haig's *Paul Kane, Artist* (1984).

83. Fort Edmonton at Christmas

from Paul Kane, *Paul Kane's Frontier*

The fort at this time of the year presented a most pleasing picture of cheerful activity: every one was busy; the men, some in hunting and bringing in the meat when the weather permitted, some in sawing boards in the saw-pit, and building the boats, about thirty feet long and six feet beam, which go as far as York Factory, and are found more convenient for carrying goods on the Saskatchawan and Red River than canoes. They are mostly built at Edmonton, because there are more boats required to take the peltries to York Factory than is required to bring goods back; and more than one-half of the boats built here never return. This system requires them to keep constantly building.

The women find ample employment in making mocassins and clothes for the men, putting up pemmi-kon in ninety-pound bags, and doing all the household drudgery, in which the men never assist them. The evenings are spent round their large fires in eternal gossiping and smoking. The sole musician of the establishment, a fiddler, is now in great requisition amongst the French part of the inmates, who give full vent to their national vivacity, whilst the more sedate Indian looks on with solemn enjoyment.

No liquor is allowed to the men or Indians; but the want of it did not in the least seem to impair their cheerfulness. True, the gentlemen of the fort had liquor brought out at their own expense; but the rules respecting its use were so strict and so well known, that none but those to whom it belonged either expected, or asked, to share it.

On Christmas-day the flag was hoisted, and all appeared in their best and gaudiest style, to do honour to the holiday. Towards noon every chimney gave evidence of being in full blast, whilst savoury steams of cooking pervaded the atmosphere in all directions. About two o'clock we sat down to dinner. Our party consisted of Mr. Harriett, the chief, and three clerks, Mr. Thebo, the Roman Catholic missionary from Manitou Lake, about thirty miles off, Mr. Rundell, the Wesleyan missionary, who resided within the pickets, and myself, the wanderer, who, though returning from the shores of the Pacific, was still the latest importation from civilised life.

The dining-hall in which we assembled was the largest room in the fort, probably about fifty by twenty-five feet, well warmed by large fires, which are scarcely ever allowed to go out. The walls and ceilings are boarded, as plastering is not used, there being no limestone within reach; but these boards are painted in a style of the most startling barbaric gaudiness, and the ceiling filled with centre-pieces of fantastic gilt scrolls, making altogether a saloon which no white man would enter for the first time without a start, and which the Indians always looked upon with awe and wonder.

The room was intended as a reception room for the wild chiefs who visited the fort; and the artist who designed the decorations was no doubt directed to "astonish the natives." If such were his instructions, he deserves the highest praise for having faithfully complied with them, although, were he to attempt a repetition of the same style in one of the rooms of the Vatican, it might subject him to some severe criticisms from the fastidious. No table-cloth shed its snowy whiteness over the board; no silver candelabra or gaudy china interfered with its simple magnificence. The bright tin plates and dishes reflected jolly faces, and burnished gold can give no truer zest to a feast.

Perhaps it might be interesting to some dyspeptic idler, who painfully strolls through a city park, to coax an appetite to a sufficient intensity to enable him to pick an ortolan, if I were to describe to him the fare set before us, to appease appetites nourished by constant outdoor exercise in an atmosphere ranging at 40° to 50° below zero.

At the head, before Mr. Harriett, was a large dish of boiled buffalo hump; at the foot smoked a boiled buffalo calf. Start not, gentle reader, the calf is very small, and is taken from the cow by the Caesarean operation long before it attains its full growth. This, boiled whole, is one of the most esteemed dishes amongst the epicures of the interior. My pleasing duty was to help a dish of mouffle, or dried moose nose; the gentleman on my left distributed, with graceful impartiality, the white fish, delicately browned in buffalo marrow. The worthy priest helped the buffalo tongue, whilst Mr. Rundell cut up the beavers' tails. Nor was the other gentleman left unemployed, as all his spare time was occupied in dissecting a roast wild goose. The centre of the table was graced with piles of potatoes, turnips, and bread conveniently placed, so that each could help himself without interrupting the labours of his companions. Such was our jolly Christmas dinner at Edmonton; and long will it remain in my memory, although no pies, or puddings, or blanc manges, shed their fragrance over the scene.

In the evening the hall was prepared for the dance to which Mr. Harriett had invited all the inmates of the fort, and was early filled by the gaily dressed guests. Indians, whose chief ornament consisted in the paint on their faces, voyageurs with bright sashes and neatly ornamented mocassins, half-breeds glittering in every ornament they could lay their hands on; whether civilised or savage, all were laughing, and jabbering in as many different languages as there were styles of dress. English, however, was little used, as none could speak it but those who sat at the dinner-table. The dancing was most picturesque, and almost all joined in it. Occasionally I, among the rest, led out a young Cree squaw, who sported enough beads round her neck to have made a pedlar's fortune, and having led her into the centre of the room, I danced round her with all the agility I was capable of exhibiting, to some highland-reel tune which the fiddler played with great vigour, whilst my partner with grave face kept jumping up and down, both feet off the ground at once, as only an Indian can dance. I believe, however, that we elicited a great deal of applause from Indian squaws and children, who sat squatting round the room on the floor. Another lady with whom I sported the light fantastic toe, whose poetic name was Cun-ne-wa-bum, or "One that looks at the Stars," was a half-breed Cree girl; and I was so much struck by her beauty, that I prevailed upon her to promise to sit for her likeness, which she afterwards did with great patience, holding her fan, which was made of the tip end of swan's wing with an ornamental handle of porcupine's quills, in a most coquettish manner.

After enjoying ourselves with such boisterous vigour for several hours, we all gladly retired to rest about twelve o'clock, the guests separating in great good humour, not only with themselves but with their entertainers.

84. Hudson's Bay Company Regale

from Paul Kane, *Paul Kane's Frontier*

July 1st.—The nine boats composing the brigade had now completed their outfit, and were all prepared for their different destinations. Mr. Lewis was to command until he arrived at his own post, Colville; but we had great difficulty in collecting the men, between sixty and seventy in number: some wanted their allowance of rum, or regale, before they started, given to the Company's men only preparatory to a long voyage. Others were bidding farewell to their Indian loves, and were hard to be found; in fact, all hesitated to give up the life of idleness and plenty in which they had been luxuriating for the last two or three weeks, for the toils and privations which they well knew were before them. However, towards evening we succeeded in collecting our crews, and Mr. Lewis promised them their regale on the first fitting opportunity. The fort gave us a salute of seven guns, which was repeated by the Company's ship lying at the store-house. The occupants of the fort crowded round us; and at last, amidst cheers and hearty wishes for our safety, we pushed off. Owing to the lateness of the hour at which we started, we only got to the Company's mills, eight miles from the fort, that evening.

July 2nd.—We started very early this morning, and the men plied their oars with unusual vigour, as they were to get their regale this evening. By 2 o'clock P.M. we had reached the Prairie de Thé, a distance of twenty-eight miles. Here we landed to let the men have their customary debauch. In the Hudson's Bay Company's service no rations of liquor are given to the men, either while they are stopping in fort or while travelling, nor are they allowed to purchase any; but when they are about commencing a long journey, the men are given what is called a regale, which consists of a pint of rum each. This, however, they are not allowed to drink until they are some distance from the post, where those who are entitled to get drunk may do so without interfering with the resident servants of the establishment.

Immediately on landing, the camp was made, fires lit, and victuals cooked; in short, every preparation for the night was completed before the liquor was given out. As soon as the men got their allowance, they commenced all sorts of athletic games; running, jumping, wrestling, &c. We had eight Sandwich Islanders amongst the crews, who afforded great amusement by a sort of pantomimic dance accompanied by singing. The whole thing was exceedingly grotesque and ridiculous, and elicited peals of laughter from the audience; gradually, as the rum began to take effect, the brigades, belonging to different posts, began to boast of their deeds of daring and endurance. This gradually led on to trying which was the best man. Numberless fights ensued; black eyes and bloody noses became plentiful, but all terminated in good humour. The next day the men were stupid from the effects of drink, but quite good-tempered and obedient; in fact, the fights of the previous evening seemed to be a sort of final settlement of all old grudges and disputes. We did not get away until 3 o'clock P.M., and only made a distance of about fourteen miles. We encamped at the foot of the Cascades, where the first portage in ascending the Columbia commences.

85 and 86. Rendezvous at Brown's Hole

In his book *Where the Old West Stayed Young* (1962) John Rolfe Burroughs includes a chapter on the early history of Brown's Hole (now known as Brown's Park), the scene of the rendezvous that is the subject of the following selections. The Brown's Hole tailors in the second selection sewed apparel like that described in James Austin Hanson's *The Mountain Man's Sketch Book* (1982), and in Ernest Lisle Reedstrom's *Historic Dress of the Old West* (1986). By the way, the Brown's Hole rendezvous is not included in the list of rendezvous at the head of this section because it was not a major rendezvous.

85. The Varied Amusements at Rendezvous

from William Thomas Hamilton, *My Sixty Years on the Plains*

The streams were now beginning to freeze up, and we started for the Brown's Hole rendezvous, arriving there the latter part of November.

Several traders had come from the States with supplies, and there was quite a rivalry among them for our furs. Bovey & Company were the most liberal buyers, and we sold them the entire lot.

Besides the trappers there were at the rendezvous many Indians—Shoshones, Utes, and a few lodges of Navajos,—who came to exchange their pelts for whatever they stood in need of. Take it all in all, it was just such a crowd as would delight the student were he studying the characteristics of the mountaineer and the Indian. The days were given to horse-racing, foot-racing, shooting-matches; and in the evening were heard the music of voice and drum and the sound of dancing. There was also an abundance of reading matter for those inclined in that direction.

86. Two Tailors at the Brown's Hole Rendezvous

from William Thomas Hamilton, *My Sixty Years on the Plains*

It must not be thought that trappers are an idle set while at the rendezvous. The reverse is true. Many of them are constantly dressing buckskin, and their mode of dressing is far superior to that of the Indians, as the skin when prepared by them will not stretch nor shrink when wet. Others are hunting deer, to keep the camp supplied with meat, or putting arms and traps in perfect condition. Most trappers make their own buckskin clothes, although there were two tailors at Brown's Hole.

87. Of Teepees and the Many Languages of the Fur Trade

from Warren Angus Ferris, *Life in the Rocky Mountains*

Warren Ferris writes in the next selection about life in Winter Quarters. The linguistic mix he describes helped shape the American English we speak today. For an explanation of that shaping process see Charles L. Cutler's *O Brave New Words!: Native American Loanwords in Current English* (1994).

The season having become far advanced, we pitched quarters in a large grove of aspen trees, at the brink of an excellent spring that supplied us with the purest water, and resolved to pass the winter here. Our hunters made daily excursions in the mountains, by which we were half surrounded, and always returned with the flesh of several black tail deer; an animal almost as numerous as the pines and cedars among which they were found. They frequently killed seven or eight individually, in the course of a day; and consequently our encampment, or at least the trees within it, were soon decorated with several thousand pounds of venison. We passed the time by visiting, feasting, and chatting with each other, or by hunting occasionally, for exercise and amusement. Our camp presented eight leathern lodges, and two constructed of poles covered with cane grass, which grows in dense patches to the height of eight or ten feet, along the river. They were all completely sheltered from the wind by the surrounding trees. Within, the bottoms were covered with reeds, upon which our blankets and robes were spread, leaving a small place in the centre for the fire. Our baggage was placed around at the bottom of the lodge, on the inside, to exclude the cold from beneath it, and each one of the inmates had his own particular place assigned him. One who has never lived in a lodge, would scarcely think it possible for seven or eight persons to pass a long winter agreeably, in a circular room, ten feet in diameter, having a considerable portion of it occupied by the fire in the centre;

but could they see us seated around the fire, cross legged like Turks, upon our beds, each one employed in cleaning guns, repairing moccasins, smoking, and lolling at ease on our elbows, without interfering with each other, they would exclaim, Indeed they are as comfortable as they could wish to be! which is the case in reality. I moved from a lodge into a comfortable log house, but again returned to the lodge, which I found much more pleasant than the other. These convenient and portable dwellings, are partially transparent, and when closed at the wings above, which answer the double purpose of windows and chimneys, still admit sufficient light, to read the smallest print without inconvenience. At night a good fire of dry aspen wood, which burns clear without smoke, affording a brilliant light, obviates the necessity of using candles. Our little village numbers twenty-two men, nine women and twenty children; and a different language is spoken in every lodge, the women being of different nations, and the children invariably learn their mothers tongue before any other. There were ten distinct dialects spoken in our camp, each of which was the native idiom of one or more of us, though French was the language predominant among the men, and Flatt-head among the women; yet there were both males and females, who understood neither. One would imagine that where such a multiplicity of tongues are spoken, a confusion, little short of that of Babel, would naturally ensue. However, it is not the case. Men who find it difficult to convey their ideas to each other, through ignorance of their opposing dialect, readily make themselves understood by avoiding difficult or abstract expressions, and accompanying their simple speech with explanatory gestures.

88. The Battle of Pierre's Hole

from Washington Irving, *The Adventures of Captain Bonneville*

Although most rendezvous were harmonious occasions, the rendezvous of 1832 erupted into the Battle of Pierre's Hole—the most legendary conflict to come out of the fur trade. More than a half-dozen contemporary accounts of the battle exist. We have included one by Washington Irving, the most famous American writer of his day. Many biographies of Irving explain that he traveled only as far west as what is now Oklahoma. He learned about the fur trade from the papers of John Jacob Astor and from the journals of Benjamin Bonneville. Mary Weatherspoon Bowden's *Washington Irving* (1981) gives a brief introduction to Irving's life and works. Readers interested in Irving's depiction of mountain men should consult Robert Edson Lee's *From West to East: Studies in the Literature of the American West* (1966), and Richard H. Cracroft's *Washington Irving: The Western Works* (1974).

On the following morning, just as they were raising their camp, they observed a long line of people pouring down a defile of the mountains. They at first supposed them to be Fontenelle and his party, whose arrival had been daily expected. Wyeth, however, reconnoitered them with a spyglass, and soon perceived they were Indians. They were divided into two parties, forming, in the whole, about one hundred and fifty persons, men, women, and children. Some were on horseback, fantastically painted and arrayed, with scarlet blankets fluttering in the wind. The greater part, however, were on foot. They had perceived the trappers before they were themselves discovered, and came down yelling and whooping into the plain. On nearer approach, they were ascertained to be Blackfeet.

One of the trappers of Sublette's brigade, a half-breed, named Antoine Godin, now mounted his horse, and rode forth as if to hold a conference. He was the son of an Iroquois hunter, who had been cruelly murdered by the Blackfeet at a small stream below the mountains, which still bears his name. In company with Antoine rode forth a Flathead Indian, whose once powerful tribe had been completely broken down in their wars with the Blackfeet. Both of them, therefore, cherished the most vengeful hostility against these marauders of the mountains. The Blackfeet came to a halt. One of the chiefs advanced singly and unarmed, bearing the pipe of peace. This overture was certainly pacific; but Antoine and the Flathead were predisposed to hostility, and pretended to consider it a treacherous movement.

"Is your piece charged?" said Antoine to his red companion.

"It is."

"Then cock it, and follow me."

They met the Blackfoot chief half way, who extended his hand in friendship. Antoine grasped it.

"Fire!" cried he.

The Flathead levelled his piece, and brought the Blackfoot to the ground. Antoine snatched off his scarlet blanket, which was richly ornamented, and galloped off with it as a trophy to the camp, the bullets of the enemy whistling after him. The Indians immediately threw themselves into the edge of a swamp, among willows and cotton-wood trees, interwoven with vines. Here they began to fortify themselves; the women digging a trench, and throwing up a breastwork of logs and branches, deep hid in the bosom of the wood, while the warriors skirmished at the edge to keep the trappers at bay.

The latter took their station in a ravine in front, whence they kept up a scattering fire. As to Wyeth and his little band of "down-easters," they were perfectly astounded by this second specimen of life in the wilderness; the men being, especially, unused to bush fighting and the use of the rifle, were at a loss how to proceed. Wyeth, however, acted as a skilful commander. He got all his horses into camp and secured them; then, making a breastwork of his packs of goods, he charged his men to remain in garrison, and not to stir out of their fort. For himself, he mingled with the other leaders, determined to take his share in the conflict.

In the meantime, an express had been sent off to the rendezvous for reinforcements. Captain Sublette, and his associate, Campbell, were at their camp when the express came galloping across the plain, waving his cap, and giving the alarm; "Blackfeet! Blackfeet! a fight in the upper part of the valley!—to arms! to arms!"

The alarm was passed from camp to camp. It was a common cause. Every one turned out with horse and rifle. The Nez Percés and Flatheads joined. As fast as a horseman could arm and mount he galloped off; the valley was soon alive with white men and red men scouring at full speed.

Sublette ordered his men to keep to the camp, being recruits from St. Louis, and unused to Indian warfare. He and his friend Campbell prepared for action. Throwing off their coats, rolling up their sleeves, and arming themselves with pistols and rifles, they mounted their horses and dashed forward among the first. As they rode along, they made their wills in soldierlike style; each stating how his effects should be disposed of in case of his death, and appointing the other his executor.

The Blackfeet warriors had supposed the brigade of Milton Sublette all the foe they had to deal with, and were astonished to behold the whole valley suddenly swarming with horsemen, galloping to the field of action. They withdrew into their fort, which was completely hid from sight in the dark and tangled wood. Most of their women and children had retreated to the mountains. The trappers now sallied forth and approached the swamp, firing into the thickets at random;

the Blackfeet had a better sight at their adversaries, who were in the open field, and a half-breed was wounded in the shoulder.

When Captain Sublette arrived, he urged to penetrate the swamp and storm the fort, but all hung back in awe of the dismal horrors of the place, and the danger of attacking such desperadoes in their savage den. The very Indian allies, though accustomed to bush-fighting, regarded it as almost impenetrable, and full of frightful danger. Sublette was not to be turned from his purpose, but offered to lead the way into the swamp. Campbell stepped forward to accompany him. Before entering the perilous wood, Sublette took his brothers aside, and told them that in case he fell, Campbell, who knew his will, was to be his executor. This done, he grasped his rifle and pushed into the thickets, followed by Campbell. Sinclair, the partisan from Arkansas, was at the edge of the wood with his brother and a few of his men. Excited by the gallant example of the two friends, he pressed forward to share their dangers.

The swamp was produced by the labors of the beaver, which, by damming up a stream, had inundated a portion of the valley. The place was all overgrown with woods and thickets, so closely matted and entangled, that it was impossible to see ten paces ahead, and the three associates in peril had to crawl along, one after another, making their way by putting the branches and vines aside; but doing it with caution, lest they should attract the eye of some lurking marksman. They took the lead by turns, each advancing about twenty yards at a time, and now and then hallooing to their men to follow. Some of the latter gradually entered the swamp, and followed a little distance in their rear.

They had now reached a more open part of the wood, and had glimpses of the rude fortress from between the trees. It was a mere breastwork, as we have said, of logs and branches, with blankets, buffalo robes, and the leathern covers of lodges, extended round the top as a screen. The movements of the leaders, as they groped their way, had been descried by the sharp-sighted enemy. As Sinclair, who was in the advance, was putting some branches aside, he was shot through the body. He fell on the spot. "Take me to my brother," said he to Campbell. The latter gave him in charge to some of the men, who conveyed him out of the swamp.

Sublette now took the advance. As he was reconnoitring the fort, he perceived an Indian peeping through an aperture. In an instant his rifle was levelled and discharged, and the ball struck the savage in the eye. While he was reloading, he called to Campbell, and pointed out to him the hole; "Watch that place," said he, "and you will soon have a fair chance for a shot." Scarce had he uttered the words, when a ball struck him in the shoulder, and almost wheeled him round. His first thought was to take hold of his arm with his other hand, and move it up and down. He ascertained to his satisfaction, that the bone was not broken. The next moment he was so faint that he could not stand. Campbell took him in his arms and carried him out of the thicket. The same shot that struck Sublette, wounded another man in the head.

A brisk fire was now opened by the mountaineers from the wood, answered occasionally from the fort. Unluckily, the trappers and their allies, in searching for the fort, had got scattered, so that Wyeth, and a number of Nez Percés, approached the fort on the northwest side, while others did the same on the opposite quarter. A cross fire thus took place, which occasionally did mischief to friends as well as foes. An Indian was shot down, close to Wyeth, by a ball which, he was convinced, had been sped from the rifle of a trapper on the other side of the fort.

The number of whites and their Indian allies, had by this time so much increased by arrivals from the rendezvous, that the Blackfeet were completely overmatched. They kept doggedly in their fort, however, making no offer of surrender. An occasional firing into the breastwork was kept up during the day. Now and then, one of the Indian allies, in bravado, would rush up to the fort, fire over the ramparts, tear off a buffalo robe or a scarlet blanket, and return with it in triumph to his comrades. Most of the savage garrison that fell, however, were killed in the first part of the attack.

At one time it was resolved to set fire to the fort; and the squaws belonging to the allies, were employed to collect combustibles. This, however, was abandoned; the Nez Percés being unwilling to destroy the robes and blankets, and other spoils of the enemy, which they felt sure would fall into their hands.

The Indians, when fighting, are prone to taunt and revile each other. During one of the pauses of the battle, the voice of the Blackfeet chief was heard.

"So long," said he, "as we had powder and ball, we fought you in the open field: when those were spent, we retreated here to die with our women and children. You may burn us in our fort; but, stay by our ashes, and you who are so hungry for fighting, will soon have enough. There are four hundred lodges of our brethren at hand. They will soon be here—their arms are strong—their hearts are big—they will avenge us!"

This speech was translated two or three times by Nez Percé and creole interpreters. By the time it was rendered into English, the chief was made to say, that four hundred lodges of his tribe were attacking the encampment at the other end of the valley. Every one now was for hurrying to the defence of the rendezvous. A party was left to keep watch upon the fort; the rest galloped off to the camp. As night came on, the trappers drew out of the swamp, and remained about the skirts of the wood. By morning, their companions returned from the rendezvous, with the report that all was safe. As the day opened, they ventured within the swamp and approached the fort. All was silent. They advanced up to it without opposition. They entered: it had been abandoned in the night, and the Blackfeet had effected their retreat, carrying off their wounded on litters made of branches, leaving bloody traces on the herbage. The bodies of ten Indians were found within the fort; among them the one shot in the eye by Sublette. The Blackfeet afterwards reported that they had lost twenty-six warriors in this battle. Thirty-two horses were likewise found killed; among them were some of those recently carried off from Sublette's party, in the night; which showed that these were the very savages that had attacked him. They proved to be an advance party of the main body of Blackfeet; which had been upon the trail of Sublette's party. Five white men and one half-breed were killed, and several wounded. Seven of the Nez Percés were also killed, and six wounded. They had an old chief, who was reputed as invulnerable. In the course of the action he was hit by a spent ball, and threw up blood; but his skin was unbroken. His people were now fully convinced that he was proof against powder and ball.

A striking circumstance is related as having occurred, the morning after the battle. As some of the trappers and their Indian allies were approaching the fort, through the woods, they beheld an Indian woman, of noble form and features, leaning against a tree. Their surprise at her lingering here alone, to fall into the hands of her enemies, was dispelled, when they saw the corpse of a warrior at her feet. Either she was so lost in grief, as not to perceive their approach; or a proud spirit kept her silent and motionless. The Indians set up a yell, on discovering her, and before the trappers could interfere, her mangled body fell upon the corpse which she had refused to abandon. We have heard this anecdote discredited by one of the leaders who had been in the battle: but the fact may have taken place without his seeing it, and been concealed from him. It is an instance of female devotion, even to the death, which we are well disposed to believe and to record.

89. A Run-in with Black Harris at the 1840 Rendezvous

from Robert Newell, *Robert Newell's Memoranda*

Rendezvous could lead to fights among trappers as well as to fights between trappers and Indians. Here mountain man Robert Newell (1807–
1869) describes an attack made on him by Black Harris at the 1840
Rendezvous. Behind the personal confrontation lay an economic conflict:
Harris was furious at Newell for undercutting Harris's price for leading a
wagon train to Oregon. For an analysis of the economic, geographical,
and ecological factors underlying the activities of mountain men see
David J. Wishart, *The Fur Trade of the American West, 1807–1840*
(1979).

I went to the Amarican randezvous Mr Drips Feab & Bridger
from St Louis with goods but times was certainly hard no beaver
and everything dull some Missionaries came along with them for the
Columbia Messers Clark Smith Littlejohn I engaged to pilot them over
the mountains with their waggons and succeeded in crossing to fort
hall thare I bought their waggons also of which I perchased and Sold
them to the H Bay Co while at Rondezvous I had Some diffiquilty
with a man by the name of Moses Harris I think he intended murder
he Shot at me about 70 or 80 yards but done no damage only to him
self. I left the randezvous our little party consisted of 9 men and 3
woman in 17 days we arived at fort hall found all well and on the
27th of September 1840 with two waggons and my family I left fort
hall for the Columbia and with Some little Difiqutly I arived at walla
walla thare I left one waggon and the other I had took down in a boat
to vancouver and have it at this time on my farm about 25 miles from
vancouver west. I arivd at the willamitte on the 15 of December 1840
and on the 25 of the Same month came to this place called the Folitine
planes I likewise brought 2 american cows with me. this is to be remembered that I Robert Newell was the first who brought waggons
across the rocky mountains and up to this 19th of April 1841

90 and 91. Rendezvous Through Outsiders' Eyes

Some of the missionaries who were present at rendezvous recorded their impressions of these often unholy events. While reading the accounts of Mary Walker (1811–1897) and Myra Eells (1805–1878) about rendezvous drunks, it is tempting to characterize the two women as sanctimonious prigs who overreacted to mountain-grown rowdiness. However, it is important to remember that the fur companies used the institutionalized debauchery of the annual rendezvous to lock the mountain men into what we in the late twentieth century would call a cycle of dependency. To better understand the feelings expressed by Walker and Eells read Barbara Leslie Epstein's *The Politics of Domesticity: Women, Evangelism, and Temperance in Nineteenth-Century America* (1981). In the second selection, W. H. Gray (1810–1889) categorizes mountain men. A member of a missionary party but not himself a missionary, he is the "Mr. Gray" mentioned in Myra Eells' account of the drunks. For other accounts by and about missionaries see Section X.

90. Rendezvous Drunks

from Mary Walker and Myra Eells, "Mrs. Elkanah Walker and Mrs. Cushing Eells"

Myra {July} 5th. Thursday. Last night were troubled exceedingly by the noise of some drunken men. About one was awakened by the barking of dogs, soon we heard a rush of drunken men coming directly towards our tent. Mr. Eells got up immediately and went to the door of the tent in a moment. Four men came swearing and blaspheming, inquiring for Mr. Gray. Asked if Mr. Richardson was at home. Mr. Eells answered their inquiries and said little else. They said they wished to settle accounts with Mr. Gray, then they should be off. They said they did [not] come to do us harm, had they attempted it, the dog would have torn them to pieces. They then began singing. Asked Mr. Eells to sing with them. He told them he did not know their tunes. They asked if they disturbed him by keeping him up. He made no reply. They said silence gave consent and went away . . . giving us no more trouble, only that we were constantly in fear lest they would come back again.

All this while, Mr. G. and myself were making preparations for our escape, while Mr. Gray was loading Mr. E's gun, his own being lent.

Capt. Bridger's company comes in about 10 o'clock, with drums and firing—an apology for a scalp dance. After they had given Capt. Drip's company a shout, 15 or 20 mountain men and Indians came to our tent with drumming, firing, and dancing. If I might make the comparison, I should say that they looked like the emissaries of the Devil worshipping their own master. They had the scalp of a Blackfoot Indian, which they carried for a color, all rejoicing in the fate of the Blackfoot in consequence of the small-pox. The dog being frightened took the trail across the river and howled so that we knew him and called him back. When he came he went to each tent to see if we were all safe, then appeared quiet. Thermometer, 90 degrees.

Mary Last night disturbed by drunkards. Rose early and washed. A large company arrived under command of Capt. Bridger. Some of them came to salute us. One man carried the scalp of a Blackfoot. The musick consisted of ten horns, accompanied by the inarticulate sound of the voice. They halowed, danced, fired [guns] & acted as strangely as they could.

Myra 6th. Friday. Last night twelve white men came, dressed and painted Indian style, and gave us a dance. No pen can describe the horrible scene they presented. Could not imagine that white men, brought up in a civilized land, can appear to so much imitate the Devil. Thermometer, 100 degrees. Cut two dresses for children. About noon, the white men and Indians gave us another dance. All writing.

Mary Some of the squaws came to get dresses cut. We were again saluted by a company on foot. The same musick, scalp, etc. Their faces were painted. White men acted like Indians. It is said that many of the white men in the Mts. try to act as much like Indians as they can & would be glad if they really were so. Several squaws were here who united in the dance. They were warmly clad, [though] the weather was excessively hot. For several nights the noise in the camp has continued nearly all night. Some of the Capts. & I suppose many of the men are drunk nearly all the time.

91. Mountain Men in General and in Particular

from W. H. Gray, *A History of Oregon*

As we have never seen a description of these semi-civilized men, that in youth had left their native countries, and found themselves thousands of miles away, in the midst of the Rocky Mountains, surrounded on all sides by wild, roving bands of savages, cut off from communication with civilization, except by the annual return of the fur company's traders, or occasional wandering to some distant trading-post, a thousand or five hundred miles from the borders of any State or settlement, we will at this time introduce to the reader several men as we found them at this American rendezvous, most of them finding their way eventually into the settlement of Oregon, and becoming active and prominent men in the organization of the provisional government, as also good citizens. Among these veteran Rocky Mountain hunters was a tall man, with long black hair, smooth face, dark eyes (inclining to turn his head a little to one side, as much as to say, "I can tell you all about it"), a harum-scarum, don't-care sort of a man, full of "life and fun in the mountains," as he expressed it. He came and paid his respects to the ladies, and said he had been in the mountains several years; he had not seen a white woman for so long he had almost forgotten how they looked. He appeared quite fond of telling "yarns." In the conversation Mrs. Whitman asked him if he ever had any difficulty or fights with the Indians. "That we did," said he. "One time I was with Bridger's camp; we were traveling along that day, and the Blackfeet came upon us. I was riding an old mule. The Indians were discovered some distance off; so all the party put whip to their horses and started to get to a place where we could defend ourselves. My old mule was determined not to move, with all the beating I could give her, so I sung out to the boys to stop and fight the Indians where we were; they kept on, however. Soon, my old mule got sight of the Blackfeet coming; she pricked up her ears, and on she went like a streak, passed the boys, and away we went. I sung out to the boys, as I passed, 'Come on, boys, there is no use to stop and fight the Indians here.' " Fun and firmness were the two prominent characteristics of this young mountain hunter. He expressed a wish and a determination to visit and settle in lower Oregon (as the Wallamet Valley was then called). He had a native wife, and one son, just beginning to speak a few words. The father seemed, on my first noticing him, to be teaching this son of his to say "God d—n you," doubtless considering this prayer the most important one to teach his son to repeat, in the midst of the wild scenes with which he was surrounded. Though, to his credit be it said, this same wild, youthful mountaineer has become a good supporter of religious society, and has a respectable family, in an interesting neighborhood, near Forest Grove, in Oregon.

We will call these mountain hunters by numbers, for convenience, as we shall refer to them in our future political sketches, in which they participated.

No. 2. A man of medium height, black hair, black whiskers, dark-brown eyes, and very dark complexion; he was formerly from Kentucky. (I am not positive.) He was quite fond of telling yarns; still, as he was not considered very truthful, we will only give the story as we have it of the manner in which he and the one we will give as No. 3 obtained their titles. 2 and 3 were traveling together; 3 was from Cincinnati, Ohio. They had reached Independence, Mo.; says 3 to 2, "Titles are very necessary here in Missouri, what titles shall we take?" "Well," says 2, "I will take *Major*." 3 says, "I will take *Doctor*." Very good. They rode up to the best hotel in the place and called for lodgings.

2. "Well, Doctor, what shall we have for supper?"

3. "I don't care, Major, so as we get something to eat."

The Major and the Doctor enjoyed their supper and have borne their titles to the present time. The Major has never been, from all I could learn of him, a very truthful man or reliable citizen. He spent several years in Oregon and in the mountains, and found his way back to Missouri. The Doctor is now a resident of Idaho. The most remarkable trait in his composition is story-telling, or yarns, and a disposition to make friends of all political parties, or join all religious sects— something of a good lord and good devil order. He appeared in those early times to belong to that party that paid him the best. He was first in the employ of the American Fur Company, but appeared to lend his influence to the Hudson's Bay Company. He also had a native wife of the Nez Percé tribe, and was considered by the Hudson's Bay Company a useful man to divide the American influence in trade with the

Indians in the mountains, and equally useful to distract and divide the political influence of the early settlers. By his connection with the natives in marriage, the Hudson's Bay Company in trade, and good lord and good devil principles, he could adapt himself to the Protestant or Catholic religion, and in this manner become a kind of representative man, something like *strong lye and aquafortis mixed*, and just about as useful as such a mixture would be. He succeeded, by political maneuvering, or as the sailors say, "boxing the compass," to fill a place and draw a salary from Uncle Sam; carrying out the principles he has acted upon in his whole life, his efforts have been to neutralize what good others might do.

No. 4. A young man from Ohio, of a serious turn of mind; at least I concluded this to be the case, from the fact that he asked of the ladies if they had any books to sell, or that they could spare. A nice pocket-bible was given him, for which he politely expressed his thanks, after offering to pay for it. The pay, of course, was declined, as a few bibles were brought along for distribution. This young man, in a few years, followed the mission party and became a settler and a prominent man in the provisional government.

No. 5. A wild, reckless, don't-care sort of a youth, with a Nez Percé wife, so thoroughly attached to Indian ideas and customs that he has felt it beneath his dignity to turn from the ancient habits of the Indian to a "more recent invention" of religion and civilization. His curiosity was a little excited, which induced him to pay his respects to the missionaries, on account of their wives. He called on them, and spoke of some day finding his way somewhere down about where the missionaries might be located; as he had bought him a Nez Percé wife, she might want to go and see her people, and he might make up his mind to go and settle. This man, from his utter disregard for all moral and civilized social relations, has coiled himself up in the tribe he adopted, and spit out his venomous influence against all moral and civil improvement, training his children so that the better portion of the natives treat them with contempt. For a time he had considerable influence in shaping government policy toward the tribe and securing his own personal Indian position, to the injury of all other interests. I am unable to say how he obtained his title of colonel, unless it was from the influence he once pretended to have with the Indians, and a disposition on the part of those of his countrymen to title those who aspire to such honors.

No. 6. What the miners nowadays would call a "plain, honest farmer," with a native wife and one child. He called on the party, took a look at their cattle, and some four years afterward, after going into Mexico and Taos, found his way to the Wallamet as a settler, with a few head of cattle, which he managed to get through. This man is a quiet and good citizen, and has a respectable family of half-native children. The accursed influence of slavery in his neighborhood has borne heavily upon his children. Whether they will be able to rise above it and stand as examples of good citizens remains for them to demonstrate.

No. 7. A short, thick-set man, with a Nez Percé wife; a good honest farmer; has done credit to himself and family in giving them every possible advantage for education and society, though the aquafortis mixture has been strong in his neighborhood; his family are respected; his Indian wife he considers as good as some of his neighbors', that don't like her or her children. In this opinion all who are not saturated with our *cultus* mixture agree with him. His title in the mountain was Squire, but I think it has been improved since he came to the settlements by adding the E to it, he having been duly elected to fill the office under the provisional, territorial, and State government. I have learned, with much regret, that the Squire of the Rocky Mountains, who had courage and strength to meet and overcome all the dangers and trials of early times, has not the courage to resist the approaches of false friends and bad whisky, which will ultimately bring himself and his family to that certain destruction that follows the debasing habit of using liquor in any shape.

No. 8. A fair, light-haired, light-complexioned, blue-eyed man, rather above the medium height, with a Nez Percé wife, came about the camp, had little or nothing to say. I am not quite certain that he had his native wife at that time, still he had one when he came into the settlement. He has a good farm, and if he avoids his false friend and the fatal habits of his neighbors, he may have a good name, which will be of more value to his children than his present social and vicious habits.

92. "A Great Majority of Scoundrels"

from Nathaniel J. Wyeth, *Correspondence and Journals of Captain Nathaniel J. Wyeth, 1831–1836*

The following letter by Nathaniel Wyeth to Francis Ermatinger (1798–1858) includes the phrase that Don Berry used as the title of his "informal history" of the Rocky Mountain Fur Company, *A Majority of Scoundrels* (1961).

Green River July 18th 1833
Mr F. Ermatinger

Dear Sir I arrived here on the 16th 9 days from your camp Saw no Indians but saw the bones of Mr More killed by the Blkfeet last year and buried them. He was one of my men who left me in Pier[r]es Hole last year. A Mr Nudd was also killed by them. All the rest arrived well in the States. I found here about 250 whites. A list of the Cos. and their Beaver which I have seen I subjoin. I should have been proud of my countrymen if you could have seen the American Fur Co. or the party of Mr. S. Campbell. For efficiency of goods, men, animals and arms, I do not believe the fur business has afforded a better example of discipline. I have sold my animals and shall make a boat and float down the Yellowstone and Missouri and see what the world is made of there. Mr. Wm Sublette and Mr Campbell have come up the Missouri and established a trading fort at each location of the posts of the Am. Fur Co. with a view to a strong opposition. Good luck to their quarrels. I have got letters from the States. The chief news are that the cholera Morbus has swept through them killing 5000 people in N York and in proportion elsewhere. Genl. Jackson president an insurrection in the Southern States on acc. of the Tariff but quelled by Bloc[k]ading their ports and the repeal of the most obnoxious parts of the same. About 25 Americans have been killed during the last year. A Snake village is here with us. I find Bonnevilles connections are responsible [A statement that he has a draft from B(onneville) for horses follows but is crossed out.] he being very short of them. He lost one entire party among the Crows that is the Horses and of course all the Beavers. A party under Bridger and Frapp also lost their horses by the Aricarees, also Harris party lost theirs by the same Inds. who have taken a permanent residence on the Platte and left the Missouri which is the reason I go by the last named river. Harris party did not interfere with any of my plans south of Snake River.

In my opinion you would have been Robbed of your goods and Beaver if you had come here altho it is the west side of the Mts. for Green River emtys into the head of the Gulph of Calafornia. I give you this as an honest opinion which you can communicate to the Co. There is here a great majority of Scoundrels. I should much doubt the personal safety of any one from your side of the house.

My Respects to Mr. Payette and believe me yr. sincere friend
Nathl J. Wyeth.

Drips and Fontenelle arrd July 8th 160 men a good supply of animals. Obtained 51 packs of 100 lbs ea. Beaver.

Rocky Mtn. Fur Co. 55 packs 55 men well supplied one party not in Beaver sent home by Mr. Campbell.

Mess. Bonneville & Co. 22½ packs. Few goods few horses and poor Capt. Cerry goes home B. remains.

Harris party now in hand 7 packs Beaver and are on foot.

Critics of the Fur Trade

Criticism of the fur trade has become as fashionable today as the wearing of beaver hats was 160 years ago. Not only do animal-rights activists protest the present-day taking of fur, revisionist historians and others level criticisms at the nineteenth-century fur trade. There is plenty to criticize. The nineteenth-century fur trade played Hell on native America, ravaged animal populations, and didn't treat the trappers themselves much better. When a historian such as Patricia Nelson Limerick, writing in *The Legacy of Conquest* (1987), brings up the American Fur Company's "avarice and . . . cruel role in the decline of the Indians" (182), it is hard to accuse her of overstating her case.

Indeed, in the light of the late twentieth century, the once-celebrated heroes of the fur trade do not shine as brightly as they once did. For all of his amazing exploits, is it still possible to unblinkingly admire a man like Kit Carson when we know the sad role he played in subduing the Navajo Nation? And if the faces of Carson and his fellow mountain-man legends *had* ended up carved into Mount Rushmore as originally planned, wouldn't there be plenty of present-day Americans protesting their placement in our national pantheon?

If so, their protests would not be new ones. For as the following selections show, at least some nineteenth-century observers saw the problems caused by the fur trade and were not afraid to put their objections on paper. Whether these nineteenth-century critics were ahead of their time or whether they were just angry ax-grinders, their writings show that what some see as a rosy, simple past was as conflicted and confused as the present. After reading an account like artist George Catlin's tirade against the fur trade, it becomes clear that conflicts between such adversaries as EarthFirst! and People for the West are nothing new under the western sun.

93. Arguments *Against* Trapping

from John B. Wyeth, *Oregon*

We have included in this anthology a number of selections by Nathaniel J. Wyeth, an entrepreneur who started from Boston in March 1832 with a twenty-man party bound for fur trapping in the West. John B. Wyeth (b. 1814?), a member of the party, was Nathaniel's eighteen-year-old nephew. Disgruntled by his uncle's leadership, John B. deserted when the party was in Pierre's Hole, and six other members of the party returned with him to Boston. The following attack on the fur trade is from *Oregon* (1833), a book that was ghostwritten by Dr. Benjamin Waterhouse (1754–1846) and published under John B. Wyeth's name.

There is a passage in the essay written by W.J.S. which we shall insert here on his authority, as it cannot be supposed that we, at this distance, should be so well acquainted with the affairs in Missouri, as one who had resided on the spot. We assume not to keep pace with the professed eulogist of Oregon, of its river, and its territory, its mild climate, its exuberant soil, and its boisterous Pacific, so inviting to the distressed poor in the neighbourhood of Boston; who are exhorted by him to pluck up stakes and courage, and march over the Rocky Mountains to wealth, ease, and independence. The passage we allude to reads thus:—"About twelve years since, it was discovered by a public-spirited citizen of St. Louis, that the supply of furs was not equal to the demand. To remedy this evil, he raised a corps of sharp-shooters, equipped them with guns, ammunition, steel-traps, and horses, and sent them into the wilderness to teach the Indians that their right was only a right of occupancy. They did the savages irreparable injury. They frightened the buffaloes from their usual haunts,—destroyed the fur-clad animals, and did more mischief than we have room to relate." He adds, sarcastically, that "the Indians were wont to hunt in a slovenly manner, leaving a few animals yearly for breeding. But that the white hunters were more thorough-spirited, and made root-and-branch work of it. When they settled on a district, they destroyed the old and young alike; and when they left it, they left no living thing behind them. The first party proving successful, more were fitted out, and every successive year has seen several armed and mounted bands of hunters, from twenty to a hundred men and more in each, pouring into the Indian hunting grounds; and *all this has been done in open and direct violation of a law of the United States, which expressly forbids trapping and hunting on Indian lands.* The consequence has been that there are now few fur-clad animals this side the mountains."

Lewis and Clarke, and some other travellers, speak of friendly Indians,—of their kindness and hospitality, and expatiate on their amiable disposition, and relate instances of it. Yet after all, this Indian friendship is very like the affection of the negroes in the Southern States for their masters and mistresses, and for their children,—the offspring merely of fear. There can be no friendship where there is such a disparity of condition. As to their presents, an Indian gift is proverbial. They never give without expecting double in return.

What right have we to fit out armed expeditions, and enter the long occupied country of the natives, to destroy their game, not for subsistence, but for their skins? They are a contented people, and do not want our aid to make them happier. We prate of civilizing and Christianizing the savages. What have we done for their benefit? We have carried among them *rum, powder* and *ball,* small-pox, starvation, and misery. What is the reason that Congress,—the great council of the nation,—the collected wisdom of these United States, has turned a deaf ear to all applications for establishing a colony on the Oregon river? Some of the members of that honorable house of legislation know that the district in question is a boisterous and inclement region, with less to eat, less to warm the traveller, and to cook with, than at the mouth of any other known river in the United States. We deem the mouth of the river St. Lawrence as eligible a spot for a settlement of peltry merchants as the mouth of the Columbia. When Lewis and Clarke were on that river, they had not a single fair day in two months. They were drenched with rain day and night; and what added to their comfortless condition was the incessant high winds, which drove the waves furiously into the Columbia river with the tide; and on its ebb, raised such commotion, and such a chopping sea, that the travellers dared not venture upon it in their boats; yet the Indians did, and managed their canoes with a dexterity which the explorers greatly admired, but could not imitate. The boisterous Pacific was among the new discoveries of our American adventurers. Had their expedition been to the warm climate of Africa, or to South America, they would have been sure of plenty to eat; but in the western region, between the Rocky Mountains and the great river of the West, the case is far otherwise.

It is devoutly to be wished that truth may prevail respecting those distant regions. Indeed the sacred cause of humanity calls loudly on its votaries to disabuse the people dwelling on these Atlantic shores respecting the Oregon paradise, lest our farmers' sons and young mechanics should, in every sense of the phrase, stray from home, and go they know not whither,—to seek they know not what. Or must Truth wait on the Rocky Mountains until some Indian historian,—some future *Clavigero* shall publish his annals, and separate facts from fiction? We esteem the *"History of the Expedition under the command of Captains Lewis and Clarke to the Sources of the Missouri, thence across the Rocky Mountains, and down to the Pacific Ocean,"* substantially correct. Their conduct towards the Indians was marked throughout with justice and humanity; and the journal of that expedition will be a lasting monument of their judicious perseverance, and of the wisdom of the government of the United States.

Reader! The book you have in your hands is not written for your amusement merely, or to fill up an idle hour, but for your instruction,—particularly to warn young farmers and mechanics not to leave a certainty for an uncertainty, and straggle away over a sixth part of the globe, in search of what they leave behind them at home. It is hoped that it may correct that too common opinion that the farther you go from home the surer you are of making your fortune. Agriculture gives to the industrious farmer the riches which he can call his own; while the indefatigable mechanic is sure to acquire a sufficiency, provided he "build not his house too high."

Industry conducted by Prudence is a virtue of so diffusive a nature that it mixes with all our concerns. No business can be managed and accomplished without it. Whatever be a man's calling or way of life, he must, to be happy, be actuated by a spirit of industry, and that will keep him from want, from dishonesty, and from the vice of gambling and lottery-dealing, and its long train of miseries.

The first and most common deviation from sober industry is a desire to roam abroad, or in one word, a feeling of *discontent,*—a making haste to be rich, without the patient means of it. These are reflections general and not particular, as it regards all such high hopes and expectations, as led to our Oregon expedition and to its disappointments. The most that we shall say of it is,—that it was an injudicious scheme arising from want of due information, and the whole conducted by means inadequate to the end in view.

Oh happy—if he knew his happy state,
The man, who, free from turmoil and debate,
Receives his wholesome food from Nature's hand,
The just return of *cultivated* land.

94 and 95. Opposition to Wanton Destruction and Trapper Excesses

Some mountain men as well as some of the British nobles who toured the West in the first half of the nineteenth century found the West's teeming wildlife and wide-open spaces an excuse for senseless animal slaughter and other forms of licentiousness. Their wanton behavior met with strong disapproval, examples of which appear in the following selections by two of America's most distinguished authors: John James Audubon (1785–1851), the famous ornithologist, and Francis Parkman (1823–1893), the famous historian and author of *The Oregon Trail* (1849). There are, of course, many studies of Audubon and Parkman; readers of this anthology might find most helpful Alice Ford, *John James Audubon: A Biography* (1988); Shirley Streshinsky, *Audubon: Life and Art in the American Wilderness* (1993); and Elmer Nathaniel Feltskog, "Francis Parkman's *The Oregon Trail*" (1966).

94. A Motley Bunch of Trappers

from John James Audubon, *Audubon and His Journals*

Having conveyed the whole of our effects on board the steamer, and being supplied with excellent letters, we left St. Louis at 11:30 A. M., with Mr. Sarpy on board, and a hundred and one trappers of all descriptions and nearly a dozen different nationalities, though the greater number were French Canadians, or Creoles of this State. Some were drunk, and many in that stupid mood which follows a state of nervousness produced by drinking and over-excitement. Here is the scene that took place on board the "Omega" at our departure, and what followed when the roll was called.

First the general embarkation, when the men came in pushing and squeezing each other, so as to make the boards they walked upon fairly tremble. The Indians, poor souls, were more quiet, and had already seated or squatted themselves on the highest parts of the steamer, and were tranquil lookers-on. After about three quarters of an hour, the crew and all the trappers (these are called *engagés*) were on board, and we at once pushed off and up the stream, thick and muddy as it was. The whole of the effects and the baggage of the *engagés* was arranged in the main cabin, and presently was seen Mr. Sarpy, book in hand, with the list before him, wherefrom he gave the names of these *attachés*. The men whose names were called nearly filled the fore part of the cabin, where stood Mr. Sarpy, our captain, and one of the clerks. All awaited orders from Mr. Sarpy. As each man was called, and answered to his name, a blanket containing the apparel for the trip was handed to him, and he was ordered at once to retire and make room for the next. The outfit, by the way, was somewhat scanty, and of indifferent quality. Four men were missing, and some appeared rather reluctant; however, the roll was ended, and one hundred and one were found. In many instances their bundles were thrown to them, and they were ordered off as if slaves. I forgot to say that as the boat pushed off from the shore, where stood a crowd of loafers, the men on board had congregated upon the hurricane deck with their rifles and guns of various sorts, all loaded, and began to fire what I should call a very disorganized sort of a salute, which lasted for something like an hour, and which has been renewed at intervals, though in a more desultory manner, at every village we have passed. However, we now find them passably good, quiet, and regularly sobered men. We have of course a motley set, even to Italians. We passed the mouth of the Missouri, and moved very slowly against the current, for it was not less than twenty minutes after four the next morning, when we reached St. Charles, distant forty-two miles. Here we stopped till half-past five, when Mr. Sarpy, to whom I gave my letters home, left us in a wagon.

April 26. A rainy day, and the heat we had experienced yesterday was now all gone. We saw a Wild Goose running on the shore, and it was killed by Bell; but our captain did not stop to pick it up, and I was sorry to see the poor bird dead, uselessly.

95. "Willing Agents of Villainy"

from Francis Parkman, *The Oregon Trail*

We being first on the ground, had appropriated all the wood within reach; so that our fire alone blazed cheerily. Around it soon gathered a group of uncouth figures, shivering in the drizzling rain. Conspicuous among them were two or three of the half-savage men who spend their reckless lives in trapping among the Rocky Mountains, or in trading for the Fur Company in the Indian villages. They were all of Canadian extraction; their hard, weather-beaten faces and bushy moustaches looked out from beneath the hoods of their white capotes with a bad and brutish expression, as if their owner might be the willing agent of any villany. And such in fact is the character of many of these men.

96. A Runaway Slave Barely Survives

from Francis Parkman, *The Oregon Trail*

In "Marriage and Settlement Patterns of Rocky Mountain Trappers and Traders" (1980), William R. Swagerty says that although "one out of every hundred trappers and traders was an Indian, 'mountain men' of African descent were almost unknown in the trade, with the exceptions of James Beckwourth and Edward Rose" (161). Yet, in the following passage, Francis Parkman tells about a runaway slave who spent some time in the mountains. Probably some runaways were not rescued as was the man Parkman describes; and other slaves would not have sought refuge in the West if they had known that slavery was an old institution there, predating the arrival of Europeans.

Several days passed, and we and the Indians remained encamped side by side. They could not decide whether or not to go to the war.

Toward evening, scores of them would surround our tent, a picturesque group. Late one afternoon a party of them mounted on horseback came suddenly in sight from behind some clumps of bushes that
lined the bank of the stream, leading with them a mule, on whose back
was a wretched negro, only sustained in his seat by the high pommel
and cantle of the Indian saddle. His cheeks were withered and
shrunken in the hollow of his jaws; his eyes were unnaturally dilated,
and his lips seemed shriveled and drawn back from his teeth like those
of a corpse. When they brought him up before our tent, and lifted him
from the saddle, he could not walk or stand, but he crawled a short
distance, and with a look of utter misery sat down on the grass. All the
children and women came pouring out of the lodges around us, and
with screams and cries made a close circle about him, while he sat
supporting himself with his hands, and looking from side to side with
a vacant stare. The wretch was starving to death! For thirty-three days
he had wandered alone on the prairie, without weapon of any kind;
without shoes, moccasons, or any other clothing than an old jacket
and pantaloons; without intelligence and skill to guide his course, or
any knowledge of the productions of the prairie. All this time he had
subsisted on crickets and lizards, wild onions, and three eggs which he
found in the nest of a prairie dove. He had not seen a human being.
Utterly bewildered in the boundless, hopeless desert that stretched
around him, offering to his inexperienced eye no mark by which to
direct his course, he had walked on in despair, till he could walk no
longer, and then crawled on his knees, until the bone was laid bare. He
chose the night for his travelling, laying down by day to sleep in the
glaring sun, always dreaming, as he said, of the broth and corn-cake
he used to eat under his old master's shed in Missouri. Every man in
the camp, both white and red, was astonished at his wonderful escape
not only from starvation but from the grizzly bears, which abound in
that neighborhood, and the wolves which howled around him every
night.

Reynal recognized him the moment the Indians brought him in.
He had run away from his master about a year before and joined the
party of M. Richard, who was then leaving the frontier for the mountains. He had lived with Richard ever since, until in the end of May he
with Reynal and several other men went out in search of some stray
horses, when he got separated from the rest in a storm, and had never
been heard of up to this time. Knowing his inexperience and helplessness, no one dreamed that he could still be living. The Indians had
found him lying exhausted on the ground.

As he sat there, with the Indians gazing silently on him, his haggard face and glazed eye were disgusting to look upon. Delorier made him a bowl of gruel, but he suffered it to remain untasted before him. At length he languidly raised the spoon to his lips; again he did so, and again; and then his appetite seemed suddenly inflamed into madness, for he seized the bowl, swallowed all its contents in a few seconds, and eagerly demanded meat. This we refused, telling him to wait until morning, but he begged so eagerly that we gave him a small piece, which he devoured, tearing it like a dog. He said he must have more. We told him that his life was in danger if he ate so immoderately at first. He assented, and said he knew he was a fool to do so, but he must have meat. This we absolutely refused, to the great indignation of the senseless squaws, who, when we were not watching him, would slyly bring dried meat and *pommes blanches*, and place them on the ground by his side. Still this was not enough for him. When it grew dark he contrived to creep away between the legs of the horses and crawl over to the Indian village, about a furlong down the stream. Here he fed to his heart's content, and was brought back again in the morning, when Jean Gras, the trapper, put him on horseback and carried him to the fort. He managed to survive the effects of his insane greediness, and though slightly deranged, when we left this part of the country, he was otherwise in tolerable health, and expressed his firm conviction that nothing could ever kill him.

97 and 98. Liquor and the Fur Trade

In *Europe and the People Without History* (1982) Eric Robert Wolf explains how, centuries before Lewis and Clark explored the West, Europeans learned to use alcohol in the fur trade. The next two selections show that some American trappers and traders understood that it was wrong to give the Indians alcohol for furs; but the practice was enormously profitable and mountain entrepreneurs found ways to rationalize it. Moreover, fur-trading companies used liquor not only to exploit Indians but also to keep non-Indian trappers in debt to the companies.

97. Trading Liquor for Furs

from Thomas D. Bonner, *Life and Adventures of James P. Beckwourth*

While I sat talking thus, one of my men entered the village bearing two ten-gallon kegs of whisky. He requested me to take one and sell it out, while he went to the other end of the village, where the Siouxs were encamped, to sell the other. I had hitherto always opposed the sale of liquor to the Indians, and, during my chieftainship of the Crows, not one drop had ever been brought into the village; but now I was restrained by no such moral obligation. I was a mere trader, hazarding my life among the savages to make money for my employers. The sale of liquor is one of the most profitable branches of a trader's business, and, since the appetite for the vile potion had already been created, my personal influence in the matter was very slight. I was no lawgiver; I was no longer in a position to prohibit the introduction of the white man's fire-water; if I had refused to sell it to the Indians, plenty more traders would have furnished it to them; and my conscientious scruples would benefit the Indians none, and would deprive my embarrassed employer of a very considerable source of profit.

Running these things hurriedly over in my own mind, I took the proffered keg, and dealt it all out within two hours. Certainly the rate of profit was high enough; if a man wants a good price for the sale of his soul to his satanic majesty, let him engage in the liquor business among the nations of the Rocky Mountains. Our liquor was a choice article. One pint of alcohol, costing, I suppose, six cents, was manufactured into five times the quantity of whisky, and this was retailed to our insatiate customers at the rate of one pint for each buffalo robe. If the robe was an extra fine one, I might possibly open my heart, and give two pints. But I felt no particular inducement to liberality in my dealings, for I thought the greatest kindness I could show my customers was to withhold the commodity entirely.

Before I had got through with my keg I had a row with an Indian, which cost him his life on the spot. While I was busy in attending the tap, a tall Sioux warrior came into my establishment, already the worse for liquor, which he had obtained elsewhere. He made some formidable strides round and near me, and then inquired for the Crow. I was pointed out to him, and, pot valiant, he swaggered up to me.

"You are a Crow?" he exclaimed.

"Yes."

"You are a great Crow brave?"

"Yes."

"You have killed a host of Siouxs?"

"No; I have killed a host of Cheyennes, but I have only killed fourteen Siouxs with my own hand."

"Look at me," said he, with drunken gasconade; "my arm is strong; I am the greatest brave in the Sioux nation. Now come out, and I will kill you."

"No," I said, "I did not come here to be killed or to kill; I came here to trade. I could kill you as easily as I could kill a squaw, but you know that you have a host of warriors here, while I am alone. They would kill me after I had killed you. But if I should come in sight of your village with twenty of my Crow warriors, you would all run and leave your lodges, women, and children. Go away; I want nothing to do with you. Your tongue is strong, but you are no brave."

I had told the Cheyennes but a few moments previously that I had been among all the nations in the country, and that it had ever been my invariable rule, when struck by a Red Man, to kill him. I was determined to prove the truth of my declaration in this instance. I had my battle-axe hanging from my wrist, and I was ready at a moment's warning. The Sioux continued his abuse of me in his own tongue, which I paid no attention to, for I supposed that, like his white brethren, he might utter a great deal of provocation in his cups, and straightway repent it when he became sober.

Finally, he became so importunate that I saw it was time to take an active part. I said, "You want to kill me, eh? I would fight with you, only I know I should be killed by the Siouxs afterward, and I should have you for my waiter in the spirit land. I would rather kill a good brave, if I kill any."

This was a very opprobrious speech, for it is their faith that when an Indian is slain who has previously slain a foe, the first-killed warrior becomes waiter in the spirit land to the one who had laid him low. Indeed, it was more than he could endure. He jerked off the cloth that was fastened round his hips, and struck me in the face with it. I grasped my battle-axe, but the blow I aimed was arrested by a lodge pole, which impended over his head, and saved him from immediate death. The lodge pole was nearly severed with the blow. I raised my arm again, but it was restrained by the Cheyennes, who had been sitting round with their heads declined during the Sioux's previous abuse.

The Sioux chief, Bull Bear, was standing near, and was acquainted with the whole particulars of the difficulty. He advanced, and chopped his warrior down, and hacked him to pieces after he fell.

"Ugh!" grunted he, as coolly as possible, "you ought to have been killed long ago, you bad Indian!"

This demonstration on my part had a good effect. The Indians examined the cut inflicted by the edge of my axe on the lodge pole, and declared mine a strong arm. They saw I was in earnest, and would do what I had threatened, and, except in one single instance, I had no farther trouble.

Influenced by my persuasions, two hundred lodges of the Cheyennes started for the Platte, Bent and myself accompanying them. On our way thither we met one of my wagons, loaded with goods, on its way to the North Fork of the Platte. There was a forty-gallon cask of whisky among its contents, and, as the Indians insisted on having it opened, I brought it out of the wagon, and broached it. Bent begged me not to touch it, but to wait till we reached the fort. I was there for the purpose of making money, and when a chance offered, it was my duty to make the most of it. On that, he left me, and went to the fort. I commenced dealing it out, and, before it was half gone, I had realized sixteen horses and over two hundred robes.

98. Liquor and Lost Fortunes

from **David L. Brown**, *Three Years in the Rocky Mountains*

The first few days after our arrival at the rendezvous, were one continued scene of wild revelry and excitement. A quantity of liquor which we had brought along with us in order to give the hunters what is termed a *good spree*, was the immediate cause of this state of things.

It has always been the custom of the American Fur Company to supply the persons in its employment, once a year, with a large amount of this pernicious stimulant; induced thereto, no doubt, by a knowledge that in the thoughtless and extravagant exhilaration, many of their best and most industrious trappers are led to squander away in a few short days the hard earned wages of whole years of almost incessant labor, danger and privation. It was really pitiable to see some of these poor fellows on recovering from a paroxism of frantic and self-induced madness, in which they had spent everything coming to them on the books of the Company,—to the amount very often of several hundred dollars,—and on the possession of which they perhaps had built their caculations of retiring from this wild and hazardous life, to the peaceful occupations of civilized society. In thus encouraging and furnishing the means of intoxication, it is not going too far to say, that many of these men have felt themselves defrauded and cheated out of their money by the Company, whose interest it was to keep them in the country, and which is especially anxious to retain in its service, all such as are due a large sum, as the risk of life is very great—from the hand of villainous Indians—and from a thousand unforeseen casualties that threaten the hunter on every side. In case of death the Company becomes executor to the deceased, and in general they appear to have been poorly rewarded for their trouble and exertions. I know not how it is, but every man who has died in that country for the last twenty-years, died in its debt, and many persons who the day and the hour preceding their death, were thought to have a large sum due them on the books of the Company, have yet been found, incredible as it may appear, to have been not only worth nothing, but a few dollars less than even *that.*

99. Smallpox

from Charles Larpenteur, *Forty Years a Fur Trader on the Upper Missouri*

Of all the effects of European-American contact with Native Americans, none is more appalling to read about than the devastation caused by smallpox, the killer of millions of Indians whose immune systems could not resist the disease. For more information about this horror see E. Wagner Stearn, *The Effect of Smallpox on the Destiny of the Amerindian* (1945), and Michael K. Trimble, *An Ethnohistorical Interpretation of the Spread of Smallpox in the Northern Plains Utilizing Concepts of Disease Ecology* (1986). Some trappers and traders tried to prevent the spread of smallpox by inoculating Native Americans; however, even that preventive measure sometimes failed, as we see in Charles Larpenteur's account of an epidemic at Fort Union on the Upper Missouri in 1837.

After my return from the Canoe camp nothing worthy of remark took place until the arrival of the steamer, late in June [1837]. The mirth usual on such occasions was not of long duration, for immediately on the landing of the boat we learned that smallpox was on board. Mr. J. Halsey, the gentleman who was to take charge this summer, had the disease, of which several of the hands had died; but it had subsided, and this was the only case on board. Our only apprehensions were that the disease might spread among the Indians, for Mr. Halsey had been vaccinated, and soon recovered. Prompt measures were adopted to prevent an epidemic. As we had no vaccine matter we decided to inoculate with the smallpox itself; and after the systems of those who were to be inoculated had been prepared according to Dr. Thomas' medical book, the operation was performed upon about 30 Indian squaws and a few white men. This was done with the view to have it all over and everything cleaned up before any Indians should come in, on their fall trade, which commenced early in September. The smallpox matter should have been taken from a very healthy person; but, unfortunately, Mr. Halsey was not sound, and the operation proved fatal to most of our patients. About 15 days afterward there was such a stench in the fort that it could be smelt at the distance of 300 yards. It was awful—the scene in the fort, where some went crazy, and others were half eaten up by maggots before they died; yet, singular to say, not a single bad expression was ever uttered by a sick Indian. Many died, and those who recovered were so much disfigured that one could scarcely recognize them. While the epidemic was at its height a party of about 40 Indians came in, not exactly on a trade, but more on a begging visit, under the celebrated old chief Co-han; and the word was, "Hurry up! Open the door!" which had been locked for many days, to keep the crazy folks in. Nothing else would do—we must open the door; but on showing him a little boy who had not recovered, and whose face was still one solid scab, by holding him above the pickets, the Indians finally concluded to leave. Not long afterward we learned that more than one-half of the party had died—some said all of them. In the course of time the fort became clear of the smallpox, but the danger of infection continued. Fort William was still standing, and the remaining houses, which were no longer inhabited, were used as hospitals for Indians, with no other attendants than some old squaws. It became the duty of John Brazo to take out the dead and dump them into the bushes, and some mornings, on asking him "How many?" he would say, "Only three, sir; but, according to appearances in the hospital, I think I shall have a full load tomorrow or next day." This seemed to be fun for Brazo, but was not for others, particularly myself, as I happened to be the trader, who was liable to be shot at any time; but, singular to say, not even a threat was made, though the tribe was reduced more than one-half by next spring [1838]. Trade continued very nearly up to the average; on being asked how it happened that there were so many robes brought in, the Indians would say laughingly that they expected to die soon, and wanted to have a frolic till the end came. The winter [of 1837–38] was spent in great suspense and fear, but, fortunately, nothing serious occurred except some few shots fired at me through the wicket during the night liquor trade; and as this had frequently happened before, it was not attributed to revenge for the smallpox.

100. Indians Murdered at an American Post

from Paul Kane, *Paul Kane's Frontier*

Scenes of brutal murder dominate the next selection. To understand the transformation of actual conflicts into narrative and fictional constructs see Louise K. Barnett's *The Ignoble Savage* (1975). In *The Conquest of America* (1984), Tzvetan Todorov explores the minds of Aztec warriors and Spanish conquistadors to show how, in his view, the conquest of the Americas was the beginning of European efforts to wipe out cultures different from those of Europe.

Big Snake's brother was the first who sat to {for} me, and while I was sketching, he told me the following anecdote of his brother, of whom he seemed to be very proud. Mr. Harriett understood the language and acted as interpreter. Some time back, Big Snake had the free admission to one of the American forts near the Rocky Mountains. Coming up one day with two other Indians, to enter the gate, it was shut rudely in his face by the orders of the commander, who had only lately arrived in the country. This his pride led him to regard as a direct insult; he rode away, and falling in with some cattle that he knew belonged to the fort, he commenced firing on them, and killed thirteen. As soon as the sentinel, who had given the offence, heard the shots, he suspected the reason, and informed the superintendent, who immediately collected his men, and sallied out with them well armed, in the direction of the firing. Big Snake being on the watch, hid himself with his two companions behind a small hill.

The party from the fort apprehending there might be a large number of Indians hid, hesitated to advance within gun-shot; but a negro of the party offered to proceed and reconnoitre. Approaching the hill with great caution, and seeing no one, he began to think they had escaped; but, when within about twenty yards of the top, Big Snake sprang up from his lair and fired, bringing him down, and the next moment bore off his scalp, and waved it in derision towards the Americans.

A short time afterwards Big Snake met a large party of Blackfeet, "pitching" towards the fort on a trade. On his arrival amongst them, he stated what he had done, and dared any one to censure his conduct on peril of making him his enemy. Although the band well knew that what he had done amounted to an open declaration of war, and would of course cut off any communication or trade with the establishment, unless they actually gave up Big Snake as a prisoner, yet they suffered their disappointment in silence rather than incur the anger of one whom they so much feared. Another band of the same tribe, ignorant of the circumstance, arrived at the fort a few days afterwards. The Americans, thinking this a good opportunity of chastising the aggressors, loaded one of their cannons with musket-balls, and while the unsuspecting Indians were standing huddled together at the gate, waiting for admittance, applied the fusee. Fortunately it did not explode, and the Indians, seeing the unusual stir and the flash, became alarmed, and fled. On a second application of the fusee, it discharged its murderous projectiles amongst the fugitives, and killed ten persons, principally women and children.

Some time after, Big Snake heard that one of the most influential Indians of the tribe had blamed him, in a speech, for involving the tribe in much inconvenience and destroying their trade. On hearing these remarks, he directly went in search of the censurer, armed with a scalping-knife, and, on coming up with him, attempted to stab him;

his foot, however, slipped in the attempt, which saved the other's life, although he received a severe wound in the side.

101. Trapping in New Mexico

from George Frederick Ruxton, *Adventures in Mexico and the Rocky Mountains*

The Spanish had established settlements in New Mexico in the early seventeenth century, and American and Canadian fur trappers who ventured into the Southwest often went to Taos and Santa Fe to trade and to enjoy the local culture, especially "Taos lightning," a whiskey made from wheat by distillers who were mostly former mountain men. In *The Taos Trappers* (1971), David J. Weber explains how, after the U.S. government tried to stop the use of liquor in the fur trade, the Taos distilleries became a major source of the whiskey used in the trade. The old trapper that George Frederick Ruxton describes in the following selection wanted coffee, a commodity that in the West was almost as precious as whiskey. For more information about the fur trade in the Southwest see Robert Glass Cleland, *This Reckless Breed of Men* (1950).

All this day I marched on foot through the snow, as Panchito made sad work of ascending and descending the mountain, and it was several hours after sunset when I arrived at Rio Colorado, with one of my feet badly frozen. In the settlement, which boasted about twenty houses, on inquiry as to where I could procure a corral and hoja for the animals, I was directed to the house of a French Canadian—an old trapper named Laforey—one of the many who are found in these remote settlements, with Mexican wives, and passing the close of their adventurous lives in what to them is a state of ease and plenty; that is, they grow sufficient maize to support them, their faithful and well-tried rifles furnishing them with meat in abundance, to be had in all the mountains for the labour of hunting.

I was obliged to remain here two days, for my foot was so badly frozen that I was quite unable to put it to the ground. In this place I found that the Americans were in bad odour; and as I was equipped as a mountaineer, I came in for a tolerable share of abuse whenever I limped through the village. As my lameness prevented me from pursuing my tormentors, they were unusually daring, saluting me, every time I passed to the shed where my animals were corralled, with cries of "Burro, burro, ven a comer hoja." (Jackass, jackass, come here and eat shucks), "Anda coxo, a ver los burros, sus hermanos" (Hallo, game-leg, go and see your brothers, the donkeys); and at last, words not being found heavy enough, pieces of adobe rattled at my ears. This, however, was a joke rather too practical to be pleasant; so, the next time I limped to the stable, I carried my rifle on my shoulder, which was a hint never to be mistaken by Mexicans, and hereafter I passed with impunity. However, I was obliged to watch my animals day and night, for, as soon as I fed them, either the corn was bodily stolen, or a herd of hogs was driven in to feed at my expense. The latter aggression I put a stop to by administering to one persevering porker a pill from my rifle, and promised the threatening crowd that I would have as little compunction in letting the same amount of daylight into them if I caught them thieving the provender; and they seemed to think me in earnest, for I missed no more corn or shucks. I saw plainly enough, however, that my remaining here, with such a perfectly lawless and ruffianly crew, was likely to lead me into some trouble, if, indeed, my life was not in absolute danger, which, from what occurred shortly after, I have now no doubt it was; and therefore I only waited until my foot was sufficiently recovered to enable me to resume my journey across the mountains.

The fare in Laforey's house was what might be expected in a hunter's establishment: venison, antelope, and the meat of the carnero cimarron, the Rocky Mountain sheep, furnished his larder; and such meat (poor and tough at this season of the year), with cakes of Indian meal, either tortillas or gorditas, furnished the daily bill of fare. The absence of coffee he made the theme of regret at every meal, bewailing his misfortune in not having at that particular moment a supply of this article, which he never before was without, and which I may here observe, amongst the hunters and trappers when in camp or rendezvous, is considered as an indispensable necessary. Coffee, being very cheap in the States, is the universal beverage of the western people, and finds its way to the mountains in the packs of the Indian traders, who retail it to the mountain-men at the moderate price of from two to six dollars the half-pint cup. However, my friend Laforey was never known to possess any, and his lamentations were only intended to soften my heart, as he thought (erroneously) that I must certainly carry a supply with me.

"Sacré enfant de Gârce," he would exclaim, mixing English, French, and Spanish into a puchero-like jumble, "voyez-vous dat I vas nevare tan pauvre as dis time; mais before I vas siempre avec plenty café, plenty sucre; mais now, God dam, I not go à Santa Fé, God dam, and mountain-men dey come aqui from autre côté, drink all my café. Sacré enfant de Gârce, nevare I vas tan pauvre as dis time, God dam. I not care comer meat, ni frijole, ni corn, mais widout café I no live. I hunt may be two, three day, may be one week, mais I eat notin; mais sin café, enfant de Gârce, I no live, parceque me not sacré Espagnol, mais one Frenchman."

102 and 103. Horses in the Fur Trade

John C. Ewers points out in *The Horse in Blackfoot Indian Culture* (1980) that "the prominent part played by horse raiding in the intertribal warfare of the late 18th and early 19th century as emphasized in fur traders' accounts suggests that the Indians' need for horses to use in hunting buffalo and transporting food and domestic articles furnished a major motive for that early warfare" (174). In the following two selections, George Catlin (1796–1872) and Robert Stuart (1785–1848) give differing European-American views on the Indian practice of horse raiding.

102. Indians *Capture* Not *Steal* Trappers' Horses

from George Catlin, *North American Indians*

These people to be sure, have in some instances plundered and robbed trappers and travellers in their country; and for that I have sometimes heard them called rascals and thieves, and rogues of the first order, &c.; yet they do not consider themselves such; for thieving in their estimation is a high crime, and considered the most disgraceful act that a man can possibly do. They call this *capturing*, where they sometimes run off a Trader's horses, and make their boast of it; considering it a kind of retaliation or summary justice, which they think it right and honourable and that they should administer. And why not? For the unlicensed trespass committed through their country from one end to the other, by mercenary white men, who are destroying the game, and catching all the beaver and other rich and valuable furs out of their country, without paying them an equivalent, or, in fact, anything at all, for it; and this too, when they have been warned time and again of the danger they would be in, if they longer persisted in the practice.

103. How Indians Stole Trappers' Horses

from Robert Stuart, *On the Oregon Trail*

Saturday 19th—We were all up at dawn, and I had just reached the river bank when I heard the Indian yell raised in the vicinity of our camp and the cry, "To Arms" there are Indians, echoed by all of our party—We had just time to snatch our arms when several Indians at full speed passed 300 yards to one side of our stations, having by their yells driven off every horse we had (notwithstanding their being tethered & hobbled); towards them we rushed, and got almost within shot of the nearest, when repeated yells in the direction from which they came made us desist from the pursuit in order to defend ourselves and baggage, for their being only a few Indians after the horses, we very readily imagined that the main body were in reserve to attack our rear, did we follow the foremost, or to plunder the Camp, if opportunity.—

At the rate the horses were going, all attempts to regain them would be unavailing, and had we pursued farther, every thing else should have been lost to a certainty, which would have undoubtedly have made our situation, if possible, far more deplorable than it really is—The savages whose yells made us return to the baggage passed soon after in the others tracks, and we could not discover that the whole party amounted to more than 20, which had we known only 3 minutes sooner, a few horses might probably have been saved & a scalp or two fallen into our hands—From a few words we heard they are beyond all doubt of the Crow nation and, I believe, the band we met at Millers river.—

This method of stealing horses is deserving of being more minutely described; one of the party rode past our camp and placed himself on a conspicuous knob, in the direction they wanted to run them off; when the others (who were hidden behind our camp), seeing him prepared, rose the warwhoop, or yell (which is the most horribly discordant howling imaginable, being in imitation of the different beasts of prey); at this diabolical noise, the animals naturally rose their heads to see what the matter was—at that instant he who had planted himself in advance put spurs to his steed, and ours, seeing him gallop off in apparent fright, started all in the same direction, as if a legion of infernals were in pursuit of them.—In this manner a dozen or two of these fellows have sometimes succeeded in running off every horse belonging to parties of perhaps 5 or 600 men; for once those creatures take fright, nothing short of broken necks, can stop their progress.—

On the whole this was one of the most daring, and intrepid actions I ever heard of among Indians, and convinces me how determined they were on having our horses, for which they would unquestionably have followed us any distance, and nothing but seeing us prepared and ready to defend ourselves prevented their attacking us where we first saw them—

104. A Critique of the Fur Trade

from George Catlin, *North American Indians*

Mountain men sometimes became the targets of criticism for the way they treated Indians. In the selection that follows, the painter George Catlin condemns the entire fur trade. However, it was a change in fashion and the near extinction of the beaver—not Catlin's or others' critiques— that brought the fur trade to an end. Yet, as Joseph R. Millichap notes in *George Catlin* (1977), the artist's "championship of the Indian probably cost him his major opportunity for financial success—the attempted sale of his entire gallery to the United States Government, which was to form the basis of a national gallery of art and science" (17).

In alluding to the cruel policy of removing the different tribes to their new country, West of the Mississippi, I would not do it without the highest respect to the motives of the Government . . . but when I go, as I have done, through every one of those tribes removed, who had learned at home to use the ploughshare, and also contracted a passion, and a taste of civilized manufactures; and after that, removed twelve and fourteen hundred miles West, to a wild and lawless region, where their wants are to be supplied by the traders, at eight or ten times the prices they have been in the habit of paying; where whiskey can easily be sold to them in a boundless and lawless forest, without the restraints that can be successfully put upon the sellers of it in their civilized neighbourhoods; and where also they are allured from the use of the ploughs, by the herds of buffaloes and other wild animals on the plains; I am compelled to state, as my irresistible conviction, that I believe the system one well calculated to benefit the interests of the voracious land-speculators and Indian Traders; the first of whom are ready to grasp at their lands, as soon as they are vacated—and the others, at the *annuities* of one hundred and twenty thousand extravagant customers. I believe the system is calculated to aid these, and perhaps to facilitate the growth and the wealth of the civilized border; but I believe, like everything else that tends to white man's aggrandizement, and the increase of his wealth, it will have as rapid a tendency to the poverty and destruction of the poor *red men*; who, unfortunately, *almost* seem *doomed*, never in any way to be associated in interest with their pale-faced neighbours.

The system of trade, and the small-pox, have been the great and wholesale destroyers of these poor people, from the Atlantic Coast to where they are now found. And no one but God, knows where the voracity of the one is to stop, short of the acquisition of everything that is desirable to money-making man in the Indian's country; or when the mortal destruction of the other is to be arrested, whilst there is untried flesh for it to act upon, either within or beyond the Rocky Mountains.

From the first settlements on the Atlantic Coast, to where it is now carried on at the base of the Rocky Mountains, there has been but one system of trade and money-making, by hundreds and thousands of white men, who are desperately bent upon making their fortunes in this trade, with the unsophisticated children of the forest; and generally they have succeeded in the achievement of their object.

The Governments of the United States, and Great Britain, have always held out every encouragement to the Fur Traders, whose traffic has uniformly been looked upon as beneficial, and a source of wealth to nations; though surely, they never could have considered such intercourse as advantageous to the savage.

Besides the many thousands who are daily and hourly selling whiskey and rum, and useless gewgaws, to the Indians on the United States, the Canada, the Texian and Mexican borders, there are, of hardy adventurers, in the Rocky Mountains and beyond, or near them, and out of all limits of laws, one thousand armed men in the annual employ of the United States' Fur Companies—and equal number in the employment of the British Factories, and twice that number in the Russian and Mexican possessions; all of whom pervade the countries of the wildest tribes they can reach, with guns and gunpowder in their hands, and other instruments of death, unthought of by the simple savage, calculated to terrify and coerce him to favourable terms in his trade: and in all instances they assume the right, (and prove it if necessary, by the superiority of their weapons), of hunting and trapping the streams and lakes of their countries.

These traders, in addition to the terror, and sometimes death, that they carry into these remote realms, at the muzzles of their guns, as well as by whiskey and the small-pox, are continually arming tribe after tribe with fire-arms; who are able thereby, to bring their unsuspecting enemies into unequal combats, where they are slain by thousands, and who have no way to heal the awful wound but by arming themselves in turn; and in a similar manner reeking their vengeance upon *their* defenceless enemies on the West. In this wholesale way, and by whiskey and disease, tribe after tribe sink their heads and lose their better, proudest half, before the next and succeeding waves of civilization flow on, to see or learn anything definite of them.

Without entering at this time, into any detailed history of this immense system, or denunciation of any of the men or their motives, who are engaged in it, I would barely observe, that, from the very nature of their traffic, where their goods are to be carried several thousands of miles, on the most rapid and dangerous streams, over mountains and other almost discouraging obstacles; and that at the continual hazard to their lives, from accident and diseases of the countries, the poor Indians are obliged to pay such enormous prices for their goods, that the balance of trade is so decidedly against them, as soon to lead them to poverty; and, unfortunately for them, they mostly contract a taste for whiskey and rum, which are not only ruinous in their prices, but in their effects destructive to life—destroying the Indians, much more rapidly than an equal indulgence will destroy the civilized constitution.

In the Indian communities, where there is no law of the land or custom denominating it a vice to drink whiskey, and to get drunk; and where the poor Indian meets whiskey tendered to him by white men, whom he considers wiser than himself, and to whom he naturally looks for example; he thinks it no harm to drink to excess, and will lie drunk as long as he can raise the means to pay for it. And after his first means, in his wild state, are exhausted, he becomes a beggar for whiskey, and begs until he disgusts, when the honest pioneer becomes his neighbour; and then, and not before, gets the name of the "poor, degraded, naked, and drunken Indian," to whom the epithets are well and truly applied.

Alfred Jacob Miller, *Auguste and his Horse* (37.1940.10).

Alfred Jacob Miller, *The Greeting* (37.1940.133).

Alfred Jacob Miller, *Moonlight—Camp Scene* (37.1940.135).

Alfred Jacob Miller, *The Trapper's Bride* (37.1940.12).

Alfred Jacob Miller, *Scene on Big Sandy River* (37.1940.20).

Alfred Jacob Miller, *The Grizzly Bear* (37.1940.32).

Alfred Jacob Miller, *The Lost Greenhorn* (37.1940.141).

Alfred Jacob Miller, *Threatened Attack* (37.1940.76).

Alfred Jacob Miller, *Trapping Beaver* (37.1940.111).

Alfred Jacob Miller, *Interior of Fort Laramie* (37.1940.150).

Alfred Jacob Miller, *Roasting the Hump Rib* (37.1940.36).

Indians

If any image of the fur trade takes precedence in popular imagination, it is that of trappers and Indians at war with each other. There is some truth behind this image, as Indians and trappers could and did fall into violent conflicts for a variety of reasons. Fighting often broke out when Indians took trappers' horses or other possessions. Trappers considered such actions theft, though from the Indian point of view horse raiding was an honorable activity—part collecting fines against poachers, part National Pastime. Sometimes the reasons for fighting were personal, such as "Liver Eatin' " Johnston's legendary vendetta against the Crows. Sometimes the conflicts between Indians and trappers were political in nature: After 1806, when a Blackfoot was killed by members of the Lewis and Clark expedition, the Blackfeet set up an organized resistance to American trappers. This Blackfoot "wall" kept American trappers out of the Upper Missouri for more than twenty years.

While images of smoking rifles and bared knives sell books and movie tickets, the mundane truth is that, among trappers and Indians, interracial marriage was more common than interracial murder. Trappers married Indian women not only for love, companionship, and help with the chores that went with living in the wilderness, but also because marrying an Indian woman established kinship ties to members of her tribe—ties that were far more effective in keeping a man alive than was a single-shot rifle. Indians likewise gained from interracial marriages. Having a white trapper or trader in the family gave Indians an economic edge at trading time, and Indian women who married trappers typically were wealthier and lived more pampered lives than their sisters who married Indian men.

Not only did trappers and Indians get along more than they fought, there were times in the history of the fur trade when Indians *were* the trappers. Fur traders valued Indian trappers both because of their skill and the fact that their labor was cheaper than non-Indian labor. The problem with Indian labor, as far as white fur traders were concerned, was that Indians weren't always willing to hunt furs or to produce them in the numbers that the fur companies demanded. The reasons for this were many and complex, as Mary K. Whelan points out in "Dakota Economics and the Nineteenth-Century Fur Trade" (1993). Some Indians didn't trap because they put a higher value on other activities such as subsistence hunting, horse raiding, and warfare. Some Indians didn't trap due to religious beliefs about animal life. Some came from societies that emphasized sharing and generosity over individual gain and so did not embrace the economic values that drove the fur trade. Those Indians who did trap did so because they needed trade goods—guns, metal pots, needles, steel knives, gunpowder, lead, cloth, and vermilion—in order to survive the technological, ecological, and political changes sweeping through the nineteenth-century West. Addiction to alcohol was another incentive to trap, and fur traders took full advantage of this in spite of government regulations against trading alcohol to Indians.

Sometimes Indians couldn't be persuaded to pursue beaver at all. One of the main reasons behind the importation of large numbers of white fur trappers into the Rocky Mountains was that the natives of the region were largely uninterested in pursuing beaver.

Of course we have to be careful when we talk about "white" fur trappers, since a number of the trappers in the Rocky Mountain had Indian blood. It is not always easy to know which trappers were Indian and which were not, as most trappers of Indian descent had European (often French) names. Another complication in separating Indians from non-Indians is the fact that some non-Indian mountain men adopted Indian language, dress, and customs to such an extent that they became, in all but ancestry, Indians.

In the selections that follow we hear only the voices of the literate. If narratives written by Indians existed, the stories would sound quite different. As it is, we must take away what lessons we can from the only direct witnesses we have.

105. The Greeting

from Alfred Jacob Miller, *The West of Alfred Jacob Miller*

The following selection shows that mountain men couldn't always tell whites from Indians.

The Greeting

In approaching our destination, one morning as we proceeded quietly along, our ears were saluted by sounds that raised the pulse immediately, and to which we had become sensitively alive. It was a tremendous Indian yell of a large body of men, and we heard the clattering of their horses as they came down the valley;—as soon however as we had sight of them, we were relieved;—it was a body of Trappers, who had heard of our approach and sallied forth to give us a greeting;—this is done by a *feu de joie* of blank cartridges and a hearty shaking of hands among the merry fellows;—for they found many of their comrades in our company, and when we encamped for the evening, our Captain gave them a grand *Carouse* in the shape of hump ribs, buffalo tongues, and mountain sheep. In addition to this, a metheglin, made of honey and alcohol, potent and fiery, was concocted and circulated among them.

The jovial fellows paid their respects to it again and again;—sung their French songs;—related their adventures,—

> Wherein they spoke of most disastrous chances,
> Of moving accidents by flood and field.

It was soon evident that they could not hold out,—in short, one after another toppled over;—the *conqueror* had it all his own way—and overpowering sleep came to their relief.

106. A Story of a Massacre

from Alexander Ross, *Adventures of the First Settlers on the Oregon or Columbia River*

Marie Dorion (1770–1850) in the account that follows was an Iowa Indian married to Pierre Dorion, Jr. (d. 1811), a mixed-blood Yankton Sioux. Regardless of her ancestry, her story of surviving and protecting her children after Indians killed their father and his trapper companions is a moving account. The events of Marie Dorion's story took place on the Boise River in 1811 but were not published until 1849. Alexander Ross, who wrote down Dorion's story, was himself one of the subjects of George Bird Grinnell's *Beyond the Old Frontier* (1913).

"About the middle of August we reached the Great Snake River, and soon afterwards, following up a branch to the right hand, where there were plenty of beaver, we encamped; and there Mr. Reed built a house to winter in. After the house was built, the people spent their time in trapping beaver. About the latter end of September, Hoback, Robinson, and Rezner came to us; but they were very poor, the Indians having robbed them of everything they had about fifteen days before. Mr. Reed gave them some clothing and traps, and they went to hunt with my husband. Landrie got a fall from his horse, lingered a while, and died of it. Delaunay was killed, when trapping: my husband told me that he saw his scalp with the Indians, and knew it from the colour of the hair. The Indians about the place were very friendly to us; but when strange tribes visited us, they were troublesome, and always asked Mr. Reed for guns and ammunition; on one occasion, they drove an arrow into one of our horses, and took a capot from La Chapelle. Mr. Reed not liking the place where we first built, we left it, and built farther up the river, on the other side. After the second home was built, the people went to trap as usual, sometimes coming home every night, sometimes sleeping out for several nights together at a time. Mr. Reed and one man generally stayed at the house.

"Late one evening, about the 10th of January, a friendly Indian came running to our house, in a great fright, and told Mr. Reed that a band of the bad Snakes, called the Dog-rib tribe, had burnt the first house that we had built, and that they were coming on whooping and singing the war-song. After communicating this intelligence, the Indian went off immediately, and I took up my two children, got upon a horse, and set off to where my husband was trapping; but the night was dark, the road bad, and I lost my way. The next day being cold and stormy, I did not stir. On the second day, however, I set out again; but seeing a large smoke in the direction I had to go, and thinking it might proceed from Indians, I got into the bushes again and hid myself. On the third day, late in the evening, I got in sight of the hut, where my husband and the other men were hunting; but just as I was approaching the place, I observed a man coming from the opposite side, and staggering as if unwell: I stopped where I was till he came to me. Le Clerc, wounded and faint from loss of blood, was the man. He told me that La Chapelle, Rezner, and my husband had been robbed and murdered that morning. I did not go into the hut; but putting Le Clerc and one of my children on the horse I had with me, I turned round immediately, took to the woods, and I retraced my steps back again to Mr. Reed's; Le Clerc, however, could not bear the jolting of the horse, and he fell once or twice, so that we had to remain for nearly a day in one place; but in the night he died, and I covered him over with brushwood and snow, put my children on the horse, I myself walking and leading the animal by the halter. The second day I got back again to the house. But sad was the sight! Mr. Reed and the men were all murdered, scalped, and cut to pieces. Desolation and horror stared me in the face. I turned from the shocking sight in agony and despair; took to the woods with my children and horse, and passed the cold and lonely night without food or fire. I was now at a loss what to do: the snow was deep, the weather cold, and we had nothing to eat. To undertake a long journey under such circumstances was inevitable death. Had I been alone I would have run all risks and proceeded; but the thought of my children perishing with hunger distracted me. At this moment a sad alternative crossed my mind: should I venture to the house among the dead to seek food for the living? I knew there was a good stock of fish there; but it might have been destroyed or carried off by the murderers; and besides, they might be still lurking about and see me: yet I thought of my children. Next morning, after a sleepless night, I wrapped my children in my robe, tied my horse in a thicket, and then went to a rising ground, that overlooked the house, to see if I could observe anything stirring about the place. I saw nothing; and, hard as the task was, I resolved to venture after dark: so I returned back to my children, and found them nearly frozen, and I was afraid to make a fire in the day time lest the smoke might be seen; yet I had no other alternative, I must make a fire, or let my children perish. I made a fire and warmed them. I then rolled them up again in the robe, extinguished the fire, and set off after dark to the house: went into the store and ransacked every hole and corner, and at last found plenty of fish scattered about. I gathered, hid, and slung upon my back as much as I could carry, and returned again before dawn of day to my children. They were nearly frozen, and weak with hunger. I made a fire and warmed them, and then we shared the first food we had tasted for the last three days. Next night I went back again, and carried off another load; but when these efforts were over, I sank under the sense of my afflictions, and was for three days unable to move, and without hope. On recovering a little, however, I packed all up, loaded my horse, and putting my children on the top of the load, set out again on foot, leading the horse by the halter as before. In this sad and hopeless condition I travelled through deep snow among the woods, rocks, and rugged paths for nine days, till I and the horse could travel no more. Here I selected a lonely spot at the foot of a rocky precipice in the Blue Mountains, intending there to pass the remainder of the winter. I killed my horse, and hung up the flesh on a tree for my winter food. I built a small hut with pine branches, long grass, and moss, and packed it all round with snow to keep us warm, and this was a difficult task, for I had no axe, but only a knife to cut wood. In this solitary dwelling, I passed fifty-three lonely days! I then left my hut and set out with my children to cross the montains; but I became snow blind the second day, and had to remain for three days without advancing a step; and this was unfortunate, as our provisions were almost exhausted. Having recovered my sight a little, I set out again, and got clear off the mountains, and down to the plains on the fifteenth day after leaving my winter encampments; but for six days we had scarcely anything to eat, and for the last two days not a mouthful. Soon after we had reached the plains I perceived a smoke at a distance; but being unable to carry my children farther, I wrapped them up in my robe, left them concealed, and set out alone in hopes of reaching the Indian camp, where I had seen the smoke; but I was so weak that I could hardly crawl, and had to sleep on the way. Next day, at noon, I got to the camp. It proved to belong to the Walla Wallas, and I was kindly treated by them. Immediately on my arrival the Indians set off in search of my children, and brought them to the camp the same night. Here we staid for two days, and then moved on to the river, expecting to hear something of the white people on their way either up or down."

107. Antoine Godin Murdered by Blackfeet

from John Kirk Townsend, *Narrative of a Journey across the Rocky Mountains to the Columbia River*

Antoine Godin (or Goddin) (d. 1836) was the Iroquois mountain man whose murder of a Blackfoot chief touched off the Battle of Pierre's Hole. While the white man described in the following narrative may have been involved in the murder of Godin as Townsend claims, it was somewhat common in the West to attribute Indian atrocities to renegade white "masterminds" whether or not there was evidence to support such charges.

Mr. M'Leod informed me of the murder of Antoine Goddin, the half-breed trapper, by the Blackfeet Indians, at Fort Hall.—A band of these Indians appeared on the shore of the Portneuf river, opposite the fort, headed by a white man named Bird.—This man requested Goddin, whom he saw on the opposite side of the river, to cross to him with a canoe, as he had beaver which he wished to trade. The poor man accordingly embarked alone, and landing near the Indians, joined the circle which they had made, and *smoked the pipe of peace with them.* While Goddin was smoking in his turn, Bird gave a sign to the Indians and a volley was fired into his back. While he was yet living, Bird himself tore the scalp from the poor fellow's head, and deliberately cut Captain Wyeth's initials, N. J. W. in large letters upon his forehead. He then hallooed to the fort people, telling them to bury the carcass if they wished, and immediately went off with his party.

This Bird was formerly attached to the Hudson's Bay Company, and was made prisoner by the Blackfeet, in a skirmish several years ago. He has since remained with them, and has become a great chief, and leader of their war parties. He is said to be a man of good education, and to possess the most unbounded influence over the savage people among whom he dwells. He was known to be a personal enemy of Goddin, whom he had sworn to destroy on the first opportunity.

108. An Indian Battle at Fort MacKenzie

from **Maximilian von Wied,** *Travels in the Interior of North America*

Germanic Prince Maximilian von Wied (1782–1867) traveled up the Missouri River in the spring of 1832, accompanied by the artist Karl Bodmer (1809–1893). Late in August 1833, while staying at Fort Mac-Kenzie, the two witnessed the battle that Maximilian describes in the following selection. For a full account of their historic trip see John C. Ewers, *Views of a Vanishing Frontier* (1984). For a look at Bodmer's art, see Bodmer, *Karl Bodmer's America* (1984).

About this time, when we began to be in want of meat in the fort, having, for some time past, had only a couple of beavers, many unfavourable reports were spread of the hostile disposition of Ninoch-Kiaiu and his adherents towards the Whites, which had, doubtless, been excited by the pernicious influence of the treacherous Bird, who was prejudiced against the Company. An Indian told us that his countrymen would demand double the usual price for the beavers, and, if that were refused, they would kill all the Americans. We did not suffer ourselves to be alarmed by such reports, which indicated the unsteady character of the Blackfeet; but the time was come when we were to be put to a more serious trial.

On the 28th of August, at break of day, we were awakened by musket-shot, and Doucette entered our room, crying, "Levez-vous, il faut nous battre," on which we arose in haste, dressed ourselves, and loaded our fowling-pieces with ball. When we entered the court-yard of the fort, all our people were in motion, and some were firing from the roofs. On ascending it, we saw the whole prairie covered with Indians on foot and on horseback, who were firing at the fort; and on the hills were several detached bodies. About eighteen or twenty Blackfoot tents, pitched near the fort, the inmates of which had been singing and drinking the whole night, and fallen into a deep sleep towards morning, had been surprised by 600 Assiniboins and Crees. When the first information of the vicinity of the enemies was received from a Blackfoot, who had escaped, the *engagés* immediately repaired to their posts on the roofs of the buildings, and the fort was seen to be surrounded on every side by the enemy, who had approached very near. They had cut up the tents of the Blackfeet with knives, discharged their guns and arrows at them, and killed or wounded many of the inmates, roused from their sleep by this unexpected attack. Four women and several children lay dead near the fort, and many others were wounded. The men, about thirty in number, had partly fired their guns at the enemy, and then fled to the gates of the fort, where they were admitted. They immediately hastened to the roofs, and began a well-supported fire on the Assiniboins.

In the fort itself all was confusion. If the men had been now and then mustered and inspected, it would have been found that the *engagés* had sold their ammunition to the Indians; they were, therefore, quite unprepared to defend themselves, and it was necessary, during the combat, to distribute powder as well among the Whites as the Indians. Mr. Mitchell and Berger, the interpreter, were employed in admitting the Blackfoot women and children, who were assembled at the door of the fort, when a hostile Indian, with his bow bent, appeared before the gate, and exclaimed, "White man, make room, I will shoot those enemies!" This exclamation showed that the attack was not directed against the Whites, but only against the Blackfeet. Mr. Mitchell immediately gave orders to his people to cease firing; notwithstanding this, single shots continued to be fired, and our Blackfeet were not to be restrained, nay, ten or twelve of our people, among whom were Doucette and Loretto, went into the prairie, and fired in the ranks of the Blackfeet, who were assembling, and every moment increasing in numbers. Loretto had shot, at the distance of eighty-six paces from the pickets, the nephew of the Assiniboin chief, Minohanne (the lefthanded), and this was the only one of the killed whom the enemy were unable to carry away, for we saw them lay many others on their horses, and take them off. In the fort itself only one man was wounded, having had his foot pierced by an arrow, and likewise a horse and a dog. If the enemy had occupied the heights on the other side of the river, they might, from that position, have killed all our people in the fort.

When the Assiniboins saw that their fire was returned, they retreated about 300 paces, and an irregular firing continued, during which several people from the neighbourhood joined the ranks of the

Blackfeet. While all this was passing, the court-yard of the fort exhibited very singular scenes. A number of wounded men, women, and children, were laid or placed against the walls; others, in their deplorable condition, were pulled about by their relations, amid tears and lamentations. The White Buffalo, whom I have often mentioned, and who had received a wound at the back of his head, was carried about, in this manner, amid singing, howling, and crying: they rattled the schischikué in his ears, that the evil spirit might not overcome him, and gave him brandy to drink. He himself, though stupefied and intoxicated, sung without intermission, and would not give himself up to the evil spirit. Otsequa-Stomik, an old man of our acquaintance, was wounded in the knee by a ball, which a woman cut out with a penknife, during which operation he did not betray the least symptom of pain. Natah-Otann, a handsome young man, with whom we became acquainted on our visit to Kutonapi, was suffering dreadfully from severe wounds. Several Indians, especially young women, were likewise wounded. We endeavoured to assist the wounded, and Mr. Mitchell distributed balsam, and linen for bandages, but very little could be done; for, instead of suffering the wounded, who were exhausted by the loss of blood, to take some rest, their relations continually pulled them about, sounded large bells, rattled their medicine or amulets, among which were the bears' paws, which the White Buffalo wore on his breast. A spectator alone of this extraordinary scene can form any idea of the confusion and the noise, which was increased by the loud report of the musketry, the moving backwards and forwards of the people carrying powder and ball, and the tumult occasioned by above twenty horses shut up in the fort.

When the enemy were still very near the fort, Mr. Mitchell had given orders to fire the cannons of the right-hand front block-house among them; but this had not been done, because the Blackfeet were partly mixed with the Assiniboins; no use, therefore, had been made of them, of which the Indians complained bitterly. The enemy gradually retreated, and concentrated themselves in several detachments on the brow of the hill . . . and this gave us an opportunity to open the gate, with due precaution, and view the destroyed tents and the bodies of the slain. The Indian who was killed near the fort especially interested me, because I wished to obtain his skull. The scalp had already been taken off, and several Blackfeet were engaged in venting their rage on the dead body. The men fired their guns at it; the women and children beat it with clubs, and pelted it with stones; the fury of the latter was particularly directed against the privy parts. Before I could obtain my wish, not a trace of the head was to be seen. Not far from the river there was a melancholy scene; old Haisikat (the stiff foot) was lamenting over his grown-up daughter, who had concealed herself in the bushes near the fort, and had been shot in mistake by Dechamp, who thought she was an enemy.

At the very beginning of the engagement, the Blackfeet had despatched messengers on horseback to the great camp of their nation, which was eight or ten miles off, to summon their warriors to their aid, and their arrival was expected every moment. Meantime, Ninoch-Kiaiu came and called on Mr. Mitchell for assistance, for they had been attacked by another party of the enemy. Hotokaneheh likewise came to the fort, and made a long and violent speech, in which he reproached the Whites with being inactive while the enemy were still in the vicinity; they ought not to confine themselves to the "defence of the fort, if they seriously desired the alliance of the Blackfeet, but endeavour to attack the common enemy in the prairie," &c. All these reproaches hurt Mr. Mitchell, and he resolved to show the Indians that the Whites were not deficient in courage. With this view he made the best hunters and riflemen mount their horses, and, in spite of our endeavours to dissuade him from this impolitic measure, he proceeded to the heights, where 150 or 200 Blackfeet kept up an irregular fire on the enemy. We who remained in the fort had the pleasure of viewing a most interesting scene. From the place where the range of hills turns to the Missouri, more and more Blackfeet continued to arrive. They came galloping in groups, from three to twenty together, their horses covered with foam, and they themselves in their finest apparel, with all kinds of ornaments and arms, bows and quivers on their backs, guns in their hands, furnished with their medicines, with feathers on their heads; some had splendid crowns of black and white eagles' feathers, and a large hood of feathers hanging down behind, sitting on fine panther skins lined with red; the upper part of their bodies partly naked, with a long strip of wolf's skin thrown across the shoulder, and carrying shields adorned with feathers and pieces of coloured cloth. A truly original sight! Many immediately galloped over the hill, whipped their tired horses, in order to take part in the engagement, shouting, singing, and uttering their war-whoop; but a great part of them stopped at the fort, received powder and balls, and, with their guns and bows, shot at the disfigured remains of the Assiniboin who was slain, and which were now so pierced and burnt as scarcely to retain any semblance of the human form. As the Indians near the fort believed themselves to be now quite safe, they carried the wounded into the leather tents, which were injured and pierced through and through by the enemy's balls, round which many dead horses and dogs were lying, and the crying and lamenting were incessant.

About one o'clock Mr. Mitchell and his people returned, much fatigued by the expedition, and the great heat, the thermometer being at 84°. Mr. Mitchell's horse had been shot through the withers; he himself fell off and hurt his arm; another horse was shot through the neck, and captured by the enemy; Bourbonnais, its rider, had escaped. All our people, however, had returned safe. The enemy had been driven back to the Maria River, where, from the want of bravery in the Blackfeet, they were able to maintain their ground behind the trees; nay, they had sometimes advanced and repulsed their enemies. They were plainly heard encouraging each other, on which they came forward in parties of twenty or thirty, and renewed the attack. It was generally observed that the Assiniboins fought better than the Blackfeet, many of whom did not leave the fort during the whole day. Mr. Mitchell, with his people, had always been in advance of the Blackfeet, and nearer to the enemy. He had often shamed the Blackfeet, whose numbers had increased to 500 or 600, calling out—"Why did they lag behind? They had reproached the Whites with cowardice, but now it was seen who were the most cowardly. Now was the time to show their courage," &c. The hunter, Dechamp, had especially distinguished himself by his bravery and well-directed fire at the enemy, of whom he had killed or wounded several. They called out to him that they knew him very well, for he is a Half Cree Indian, and had many relations among the enemy. He had been several times in the heat of the action, and a Blackfoot gave him his horse, on which he saved himself. During this engagement Kutonapi came to Mr. Mitchell, and asked him for a paper, which he had received on the conclusion of the treaty with the Fur Company; and, being told that it was in the fort, he said, "Oh, if I had it here, it would secure me against every ball!" The Indians had fired quite at random, otherwise the loss must have been much greater on both sides. We learnt, in the sequel, that the Assiniboins had three killed, and twenty severely wounded. Many Indians took Mr. Mitchell by the hand, welcomed him as their friend and ally, and offered him several horses, which he did not accept.

After dinner, Doucette, Dechamp, and Berger again rode in quest of the enemy, who still occupied the valley of the Maria River, and many Blackfeet came back, boasting of their heroic exploits. Old Pioch (*qy.* Ninoch?) Kiaiu came full of joy, and told us that "no ball had touched him; doubtless, because Mr. Bodmer had taken his portrait a few days before." In the afternoon a number of Blackfeet arrived, and the dust raised by their horses was visible at a great distance in the prairie. The fort was filled with them; and they were refreshed with water and tobacco. We visited the wounded in their tents, had the blood washed from their wounds, and their hair, which was clotted with it, cut off; and gave them medicines and plaster, and, instead of brandy, which they asked for, sugar and water to refresh them. A child had died of its wounds; they had daubed its face with vermilion. After the exertions of this day, both Indians and Whites were covered with perspiration and dust, and quite exhausted.

109. A Mountain Man Shot with a Bullet and an Arrow

from Nathaniel J. Wyeth, *The Journals of Captain Nathaniel J. Wyeth's Expeditions to the Oregon Country, 1831–1836*

Horse raiding probably accounted for more violence between mountain men and Indians than did any other cause. In the event described below, a mountain man gets the worst of such an encounter.

Aug. 1st. Same camp find Mr. Bonneville camped a few miles above us. On farther inquiry I changed my opinion expressed above in regard to the Indians who stole the horses I think they were 15 Snakes who left our camp at Green river a few days before we left that place. The case was this. Mr. Bridger sent 4 men to this river to look for us *viz* Mr. Smith, Thomson, [J.B.] Charboneau a half breed and Evans. Two days before it happened 15 Inds came to them and after smoking departed the second day after they were gone Thompson having been out hunting [tied] his horse to the others and thought he would sit down by them until it was time to water them and having been on guard much of the time previous fell asleep he was waked by a noise among the horses which he supposed to [be] his comrades come to water them raising his head and opening his eyes the first thing that presented itself to his sight was the muzzle of a gun in the hands of an Indian it was immediately discharged and so near his head that the front piece of his cap alone saved his eyes from being put out by the powder the Ball entered the head outside of the eye and breaking the cheek bone passing downward and lodged behind the ear in the neck this stunned him and while insensible an arrow was shot into him on the top of the shoulder downward which entered about 6 inches, the Inds. got 7 horses all there were. charboneau pursued them on foot but wet his gun in crossing a little stream and only snapped twice.

110. Richardson's Run-in with the Otos

from John Kirk Townsend, *Narrative of a Journey across the Rocky Mountains to the Columbia River*

In accounts like the following, we get only one side of the story of con-flicts between trappers and Indians. Although we don't have the Indian response to such tales, we can at least try to gain greater knowledge and understanding of their culture in order to understand the roots of the conflict. To better understand the Otos see William Whitman, *The Oto* (1937), and Anna Lee Walters, *Talking Indian* (1992).

While we were at breakfast three Indians of the Otto tribe, came to our camp to see, and smoke with us. These were men of rather short stature, but strong and firmly built. Their countenances resemble in general expression those of the Kanzas, and their dresses are very simi-lar. We are all of opinion, that it is to these Indians we owe our diffi-culties of last night, and we have no doubt that the three missing horses are now in their possession, but as we cannot prove it upon them, and cannot even converse with them, (having no interpreters,) we are compelled to submit to our loss in silence. Perhaps we should even be thankful that we have not lost more.

While these people were smoking the pipe of peace with us, after breakfast, I observed that Richardson, our chief hunter, (an experi-enced man in this country, of a tall and iron frame, and almost child-like simplicity of character, in fact an exact counterpart of *Hawk-eye* in his younger days,) stood aloof, and refused to sit in the circle, in which it was always the custom of the *old hands* to join.

Feeling some curiosity to ascertain the cause of this unusual diffidence, I occasionally allowed my eyes to wander to the spot where our sturdy hunter stood looking moodily upon us, as the calamet passed from hand to hand around the circle, and I thought I perceived him now and then cast a furtive glance at one of the Indians who sat opposite to me, and sometimes his countenance would assume an expression almost demoniacal, as though the most fierce and deadly passions were raging in his bosom. I felt certain that hereby hung a tale, and I watched for a corresponding expression, or at least a look of consciousness, in the face of my opposite neighbor, but expression there was none. His large features were settled in a tranquillity which nothing could disturb, and as he puffed the smoke in huge volumes from his mouth, and the fragrant vapor wreathed and curled around his head, he seemed the embodied spirit of meekness and taciturnity.

The camp moved soon after, and I lost no time in overhauling Richardson, and asking an explanation of his singular conduct.

"Why," said he, "that *Injen* that sat opposite to you, is my bitterest enemy. I was once going down alone from the rendezvous with letters for St. Louis, and when I arrived on the lower part of the Platte river, (just a short distance beyond us here,) I fell in with about a dozen Ottos. They were known to be a friendly tribe, and I therefore felt no fear of them. I dismounted from my horse and sat with them upon the ground. It was in the depth of winter; the ground was covered with snow, and the river was frozen solid. While I was thinking of nothing but my dinner, which I was then about preparing, four or five of the cowards jumped on me, mastered my rifle, and held my arms fast, while they took from me my knife and tomahawk, my flint and steel, and all my ammunition. They then loosed me, and told me to be off. I begged them, for the love of God, to give me my rifle and a few loads of ammunition, or I should starve before I could reach the settlements. No—I should have nothing, and if I did not start off immediately, they would throw me under the ice of the river. And," continued the excited hunter,—while he ground his teeth with bitter, and uncontrollable rage,—"that man that sat opposite to you was the chief of them. He recognised me, and knew very well the reason why I would not smoke with him. I tell you, sir, if ever I meet that man in any other situation than that in which I saw him this morning, I'll shoot him with as little hesitation as I would shoot a deer. Several years have passed since the perpetration of this outrage, but it is still as fresh in my memory as ever, and I again declare, that if ever an opportunity offers, I will kill that man." "But, Richardson, did they take your horse also?" "To be sure they did, and my blankets, and every thing I had, except my clothes." "But how did you subsist until you reached the settlements? You had a long journey before you." "Why, set to *trappin'* prairie squirrels with little nooses made out of the hairs of my head." I should remark that his hair was so long, that it fell in heavy masses on his shoulders. "But squirrels in winter, Richardson, I never heard of squirrels in winter." "Well but there was plenty of them, though; little white ones, that lived among the snow." "Well, really, this was an unpleasant sort of adventure enough, but let me suggest that you do very wrong to remember it with such blood-thirsty feelings." He shook his head with a dogged and determined air, and rode off as if anxious to escape a lecture.

111. Of Battles and Scalping

from Raymond W. Thorp and Robert Bunker, *Crow Killer*

Known as "Liver-eating Johnson" to his fellow trappers, John Johnston (1823–1900) had a reputation both as a killer of Crow Indians and as a cannibal. According to legend, Johnston sought vengeance against the entire Crow nation for the murder of his pregnant wife. If the account which follows is accurate, Johnston's killings were not limited to Crow Indians. Vardis Fisher made Johnston's life the basis for his novel *Mountain Man* (1965), which served in turn as the basis for Sidney Pollack's 1972 movie *Jeremiah Johnson*.

"Allus remember, young un," Hatcher told him repeatedly, "ye must never give a red coon a chanst." Or again, "Allus be the fust ter count coup. Otherwise ye'll be nowhar!" Johnston was soon enough to prove that he could follow such good advice.

For along in the middle of one afternoon, as they were entering the foothills, a dozen Arapahos swept down upon them. At first fire Johnston caught an arrow in the flesh of his right shoulder, but despite this he felled one of the attackers while Hatcher downed two—before the others fled out of rifle range. The young trapper started forward for the coup but found himself peremptorily halted.

"We'll git that arrer out fust," said Hatcher; and with his Bowie knife he removed it, along with a quantity of flesh. Johnston stood stoically the while: "Now cuss me fer a Kiowa," said the Mountain Man, "haven't ye got no feelin's? Thet stun wuz deep!" Johnston's only reply was to load his rifle. ("Never come up on a dead Injun wi' an unloaded gun," Hatcher had taught him.) They advanced, leading their horses, toward the fallen Indians.

Hatcher took advantage of the occasion to expound upon Arapaho character: "These red coons," he said, "air treacherouser than most."

"One is still a-livin'," his partner told him.

For answer Hatcher drew his Bowie, and as Johnston pointed, the wounded brave attempted to draw his scalping knife. He was too late: the Mountain Man's blade was buried to the hilt in his chest.

"Now," said Hatcher, "let's git on."

He sank his Bowie into the soft earth and pulled it out again, clean and bright. Coolly he placed one moccasined foot on his victim's face, then reached down and twisted the scalplock around one hand, slowly, for Johnston to see. Now with the point of his knife he made a quick circle around the base of the topknot, and yanked upward. The scalp came off cleanly, with a snap like that of a whiplash. Whirling it round several times to clean it of excess gore, Hatcher deftly slipped the topknot through the ring at his belt, pulling it until the bloody side faced the sky.

"Dries quicker this way," he said, "now let's see ye try one."

As Johnston bent to his task, he was aware that the old trapper's frosty stare was boring into his back. But he was an apt pupil, and now he cut as clean and sure as his teacher. As he snapped the trophy, Hatcher spoke in some doubt:

"Never skelped a wil' Injun afore, lad?"

"Never seen one afore."

"Then cuss me fer a Kiowa! Ye air better built fer this work than any man I ever seed." The old trapper looked off toward the mountains and added: "Fust time I skinned a red coon I wuz cold an' shuk all over." He turned to peel the remaining scalp, then watched as Johnston mounted his horse and looped the topknot through the bridle.

"Slicin' a man don't bother me none," said Johnston; and Hatcher was to remark later on his partner's expressionless eyes.

112. Joe Meek Tells of Being Captured by Indians

from Frances Fuller Victor, *River of the West*

The story Joe Meek tells in the next selection is part of a long tradition of Indian captivity narratives. To learn more about that tradition see any of the 296 titles in the *Garland Library of Narratives of North American Indian Captivities.*

From the mountains about the head-waters of the Snake River, Meek returned, with Bridger's brigade to the Yellowstone country, where he fell into the hands of the Crows. The story as he relates it, is as follows:

"I war trapping on the Rocky Fork of the Yellowstone. I had been out from camp five days; and war solitary and alone, when I war discovered by a war party of Crows. They had the prairie, and I war forced to run for the Creek bottom; but the beaver had throwed the water out and made dams, so that my mule mired down. While I war struggling in the marsh, the Indians came after me, with tremendous yells; firing a random shot now and then, as they closed in on me.

"When they war within about two rods of me, I brought old *Sally*, that is my gun, to my face, ready to fire, and then die; for I knew it war death this time, unless Providence interfered to save me: and I didn't think Providence would do it. But the head chief, when he saw the warlike looks of *Sally*, called out to me to put down my gun, and I should live.

"Well, I liked to live,—being then in the prime of life; and though it hurt me powerful, I resolved to part with *Sally*. I laid her down. As I did so, the chief picked her up, and one of the braves sprang at me with a spear, and would have run me through, but the chief knocked him down with the butt of my gun. Then they led me forth to the high plain on the south side of the stream. There they called a halt, and I was given in charge of three women, while the warriors formed a ring to smoke and consult. This gave me an opportunity to count them: they numbered one hundred and eighty-seven men, nine boys, and three women.

"After a smoke of three long hours, the chief, who war named 'The Bold,' called me in the ring, and said:

" 'I have known the whites for a long time, and I know them to be great liars, deserving death; but if *you* will tell the truth, you shall live.'

"Then I thought to myself, they will fetch the truth out of me, if thar is any in me. But his highness continued:

" 'Tell me whar are the whites you belong to; and what is your captain's name.'

"I said 'Bridger is my captain's name; or, in the Crow tongue, *Casapy*,' the 'Blanket chief.' At this answer the chief seemed lost in thought. At last he asked me—

" 'How many men has he?'

"I thought about telling the truth and living; but I said 'forty,' which war a tremendous lie; for thar were two hundred and forty. At this answer The Bold laughed:

" 'We will make them poor,' said he; 'and you shall live, but they shall die.'

"I thought to myself, 'hardly;' but I said nothing. He then asked me whar I war to meet the camp, and I told him:—and then how many days before the camp would be thar; which I answered truly, for I wanted them to find the camp.

"It war now late in the afternoon, and thar war a great bustle, getting ready for the march to meet Bridger. Two big Indians mounted my mule, but the women made me pack moccasins. The spies started first, and after awhile the main party. Seventy warriors traveled ahead of me: I war placed with the women and boys; and after us the balance of the braves. As we traveled along, the women would prod me with sticks, and laugh, and say 'Masta Sheela,' (which means white man,) 'Masta sheela very poor now.' The fair sex war very much amused.

"We traveled that way till midnight, the two big bucks riding my mule, and I packing moccasins. Then we camped; the Indians in a ring, with me in the centre, to keep me safe. I didn't sleep very well that night. I'd a heap rather been in some other place.

"The next morning we started on in the same order as before: and the squaws making fun of me all day; but I kept mighty quiet. When we stopped to cook that evening, I war set to work, and war head cook, and head waiter too. The third and the fourth day it war the same. I felt pretty bad when we struck camp on the last day: for I knew we must be coming near to Bridger, and that if any thing should go wrong, my life would pay the forfeit.

"On the afternoon of the fourth day, the spies, who war in advance, looking out from a high hill, made a sign to the main party. In a moment all sat down. Directly they got another sign, and then they got up and moved on. I war as well up in Indian signs as they war; and I knew they had discovered white men. What war worse, I knew they would soon discover that I had been lying to them. All I had to do then war to trust to luck. Soon we came to the top of the hill, which overlooked the Yellowstone, from which I could see the plains below extending as far as the eye could reach, and about three miles off, the camp of my friends. My heart beat double quick about that time; and I once in a while put my hand to my head, to feel if my scalp war thar.

"While I war watching our camp, I discovered that the horse guard had seen us, for I knew the sign he would make if he discovered Indians. I thought the camp a splendid sight that evening. It made a powerful show to me, who did not expect ever to see it after that day. And it *war* a fine sight any how, from the hill whar I stood. About two hundred and fifty men, and women and children in great numbers, and about a thousand horses and mules. Then the beautiful plain, and the sinking sun; and the herds of buffalo that could not be numbered; and the cedar hills, covered with elk,—I never saw so fine a sight as all that looked to me then!

"When I turned my eyes on that savage Crow band, and saw the chief standing with his hand on his mouth, lost in amazement; and beheld the warriors' tomahawks and spears glittering in the sun, my heart war very little. Directly the chief turned to me with a horrible scowl. Said he:

" 'I promised that you should live if you told the truth; but you have told me a great lie.'

"Then the warriors gathered around, with their tomahawks in their hands; but I war showing off very brave, and kept my eyes fixed on the horse-guard who war approaching the hill to drive in the horses. This drew the attention of the chief, and the warriors too. Seeing that the guard war within about two hundred yards of us, the chief turned to me and ordered me to tell him to come up. I pretended to do what he said; but instead of that I howled out to him to stay off, or he would be killed; and to tell Bridger to try to treat with them, and get me away.

"As quick as he could he ran to camp, and in a few minutes Bridger appeared, on his large white horse. He came up to within three hundred yards of us, and called out to me, asking who the Indians war.

I answered 'Crows.' He then told me to say to the chief he wished him to send one of his sub-chiefs to smoke with him.

"All this time my heart beat terribly hard. I don't know now why they didn't kill me at once; but the head chief seemed overcome with surprise. When I repeated to him what Bridger said, he reflected a moment, and then ordered the second chief, called Little-Gun, to go and smoke with Bridger. But they kept on preparing for war; getting on their paint and feathers, arranging their scalp locks, selecting their arrows, and getting their ammunition ready.

"While this war going on, Little-Gun had approached to within about a hundred yards of Bridger; when, according to the Crow laws of war, each war forced to strip himself, and proceed the remaining distance in a state of nudity, and kiss and embrace. While this interesting ceremony war being performed, five of Bridger's men had followed him, keeping in a ravine until they got within shooting distance, when they showed themselves, and cut off the return of Little-Gun, thus making a prisoner of him.

"If you think my heart did not jump up when I saw that, you think wrong. I knew it war kill or cure, now. Every Indian snatched a weapon, and fierce threats war howled against me. But all at once about a hundred of our trappers appeared on the scene. At the same time Bridger called to me, to tell me to propose to the chief to exchange me for Little-Gun. I explained to The Bold what Bridger wanted to do, and he sullenly consented: for, he said, he could not afford to give a chief for one white dog's scalp. I war then allowed to go towards my camp, and Little-Gun towards his; and the rescue I hardly hoped for war accomplished.

"In the evening the chief, with forty of his braves, visited Bridger and made a treaty of three months. They said they war formerly at war with the whites; but that they desired to be friendly with them now, so that together they might fight the Blackfeet, who war everybody's enemies. As for me, they returned me my mule, gun, and beaver packs, and said my name should be *Shiam Shaspusia*, for I could out-lie the Crows."

113. An Escape from the Blackfoot Indians

from Alfred Jacob Miller, *The West of Alfred Jacob Miller*

Black Harris's stories spread far beyond the frontier, and in 1837 the painter Alfred Jacob Miller depicted Harris and a companion escaping from Blackfoot Indians. Miller had been hired by a British peer, Sir William Drummond Stewart (1795–1871), to paint scenes from his expedition to the Rocky Mountains; and Miller's explanatory notes—like the following about Black Harris—add interesting details to his pictorial record. As for the point of view of the Blackfeet, historians are still debating whether it is possible to imagine what the Indians of that era thought about the mountain men. A study such as Oscar Lewis's *The Effects of White Contact upon Blackfoot Culture, with Special Reference to the Role of the Fur Trade* (1942) at least goes beyond the mountain man's limited view. And one of the best American novels of the twentieth century, *Fools Crow* (1986), by James Welch, gives us a sense of what life was like for the Blackfeet before they were forced onto reservations.

Escape from Blackfeet

Black Harris and his brother Trapper are here making their escape from the terrible Blackfeet, the *bête noires* of the Rocky Mountains, the word is "*sauve qui peut*," and spur and whip are both in requisition.

This Black Harris always created a sensation at the camp fire, being a capital *raconteur*, and having had as many perilous adventures as any man probably in the mountains. He was of wiry form, made up of bone and muscle, with a face apparently composed of tan leather and whip cord, finished off with a peculiar blue-black tint, as if gunpowder had been burnt into his face.

In riding expresses for the Fur Co[y], in which he had no equal;—he told us that in running the gauntlet among hostile Indians, he laid by in the day for sleep, and rode hard all night. At times, he would raise the envy of the Trappers by recounting a discovery he had made somewhere in the Black hills of a "putrified" (petrified) Forest, and wind up with some horrible stories of butcheries among the Indians in which he bore a hand.

114. "The Most Filthy Indians We Have Seen"

from Myra Eells, "Journal of Myra F. Eells"

As a professed Christian and a missionary, Myra Eells's attitudes towards Indians were supposed to be charitable. This did not prevent her from expressing her negative impressions of Indians, however. To better understand the attitudes illustrated by Eells's comments see Genevieve McCoy, "Sanctifying the Self and Saving the Savage: The Failure of the ABCFM Oregon Mission and the Conflicted Language of Calvinism" (1991).

Sunday, July 22nd.—The Indians are about our tent before we are up and stay about us all day; think they are the most filthy Indians we have seen—some of them have a buffalo robe on them, though many of them are as naked as when born. Mr. Walker read a sermon, and although they could not understand a word, they were still and paid good attention. They appeared amused with our singing.

115. Aged Indians Left to Die

from George C. Yount, *George C. Yount and His Chronicles of the West*

Studies such as James J. Farrell's *Inventing the American Way of Death, 1830–1920* (1980) show that attitudes toward death and dying are culturally determined and change over time. In the next selection, the shock expressed by the whites at the Indians' treatment of their aged tribal members is understandable, given the difference in cultures. By the beginning of the twentieth century, some Americans had gained a greater understanding of native cultures. Contrast the following selection with Jack London's short story "The Law of Life," which was first published in March 1901 in *McClure's Magazine*. London also describes leaving the aged to die, but he tells the story from the point of view of a dying old man who expresses a stoic acceptance of his fate.

At or near the mouth of the Gila, a spectacle was presented distressing beyond what humanity is often called to witness—Somewhere in that remote and dreary region reside a tribe of savages [Cocopa Indians] more barbarous than almost any other. They appear lost to all the attributes of humanity—They appear to retain no idea of kindred relationship, of paternal, fraternal or filial regard—They are the ultimatum of human degradation—These people have a method of disposing of the old and superannumated of their tribe, quite peculiar to themselves, revolting to the heart of man, and destitute of the least possible degree of natural affection they do it as a calm business transaction.

Waiting for Death

Our trappers found seven of these decrepit victims, four men and three women, brought by their children to a secluded spot, quite surrounded and hemmed in with the above described hempvine, absolutely impenetrable save a narrow path which the Indians had cut, and filled up again when they left, in such a manner that the old people could not again open it—So advanced in age and decrepit were they that they could be only a burden to their children to feed and nourish them; and this is the method in that tribe, of relieving themselves from such a tax—These aged fathers and mothers were in a state of perfect nudity, lying on the bare ground, without a morsel of food, and too much enfebled even to creep to the River for water, to slack the burning thirst, of a tropical sun—Thus they lay waiting for death to end their sufferings—Emaciated to the last degree, they moaned and wept, and begged of the trappers some morsel of nourishment, or water to moisten their lips—The party fed them, gave them water and sat down then to weep; when they discovered that the vermine were already crawling in and out of their blistered skin—some of them had not remaining strength to carry to their own mouths the food bestowed, and it was necessary to place it in their mouths—After having ministered to these wretched creatures all in their power, our trappers turned their backs, stopped their ears and fled—By thus feeding them they had only prolonged their sufferings, and no one had a heart to look back, as they abandoned a scene so awful. The poor wretched laid themselves down together and were seen no more—They could moan, but tears they had none—

116. Indians and Half-Breeds Torture a Buffalo

from Washington Irving, *The Adventures of Captain Bonneville*

In contrast to the popular notion that all Indians displayed a reverent attitude toward animal life at all times, Washington Irving here provides evidence that Indians could be both cruel to animals and wasteful of animal resources. But while Irving is not the only witness to offer such evidence, it is worth noting that in describing the incident that follows Irving could have been influenced as much by the bullfights he saw during his time as a diplomat in Spain as he was by anything he actually witnessed during his western travels.

Among the Indians and half-breeds of the party, were several admirable horsemen and bold hunters; who amused themselves with a grotesque kind of buffalo bait. Whenever they found a huge bull in the plains, they prepared for their teasing and barbarous sport. Surrounding him on horseback, they would discharge their arrows at him in quick succession, goading him to make an attack; which, with dexterous movement of the horse, they would easily avoid. In this way, they hovered round him, feathering him with arrows, as he reared and plunged about, until he was bristled all over like a porcupine. When they perceived in him signs of exhaustion, and he could no longer be provoked to make battle, they would dismount from their horses, approach him in the rear, and seizing him by the tail, jerk him from side to side, and drag him backwards; until the frantic animal, gathering fresh strength from fury, would break from them, and rush, with flashing eyes and a hoarse bellowing, upon any enemy in sight; but in a little while, his transient excitement at an end, would pitch headlong on the ground, and expire. The arrows were then plucked forth, the tongue cut out and preserved as a dainty, and the carcass left a banquet for the wolves.

117. White Indians

from Rufus B. Sage, *Scenes in the Rocky Mountains*

By the beginning of the nineteenth century, one long-standing myth of the West was the belief that Europeans had arrived there before Columbus and had started a race of "white Indians." One variant of the myth held that a Welshman named Madoc had come to the New World and that his descendants were the Mandan Indians. The British Romantic poet Robert Southey received his inspiration for his poem *Madoc* (1807) from the myth. Richard Deacon's *Madoc and the Discovery of America* (1967) shows that the evidence in support of this myth is flimsy or non-existent. Rufus B. Sage was an itinerant Connecticut newspaperman before going off to live for several years as a mountain man.

In narrating the events of their long excursion, an account was given of visiting the Munchies, a tribe of *white Indians*.

What added much to the interest I felt in this part of their story, was the recollection of an article which went the newspaper rounds several years since, stating the existence of such a tribe. I had disbelieved it at the time; but this, and subsequent corroborative evidence, has effectually removed from my mind all doubts upon the subject.

Our trappers had remained with the Munchies for four weeks, and spoke of them in high terms.

In reference to their color they were represented as being of a much fairer complexion than Europeans generally, a thing easily explained if we remember this one fact, i.e., my informants must have spoken comparatively, taking themselves as the true representatives of that race, when in reality their own color, by constant exposure to the weather, had acquired a much darker hue than ordinary; then drawing their conclusion from a false standard, they were led to pronounce the fair natives much fairer, as a body, than the whites.

By information derived from various sources, I am enabled to present the following statement relative to this interesting people:

The Munchies are a nation of *white aborigines*, actually existing in a valley among the Sierra de los Mimbros chain, upon one of the affluents of the Gila, in the extreme northwestern part of the Province of Sonora.

They number about eight hundred in all. Their country is surrounded by lofty mountains at nearly every point, and is well watered and very fertile, though of limited extent. Their dwellings are spacious apartments nicely excavated in the hill-sides, and are frequently cut in the solid rock.

They subsist by agriculture, and raise cattle, horses, and sheep. Their features correspond with those of Europeans, though with a complexion, perhaps, somewhat fairer, and a form equally if not more graceful.

Among them are many of the arts and comforts of civilized life. They spin and weave, and manufacture butter and cheese, with many of the luxuries known to more enlightened nations.

Their political economy, though much after the patriarchal order, is purely republican in its character. The old men exercise the supreme control in the enactment and execution of laws. These laws are usually of the most simple form, and tend to promote the general welfare of the community. They are made by a concurrent majority of the seniors in council,—each male individual, over a specified age, being allowed a voice and a vote.

Questions of right and wrong are heard and adjudged by a committee selected from the council of seniors, who are likewise empowered to redress the injured and pass sentence upon the criminal.

In morals they are represented as honest and virtuous. In religion they differ but little from other Indians.

They are strictly men of peace, and never go to war, nor even, as a common thing, oppose resistance to the hostile incursions of surrounding nations. On the appearance of an enemy, they immediately retreat, with their cattle, horses, sheep, and other valuables, to mountain caverns, fitted at all times for their reception,—where, by barricading the entrances, they are at once secure without a resort to arms.

In regard to their origin they have lost all knowledge or even tradition, (a thing not likely to have happened had they been the progeny of Europeans at any late period,—that is, since the time of Columbus;) neither do their characters, manners, customs, arts, or government savor of modern Europe.

Could a colony or party of Europeans in the short period of three centuries and a half lose all trace of their origin, religion, habits, arts, civilization, and government? Who, for a moment, would entertain an idea so estranged to probability?

And yet the Munchies cannot be real Indians,—they must be of European descent, though circumstances other than complexion afford no evidence of identity with either race. Where, then, shall we place them?—from whence is their origin?

We are forced to admit the weight of circumstantial testimony as to their having settled upon this continent prior to its discovery by Columbus. Here we are led to inquire, are they not the remote descendants of some colony of ancient Romans?

That such colonies did here exist in former times, there is good reason for believing. The great lapse of time and other operative causes combined, may have transformed the Munchies from the habits, customs, character, religion, arts, civilization, and language of the Romans, to the condition in which they are at present found.

118. The Lone Sentinel: A Dead Indian Adulterer

from **Warren Angus Ferris,** *Life in the Rocky Mountains*

We know from Mark Twain's *Life on the Mississippi* (1883) that whites used Indian legends or tales for moralistic purposes. That this was the case even earlier is shown in the following account.

At day break we resumed our weary march, forced our way, though with great difficulty through a chaos of snow banks, rocks and fallen pines, to the east side of the mountain, and at last descended to the source of Ham's Fork, on which we passed the night. The next day we reached an open valley of considerable extent, decked with groves of aspen, and beds of willows, and grazed by a numerous herd of buffalo. Midway of this valley, on the western side, is a high point of rock, projecting into the prairie and overlooking the country to a great distance. Imagine our surprise when we beheld a solitary human being seated on the very pinnacle of this rock, and apparently unconscious of our approach, though we were advancing directly in front of him,—

and he so elevated that every object however trifling, within the limit of human vision seemed to court his notice; and what made it still more singular, there was evidently no person in or near the valley except ourselves. We halted before him, at a short distance, astonished to see one solitary hero, who seemed to hide himself from he knew not what—friends or foes; but firm as the giant rock on which he sat as on a throne, seemed calmly to await our approach, then to hurl the thunder of his vengeance upon us, or fall gloriously like another Warwick, disdaining to ask what he can no longer defend. With mingled feelings of respect and awe we approached this lord of the valley, gazed admiringly up at the fixed stolidity of his countenance, and lo! *he was dead.*

I afterwards learned that this Indian was taken in the act of adultery with the wife of another, and put to death by the injured husband. He was a Shoshone, and was placed in this conspicuous position by the chief of the tribe, as a warning to all similar offenders.

119. A Spanish Massacre of Helpless Indians

from **Zenas Leonard**, *Narrative of the Adventures of Zenas Leonard*

The following description of cold-blooded murder shows that mountain men could be shocked and repelled by violence. Even so, the violence described in many mountain-man narratives provides support for the revisionist views expressed in works like Patricia Nelson Limerick's *The Legacy of Conquest* (1987) and Richard Slotkin's trilogy: *Regeneration Through Violence* (1973), *The Fatal Environment* (1985), and *Gunfighter Nation* (1992).

28th. To-day a party of Spaniards arrived at our encampment on search of a party of Indians who had eloped from the St. Juan Missionary station, and taken with them 300 head of horses—which we supposed to be the party seen by us on the 26th. These men stayed with us all night and the next morning some of our men joined the Spaniards in the chase, who were to get one half of the horses as a compensation for their trouble, if lucky enough to find them. These men followed the Indians to the foot of a large mountain, where they discovered several smokes rising out of the forest along the base of the mountain in a thicket of timber. From the smoke that arose, they thought the whole Indian force was concentrated, and the Spanish and American force surrounded the spot in battle array, determined to give the offenders a severe chastisement at once. When all the preparations were made, the word to fire was given. But instead of the lamentations of wounded Indians, and the frantic prancing of frightened horses, nothing but a dead silence answered the discharge of their artillery.— They then dismounted and went into the thicket, where they found a large portion of their horses well butchered, and partly dried and a few old and feeble Indians, with some squaws and children. The Indians having killed some of the horses, were engaged in drying the meat,— but on seeing the white men approach, fled to the mountain, leaving nothing behind but what is above stated. The disappointment of the Spaniards now exceeded all bounds, and gave our men some evidence of the depravity of the Spanish character. By way of revenge, after they found that there was no use in following the Indians into the mountain, the Spaniards fell to massacreing, indiscriminately, those helpless creatures who were found in the wigwams with the meat, and cutting off their ears. Some of them were driven into a wigwam, when the door was barricaded, and a large quantity of combustible matter thrown on and around the hut, for the purpose of setting fire to it, and burning them all together. This barbarous treatment our men would not permit and they went and released the prisoners, when the Spaniards fell to work and despatched them as if they were dogs. When this tragedy was completed they all returned to our encampment on the 31st.

On their arrival at our camp, the Spaniards told me that their object in taking off the ears, was to show the Priests and Alcaldes, that they had used every effort to regain the stolen property. These people also informed me that the Indians of this country are in the habit of coming in large droves to the missionary stations, & make the most sincere professions of religion, until they gain the confidence of the priests, when they will suddenly decamp, and take off all the horses they can get, to the mountain, where they remain as long as their meat lasts—when they will send another detachment, whose duty it is to do likewise. They prefer eating domesticated horses because the act of stealing them gives their flesh a superior flavour—and it would be less trouble for them to catch wild horses, if they could thus gratify their stealing propensities.

120. How the Crows Crossed a River

from Thomas James, *Three Years Among the Indians and Mexicans*

The following selection describes how Indians crossed rivers. For more about the history of mountain men and the rivers of the West see selected volumes in the *Rivers of America Series*, especially Dale L. Morgan, *The Humboldt: Highroad of the West* (1943); Maxwell Struthers Burt, *Powder River: Let 'Er Buck* (1938); Frank Waters, *The Colorado* (1946); and Stewart Holbrook, *The Columbia* (1974).

Their manner of crossing the river was singular, and reminded me of the roving Tartars. They stripped themselves entirely naked and every ten piled their accouterments together, blankets, saddles, weapons, &c. on a tent skin made of buffalo robes, and tying it up in a large round bundle threw it into the river and plunged after it, some swimming with these huge heaps, floating like corks, and others riding the horses or holding by the tails till they had all crossed the river. Arrived on the opposite bank, which they reached in little less time than I have taken to describe their passage, they dressed, mounted their horses, and marched off two and two as before, and were quickly out of our sight.

121. A Mandan Sun Dance

from Abner Levi Blackburn, "Lou Devon's Narrative"

Abner Levi Blackburn (1827–1904) gives us his version of a campfire tale he heard in 1847 from Lou Devon, a mysterious man who (if he existed at all) was born in Montreal in 1822. Devon's story is reminiscent of a scene from the movie *A Man Called Horse* (1970), which is based on a short story by Montana author Dorothy Johnson. For information about

Johnson and the source for her story see Judy Alter, *Dorothy Johnson* (1980).

I was born in Montreal in the year 1822. My parents moved to Salt St Maryes [Sault Ste. Marie] when I was eight years old. They both died with the small pox three years afterwards and my uncle took me to his home in the neighborhood. He joined the Hudson['s] Bay Company. [He] went trapping and took me along with him.

Trapt on the Red River, [the] Columbia, and the head watters of the Missouri and other streams. For about five years a small party of us went on the mountains and [then] we were attackted by a savage band of Indians. They killed my uncle and three others of our party and took me prisoner and took me along with them.

We traveled south several days and come to their village. It was the Mandan nation of Indians. They kept close watch over me for some time and set me to carrying wood, for it was cold weather. I worked with some squaws and boys. I had not much clothing. The Indians had nearly stript me clean and [I] slept with the dogs to keep warm. Helpt the squaws in all kinds of drudgery, tanning buffalow robes and deer skins and other chores.

I made up my mind when warm weather come to escape from captivity. I got manny a beating from my captors dureing the winter. They began to treat me better after [a] while and tak[e] me out to hunt and to carry in the game for them. I could beat them hunting and they had a better opinion of me. They learnt I could beet them at anny thing [and] they wanted me to join their tribe, and [I] could speak their toung verry well. [I] now began to get used to their ways and learned them manny new things. Went hunting with [th]em. They gave me back my gun [that] they took from me when captured, but they kept a very close watch over me yet. I killed a brown bear that come verry near catching one of the braves and they thought I was a mighty brave. They treated me much better.

We had a feast of bear, horse, and dog meat. The spring had come. The grass was good and everry thing was nice. A friendly tribe, the Crows, a cheif and a few braves, come to smoke the pipe of peace. This time [we] had a big feast. Killed two of the Crows horses and some of our dogs and two large Elks. Made all ready. Put up a high pole in the center of the ring and hung war trophies and scalps on it. They were going to make me and four young bucks wariers. They slit our backs and breasts with knives and passed thongs through under the skin and tied old buffalow heads to us and tied each one to the center pole and [we were to] dance arround the pole until the skin tore loose. And the show commenced. The[y] were dressed in all the paint and feathers. [They] beat the drum and [played] a kind of fife, yelled and danced, and a perfect hell turned loose and other ceremonies going on at the same time.

The blood [was] streaming down our breasts and backs while we were dancing arround the pole. I knew it was going to be hard on me and began to look arround for something to cut loose with. Saw a flint arrow head close by and picked it up on the sly and when there was a chance, [I] would saw on the skin a little at a time. By and by one head dropt off. That encouraged me. I jumpt and yelled and ran against the pole and another dropt off. The wariers gave a hoop. The one on my back I thought would kill me and [I] gave the skin a scrape when no one was looking. Gave a hoop [and] ran against the pole. [Went] arround a few jumps more [and] tore loose and I was a brave. They put me in the sweat house to cure up. Two young bucks fainted and lay down. They were cut loose and were called squaw men. The other two tore loose on the square.

After we healed up, [we] had a war dance. Painted up to look [like] Devils and went [to] hunt the Blackfeet. They were our enemyes at this time. They had stole some horses that fall before from us and we were a going to get even on them. Went into their country and sneaked arround for a while and found them too strong for us. Stole five horses and come back without anny scalps. The tribe were disipointed because we brought no trophies of victory, but the horses suited them verry well.

In about two weeks warriers, squaws, dogs, and all went south on a buffalow hunt. We found some Crow Indians there and run them off. Killed all the buffalow we wanted and dried the meat and saved some of their skins. Went over to another place to fish. There was plenty of good [fish] in this river, but it is verry [dangerous, with] rappids, steep banks, and falls.

I was fishing and setting on a large rock. Was thinking about makeing my escape from the Indians, for I had not given up [watching for] a good chance to get away. Looking up the rappids of the stream, I saw some Indian girls picking berries that hung out over the stream. Heard a cry [and] looked again. The bush had broken and one fell in the watter. She had cau[gh]t hold of a stick of wood but the rappids drew her down over the falls and she disappeard beneath the foam. She rose shortly, holding on to the piece of wood. She went arround in the whirl pool. By this time I had come to her resque and threw her a long grape vine so she could reach it. When she come around to it, she cau[gh]t the vine and [I] pulled her out. She was so weak she could not stand for some time.

The other young squaws ran screaming to camp. She belonged to our cheif. He was her uncle, Sutek Sacote, or Lame Cougar in English. He told me to tak[e] her for she was mine for saveing her. And [I] did not care about takeing [her] at this time and concluded to wait a while. Her name in Indian was Sinute Kota, in English [she] was the Leaping Faun. This Indian girl would never leave me afterwards, [but] only for a short time, when she would return and sit by my side. When I went hunting she appeard lost. When I returned she would come to me and combe my hair with her long fingers. I could not help it. In time I could not do without her, for she had me. And I was gone on the Leaping Faun and I gave up trying to escape, for this was the best place after all.

122. A Crow Chief Fasts Until His People Return Pelts

from Robert Campbell, *A Narrative of Colonel Robert Campbell's Experiences in the Rocky Mountain Fur Trade from 1825 to 1830*

Because the next story is such a striking example of upright and noble conduct, it is a shame that it is not as well known as the many stories that emphasize violence and conflict between trappers and Indians. Exemplary morality was instilled in Native American children, as Claude Andrew Nichols explains in *Moral Education among the North American Indians* (1972).

(1829) I was then with Long Hair, principal chief of the Crows. They had brought in some scalps and were having great rejoicings. They held a great dance, in which the braves boasted of their exploits. Among other things they boasted of having found my cache. The old Chief then came into my lodge and said to me "Have you been catching beaver?" "Yes!" I answered.

"What did you do with it?" asked the chief.

"Put it in the ground," said I.

"Where is it?" he enquired.

I drew a plan of the g{r}ound, where my beaver had been cached.

The old chief then said, "You talk straight about it!"

He said for four years they had had no Whites trading among them and a War party found this place where the beaver was cached. "They opened it," said the chief, "and brought some along." They tell me they brought 150 skins. Now don't let your heart be sad. You are in my lodge and all these skins will be given back to you.

I'll neither eat, drink or sleep till you get all your skins. Now count them as they come in!

He then mounted his horse and harangued the village, saying to his people that he had been a long time without traders, and they must not keep one skin back.

Then the old squaws and old men would come and pitch the beaver skins into my lodge, until nearly all were returned.

The son-in-law of the chief, said to me, "Tell the old chief the skins were all in, and if any are missing, I'll give you the balance." I then told the old chief, the skins were all in, and the next day I invited two or three men into my lodge to satisfy him from their inspection, that the skins were all right; the old chief becoming satisfied, then broke his fast.

123. Nez Percé Virtues

from Washington Irving, *The Adventures of Captain Bonneville*

Of all those who wrote about the mountain men during the nineteenth century, Washington Irving was certainly the best known. He and the other writers included in this anthology are part of a western American literary tradition that flourishes to this day. An invaluable resource for anyone interested in this rich literature is *A Bibliographical Guide to the Study of Western American Literature* (1995), edited by Richard W. Etulain and N. Jill Howard.

Indeed, it would have been impossible to provide for the whole party in this neighborhood. It was at the extreme western limit of the buffalo range, and these animals had recently been completely hunted out of the neighborhood by the Nez Percés, so that, although the hunters of the garrison were continually on the alert, ranging the country round, they brought in scarce game sufficient to keep famine from the door. Now and then there was a scanty meal of fish or wild fowl, occasionally an antelope; but frequently the cravings of hunger had to be appeased with roots, or the flesh of wolves and muskrats. Rarely could the inmates of the cantonment boast of having made a full meal, and never of having wherewithal for the morrow. In this way they starved along until the 8th of October, when they were joined by a party of five families of Nez Percés, who in some measure reconciled them to the hardships of their situation, by exhibiting a lot still more destitute. A more forlorn set they had never encountered: they had not a morsel of meat or fish; nor any thing to subsist on, excepting roots, wild rosebuds, the barks of certain plants, and other vegetable productions; neither had they any weapon for hunting or defence, excepting an old spear: yet the poor fellows made no murmur nor complaint; but seemed accustomed to their hard fare. If they could not teach the white man their practical stoicism, they at least made them acquainted with the edible properties of roots and wild rosebuds, and furnished them a supply from their own store. The necessities of the camp at length became so urgent, that Captain Bonneville determined to despatch a party to the Horse Prairie, a plain to the north of his cantonment, to procure a supply of provisions. When the men were about to depart, he proposed to the Nez Percés that they, or some of them, should join the hunting party. To his surprise, they promptly declined. He inquired the reason for their refusal, seeing that they were in nearly as starving a situation as his own people. They replied that it was a sacred day with them, and the Great Spirit would be angry should they devote it to hunting. They offered, however, to accompany the party if it would delay its departure until the following day; but this the pinching demands of hunger would not permit, and the detachment proceeded.

A few days afterwards, four of them signified to Captain Bonneville that they were about to hunt. "What!" exclaimed he, "without guns or arrows; and with only one old spear? What do you expect to kill?" They smiled among themselves, but made no answer. Preparatory to the chase, they performed some religious rites, and offered up to the Great Spirit a few short prayers for safety and success; then, having received the blessings of their wives, they leaped upon their horses and departed, leaving the whole party of Christian spectators amazed and rebuked by this lesson of faith and dependance on a supreme and benevolent Being. "Accustomed," adds Captain Bonneville, "as I had heretofore been, to find the wretched Indian revelling in blood, and stained by every vice which can degrade human nature, I could scarcely realize the scene which I had witnessed. Wonder at such unaffected tenderness and piety, where it was least to have been sought, contended in all our bosoms with shame and confusion, at receiving such pure and wholesome instructions from creatures so far below us in all the arts and comforts of life." The simple prayers of the poor Indians were not unheard. In the course of four or five days they returned, laden with meat. Captain Bonneville was curious to know how they had attained such success with such scanty means. They gave him to understand that they had chased the herds of buffalo at full speed, until they tired them down, when they easily despatched them with the spear, and made use of the same weapon to flay the carcasses. To carry through their lesson to their Christian friends, the poor savages were as charitable as they had been pious, and generously shared with them the spoils of their hunting: giving them food enough to last for several days.

A further and more intimate intercourse with this tribe, gave Captain Bonneville still greater cause to admire their strong devotional feeling. "Simply to call these people religious," says he, "would convey but a faint idea of the deep hue of piety and devotion which pervades their whole conduct. Their honesty is immaculate, and their purity of purpose, and their observance of the rites of their religion, are most uniform and remarkable. They are, certainly, more like a nation of saints than a horde of savages."

Animals

In his "Account of the Discovery of the Buffalo, 1599 . . ." Vicente de Saldívar Mendoza describes an attempt by the Spaniards of New Mexico to domesticate buffalo. According to Saldívar Mendoza, the Spanish began by building a winged corral and then attempted to round up buffalo just as they would domestic cattle. The obstinate buffalo refused to behave like cattle and, as might be expected, the Spaniards' grandiose plans for acquiring animal wealth were soon trampled. Quite literally. What is clear from Saldívar Mendoza's account is that the Spaniards' idea of the proper relationship between humans and animals did not agree with any ideas the buffalo may have had.

Coming along more than two hundred years later, the mountain men had more realistic expectations about the West's wildlife. Unlike the early Spaniards, they did not believe that contact with "civilized" men would cause wildlife to become less wild. The mountain men did, however, carry with them the notion that animals were a source of wealth, a resource to be used just as minerals, timber, or any other resource is used. The skin of an animal was not the property of the animal attached to it. It was legal tender. Coin of the realm. Mountain money. For modern people, well fed on a diet of supermarket beef, nature films, and cartoon rabbits, the attitude of the mountain men toward animals may seem hardhearted. And, by modern standards, it is. But when your livelihood depends on catching a living creature with a steel trap that either drowns it or holds it fast until you come along to give it a belated bash to the head, you can't afford a soft heart. That would be economically incompatible with your profession.

The economic downside to the mountain man's hard heart was that it allowed him to trap the beaver to the brink of extinction, thereby insuring the extinction of the mountain-man way of life. But before feeling morally superior to the trappers who perpetrated such vast slaughter, we should look carefully at our own practices. As Gary Snyder says in *The Practice of the Wild* (1990), "the attitude toward animals, and their treatment, in twentieth-century American industrial meat production is literally sickening, unethical, and a source of boundless bad luck for this society" (21).

The mountain man's making a commodity of the beaver perhaps explains why the fur trade produced so little writing about the beaver as living creature. As the selections that follow suggest, when mountain men and their followers wrote about animals, they tended to write either about buffalo—the most spectacular and important food animal of the old West—or about wolves and bears—predatory animals that posed real or imaginary threats to trappers and their livestock.

124. A Rabid Wolf

from Frances Fuller Victor, *River of the West*

Mountain men could get liquor only at infrequent intervals, usually at the annual rendezvous. As Joe Meek confesses in the following sketch, some of them got "powerful drunk" when they had anything alcoholic on hand—drunk enough to become vulnerable to wild animals.

The rendezvous, at this time, furnished him a striking example of some of the ways of mountain-men, least to their honorable fame; and we fear we must confess that our friend Joe Meek, who had been gathering laurels as a valiant hunter and trapper during the three or four years of his apprenticeship, was also becoming fitted, by frequent practice, to graduate in some of the vices of camp life, especially the one of conviviality during rendezvous. Had he not given his permission, we should not perhaps have said what he says of himself, that he was at such times often very "powerful drunk."

During the indulgence of these excesses, while at this rendezvous, there occurred one of those incidents of wilderness life which make the blood creep with horror. Twelve of the men were bitten by a mad wolf, which hung about the camp for two or three nights. Two of these were seized with madness in camp, sometime afterwards, and ran off into the mountains, where they perished. One was attacked by the paroxysm while on a hunt; when, throwing himself off his horse, he struggled and foamed at the mouth, gnashing his teeth, and barking like a wolf. Yet he retained consciousness enough to warn away his companions, who hastened in search of assistance; but when they returned he was nowhere to be found. It was thought that he was seen a day or two afterwards, but no one could come up with him, and of course, he too, perished. Another died on his journey to St. Louis; and several died at different times within the next two years.

At the time, however, immediately following the visit of the wolf to camp, Captain Stuart was admonishing Meek on the folly of his ways, telling him that the wolf might easily have bitten him, he was so drunk.

"It would have killed him,—sure, if it hadn't *cured* him!" said Meek,—alluding to the belief that alcohol is a remedy for the poison of hydrophobia.

125. A Mad Wolf Bites Men and a Bull

from Charles Larpenteur, *Forty Years a Fur Trader on the Upper Missouri*

The "mad wolf" in the following selection almost certainly had rabies. For information about this terrible disease see George M. Baer's *The Natural History of Rabies* (1975).

A day or so later we learned that a mad wolf had got into Mr. Fontenelle's camp about five miles from us, and had bitten some of his men and horses. My messmates, who were old hands, had heard of the like before, when men had gone mad. It was very warm, toward the latter end of July; we were in the habit of sleeping in the open air, and never took the trouble to put up the tent, except in bad weather; but when evening came the boys set up the tent. Some of the other messes asked, "What is that for?" The reply was, "Oh, mad wolf come—he bite me." When the time came to retire the pack saddles were brought up to barricade the entrance of our tent, the only one up in camp, excepting that of the boss. After all hands had retired nothing was heard in the camp except, now and then, the cry of "All's well," and some loud snoring, till the sudden cry of, "Oh, I'm bitten!"—then immediately another, and another. Three of our men were bitten that night, all of them in the face. One poor fellow, by the name of George Holmes, was badly bitten on the right ear and face. All hands got up with their guns in pursuit of the animal, but he made his escape. When daylight came men were mounted to go in search, but nothing could be seen of him. It was then thought that he had gone and was not likely to return, and no further precaution was taken than the night before. But it seems that Mr. Wolf, who was thought far away, had hidden near camp; for about midnight the cry of "mad wolf" was heard again. This time the animal was among the cattle and bit our largest bull, which went mad afterward on the Bighorn, where we made the boats. The wolf could have been shot, but orders were not to shoot in camp, for fear of accidentally killing some one, and so Mr. Wolf again escaped.

126. A Grizzly Bear Punctures a Man's Eye

from Thomas James, *Three Years Among the Indians and Mexicans*

Here is another gory grizzly story. Naturalists maintain that grizzlies attacked most often when they had been provoked by being shot or shot at. For more information about these magnificent animals see Stephen Herrero, *Bear Attacks* (1985), and a collection edited by John A. Murray, *The Great Bear* (1992).

Soon after this time Marie and St. John, my two Canadian companions on the route from my winter quarters on the Missouri to the Big Horn, came to the fort at the Forks. Marie's right eye was out and he carried the yet fresh marks of a horrible wound on his head and under his jaw. After I had left them at the Big Horn to come to the Forks, they came on to the Twenty-five Yard River, the most western branch of the Yellowstone, for the purpose of trapping. One morning, after setting his traps, Marie strolled out into the prairie for game and soon perceived a large white bear rolling on the ground in the shade of a tree. Marie fired at and missed him. The bear snuffed around him without rising, and did not see the hunter until he had re-loaded, fired again, and wounded him. His Majesty instantly, with ears set back, flew towards his enemy like an arrow, who ran for his life, reached a beaver dam across the river, and seeing no escape by land, plunged into the water above the dam. The bear followed and soon proved himself as much superior to his adversary in swimming as in running. Marie dove and swam under the water as long as he could, when he rose to the surface near the bear. He saved himself by diving and swimming in this manner several times, but his enemy followed close upon him and watched his motions with the sagacity which distinguishes these animals. At last he came up from under the water directly beneath the jaws of the monster, which seized him by the head, the tushes piercing the scalp and neck under the right jaw and crushing the ball of his right eye. In this situation, with his head in the bear's mouth and he swimming with him ashore, St. John, having heard his two shots in quick succession, came running to his rescue. St. John levelled his rifle and shot the bear in the head, and then dragged out Marie from the water, more dead than alive. I saw him six days afterwards, with a swelling on his head an inch thick, and his food and drink gushed through the opening under his jaw made by the teeth of his terrible enemy.

127 and 128. The Hunting of Other Animals

The next two selections show that the fur trade included the hunting of animals other than beaver and buffalo. The sea otter, which like the beaver was hunted to the brink of extinction, ended up having an unforeseen impact on the fur trade. According to Richard White in his article "Animals and Enterprise" (1994), sea otter pelts were traded to China for silk, thus contributing to the rise of the silk hat over the beaver hat (247).

127. Sea Otter Hunting

from Job Francis Dye, *Recollections of a Pioneer, 1830–1852*

Now, I found myself in California, in a strange land, and among strangers speaking a different language, with only about $130 in my pocket. My purpose, in the first place for coming to the sea-coast of California, was to hunt and kill sea-otter, the skins of which were then worth from $25 to $45 each, in Los Angeles and in China, and $100 in the city of Mexico. On my arrival in Santa Barbara, I purchased a whale-boat and made a short trip up the coast, but had bad luck, only securing one otter-skin. I then fitted out again and went over to the Islands of San Miguel and Santa Rosa, where I spent about three months, under a license from Don Roberto Pardo, with the understanding that I was to furnish the boat while he procured the license which I could not have otherwise being a foreigner, and that the provisions and out-fit was to be supplied, mutually between us, each providing an equal share. The hunters were to have one-half of what they killed, as remuneration. When we commenced the enterprise, Don Roberto had no money, so I furnished the entire out-fit, and paid all expenses incurred. On my return, I had about twenty-four otter-skins which were worth $720, and the "Don" claimed one-half of the skins free of expense. To this unjust claim I would not agree, so he sued and brought me before his compadre, Don Anastacio Carrillo, where he got judgment for the skins that I had brought in. I became a little indignant, told them the decision was unjust, and the Judge might as well put his hand in my pocket and take out the money. Carrillo threatened to put me in jail if I said that again. I had to give Pardo one half the skins, and paid all the expenses of hiring and feeding my men. Thus in a moment, I lost five months time, all my valuable furs, the $130 I had advanced, and worst of all my license, which had been rescinded; all was gone. I dare not hunt without a license, and my boat was of no further use to me unless I hunted sea-otter, so I abandoned it and the business, and started up the coast toward San Luis Obispo.

128. A Carcagieu, or Wolverine

from George Frederick Ruxton, *Adventures in Mexico and the Rocky Mountains*

I had heard most wonderful accounts from the trappers of an animal, the existence of which was beyond all doubt, which, although exceedingly rare, was occasionally met with in the mountains, but, from its supposed dangerous ferocity, and the fact of its being a cross between the devil and a bear, was never molested by the Indians or white hunters, and a wide berth given whenever the animal made its dreaded appearance. Most wonderful stories were told of its audacity and fearlessness; how it sometimes jumps from an overhanging rock on a deer or buffalo, and, fastening on its neck, soon brings it to the ground;

how it has been known to leap upon a hunter when passing near its place of concealment, and devour him in a twinkling—often charging furiously into a camp, and playing all sorts of pranks on the goods and chattels of the mountaineers. The general belief was that the animal owes its paternity to the old gentleman himself; but the most reasonable declare it to be a cross between the bear and wolf.

Hunting one day with an old Canadian trapper, he told me that, in a part of the mountains which we were about to visit on the morrow, he once had a battle with a "carcagieu," which lasted upwards of two hours, during which he fired a pouchful of balls into the animal's body, which spat them out as fast as they were shot in. To the truth of this probable story he called all the saints to bear witness.

Two days after, as we were toiling up a steep ridge after a band of mountain-sheep, my companion, who was in advance, suddenly threw himself flat behind a rock, and exclaimed in a smothered tone, signalling me with his hand to keep down and conceal myself, "Sacré enfant de Gârce, mais here's von dam carcagieu!"

I immediately cocked my rifle, and, advancing to the rock, and peeping over it, saw an animal, about the size of a large badger, engaged in scraping up the earth about a dozen paces from where we were concealed. Its colour was dark, almost black; its body long, and apparently tailless; and I at once recognised the mysterious beast to be a "glutton." After I had sufficiently examined the animal, I raised my rifle to shoot, when a louder than common "Enfant de Gârce" from my companion alarmed the animal, and it immediately ran off, when I stood up and fired both barrels after it, but without effect; the attempt exciting a derisive laugh from the Canadian, who exclaimed, "Pe gar, may be you got fifty balls; vel, shoot 'em all at de dam carcagieu, and he not care a dam!"

The skins of these animals are considered "great medicine" by the Indians, and will fetch almost any price. They are very rarely met with on the plains, preferring the upland valleys and broken ground of the mountains, which afford them a better field for their method of securing game, which is by lying in wait behind a rock, or on the steep bank of a ravine, concealed by a tree or shrub, until a deer or antelope passes underneath, when they spring upon the animal's back, and, holding on with their strong and sharp claws, which they bury in the flesh, soon bring it bleeding to the ground. The Indians say they are purely carnivorous; but I imagine that, like the bear, they not unfrequently eat fruit and roots, when animal food is not to be had.

129. A Bullet Won't Penetrate a Buffalo Skull

from John Kirk Townsend, *Narrative of a Journey across the Rocky Mountains to the Columbia River*

Perhaps no one in the history of the West was more amazed than those fortunate Easterners who crossed the Mississippi and beheld huge herds of bison for the first time. Even mountain men who had been in the West for many years were still fascinated by buffalo, and this fascination sometimes prodded them to subject buffalo to experiments like the one John Kirk Townsend describes below. *Heads, Hides, and Horns* (1985) by Larry Barsness and *The Buffalo Book* (1974) by David Dary are good sources of buffalo facts and lore.

On the 20th, we moved our camp to a spot about twelve miles distant, where Richardson, with two other hunters, stopped yesterday and spent the night. They had killed several buffalo here, and were busily engaged in preparing the meat when we joined them. They gave us a meal of excellent cow's flesh, and I thought I never had eaten anything so delicious. Hitherto we have had only the bulls which are at this season poor and rather unsavory, but now we are feasting upon the *best food in the world*.

It is true we have nothing but meat and good cold water, but this is all we desire: we have excellent appetites, no dyspepsia, clear heads, sharp ears, and high spirits, and what more does a man require to make him happy?

We rise in the morning with the sun, stir up our fires, and *roast* our breakfast, eating usually from one to two pounds of meat at a morning meal. At ten o'clock we lunch, dine at two, sup at five, and lunch at eight, and during the night-watch commonly provide ourselves with two or three "hump-ribs" and a marrow bone, to furnish employment and keep the drowsy god at a distance.

Our present camp is a beautiful one. A rich and open plain of luxuriant grass, dotted with buffalo in all directions, a high picturesque hill in front, and a lovely stream of cold mountain water flowing at our feet. On the borders of this stream, as usual, is a dense belt of willows, and under the shade of these we sit and work by day, and sleep soundly at night. Our meat is now dried upon scaffolds constructed of old timber which we find in great abundance upon the neighboring hill. We keep a fire going constantly, and when the meat is sufficiently dried, it is piled on the ground, preparatory to being baled.

21st.—The buffalo appear even more numerous than when we came, and much less suspicious than common. The bulls frequently pass slowly along within a hundred yards of us, and toss their shaggy and frightful looking heads as though to warn us against attacking or approaching them.

Towards evening, to-day, I walked out with my gun, in the direction of one of these prowling monsters, and the ground in his vicinity being covered densely with bushes, I determined to approach as near him as possible, in order to try the efficacy of a ball planted directly in the centre of the forehead. I had heard of this experiment having been tried without success and I wished to ascertain the truth for myself.

"Taking the wind" of the animal, as it is called, (that is, keeping to leeward, so that my approach could not be perceived by communicating a taint to the air,) I crawled on my hands and knees with the utmost caution towards my victim. The unwieldy brute was quietly and unsuspiciously cropping the herbage, and I had arrived to within feet of him, when a sudden flashing of the eye, and an impatient motion, told me that I was observed. He raised his enormous head, and looked around him, and so truly terrible and grand did he appear, that I must confess, (in your ear,) I felt awed, almost frightened, at the task I had undertaken. But I had gone too far to retreat; so, raising my gun, I took deliberate aim at the bushy centre of the forehead, and fired. The monster shook his head, pawed up the earth with his hoofs, and making a sudden spring, accompanied by a terrific roar, turned to make his escape. At that instant, the ball from the second barrel penetrated his vitals, and he measured his huge length upon the ground. In a few seconds he was dead. Upon examining the head, and cutting away the enormous mass of matted hair and skin which enveloped the skull, my large bullet of twenty to the pound, was found completely flattened against the bone, having carried with it, through the interposing integument, a considerable portion of the coarse hair, but without producing the smallest fracture. I was satisfied; and taking the tongue, (the hunter's perquisite,) I returned to my companions.

This evening the roaring of the bulls in the *gang* near us is terrific, and these sounds are mingled with the howling of large packs of wolves, which regularly attend upon them, and the hoarse screaming of hundreds of ravens flying over head. The dreaded grizzly bear is also quite common in this neighborhood; two have just been seen in some bushes near, and they visit our camp almost every night, attracted by the piles of meat which are heaped all around us. The first intimation we have of his approach is a great *grunt* or *snort*, unlike any sound I ever heard, but much more querulous than fierce; then we hear the scraping and tramping of his huge feet, and the snuffing of his nostrils, as the savory scent of the meat is wafted to them. He approaches nearer and nearer, with a stealthy and fearful pace, but just as he is about to accomplish the object of his visit, he suddenly stops short; the snuffing is repeated at long and trembling intervals, and if the slightest motion is then made by one of the party, away goes "*Ephraim*," like a cowardly burglar as he is, and we hear no more of him that night.

130. Depletion of the Buffalo

from John James Audubon, *Audubon and His Journals*

Much of the West's wildlife began a precipitous decline under the impact of the fur trade. In the next selection, written in 1843, ornithologist John James Audubon assesses the buffalo's future. Paul R. Ehrlich's *Extinction: The Causes and Consequences of the Disappearance of Species* (1981) and Dan Flores's "Bison Ecology and Bison Diplomacy" (1991) help to explain why Audubon was correct to be concerned about the fate of the buffalo.

Provost tells me that Buffaloes become so very poor during hard winters, when the snows cover the ground to the depth of two or three feet, that they lose their hair, become covered with scabs, on which the Magpies feed, and the poor beasts die by hundreds. One can hardly conceive how it happens, notwithstanding these many deaths and the immense numbers that are murdered almost daily on these boundless wastes called prairies, besides the hosts that are drowned in the freshets, and the hundreds of young calves who die in early spring, so many are yet to be found. Daily we see so many that we hardly notice them more than the cattle in our pastures about our homes. But this cannot last; even now there is a perceptible difference in the size of the herds, and before many years the Buffalo, like the Great Auk, will have disappeared; surely this should not be permitted.

Missionaries

In 1833, four curious Nez Percé and Flathead Indians arrived in St. Louis, Missouri, to learn what they could of the Christian religion. The story of these Indians' quest set off a flurry of missionary activity among the churches of the eastern United States. Some of the first missionaries to travel west as a result of this activity were the Walkers, Eells, Whitmans, and Spaldings—Presbyterian missionary couples who would leave behind some of the best "outsider" accounts of the mountain men.

These missionaries, and others like them, used mountain-man rendezvous and fur-trading posts to rest and resupply on their long journeys to the Pacific Northwest. Missionaries traveled with mountain men when they could and hired them as guides when necessary. At times they preached to the mountain men and supplied them with Bibles, and some mountain men ended up as residents of the communities that grew up around the early missions.

This is not to say that the relationship between mountain men and missionaries was always a love fest. Though there were some highly religious mountain men (the most notable being Jedediah Smith), the nineteenth-century expression "No Sunday west of St. Louis" certainly applied to the Rocky Mountain fur trade. Wild and woolly trappers did not submit easily to the restraints of nineteenth-century religion—especially during the free-for-all of rendezvous, the time when trappers were most likely to come in contact with missionaries. On the other hand, missionaries considered themselves the spiritual guardians of the Indians and, as such, had good reason to think little of trappers who debased the natives with alcohol and other unholy enticements.

The conflicts between mountain men and missionaries are reflected in many of the selections that follow. And while it is easy to criticize missionaries as impractical idealists who made tremendous blunders in their dealings with both mountain men and Indians, it is important to remember what Cathy Luchetti says in *Under God's Spell: Frontier Evangelists 1772–1915* (1989):

> Whatever their talents, whatever their trades, the western-bound evangelists differed from those who stayed behind by the specific lineament of what Catholics termed vocation and Protestants named "The call." For both, it was a lifelong commitment to forgo financial gain, worldly comfort, and even respect, often along with church protection and family ties, to further the social good of mankind and fulfill an inward duty that was, to the evangelist, clearly mandated from above. (3)

For more information on western missionaries as well as a good selection of accounts written by them, Luchetti's *Under God's Spell* is an excellent starting point.

131. Some Mountain Men's View of Missionaries

from W. H. Gray, *A History of Oregon*

The welcome extended by mountain men to missionaries was not always uncritical, as W. H. Gray (not himself a missionary, but one of their party) tells us in the next selection. For a history of the Whitman party see Clifford Merrill Drury, *Marcus and Narcissa Whitman, and the Opening of Old Oregon* (1973).

Doctor Marcus Whitman, they considered, on the whole, was a good sort of a fellow; he was not so hide-bound but what he could talk with a common man and get along easily if his wife did not succeed in "*stiffening*," starching him up; he would do first-rate, though there appeared considerable doubt in their minds, whether, from her stern, commanding manner, she would not eventually succeed in stiffening up the Doctor so that he would be less agreeable. Mrs. Whitman, they thought, was a woman of too much education and refinement to be thrown away on the Indians. "She must have had considerable romance in her disposition to have undertaken such an expedition with such a common, kind, good-hearted fellow as the Doctor. As to Spalding, he is so green he will do to spread out on a frog-pond; he may do to preach to Indians, but mountain men would have to be fly-blown before he could come near them. Mrs. Spalding is a first-rate woman; she has not got any starch in her; it is strange she ever picked up such a greenhorn as she has for a husband; she will do first-rate to teach the Indians, or anybody else; she has got good common sense, and doesn't put on any frills. As to Gray, he is young yet, is not quite so green as Spalding; he seems inclined to learn a little; by the time he goes to the Columbia River and travels about more, he will know a good deal more than he does now. He may do well in his department if he 'keeps his eye skinned.'"

I suppose by this expression was meant a sharp look out for

swindlers, rogues, and thieves, to see that they do not lie, cheat, and steal, every opportunity they may have, or at least that you do not allow them to take your property under false pretenses. Be that as it may, the general conclusion was, that, as this mission party had succeeded in getting thus far on their journey, they might get still further, and perhaps (most were certain) make a failure, either by being sent out of the country by the Hudson's Bay Company, or destroyed by the Indians. Good wishes and hopes that they might succeed were abundant from all, as was plainly expressed, and a disposition, in case the mission succeeded in establishing themselves, to find their way down into the Columbia River Valley with their native families, and become settlers about the mission stations. Lightly as these frank, open expressions of good wishes and future ideas of the mountain hunter may appear, the missionaries saw at once there was the germ of a future people to be gathered in the Columbia River Valley, probably of a mixed race.

132. Bibles for Trappers

from Narcissa Whitman, "The Coming of the White Women"

Missionary couples worked to bring civilization, as they saw it, to the wilderness. Narcissa Whitman (1808–1847) writes about such work in the following passage.

This is a cause worth living for—Wherever we go we find oppertunities of doing good—If we had packed one or two animals with bibles & testaments we should have had abundant oppertunity of disposing of them to the traders & trappers of the mountain who would have received them greatfully Many have come to us for tracts & bibles which we could not supply. We have given away all we have to spare. When they return from hunting they have leisure for reflection and reading if they have the means, which might result in the salvation of their souls. A missionary might do good in this field one who would be willing to come & live as they do

133. Jim Bridger's Party Salutes a Missionary

from Sarah Gilbert White Smith, "Diary of Sarah White Smith"

Like those mountain men who had a working conscience, missionary women disapproved of some of what they saw in the Rocky Mountains. Here, Sarah Smith (1813–1855) disapproves of a reported attack led by Jim Bridger. Unfortunately, Sarah Smith's account is not the only narrative that describes appalling attacks involving mountain men. Smith's diary is part of a large body of Western American literature that is the subject of Kathleen Boardman's "Paper Trail: Diaries, Letters, and Reminiscences of the Overland Journey West."

5th. Thurs. Mr. S. & myself have taken a pleasure ride this morning of some miles, breakfasted at 10. Received a salute from some of Bridger's party who have just arrived. This company consists of about 100 men & perhaps 60 Indian females & a great number of half breed children. Their arrival was attended with firing of guns & noisy shouts. Thought perhaps that we would be interested, therefore came & saluted us with firing, drumming, singing & dancing. Their appearance was rude & savage, were painted in a most hideous manner. One carried a scalp of the Black Foot in his hand. It is dreadful to hear how the whites treat the Indians. Bridger's party have just been among the Black Foot tribe. This tribe have long been a terror to neighboring tribes & to the whites, but now their number is much reduced by the smallpox & it is still raging. The Indians made no attack on B's party but this party attacked them & shot 15 of them dead without excuse but to please their wicked passions. Thus sending 15 souls to eternity & to the bar of God unprepared. A man told me of it who had a part in the horrid scene. Said that one they shot and wounded but not killed. Said that this Indian grasped the limb of a white man who stood near & made signs begging that his life might be spared while others dragged him away & cut his body in pieces regardless of his groans & entreaties. This fellow seemed to exult in it.

134. Joe Meek Preaches and Gets a New Wife

from Frances Fuller Victor, *River of the West*

The Mr. and Mrs. Spalding mentioned in the following account are the missionaries Henry Harmon Spalding (1803–1874) and Eliza Hart Spalding (1807–1851). Among other achievements, the Spaldings used the first printing press in the West to publish a Nez Percé grammar and other Nez Percé texts. Full accounts of the Spaldings and their press can be found in Clifford Merrill Drury, *Henry Harmon Spalding* (1936); and Wilfred P. Schoenberg, *The Lapwai Mission Press* (1994).

Here again Meek parted company with the main camp, and went on an expedition with seven other trappers, under John Larison, to the Salmon River: but found the cold very severe on this journey, and the grass scarce and poor, so that the company lost most of their horses.

On arriving at the Nez Perce village in the Forks of the Salmon, Meek found the old chief *Kow-e-so-te* full of the story of the missionaries and their religion, and anxious to hear preaching. Reports were continually arriving by the Indians, of the wonderful things which were being taught by Mr. and Mrs. Spalding at Lapwai, on the Clearwater, and at Waiilatpu, on the Walla-Walla River. It was now nearly two years since these missions had been founded, and the number of converts among the Nez Perces and Flatheads was already considerable.

Here was an opening for a theological student, such as Joe Meek was! After some little assumption of modesty, Meek intimated that he thought himself capable of giving instruction on religious subjects; and being pressed by the chief, finally consented to preach to *Kow-e-so-te*'s people. Taking care first to hold a private council with his associates, and binding them not to betray him, Meek preached his first sermon that evening, going regularly through with the ordinary services of a "meeting."

These services were repeated whenever the Indians seemed to desire it, until Christmas. Then, the village being about to start upon a hunt, the preacher took occasion to intimate to the chief that a wife would be an agreeable present. To this, however, *Kow-e-so-te* demurred, saying that Spalding's religion did not permit men to have two wives: that the Nez Perces had many of them given up their wives on this account; and that therefore, since Meek already had one wife among the Nez Perces, he could not have another without being false to the religion he professed.

To this perfectly clear argument Meek replied, that among white men, if a man's wife left him without his consent, as his had done, he could procure a divorce, and take another wife. Besides, he could tell him how the Bible related many stories of its best men having several wives. But *Kow-e-so-te* was not easily convinced. He could not see how, if the Bible approved of polygamy, Spalding should insist on the Indians putting away all but one of their wives. "However," says Meek, "after about two weeks' explanation of the doings of Solomon and David, I succeeded in getting the chief to give me a young girl, whom I called Virginia;—my present wife, and the mother of seven children."

135. Reverend Parker's Hypocrisy

from Frances Fuller Victor, *River of the West*

In an earlier selection, the Rev. Samuel Parker (1779–1855) expressed his views of Kit Carson and mountain men in general. In the next selection, Joe Meek tells what the mountain men thought of the Rev. Mr. Parker.

The Rev. Samuel Parker preached, and the men were as politely attentive as it was in their reckless natures to be, until, in the midst of the discourse, a band of buffalo appeared in the valley, when the congregation incontinently broke up, without staying for a benediction, and every man made haste after his horse, gun, and rope, leaving Mr. Parker to discourse on vacant ground.

The run was both exciting and successful. About twenty fine buffaloes were killed, and the choice pieces brought to camp, cooked and eaten, amidst the merriment, mixed with something coarser, of the hunters. On this noisy rejoicing, Mr. Parker looked with a sober aspect:

and following the dictates of his religious feeling, he rebuked the sabbath-breakers quite severely. Better for his influence among the men, if he had not done so, or had not eaten so heartily of the tender-loin afterwards, a circumstance which his irreverent critics did not fail to remark, to his prejudice; and upon the principle that the "partaker is as bad as the thief," they set down his lecture on sabbath-breaking as nothing better than pious humbug.

Dr. Marcus Whitman was another style of man. Whatever he thought of the wild ways of the mountain-men he discretely kept to himself, preferring to teach by example rather than precept; and showing no fastidious contempt for any sort of rough duty he might be called upon to perform. So aptly indeed had he turned his hand to all manner of camp service on the journey to the mountains, that this abrogation of clerical dignity had become a source of solicitude, not to say disapproval and displeasure on the part of his colleague; and it was agreed between them that the Doctor should return to the states with the St. Louis Company, to procure recruits for the promising field of labor which they saw before them, while Mr. Parker continued his journey to the Columbia to decide upon the location of the missionary stations. The difference of character of the two men was clearly illustrated by the results of this understanding. Parker went to Vancouver, where he was hospitably entertained, and where he could inquire into the workings of the missionary system as pursued by the Methodist missionaries. His investigations not proving the labor to his taste, he sailed the following summer for the Sandwhich Islands, and thence to New York; leaving only a brief note for Doctor Whitman, when he, with indefatigable exertions, arrived that season among the Nez Perces with a missionary company, eager for the work which they hoped to make as great as they believed it to be good.

136. "One of the Most Beautiful Prospects"

from Sarah Gilbert White Smith, "Diary of Sarah White Smith"

Although in an earlier selection included in this book missionary Sarah Smith didn't have anything good to say about bloodthirsty mountain men, the following entries from her diary show that she appreciated the natural beauty of the mountain West. One of the categories of nature writing is that which describes travel and adventure, and Sarah Smith's diary entries are a nascent form of that subgenre. For more information about, and examples of, this literary genre see Thomas J. Lyon's anthology *This Incomperable Lande* (1989).

4th. Mon. Yesterday we witnessed one of the most beautiful prospects I ever saw & some truly grand. We followed around among the bluffs. Saw their ragged sides & the deep indentations made by falling water. Passed among beautiful groves of pine trees, foliage of the deepest green. We crossed some beds of sand, where some beautiful river had once flowed & where now is only left a rill to tell us what has been. Passed some delightful plains studded with beautiful pines & some lofty bluffs whose towering tops & ragged sides presented an appearance of grandeur rather than beauty. Today the scene has been indeed grand. Our course has been more mountainous than yesterday. Have rode where it was so steep I was obliged to hold to my saddle lest I should fall over my horses head and again ascended where I must hold by her mane to keep from slipping off backward but I enjoyed it much. Of course we went where the waggons could not. Travelled 25 miles, 10½ hours.

June 5th. Tuesday. Travelled today about 15 miles over mountains & ravines. The scenery grand. Many of the bluffs appeared to be composed of red sandstone. The hills which we see on every side of us are I think rightly named Black Hills for they indeed present a very dark appearance, most of them being covered with pines of a heavy green.

6th. Wed. Move at 4 this morning as usual. Took breakfast of buffalo & again commenced travelling. Our leader told us if we would leave the company and follow him, he would lead us 4 miles, where the wagons would go to. So Mr. & Mrs. Eells, Mr. S. & myself with the pack animals concluded to follow him. He took us over awful places, mountains & deep ravines where in many places we dare not ride the horses, & then he did not know where the company would camp for noon but guessed at it & the company did not come there but so near that we could see them. We had a fine time, had all the food with us. Cooked our dinner & ate it alone. Then started to meet the company. Came to them about 2. Soon left them again, witnessed some most romantic scenery. Crossed deep ravines, rode along the side of one high bluff that overhung the water. Encamped about 4 on the Platte. Travelled at least 20 miles, 9½ hours.

SECTION XI

Fur Trappers in Fiction

Including a section entitled "Fur Trappers in Fiction" does not, by any means, indicate that everything else in this book should be taken as fact. We are well aware, for example, that the visit to Hell described in Section I is not supported by the historical record. Nor by the theological record, either. What we have included in this section are examples of early, overt attempts to fictionalize the mountain-man experience. The reason we point this out is that many students of the West who focus on the *facts* of western history tend to have an underdeveloped awareness of how fiction sometimes assumes the status of fact and of how facts sometimes become embroidered into fiction. For the logical, clearheaded Westerner, Fact is Fact, Fiction is Fiction, and never the twain shall meet. What is missed in this equation, however, is the all-too-common truth that what we often accept as unvarnished fact has been well lacquered with fiction—some of it highly ideological.

For example, in his article "The Art of the Mountain Man Novel," David Stouck has noted that the earliest novels about mountain men, including Timothy Flint's *The Shoshonee Valley* (1830) and David Coyner's *The Lost Trappers* (1847), tend to portray mountain men "as essentially crude, lawless men concerned only with satisfying their most basic instincts" (211). While this view of the mountain man may have been fashionable in its day (and may have become once again fashionable in the present day), it is far from being fact—as we hope at least *some* of the selections in this anthology show. David Stouck also points out, in the same article, how novels of the mountain man soon changed direction to portray mountain men as what we today might call super heroes—almost infallible knights of the wilderness who represent all that is good. Again, this is an ideological view of the mountain man that is as far from the truth as are the earlier (and later) attempts to portray him as a barbarian.

Such fictionalizations are, in the case of the mountain men, readily confused with fact because the mountain-man novel is so closely tuned to historical events. Real mountain men such as Kit Carson, Jim Bridger, and John Colter frequently turn up as characters in mountain-man fiction. Similarly, real incidents, such as Hugh Glass's encounter with the bear, are woven into the plots of novels and stories. When the historical emphasis of the mountain-man novel is coupled with the tendency of "factual" mountain-men accounts to include invented tales as part of their fabric, it is no wonder that separating fact from fiction becomes so complicated.

Those interested in understanding the fictionalization of fact in the mountain-man novel should consult the two chapters in *A Literary History of the American West,* edited by J. Golden Taylor, et al. (1987), that survey the "true-life" narratives of the era and the early forms of the Western American novel; the first chapter is J. Golden Taylor's "Across the Wide Missouri: The Adventure Narrative from Lewis and Clark to Powell"; the second is James K. Folsom's "Precursors of the Western Novel."

The selections that follow are all from nineteenth-century mountain-man novels. Some of the selections were written by authors with considerable first-hand experience of the mountain men. Some were not. We have not included selections from any twentieth-century mountain-man novels, but these novels are listed in the bibliography.

137. Zeke Williams Uses an Axe to Drive a Grizzly Bear from His Canoe

from David H. Coyner, *The Lost Trappers*

Mountain-man life quickly attracted the attention of novelists watchful for fascinating subjects. David H. Coyner (1807–1892) was one such novelist, loosely basing his *The Lost Trappers* (1847) on the life of trapper Ezekiel Williams, who flourished in the mountains from 1807 to 1827. Obscure wordsmiths like Coyner were not the only authors to attempt mountain-man novels; Edgar Allan Poe, after reviewing a number of books about the fur trade, tried his hand at a fictional account, unfortunately one he never finished.

Captain Williams never used his rifle to procure meat, except when it was absolutely necessary, and when it could be done with perfect safety. On one occasion, when he had no beaver flesh, upon which he generally subsisted, he killed a deer, and after refreshing an empty stomach with a portion of it, he placed the carcass, which he had cut up, in one end of his canoe. As it was his invariable custom to sleep in his canoe, the night after he had laid in a supply of venison he was startled in his sleep by the trampling of something in the bushes on the bank. Tramp, tramp, tramp went the footstep, as it approached the canoe. Captain Williams first thought it might be an Indian that had found out his locality, but an Indian would not approach him in that careless manner. Although there was a beautiful star-light, yet the shade of the trees and a dense undergrowth, made it very dark on the bank of the river. Captain Williams always adopted the precaution of tieing his canoe to shore with a piece of raw hide about twenty feet long, which let it swing from the bank about that distance. This precaution he adopted at night, that in an emergency he might cut the cord that bound him to the shore, and glide off without any noise. During the day he hid his canoe in the willows. As the sound of the footsteps grew more and more distinct, the captain observed a huge grizzly bear approach the edge of the water and hold up its head as if scenting something. He then let his huge body into the water and made for the canoe. Captain Williams snatched up his axe as the most suitable means of defending himself in such a scrape, and stood with it uplifted and ready to drive it into the head of the huge aggressor. The bear reached the canoe, and immediately placed his fore paws upon the hind end of it, and nearly turned it over. Captain Williams struck one of his feet with the edge of the axe, which caused him to relax his hold with that foot. He, however, held on with the other foot, and Captain Williams inflicted another blow upon his head, which caused him to let the canoe go entirely.

138. Kit Carson Goes to the Rescue!

from Charles E. Averill, *Kit Carson, The Prince of the Gold Hunters*

An earlier selection in this anthology describes how Kit Carson found, among the effects of a woman he had failed to rescue, a dime novel in which he figured as the hero. In *Virgin Land* (1950), Henry Nash Smith says the novel that Carson found was probably "a thriller called *Kit Carson, The Prince of the Gold Hunters* [1849], by one Charles Averill" (94). No one can be absolutely sure which dime novel it was because, as Daryl Jones says in *The Dime Novel Western* (1978): "From the early 1860s through the 1890s Carson appeared in more than seventy original tales and reprints written by a host of dime novelists" (58). A chapter from Averill's book follows. The melodramatic style and improbable action Averill employs are completely typical of the dime-novel tradition. For more on the role of Kit Carson as dime-novel hero see "Frémont and Carson: Heyward and Hawkeye in California" in Richard Slotkin's *The Fatal Environment* (1985).

Another Thrilling Prairie Adventure—The Indians—The Pursuit—Kit Carson, the Prince of the Gold Hunters—The Stratagem of the Savages.

"But who that chief? his name on every shore
Is famed and feared—they ask and know no more." BYRON.

Entirely unconscious our unfortunate friend Lincoln remained, for how long a time he knew not, neither do we know; and but for a single, unlooked for incident, it is more than probable he would have awaited, in the hopeless inanition of despair, for death to come to his relief, and thus spare him the horrors of an existence dragged out in all the tortures of slow starvation.

Providence, whose ways are ever inscrutable, is said to interpose oftenest when hope has given place to utter despondency; and yet, in the present instance, that interposition—if interposition of Providence it was, came in a strange shape certainly.

What first aroused the despairing and hopeless man to outward objects once more, was the confused sound of discordant voices, intermingled in a strange chorus of cries and yells, and the hurried trampling of many feet around.

Suddenly opening his eyes to the light and blinded by it as he staggered to his feet, it was fully a moment before he could see any surrounding objects clearly. But, ere he did so, a yell, so wild, so shrill, so deafening that it almost stunned him, broke suddenly on his astonished ears.

Dashing his hands instinctively across his eyes to dispel the mist that hung before them, the sight that his vision the next instant took in, caused him to recoil, with a bound, from the spot.

Around, on every side, he beheld himself encircled by a troop of wild figures, in fantastic and savage costumes, who were dancing about him and gesticulating with every sign of ferocious delight. It was by a war tribe of Indians that he was surrounded; and the dreadful yell that he had just heard, was the thrilling war whoop of the American Aborigines.

It was uttered just as he tottered to his feet—for the Indians, it seemed, from his former motionless and prostrate position, had supposed him dead. Convinced by his sudden rise, of their mistake, they closed up with fresh shouts around him, completely hemming him in!

He had seen but few of the red race, and these only the friendly tribes through whose territory he had passed on the Missouri frontier; but he had read much of the aboriginal character and habits, and he knew at once, from their fantastic dress and painted faces, that he had, unfortunately, fallen in with a war-party.

He saw that it was with a savage tribe, unfriendly to the whites, he had now to deal; and was aware that he must expect the worst. His capture, he believed, would be but the precursor of his death; and with this peril came back the love of existence, the desire of life.

One quick, flashing glance he sent around him; his heart sunk within him as that look took in the score of savage forms, with their deadly weapons and war-paint, encompassing him as in a net. Escape, it was evident to him was impossible; but he felt convinced his life might be for the present safe, that he would only be reserved for his final doom, and that by tortures the most fearful.

He determined, therefore, since to elude them was hopeless, to force them to take his life at once, and thus by a sudden and speedy death, avoid the tortures which otherwise would be in store for him.

Thus desperately resolving, just as an aged chief advanced, with signs of amity, from the throng, he waited only until the Indian was within a few feet of him, then, springing suddenly upon him, he snatched the tomahawk from his belt, and dashing swiftly past the surprised old man, cut his way, in a single instant, through the startled savages, who immediately gave way before the whirling hatchet, which took them completely unawares.

The living wall was broken as if by magic and Lincoln darted beyond the group that surrounded him, and fled with a fleet foot down the course of the river which he had mistaken for the Sacramento.

The flying man looked behind him; and a score of sinewy forms were in pursuit, and a score of barbed arrows were drawn to the head. Internally he blessed Heaven for it—it was the death he sought.

But the same Heaven willed it otherwise. The voice of the old chief, who had been so daringly despoiled of his tomahawk, was now heard calling, in a peremptory tone to his party.

He spoke in the Indian tongue, words incomprehensible to Lincoln; but the latter conjectured their meaning, when a second backward glance shewed him that each upraised tomahawk and pointed arrow were lowered, though still every one of the pursuers kept on upon his track—their object was to take him alive.

He knew it, he saw it—and in the same breath determined that it should not be. On, on, along the river's margin he fled—on, still on, until he should come to a convenient spot for the execution of his purpose; while onward, likewise onward, yet faster, and each moment gaining on him, came the yelling Indians.

He saw that he was losing ground and soon must be overtaken. Suddenly he paused—halted—turned on the river side; his pursuers uttered a simultaneous shout of triumph; they believed he was about to surrender—they were deceived.

One bold, headlong plunge, one reckless leap from the brink of the stream, and the pursued dived beneath the water, and ten feet from the spot, reappeared upon the surface.

The reader will have anticipated, already, his purpose. It was to swim the river as long as exhausted nature would allow, and then perish by drowning rather than fall into their hands!

One after another, full a dozen of the Indians plunged into the stream after the fugitive. They were accustomed to the element and swam like ducks, in comparison with the latter, who was impeded by his heavy clothes and though a skillful swimmer, made but indifferent progress.

Still, he had greatly the start of them, and having succeeded, by a dexterous manœuvre in freeing himself of his cumbrous boots, he held his way steadily for no inconsiderable distance. Nevertheless, he swam under fearful disadvantages, and the most active of his pursuers was coming, at every stroke, closer upon him.

He redoubled his exertions, he strained every nerve; the foremost savage was within his length of him—could almost touch him. Completely exhausted, incapable of further exertion, the hunted swimmer threw up his arms, gave one last look to Heaven, and then sunk beneath the surface, just as the foremost savage reached his hand to seize him.

The waves of the river, the forest around, echoed to the sharp crack of a rifle, and the foremost pursuer rolled a corpse upon his back.

Ere the death-yell of the slain Indian had been borne on the breath of the wind past the savages in his rear, there was a deep-voiced hurrah from the opposite bank, and then a sudden splash, as the form of a man plunged head foremost into the river, and swam under water to the scene of the blood crimsoned waters, escaping by this means the shower of arrows that darkened the air, discharged at him from the shore on which the larger portion of the savages had remained; but who, on the death of the foremost of the pursuing swimmers, with yells of vengeance also took the water, to the aid of their comrades, the old chief following last.

The next moment the man whose shot had been the Indian's death warrant, was visible for an instant at the surface, as he rose for air, with the exhausted form of the half-drowned Lincoln in his arms, and then boldly and stoutly, with his burden skillfully sustained, struck out for the neighboring shore—reached it, and laid the fellow-being he had saved on the sod.

Gasping, in partial strangulation, for a moment or two, the poor youth was scarce conscious until he felt its restorative properties, that a draught of brandy had been poured, by the same friendly hand, down his throat; the invigorating effect, however, was immediate, and by a strong effort he rose staggering to his feet, still struggling for air and breath to ejaculate, brokenly,—

"Who—who are you, kind sir? God—God bless you! You—you have saved my life."

He had but time to see that his gallant preserver was a man of powerful proportions and Herculean stature, dressed in the rude deer skin suit of a western hunter, when a grasp of the arm from his Heaven-sent friend called his attension to the river and the foe, from death by both of which he had been so marvellously reprieved.

He heard, too, the voice of the hunter, in a clear, full tone, with his frontiersman's accent,—

"See, stranger; there the red devils come. Take another pull at the liquor, and keep a keen eye ahead—you'll need both soon. The critters are after us, there's no mistake. Hold my powder horn for me, stranger, while I jest pick off a couple of these infarnal varmints, with *Old Sacramento!*"

And as, in this easy, unconcerned way, he spoke, true to his word, he levelled his rifle at one of the advancing savages, now nearly abreast in the midle of the river, and rapidly making for the shore where stood the hunter; who, marking his victim, with unerring aim, fired.

The next instant was the savage's last, and the waters of the peaceful river were crimsoned with the life-blood of a second red man. The rifle of the stout hunter was double barrelled, and immediately turning the muzzle on a third foe, he discharged the remaining bullet with the same deadly effect of their predecessors.

The Indians, yelling like so many demons, infuriated at the death of their three ill-fated comrades, eager to avenge their doom, strained every sinew to reach the bank, but the river was wide, the hunter's eye was quick, and his bullet ever true.

Loading and reloading, again and again, with the wonderful celerity of long experience one after another, he picked off seven more of the howling savages, coolly reserving his fire, in each instance, until the breast of the intended victim was, at every other moment raised, in the act of respiration, above the surface, when, strait to the exposed mark, ere again it was submerged, in making the forward stroke, the eagle eye and sure hand sent the lead quivering home.

The skill, the cool courage, the inflexible resolution of the strange hunter, filled the excited Lincoln with admiration and surprise. He could scarce believe his senses as he beheld, one by one, the numbers of the savages thinned so rapidly, and heard the mournful lamentations of the survivors over their fallen braves, and then the well-nigh superhuman howls of hate and vengeance that followed as they struggled yet more desperately to gain the shore, which the nearest had now nearly reached.

"Hark'ye, stranger," cried the deep voice of the hunter, hurried, "in a minute more we shall have the pesky redskins on us.—The born devils swim like sea otters—their turn is coming now—and what's more, they know it."

"Ha!" cried Lincoln, "is there no way of escape?"

But ere there was time for an answer the most brief, a tomahawk was seen whizzing through the air, as the first Indian gained the dry land, passing, with fearful rapidity close to the head of the hunter, who had coolly bent his neck as he marked the enemy's purpose and saw the murderous missile flashing in the sunlight, suffering it pass by, where, but for the sudden movement it would have brained him.

"Quick! Quick! look to your pistols, sir," shouted the intended victim of the iron messenger, as he dropped his purposed murderer dead on the bank, up which the Indians were scrambling.

"Quick," he added, "and I hope your pistols will stand you in as good stead as Old Sacramento here."

And clubbing his good rifle as he spoke, he swung it with gigantic force twice round his head, and then, with a wide sweep of the ponderous butt to and fro right in their midst, he scattered the savages, stunned and bleeding, like chaff, before his iron arm.

The Indians gave back a moment in confusion, evidently astonished at the extraordinary bravery and strength their powerful antagonist had displayed. This momentary wavering was an advantage which the hunter did not fail to improve.

"Back, back, for your life! Get behind the trees," rang in Lincoln's ear, while he felt himself drawn backward.

Yielding to the impulse, he at the same instant lifted his heavy horse pistol, levelled it in the direction of the savages, and, as he found himself dragged behind the shelter of a great oak, saw an Indian bound into the air, then bite the dust.

The latter paused, as if in deliberation; the voice of the aged chief, who had been the last to gain the spot, was heard among them; and hunter and traveller, from their temporary shelter, could observe the savages in loud vociferation.

The hunter's grasp tightened on Lincoln's arm,—

"They're taking counsel, stranger, what's best to be done. Hark! I know their onnat'ral tongue. They want to tomahawk us on the spot—but the old chief says no—we must be taken alive. I suspicions why, stranger—but keep close—we may see our way out o' this yet."

"My noble fellow, why, in the first place, peril your life to save mine?"

The other looked at him almost indignantly as he said,—

"What! d'ye think I'd see a man murdered by a legion o' red skins, and not move a hand or foot to help him? No, no, stranger, not while my name's————humph!" and he instantly checked himself. "I mus-tn't let them red devils hear that—they'd skin me alive, if they only guessed it, I reckon. I've seen a much worse strait than this, many a time in my life; all I care for is Ed'ard—if he's safe it's little I————"

"Carson—Carson! for God's sake beware! Treachery!" shouted a voice that caused both to turn, as if at a serpent's sting, their startled looks behind.

Directly in the hunter's rear, not six feet from his back, creeping stealthily along thro' the thin brushwood upon his hands and knees, a gaunt Indian met the eye that was turned too suddenly upon him to allow a change of posture ere he was perceived.

But the keen glance of the hunter, only an instant resting on him, seemed to be anxiously seeking out some second object in the back-ground, behind the crouching savage; and the moment was seized upon by the latter, with the alertness of his race, to spring from his crawling attitude, at one long bound, on the apparently unguarded man, with hunting knife upraised.

The very instant that it flashed in the broad light above that mas-sive chest the report of a gun-shot echoed along the reverberating at-mosphere, and as the treacherous assailant fell a dead man at the hunter's feet, with the assassin's knife still grasped in his hand, the light form of a youth, with a Spanish carbine in his hand, leaped across the lifeless body and threw himself upon the neck of the frontiersman, exclaiming—

"Thank God! my friend, my noble benefactor, I was in time to save your precious life."

"Ha! it was you, then, Edward?—the voice was your own?" ejacu-lated the hunter, as he returned, with more than manly fervor, the embrace of the youth. "I am sorry, very sorry, boy, that you have exposed yourself to hazard, by coming hither at this time. I was thank-ing my stars a moment ago, boy, that you were not by my side when I fell in with those yelling red-skins yonder—that you, at all events, were out of harm's way—and the first thing I know, here you are."

"But you were in danger, dear Carson!—how could I stay?" urged the boy, earnestly. "True, you left me at our camp a quarter of a mile distant, to find a deer for our supper; but I heard the repeated firing, and I thought something must have happened to you. I knew the Pawnees were prowling around; and if the hunters had not been all gone from the camp in search of the Indians, I should have brought them along; I could not, would not stay—luckily the fire guided me hither in season to slay your enemy. O my God!—O my God! it is the first human blood on my hands!"

And the young boy, with a tremulous voice and a shuddering of the frame, turned away his head, and leaned it on the shoulder of the hunter, who was seen by Eugene to dash a manly tear from his eye, as though ashamed of the emotion, while he ejaculated in a moved tone,—

"Bless you, my boy, bless you!"

139 and 140. Mountain-Man Names on the Land

Far less melodramatic, though more moving, are the following fictional accounts, both of which deal with the very real practice of naming geographical features after comrades. For more about mountain-man naming see George R. Stewart, *Names on the Land* (1958).

139. Black George's Account of Jim Cotton's Demise

from Emerson Bennett, *The Prairie Flower*

"Yes, but everything beautiful hereabouts gits sp'ilt to them as knows it a few," chimed in the old hunter, blowing the smoke deliberately from his mouth. "Now, I've no doubt this here place looks purty to you, but I've seen blood run hereaways—augh!"

"Indeed," I exclaimed, advancing to the old trapper, as did each of the others, with the exception of Tom, who, having squatted himself some little distance off and lit his pipe, seemed wholly absorbed with thoughts of his own. "Then there has been fighting here in days gone by?" I pursued.

"Well, thar has, hoss," was the response. "Ye see that ar creek, don't ye?" pointing to it with the stem of his pipe.

"Ay."

"Well, it looks purty enough to one as don't know, but this coon's seen them waters red afore now."

"Tell us the tale," said Huntly.

"Why it's long, Bosson, and we haint got time to throw away—so I'll hev to let it slide, I'm thinkin. Howsomever, I'll gin ye the gist on't, and I spose that'll do as well. That creek you see yonder's bin called Cotton's Creek ever sence that time, and the reason on't is, case a powerful good chap called Jim Cotton, or "Snake-Eye," got rubbed out thar by the cussed Pawnees. Me and him, and Jake Strader, and Sigh Davis, had bin down to St. Louey, and sold our beavers to the Nor-Westers, (and them was the days when they fetched somethin—five dollar a plew, old or young uns, instead o' a dollar a pound—augh!) and coming out to Independence with the 'rocks' in our pockets, we got on a regular spree, and spent a few—but not all—and a infernal Greaser somehow git tin wind on't, and findin out jest which way we's a-goin, put out ahead, and got some five or six Pawnees to jine him, and come down here to cache for us.

"Well, in course we wasn't thinkin o' nothin dangerous, case our bottles warn't all emptied, and we felt happy enough. Jest down here we stopped to water and rest like we're doin now, when all at once that ar bush you see yonder near the bank, let out seven bullets right among us. Jim Cotton was throwed cold, and never kicked arter, poor feller! Jake Strader got arm broke, Sigh Davis a ball through his shoulder, and me one right into my calf. Then thinkin they throwed the majority, the oudacious skunks come tearin and yellin like sin, old Greaser on the lead. A part broke for us, and the rest for our animals, so as ef they didn't 'count a coup' they could put us 'afoot.'

" 'Heyars hair, and a chance for dry powder—gin 'em h——!' sez I; and I ups with old Sweetlove, and throwed old Greaser cold, right in his tracks—so cold he never knowed what made meat of him, Greaser didn't.

"Well, jest as mine went I heerd two more pops, and blow me for a liar ef two more of the ———— rascals didn't drap purty! How they'd done it—especially Jake Strader with his broken arm—got me all of a heap; but done it they had, sartin as winkin; and thar the varmints lay, a-kickin like darnation. Now thar was only four left and grabbin Jim Cotton's rifle, afore they knowed what I was about, I laid another han'some. Now we was even, and I hollered to the skunks to come on and show fair fight, and I'd eyther lick the three or gin 'em my scalp. But they hadn't no notion o' tryin on't, the cowards! but turned and 'split' as ef the arth was agoin to swaller 'em.

"'Hurraw for us beavers!' I sez; 'and let us go hair-raisin;' and with that I takes my butcher and walks into the varmints; and them as wasn't dead I carved; and arter I'd done, me and Sigh—for Jake couldn't work well—we hove the meat into the water, christening it Cotton's Creek; then we dug a hole nigh 'bout whar you're standing, put in poor Jim, kivered him over, and jest as we was, all wounded, we mounted our critters and put out."

140. How Scott's Bluff Got Its Name

from Emerson Bennett, *The Prairie Flower*

Pursuing our journey, we encamped in the evening on Scott's Bluffs, where we found a good spring, and plenty of grass for our animals. As wood was abundant here, we started a fire, and while sitting around discussing our meat and smoking our pipes, the old trapper, who had not been loquacious for several days, observed:

"Strangers, heyar's what can't look round this spot without feelin badly—I'll be dog-gone ef I can!"

"And why so?" I asked.

"Case one o' the almightiest best fellers you ever seed, went under here. I knowed him like a trump; and he was one o' them chaps you could bear to talk about—real mountain grit, with a hand that u'd make your fingers ache when he squeezed 'em, and a fist that could knock a hole into your upper story and let in the atmospheric ef he didn't like ye. Yes, he was one o' the purtiest men that ever raised hair, throwed buffler, trapped beaver, swallered "boudins," or I'm a liar. But all wouldn't do. Death sot his trap and cotched him, and left jest a few floatin sticks in the shape o' bones to let us know he was a goner. He died right down thar, 'bout six paces from whar you're settin."

"Tell us the story."

"It's purty easy told. Him and a heap o' other fellers had bin up on a right smart trade with the Injins, and was comin down this way, going to the States, when a lot o' the cussed varmints jumped on to 'em and stole every blessed thing they had, even to thar guns, powder, meat, and be —— to 'em. Well, Jimmy Scott—him as I's tellin about—he hadn't bin well for a week, and gittin aground o' fodder fetched him right over the coals. He kicked mighty hard at first; but findin it wasn't no use, he gin in, and told them as was with him that his time was up, and he would hev to do the rest o' his trappin in another country, and that they'd best put out while they'd got meat enough on thar bones to make wolves foller 'em. They hated to leave him like darnation—but they had to do it; and so they sot him up again a rock and vamosed. This was about a mile down on tother side thar; and arter they'd gone, Jimmy got up and paddled here, whar he laid down and went a wolfin. Nobody ever seed Jimmy Scott arterwards—but they found his floatin sticks here, and gin this the name o' Scott's Bluffs."

141. An Execution

from William Drummond Stewart, *Edward Warren*

William Drummond Stewart (1795–1871) was a British nobleman who served as an officer under Wellington at the battle of Waterloo. Stewart's experiences as a well-heeled tourist and observer of the fur trade provided the basis for his novel *Edward Warren* (1854). The Romantic novels of Stewart's fellow Scotsman Sir Walter Scott also may have had some effect on the style and substance of the novel.

Towards the outside of the village to which we were moving, there was a small mound with an abrupt bank, once probably washed by the stream which now flowed at a slight distance, round which, and along whose ridge, a dense crowd had gathered; and to the music of the old men the dancing of the squaws before the scalp of Goddard was distinctly to be seen as we came up; and above the heads of the actors in this scene was waving up and down the dark hair and bloody skin, the inside of which, as it turned distended on a hoop, glared red when fronting the sun.

There, upon the bank, sat the great chief and those immediately connected with him; also the same trader whom I had seen in the lodge in the morning. David, while I had lingered, preceded me, and was already seated, and somewhat to my disgust, by that ominous individual, who seemed to haunt me. They were already in deep converse.

The sun shone out, and the busy camp dispelled, to a certain degree, the dark feelings of misgiving or presage hitherto brought up by his appearance, and I found a man about forty, in a dress which might have suited a mountaineer of the Tyrol—the conical hat, the green coat, the Indian leggings, and moccasins, only substituted to suit the fashion of the country. He never raised his eye, but the features were regular, and but for a certain expression which they wore of a character it was impossible to define, otherwise than I have attempted by describing their effect upon myself, might be considered handsome, now that I had a fair opportunity of examining them.

Some of the war party, who had sustained a loss almost amounting to a defeat, had come in begrimed in the sombre hue which is adopted in desperate enterprises. They had been the captors of Hi-Hi; the steambaths, from which they had emerged, restored them to their natural colour, embellished by the rouge and adorned by painted robes picturing exploits which there was not time to mark by distinctive emblem on the skin. They came up in time to claim their place in the triumph of taking a prisoner, if not achieving a victory.

Hi-Hi had been taken by surprise—though not without resistance, and the reason of his being now the object of public vengeance was that beneath his girdle had been found the scalps before mentioned.

On the other side of the medicine man was the trader from the whites; and I remarked that the great chief joined in their conversation, while one of those whom I had remarked in the lodge where I had smoked, took me by the hand and led me to a seat on the opposite side from the whites. Here and there among the crowd I met a friendly glance from some one I thought I had before seen, and the men seated next me each gave their hands, after pressing them to their hearts.

But that eye of evil omen was still there, in some degree blighting this re-assuring reception. But a wave of the hand of the chief, as if granting some boon to my friend David, interrupted any reflections I might have made upon my own situation, as a movement among the crowd at the same time drew the general attention to the side from which the victim was to appear. I own I felt my heart beat, as some women were with difficulty restrained from breaking through the compact guard which had formed itself around his smaller form, and as yet concealed it from view; but a word or two from the chief, and the space around was cleared into a large circle, leaving Hi-Hi alone in its centre.

"Let us know from whom you stole the scalps which were found upon you," said the great chief.

"Why do you not give me the scalp of the warrior I struck down before the eyes of your braves?" answered the prisoner, with a calm assurance of tone, which first emboldened me to look upon him.

I had felt loath to see the gentle boy in the ruthless hands of these strong and fierce men, scarcely restraining that eagerness for vengeance which is the natural feeling of the savage, if not of the civilized man.

It was barely possible to recognize in the form before us the slight young Chochoco; away from the tall warriors around, and not being brought into immediate contrast with their height, his stature seemed to be increased; his form had assumed a nobleness of port I had thought it incapable of wearing—the head borne high and the eye dilated—he appeared possessed by some mightier spirit sustaining and exalting him above his former self. There was evident satisfaction in the look by which he recognized his friend David, as well as myself, though he never allowed it to relax from the lofty tone it now bore, to meet that ordeal which every Indian looks to as to stamp him worthy of the name of man.

"A great brave," resumed the chief, "may be killed by a creeping snake."

"It was the Snake who stood, and the Blackfoot crept on his belly. Is it so long since two Blackfeet braves were killed by the knife of the little Snake chief, when he had lost his horse and he had no gun? The chief sees things which are passed with but one eye; but I will show him, if he will untie my hands."

"Why should I let your hands be free? Where is your gun?" said the chief, with grave contempt.

"I have left two guns, which belonged to two great warriors, among the branches of a young pine; I took them alone (five Blackfeet took mine) would the braves of the Blackfeet like to see them, that they might know from whom they were taken?"

"They would be hard to find, and the Chochoco might have to live too long in searching for them. The Blackfeet have many braves."

"Yes, they may have many; I can count three," said the youth, holding up three fingers.

At this moment the medicine man, seeing that it would be difficult to contain the fury which these taunts were inflaming, passed into the space yet open, in the centre of which the prisoner stood.

The great chief said a few words, and the front rank of the circle seated themselves.

"You will tell my people," said Hi-Hi, "what I have done, and how I die?"

"Yes, my poor boy," said his friend; but as he looked at the youth, and saw the proud reproachful look at the word "boy," he corrected himself, and added, "My son is a warrior, though so few snows have passed since his birth. I will tell his people."

A beam of satisfaction shone on the countenance of the prisoner—a face though so young—lit by the beams of its last sun coming aslant over those mountains in which he had lived, and those deep valleys he loved, and their fastnesses, which, if his feet were free, would defy re-capture, or even pursuit.

142, 143, and 144. Mayne Reid Writes of the Fur Trappers

As previously noted, the glories of mountain life attracted novelists who constructed fictional mountain-man narratives for an audience hungry for more. One of those novelists, Mayne Reid (1818–1883), traveled the West with fur trappers in the early 1840s. Born in Ballyroney, Northern Ireland, Reid has been called "an innovator in the field of popular literature." His twentieth-century biographer Joan Steele claims in *Captain Mayne Reid* (1978): "In the mid-nineteenth century, his name was a household word—today he has faded into obscurity. The man, his work, and his audience are important not only as an historical curiosity, but also as a means of understanding the popular literature of our own time" (9). The following three selections, all from Reid's *The Scalp Hunters* (1851), illustrate Steele's assertion that the novel has elements of sensationalism and savagery but that it does present "some basic truths of human nature as well as natural history" (65).

To get an idea of how much readers' tastes and writers' styles changed between the nineteenth and the twentieth centuries, compare the excerpts from *The Scalp Hunters* with a twentieth-century mountain-man novel such as Harvey Fergusson's *Wolf Song* (1927). For more discussion of Reid's novel and others like it see Edwin Gaston, *The Early Novel of the Southwest* (1961).

142. A Most Picturesque Indian

from Mayne Reid, *The Scalp Hunters*

I had returned to my blanket, and was about to stretch myself upon it, when the whoop of a "gruya" drew my attention. Looking up, I saw one of these birds flying towards the camp. It was coming through a break in the trees that opened from the river. It flew low, and tempted a shot with its broad wings, and slow lazy flight.

A report rang upon the air! One of the Mexicans had fired his escopette; but the bird flew on, plying its wings with more energy, as if to bear itself out of reach.

There was a laugh from the trappers, and a voice cried out—

"Yur cussed fool! d' yur think 'ee kud hit a spread blanket wi' that beetle-shaped blunderbox? Pish!"

I turned to see who had delivered this odd speech. Two men were poising their rifles, bringing them to bear upon the bird. One was the young hunter whom I have described. The other was an Indian whom I had not seen before.

The cracks were simultaneous; and the crane, dropping its long neck, came whirling down among the trees, where it caught upon a high branch and remained.

From their position, neither party knew that the other had fired. A tent was between them; and the two reports had seemed as one. A trapper cried out—

"Well done, Garey! Lord help the things that's afore old Kil bar's muzzle, when you squints through her hind sights."

The Indian just then stepped round the tent. Hearing this side speech, and perceiving the smoke still oozing from the muzzle of the young hunter's gun, he turned to the latter with the interrogation—

"Did *you* fire, sir?"

This was said in well accentuated and most un-Indian like English, which would have drawn my attention to the man, had not his singularly imposing appearance riveted me already.

"Who is he?" I inquired from one near me.

"Don't know—fresh arriv," was the short answer.

"Do you mean he's a stranger here?"

"Just so. He kumd in thar awhile agone. Don't b'lieve anybody knows him. I guess the captain does; I seed them shake hands."

I looked at the Indian with increasing interest. He seemed a man of about thirty years of age, and not much under seven feet in height! He was proportioned like an Apollo; and, on this account appeared smaller than he actually was. His features were of the Roman type; and his fine forehead, his aquiline nose and broad jaw-bone, gave him the appearance of talent, as well as firmness and energy. He was dressed in a hunting shirt, leggings and moccasons; but all these differed from any thing worn either by the hunters, or their Indian allies. The shirt itself was made out of the dressed hide of the red deer; but differently prepared to that used by the trappers. It was bleached almost to the whiteness of a kid glove! The breast—unlike theirs—was close, and beautifully embroidered with stained porcupine quills. The sleeves were similarly ornamented; and the cape and skirts were trimmed with the soft snow-white fur of the ermine. A row of entire skins of that animal hung from the skirt border, forming a fringe both graceful and costly. But the most singular feature about this man was his hair. It fell loosely over his shoulders, and swept the ground as he walked! It could not have been less than seven feet in length. It was black, glossy, and luxuriant; and reminded me of the tails of those great Flemish horses, I had seen in the funeral carriages of London.

He wore upon his head the war-eagle bonnet, with its full circle of plumes—the finest triumph of savage taste. This magnificent head-dress added to the majesty of his appearance.

A white buffalo robe hung from his shoulders, with all the graceful draping of a toga. Its silky fur corresponded to the order of his dress, and contrasted strikingly with his own dark tresses.

There were other ornaments about his person. His arms and accoutrements were shining with metallic brightness; and the stock and butt of his rifle were richly inlaid with silver.

I have been this minute in my description, as the first appearance of this man impressed me with a picture that can never be effaced from my memory. He was the *beau ideal* of a picturesque and romantic savage; and yet there was nothing savage either in his speech or bearing. On the contrary, the interrogation which he had just addressed to the trapper was put in the politest manner. The reply was not so courteous.

143. A Dog's Revenge

from Mayne Reid, *The Scalp Hunters*

An arrow whizzed past my head as he came up, but in his hurry he had aimed badly.

Our horses' heads met. They stood muzzle to muzzle with eyes dilated—their red nostrils streaming into each other. Both snorted fiercely, as if each was imbued with the wrath of his rider. They seemed to know that a death strife was between us.

They seemed conscious, too, of their own danger. They had met at the very narrowest part of the ledge. Neither could have turned or backed off again. One or other must go over the cliff—must fall through a thousand feet into the stony channel of the torrent!

I sat with a feeling of utter helplessness. I had no weapon with which I could reach my antagonist—no missile. *He* had his bow; and I saw him adjusting a second arrow to the string!

At this crisis, three thoughts passed through my mind—not as I detail them here—but following each other like quick flashes of lightning. My first impulse was to urge my horse forward; trusting to his superior weight to precipitate the lighter animal from the ledge. Had I been worth a bridle and spurs, I would have adopted this plan. But I had neither; and the chance was too desperate without them. I abandoned it for another. I would hurl my tomahawk at the head of my antagonist. No! The third thought—I will dismount, and use my weapon upon the mustang.

This last was clearly the best; and obedient to its impulse, I slipped down between Moro and the cliff. As I did so, I heard the "hist" of another arrow passing my cheek. It had missed me from the suddenness of my movements.

In an instant, I squeezed past the flanks of my horse; and glided forward upon the ledge, directly in front of that of my adversary.

The animal, seeming to guess my intentions, snorted with affright and reared up; but was compelled to drop again into the same tracks.

The Indian was fixing another shaft. Its notch never reached the string. As the hoofs of the mustang came down upon the rock, I aimed my blow. I struck the animal over the eye. I felt the skull yielding before my hatchet; and the next moment horse and rider, the latter screaming and struggling to clear himself of the saddle, disappeared over the cliff.

There was a moment's silence—a long moment—in which I knew they were falling—falling down that fearful depth. Then came a loud plash—the percussion of their united bodies on the water below!

I had no curiosity to look over, and as little time. When I regained my upright attitude—for I had come to my knees in giving the blow—I saw the vidette just leaping upon the platform. He did not halt a moment, but advanced at a run, holding his spear at a charge.

I saw that I would be impaled, unless I could parry the thrust. I struck wildly, but with success. The lance blade glinted from the head of my weapon. Its shaft passed me; and our bodies met with a concussion that caused us both to reel upon the very edge of the cliff!

As soon as I had recovered my balance, I followed up my blows, keeping close to my antagonist—so that he could not again use his lance. Seeing this, he dropped the weapon, and drew his tomahawk. We now fought hand to hand; hatchet to hatchet!

Back and forward along the ledge we drove each other—as the advantage of the blows told in our favour, or against us.

Several times we grappled, and would have pushed each other over; but the fear that each felt of being dragged after mutually restrained us; and we let go, and trusted again to our tomahawks.

Not a word passed between us. We had nothing to say—even could we have understood each other. But we had no boast to make—no taunt to urge—nothing before our minds, but the fixed dark purpose of murdering each other!

After the first onset, the Indian had ceased yelling, and we both fought with the intense earnestness of silence.

There were sounds though; an occasional sharp exclamation; our quick high breathing; the clinking of our tomahawks; the neighing of our horses; and the continuous roar of the torrent. These were the symphonies of our conflict.

For some minutes we battled upon the ledge. We were both cut and bruised in several places; but neither of us had as yet received or inflicted a mortal wound.

At length, after a continuous shower of blows, I succeeded in beating my adversary back, until we found ourselves out upon the platform. There we had ample room to wind our weapons; and we struck with more energy than ever. After a few strokes, our tomahawks met with a violent concussion, that sent them flying from our hands.

Neither dare stoop to regain his weapon; and we rushed upon each other with naked arms, clutched, wrestled a moment, and then fell together to the earth.

I thought my antagonist had a knife. I must have been mistaken; else he would have used it. But without it, I soon found that in this species of encounter he was my master. His muscular arms encircled me, until my ribs cracked under the embrace. We rolled along the ground, over and over each other. O God! we were nearing the edge of the precipice!

I could not free myself from his grasp. His sinewy fingers were across my throat. They clasped me tightly around the trachea—stopping my breath. He was strangling me!

I grew weak and nerveless. I could resist no longer. I felt my hold relax. I grew weaker and weaker. I was dying—I was—O God—I—O Heaven pard—on—Oh——

* * * * * * * *

I could not have been long insensible, for when consciousness returned, I was still warm—sweating from the effects of the struggle—and my wounds were bleeding freshly and freely! I felt that I yet lived. I saw that I was still upon the platform; but where was my antagonist? Why had he not flung me over the cliff?

I rose upon my elbow, and looked around. I could see no living thing, but my own horse and that of the Indian, that galloped over the platform, kicking and plunging at each other.

But I heard sounds; sounds of fearful import; like the hoarse angry worrying of dogs, mingling with the cries of a human voice; a voice uttered in agony!

What could it mean? I saw that there was a break in the platform; a deep cut in the rock, and out of this the sounds appeared to issue.

I rose to my feet, and tottering toward the spot, looked in. It was an awful sight to look upon. The gully was some ten feet in depth; and at its bottom, among the weeds and cacti, a huge dog was engaged in tearing something that screamed and struggled. It was a man—an Indian. All was explained at a glance. The dog was Alp—the man was my late antagonist!

As I came upon the edge, the dog was on top of his adversary, and kept himself uppermost by desperate bounds from side to side—still dashing the other back as he attempted to rise to his feet. The savage was crying in despair. I thought I saw the teeth of the animal fast in his throat; but I watched the struggle no longer. Voices from behind caused me to turn round. My pursuers had reached the canon, and were urging their animals along the ledge!

I staggered up to my horse; and, climbing upon his back, once more directed him to the terrace—that part which led outward. In a few minutes I had cleared the cliff, and was hurrying down the mountain. As I approached its foot I heard a rustling in the bushes, that, on both sides, lined the path. Then an object sprang out a short distance behind me. It was the San Bernard.

As he came alongside, he uttered a low whimper; and once or twice wagged his tail. I knew not how he could have escaped, for he must have waited until the Indians reached the platform, but the fresh blood that stained his jaws, and clotted the shaggy hair upon his breast, showed that he had left one with but little power to detain him.

On reaching the plain, I looked back. I saw my pursuers coming down the face of the sierra; but I had still nearly half a mile of start; and, taking the snowy mountain for my guide, I struck out into the open prairie.

144. The Phantom City

from Mayne Reid, *The Scalp Hunters*

We had now entered the great desert which stretches northward from the Gila, away to the head quarters of the Colorado. We entered it without a guide—for not one of the band had ever traversed these unknown regions. Even Rube knew nothing about this part of the country. We were without compass too, but this we needed not. There were few in the band who could not point to the north, or the south, within the variation of a degree—few of them but could—night or day—tell, by the heavens, within ten minutes of the true time! Give them but a clear sky—with the "signs" of the trees and rocks—and they needed neither compass nor chronometer. A night spent beneath the blue heaven of the prairie-uplands and the mountain "parks"— where a roof rarely obstructed their view of the azure vault—had made astronomers of these reckless rovers!

Of such accomplishments was their education—drawn from many

a perilous experience. To me, their knowledge of such things seemed "instinct."

But we had a guide as to our directions, unerring as the majestic needle; we were traversing the region of the "polar plant" the planes of whose leaves, at almost every step, pointed out our meridian! It grew upon our track; and was crushed under the hoofs of our horses, as we rode onward.

For several days, we travelled northward through a country of strange looking mountains, whose top shot heavenward in fantastic forms and groupings. At one time we saw shapes semiglobular like the domes of churches. At another, Gothic turrets rose before us; and the next opening brought in view, sharp needle-pointed peaks, shooting upward in the blue sky! We saw columnar forms supporting others that lay horizontally—vast boulders of trap-rock suggesting the idea of some antediluvian ruin—some temple of gigantic Druids!

Along with the singularity of formation, was the most brilliant coloring. There were stratified rocks, red, white, green, and yellow—as vivid in their hues as if freshly touched from the palette of the painter!

No smoke had tarnished them since they had been flung up from their subterranean beds. No cloud draped their naked outlines. It was not a land of clouds, for as we journeyed among them, we saw not a speck in the heavens. Nothing above us, but the blue and limitless ether!

I remembered the remarks of Seguin.

There was something inspiriting in the sight of these bright mountains—something like-life—that prevented us from feeling the extreme and real desolation by which we were surrounded. At times, we could not help fancying that we were in a thickly populated country—a country of vast wealth and civilization—as appeared from its architectural grandeur! Yet in reality we were journeying through the wildest of earth's dominions—where no human foot ever trod, excepting such as wear the mocasson—the region of the "wolf" Apache, and the wretched Yamparico!

We travelled up the banks of the river, and, here and there, at our halting places, searched for the shining metal. It could be found only in small quantities; and the hunters began to talk loudly of the Prieto. There, according to them, the yellow gold lay in "lumps."

On the fourth day after leaving the Gila, we came to a place where the San Carlos canoned through a high sierra. Here we halted for the night. When morning came we found we could follow the river no farther, without climbing over the mountain; and Seguin announced his intention of leaving it, and striking eastward. The hunters responded to this declaration with a wild hurrah! The golden vision was again before them.

We remained at the San Carlos until after the noon heat—recruiting our horses by the stream. Then mounting, we rode forward into the plain. It was our intention to travel all night, or until we reached water—as we knew that without this, halting would be useless.

We had not ridden far, until we saw that a fearful "Jornada" was before us—one of those dreaded "stretches" without grass, wood, or water. Ahead of us we could see a low range of mountains, trending from north to south; and beyond these, another range still higher than the first. On the farther range there were snowy summits. We saw that they were distinct chains, and that the more distant was of great elevation. This we knew from the appearance upon its peaks of the "eternal snow."

We knew, moreover, that at the foot of the snowy range we should find water—perhaps the river we were in search of—but the distance was immense. If we did not find it at the nearer sierra, we would have an adventure—the danger of perishing from thirst. Such was the prospect!

We rode on over the arid soil—over plains of lava, and cut-rock, that wounded the hoofs of our horses, laming many. There was no vegetation around us, except the sickly green of the artemisia, or the fetid foliage of the creosote plant. There was no living thing to be seen—save the brown and hideous lizard, the rattle-snake, the desert crickets that crawled in myriads along the parched ground, and were crunched under the hoofs of our animals! "Water!" was the word that began to be uttered in many a language.

"Water," cried the choking trapper.

"L'eau!" ejaculated the Canadian.

"Agua! agua!" shouted the Mexican.

We were not twenty miles from the San Carlos, before our gourd canteens were as dry as a shingle! The dust of the plains and the hot atmosphere, had created unusual thirst; and we had soon emptied them.

We had started late in the afternoon. At sundown the mountains ahead of us did not seem a single mile nearer! We travelled all night, and when the sun rose again, we were still a good distance from them! Such is the illusive character of this elevated and crystal atmosphere.

The men mumbled as they talked. They held in their mouths

leaden bullets, and pebbles of obsidian—which they chewed with a desperate fierceness.

It was some time after sunrise, when we arrived at the mountain foot. To our consternation, no water could be found!

The mountains were a range of dry rocks—so parched-like and barren, that even the creosote bush could not find nourishment along their sides. They were as naked of vegetation as when the volcanic fires first heaved them into the light!

Parties scattered in all directions, and went up the ravines, but after a long while spent in fruitless wandering, we abandoned the search in despair.

There was a pass that appeared to lead through the range, and entering this, we rode forward in silence and with gloomy thoughts.

We soon debouched on the other side, when a scene of singular character burst upon our view.

A plain lay before us, hemmed in on all sides by high mountains. On its farther edge was the snowy ridge, whose stupendous cliffs rose vertically from the plain, towering thousands of feet in height. Dark rocks seemed piled upon each other, higher and higher until they became buried under robes of spotless snow!

But that which appeared most singular was the surface of the plain. It was covered with a mantle of virgin whiteness—apparently of snow—and yet the more elevated spot from which we viewed it was naked, with a hot sun shining upon it! What we saw in the valley then could not be snow.

As I gazed over the monotonous surface of this plain, and then looked upon the chaotic mountains that walled it in, my mind became impressed with ideas of coldness and desolation. It seemed as if every thing was dead around us, and nature was laid out in her winding sheet! I saw that my companions experienced similar feelings—but no one spoke; and we commenced riding down the pass that led into this singular valley.

As far as we could see, there was no prospect of water on the plain; but what else could we do than cross it? On its most distant border, along the base of the snowy mountains, we thought we could distinguish a black line—like that of timber—and for this point we directed our march.

On reaching the plain, what had appeared like snow, proved to be soda! A deep incrustation of this lay upon the ground—enough to satisfy the wants of the whole human race—yet there it lay, and no hand had ever stooped to gather it!

Three or four rocky buttes were in our way, near the debouchure of the pass. As we rounded them, getting farther out into the plain, a wide gap began to unfold itself, opening through the mountains. Through this gap the sun's rays were streaming in—throwing a band of yellow light across one end of the valley. In this the crystals of the soda, stirred up by the breeze appeared floating in myriads.

As we descended, I observed that objects began to assume a very different aspect from what they had exhibited from above. As if by enchantment, the cold snowy surface all at once disappeared. Green fields lay before us, and tall trees sprang up covered with a thick and verdant frondage!

"Cottonwoods!" cried a hunter, as his eye rested on these still distant groves.

"Tall saplins at that—Wagh!" ejaculated another.

"Water thar, fellers, I reckin," remarked a third.

"Yes sirree! yer don't see such sprouts as them growing out o' a dry peraira. Look! hilloa!"

"By Gollies, yonder's a house!"

"A house? one—two—three—a house? thar's a whole town, if thar's a single shanty. Gee! Jim, look yonder. Wagh!"

I was riding in front with Seguin; the rest of the band strung out behind us. I had been for some time gazing upon the ground, in a sort of abstraction, looking at the snow-white efflorescence, and listening to the crunching of my horse's hoofs through its icy incrustation. These exclamatory phrases caused me to raise my eyes. The sight that met them was one that made me rein up with a sudden jerk. Seguin had done the same, and I saw that the whole band had halted with a similar impulse!

We had just cleared one of the buttes, that had hitherto obstructed our view of the great gap. This was now directly in front of us; and along its base on the southern side, rose the walls and battlements of a city—a vast city judging from its distance and the colossal appearance of its architecture! We could trace the columns of temples, and doors, and gates, and windows, and balconies, and parapets, and spires! There were many towers rising high over the roofs; and in the middle was a temple-like structure, with its massive dome towering far above all the others!

I looked upon this sudden apparition with a feeling of incredulity. It was a dream, an imagination, a *mirage*! Ha! it was a *mirage*.

But no! The mirage could not effect such a complete picture. There were the roofs, and chimneys, and walls, and windows! There were the parapets of fortified houses, with their regular notches and embra-zures! It was a reality. It *was* a city!

Was it the Cibolo of the Spanish Padré? Was it that city of golden gates, and burnished towers? Was the story of the wandering priest after all true? Who had proved it a fable? Who had ever penetrated this region, the very country in which the ecclesiastic represented the golden city of Cibolo to exist?

I saw that Seguin was puzzled, dismayed, as well as myself! He knew nothing of this land. He had never witnessed a mirage like that!

For some time we sat in our saddles, influenced by strong emo-tions. Shall we go forward? Yes! We must reach water. We are dying of thirst; and, impelled by this we spur onward.

We had ridden only a few paces farther, when the hunters uttered a sudden and simultaneous cry! A new object—an object of terror—was before us! Along the mountain foot appeared a string of dark forms. *They were mounted men!*

We dragged our horses to their haunches, our whole line halting as one man!

"Injuns!" was the exclamation of several.

"Indians they must be," muttered Seguin. "There are no other here—Indians! No! There never were such as them. See! they are not men! Look! their huge horses; their long guns; *they are giants!* By heaven!" continued he, after a moment's pause, "they are bodiless! *They are phantoms!*"

There were exclamations of terror from the hunters behind.

Were these the inhabitants of the city? There was a striking propor-tion in the colossal size of the horses and the horsemen!

For a moment I was awe-struck like the rest. Only a moment. A sudden memory flashed upon me. I thought of the Hartz mountains, and their demons. I knew that the phenomena before us could be no other—an optical delusion—a creation of the *mirage.*

I raised my hand above my head. The foremost of the giants imi-tated the motion!

I put spurs to my horse, and gallopped forward. So did he, as if to meet me! After a few springs, I had passed the refracting angle; and, like a thought, the shadowy giant vanished into air!

The men had ridden forward after me; and having also passed the angle of refraction, saw no more of the phantom host.

The city, too had disappeared; but we could trace the outlines of many a singular formation in the trap-rock strata that traversed the edge of the valley.

The tall groves were no longer to be seen; but a low belt of green willows—real willows—could be distinguished along the foot of the mountain within the gap! Under their foliage there was something that sparkled in the sun like sheets of silver. *It was water!* It was a branch of the Prieto!

Our horses neighed at the sight; and shortly after we had alighted upon its banks, and were kneeling before the sweet spirit of the stream!

145. A Trapper's White Wife Has to Accept His Indian Wife

from Timothy Flint, *The Shoshonee Valley*

Timothy Flint was born in North Reading, Massachusetts, in 1780. Although he later traveled as far west as Missouri (where he met Daniel Boone), Flint died in his hometown in 1840. According to James K. Folsom, Flint's *The Shoshonee Valley* is an unjustly neglected novel that "represents Flint's final attempt to come to philosophical terms with the meaning of the advance of civilization." (*Timothy Flint*, 136). In the following selection from the novel, Flint seems to have shaped his fiction to bring about poetic justice. For a historian's study of the subject see Sylvia Van Kirk, *"Many Tender Ties": Women in Fur-Trade Society in Western Canada, 1670–1870* (1980).

All this she stated in a subdued and quiet tone, that won strongly on the heart of her husband, who, in truth, liked his Indian wife best. But the new comer was a small, brisk, sharp-faced woman, with red hair, a curved nose, and thin lips, who had, in bygone days in New York, drawn forth upon Hatch the famous proverb, touching the superior points of the gray nag. As the petition of the red skin wife and mother was stated to her, the object of debate stood before her, meekly holding one of her children in one hand and the other at the breast, looking steadily in her face with intense interest, to divine by her looks and tones, for her language she understood not, what fate was in reserve for her. The white wife required no time for deliberation. She raised her shrill voice, and peremptorily insisted, as a preliminary step in the new domestic arrangement, that her red rival should be discharged, in her phrase, bag and baggage. Perhaps, it was the first time in his life, that Hatch blushed in earnest, and his face glowed to the color of his red whiskers, when he explained this hard necessity to his Shoshonee wife, in her own speech. Obedience in these usages is implicit and without reserve. She once more shed silent tears, turned round, and wistfully surveyed her late peaceful and happy empire, as if taking a final leave. Wiping her eyes with her long black locks, she then sternly walked forth, leading one child, and holding the other to her breast. As soon as she was abroad, she began, in the deep, monotonous Indian death wail, to sing, "The proud white skin has come, and my poor babes and I go to the land of spirits." Such was the burden of her strain, as she walked on with her charge to the Sewasserna. She paused a moment on the bank. She kissed her little ones, and the tears streamed down her cheeks, while she looked alternately in their faces, and then towards her late residence, the domestic smoke of which was peacefully curling aloft. Her purpose for a moment seemed to falter. But the lament arose strong and full again. "We go to the land of spirits," she said, and threw herself into the stream, with both her babes in her arms. Her husband and a number of Indians had observed her departure, and divining her purpose, had followed her at a distance. In a moment some of the best swimmers plunged in after her.— They drew her up by her locks, holding in the spasmodic grasp of affection and death, fast to her babes. The three were brought, though apparently lifeless, to the bank. All soon gave proofs of resuscitation. The first movement of returning life in the mother was, to raise herself a little from her recumbent posture, open the blue lips of her half expiring babe, and give it the breast, imploring the husband not to drive her from him. "See," said she, "the pretty one looks like its father. Why will you have me kill it? Only let me remain in the house, and tend my little ones, and I will be as a faithful slave to the proud white skin." It was a scene to move the hearts of the Shoshonee. Tears even started under the red eye lashes of Hatch. A harsh, but decisive murmur from all the Indians present, the purport of which he but too well understood, notified him, that, in this case, he no longer had an alternative. He uttered an oath, "that the white wife should know her driver for this once." He did more. He took the eldest child in his arms, and gallantly led on his Shoshonee spouse, now gaily holding the other to her bosom. The Indians followed, murmuring applauses. He arrived at the house, and saluted his white wife, who had come to the door, to learn the object of this triumphal procession. "Mein Gott and Saviour," said he, "dey will roast me alive. You take her in, madam, well and good; you refuse, and by mein Gott and Saviour, I trive you off, and keep mein good red skin." The New York madam saw the aspect of things, and well understood the looks and gestures of the listening Indians. Her terrified consent was prompt and ample. The recovered mother and children re-entered the house, and Baptiste observed with a knowing shrug, "Ma foi, Hatch no need go to l'infer for his purgatory. He get him between he's two vives." At the joyful termination of this affair, the Indians marched off with acclamations.

146 and 147. Wolves in Fur Trapper Literature

The incidents described in the next two selections seem incredible, especially since they are from period novels. Were such scenes witnessed in the American West in the years before wildlife populations were reduced to the low numbers now common? Perhaps. Still, we should be mindful of Barry Lopez's cautionary note in his *Of Wolves and Men* (1978): "Everything we have been told about wolves in the past should have been said, I think, with more care, with the preface that it is only a perception in a particular set of circumstances, that in the end it is only an opinion" (4).

146. A Wolf Pack Eats a Buffalo While Chasing It

from David H. Coyner, *The Lost Trappers*

June 5th. This afternoon something in motion was discovered on the prairie ahead of the company, but so far off, they were not able to determine what it was. As they approached it, Captain Williams, by the aid of a glass, ascertained that it was a band of wolves in full chase after a buffalo coming directly towards the party. As all were anxious to see the race, and how it would terminate, they placed themselves in a position not to be noticed very readily by the wolves, and, in a few minutes, they had a fair view of the whole affair. The buffalo proved to be a well grown young bull, in fine condition. There were about twelve wolves of the largest kind, and must have had a long and a tight race, as they seemed (both wolves and buffalo) very much fatigued. As they ran the wolves were close around the buffalo, snapping and snatching all the time; but they were observed not to seize and hold on like a dog. Their mode of taking the buffalo is to run them down; and when they are completely out of breath, by a constant worrying and snatching kept up by all hands, they drag their victim to the ground, and then fill themselves with his flesh, sometimes before he is entirely dead.

Indeed in this case they seemed to feed upon their victim as they ran, for every thrust they made at him they took away a mouthful of his flesh, which they gulped as they ran, and by the time they had brought him to the ground, the flesh of his hind quarters was taken away to the bone. So eager were they in the chase, and so fierce was the contest, that they did not observe the company until they rode up within ten steps from them, and even then they did not appear to be much frightened, but scampered off a short distance and sat down and licked their lips, and waited with much impatience to be permitted to return to their hard-earned feast. The buffalo had suffered violence in every part. The tendons of his hind legs were cut asunder; the tuft of hair at the end of the tail was taken away, with part of the tail; pieces of hide and flesh, as large as a man's hand, were jerked out of his sides in several places; his ears were much torn, and in the battle he lost one of his eyes. Just before they succeeded in bringing him to the ground, one of the pack, a very large gray wolf, was seen to spring upon his back, tear out a mouthful of his hump, and then bound off. Having gratified their curiosity, the men withdrew, and the hungry pack in a moment set in, with fresh rapacity, tearing away and gulping the bloody flesh of their victim, that still faintly struggled for life.

147. Our Hero Chased by a Wolf Pack

from **William Drummond Stewart**, *Edward Warren*

I had got some little distance from the river, when I observed several wolves, who seemed to eye with some covetousness my wounded horse. I hardly heeded them at first, but after a time it appeared as if they increased in numbers, until they became like a pack of hounds, keeping about sixty yards behind, and getting fresh recruits as they came along. I led the roan, and the other seemed to feel that he was the object of attraction, and limped up close to his companions. It was his uneasiness which first drew my serious attention to the pursuit. I had read of attacks on villages by these beasts, and of the eating up of travellers on the roads in the south of France, and in Russia, and began to fear that the gallant beast who had borne me so well in my attack upon the bear, must, however unwillingly, be made a sacrifice of to save the rest. I knew a shot, or ten shots, would be useless, but I felt that I could not abandon the poor animal, who almost looked for protection from me, without doing my best to save him.

Happily, the sage was in some places pretty thick, and there the pack trailed; and while the horses ran on before—for I had loosened the roan—I lingered, to check as much as possible the head of the advancing column, and at the same time kept up a tolerably sharp trot.

A buffalo track, somewhat in the direction I wished to hold, led us on, and while it lasted I had less trouble, but after having rounded a little butte, it gave out, and I had to herd the horses, and bring them back to the course, from which they were continually diverging.

Things were becoming serious, and the leading wolves were not thirty paces behind; and, in a charge, I did not feel secure that they would all confine themselves to the wounded of the party, and that I should not, as being on the slowest animal of the lot, become an object of pursuit in the second degree. However, I must say my feeling of horror at being within reach of the wounded horse and hearing his cries, was the predominant one, and I waved my lasso and urged him on before, at the same time shouting to encourage his speed. For the moment this new sound, so strange to these wild wastes, checked our pursuers; but they came on again, as if ashamed of having given way to the voice of man.

The moment was almost come to urge my horse and follow the roan in a sauve qui peut—it had become almost a scurry, but as the pace increased, I felt the distance was never lessened; then came a gulley, down which the loose horses rushed, and as the side was steep, the voracious pack was obliged again to lessen their front to get across at a path; but it was only a moment's reprieve.

It was now requisite to take my line and ride for it; the ground was broken by occasional grips, and was loose and soft, and in so far unfavourable to the heavier animals. We were at three parts speed; the poor invalid went gallantly, but the pain it gave him was evident, and he began to shew by perspiration the dread of his coming fate.

I had never taken my eyes off the immediate spot we occupied, the wolves and the horses, but now, seeing the hour was come, with that sense of the last pang in danger, which those who have seen it near must have experience, I gazed up to the heavens, and then around, as if in search of some unknown aid in extremest need, or eternal adieu—there was nothing; and without further look where pity would be of no avail, I dashed my heels against my horse's flanks to take an independent line, and run for my life.

I saw with what an easy swinging pace my favourite roan cleared the rough surface while I was straining to save myself—of what use to own him now, with his gallant stride; the turn I took to separate from the victim I had destined to this sad sacrifice had also given some advantage to our pursuers, and I could see the red and hanging jaws gathering upon us; but again came a hollow, broader than the rest, and down it came half-a-dozen bulls, who had caught our wind before seeing us; they were almost in a course to cross our path had they continued, but swerved on our descending the bank; the opposite side was steep, and checked their pace, and I was upon them before they were half up. A shot through the lungs, and one of them faltered, spurting blood from his nose; my pistol broke the leg of the last as he crowned the height. I rushed after him, and he turned to fight; the first I found stopped, and staggering in his death throe, and as I left the latter between me and the herd, they were upon him before his attention had been turned to the new assailants—the warm blood had taken them off and saved us.

148. Kit Carson Kills Two Indians in a Single Charge

from Emerson Bennett, *The Prairie Flower*

We end this section on mountain men in fiction as we began it, with an incredible tale about Kit Carson.

No wonder Kit Carson was famous—for he seemed a whole army of himself. A bare glimpse of one of his feats astonished me, and for the moment almost made me doubt my senses. Two powerful Indians, hard abreast, weapons in hand, and well mounted, rushed upon him at once, and involuntarily I uttered a cry of horror, for I thought him lost. But no! With an intrepidity equalled only by his activity, a weapon in either hand, he rushed his horse between the two, and dodging by some unaccountable means the blows aimed at his life, buried his knife in the breast of one, and at the same moment his tomahawk in the brain of the other. One frightful yell of rage and despair, and two riderless steeds went dashing on.

Farewell to the Mountain-Man Life

As we pointed out in the introduction, the heyday of the mountain man was amazingly short. Any number of long-lived mountain men spent more years remembering their lives as trappers than they ever spent trapping. The selections that follow give some idea of what surviving trappers did in their later years as well as some idea of how former trappers longed for their vanished way of life.

Almost one hundred and fifty years have passed since trapping beaver was an important industry in the West. Compared to later in dustries mining, timber, agriculture, energy, defense, tourism—all the furs ever taken west of the hundredth meridian are barely a dot on the West's economic map. This is history.

The *story* of the mountain men, on the other hand, has had a tremendous impact on the West's mental map, an impact out of all proportion to the historical importance of the fur trade. The story of the mountain men has affected the western mind directly, as is evidenced by the fascination with mountain men that continues to this day. The story of the mountain men has also affected the western mind indirectly through its reincarnations in the story of the cowboy, the ranger, the logger, the Hell's Angel, the monkey wrencher—or whatever tough, untamed character catches the western imagination. This is the power of story. This is what we have tried to convey through the narratives included in this book. We hope you have learned from these stories, and we hope that you have enjoyed them, too.

149. Yount's Dream of the Donner Party

from George C. Yount, *George C. Yount and His Chronicles of the West*

As previous selections have made clear, mountain men sometimes became involved in other historic events taking place in the American West. At such times, they often called upon the wilderness skills they had developed as trappers. George C. Yount recounts his efforts to bring relief to the survivors of the Donner party. Vardis Fisher's *The Mothers* (1943) is a novel based on the Donner calamity. For a historical account see George R. Stewart, *Ordeal by Hunger* (1960).

Yount, Sutter and Vallejo were foremost in sending relief to the stricken Donner Party. "Yount . . . after being informed of those sufferings, found it difficult to sleep quietly . . . until measures had been taken for their relief—At the first arrival of those melancholy tidings there had been much discussion among the neighboring Rancheros, as to the best & most feasible method of procedure, during the day; & after much reflection, he retired to rest—All the accounts hitherto received were vague & indefinite. It was impossible to determine where the sufferers might be found, & what rout would be most likely to lead to them—Oppressed & exhausted with anxiety, he soon fell asleep, & dreams '& visions of his head upon his bed troubled him' exceedingly. He dreamed that he was present among those sufferers—that he there witnessed a degree of distress beyond all . . . imagination—" He dreamed that he saw them eating the bodies, that the snow was more than twenty feet deep, that snowshoes would be required to reach them, that provisions must be carried on the backs of men on snowshoes. Yount "arose in the morning, &, waiting not even for a morning repast, he dispatched messengers eighteen miles in one direction to Gen. Vallejo, twelve miles in another direction to a noble spirited man [James F. Reed], whose wife it was supposed might be among the sufferers, to take command of an outfit—"

He also sent ahead to Sutter for bread, of which he had an insufficient supply. And he had his butchers dress, jerk and pack up a lot of beef.

Survivors "were brought in to Yount's, where they were fed . . . with the choicest wheat, & his numerous beeves were slaughtered daily"—to feed and clothe and make them well again.

150. A Mountain Man's Lament

from Howard L. Conard, *"Uncle Dick" Wootton*

While some mountain men suffered early, violent deaths, others managed to survive to a ripe old age. "Uncle Dick" Wootton was one of the survivors, though in the following selection he looks back and laments the passing of the glory days of fur trapping. Novelists make good use of such laments; an especially good example can be found in A. B. Guthrie, Jr.'s eponymous novel *The Big Sky* (1947).

"The railroad took the place of the stage line in 1878, and since that time I have lived in a different atmosphere from that in which I formerly lived. I almost feel that I am no longer on the frontier, and that there is no frontier to go to. In my old age, I have been brought back into civilization, and I find just one unpleasant feature about it.

While I am not so foolish as to lose sight of the fact that I have grown old, and as a consequence am no longer suited to an adventurous life myself, I still fancy that I should like to live amidst such surroundings as we had in this country twenty-five years ago, so that visitors could drop in every day or two to see me, who would have something to talk about.

If the buffalo had not all been killed, if there were more deer and bear in the mountains, if the stage lines were still running, and the Indians had not been driven out of the country, the young fellows who visit me, would now and then be able to tell a story worth hearing.

As it is, I have to do pretty much all the story telling myself, except when I happen to meet somebody who tells me about the cities that have grown up on the plains where I used to hunt buffalo, and along the streams where I used to set my beaver traps. Every once in a while

I meet a man too, who tells me about the gold or silver that has been dug out of the mountains that I used to tramp over when trading with the Indians, and that interests me almost as much as if I had found it myself.

Then another man comes along who happened to know one of the "old-timers," with whom I had slept in camp perhaps a hundred times, and when I inquire about my old friend, I hear something which has a sort of melancholy interest for me.

I learn that my old-time companion is dead, and that the lawyers are dividing up his estate among themselves; or in other words, that the heirs are engaged in a legal dispute over the disposition to be made of his property, which amounts to the same thing as dividing it among the lawyers.

I don't feel very old, but when I look about me for my associates of the "forties," I find that only the mountains and I are left, and before long it will be only the mountains.

151. The Hunter's Farewell

from Osborne Russell, *Journal of a Trapper*

The final selection may not be great poetry, but it does capture the sense of loss many trappers must have felt when the fur-trapping days were only a memory.

The Hunter's Farewell

Adieu ye hoary icy mantled towers
That ofttimes pierce the onward fleeting mists
Whoer feet are washed by gentle summer showers
While Phoebus' rays play on your sparkling crests
The smooth green vales you seem prepared to guard
Beset with groves of ever verdant pine
Would furnish themes for Albions noble bards
Far 'bove a hunters rude unvarnish'd rhymes

Adieu ye flocks that skirt the mountains brow
And sport on banks of everliving snow
Ye timid lambs and simple harmless Ewes

Who fearless view the dread abyss below—
Oft have I watched your seeming mad career
While lightly tripping o'er those dismal heights
Or cliffs o'erhanging yawning caverns drear
Where none else treads save fowls of airy flight

Oft have I climbed those rough stupendous rocks
In search of food 'mong Nature's well fed herds
Untill I've gained the rugged mountain's top
Where Boreas reigned or feathered Monarchs soar'd
On some rude cragg projecting from the ground
I've sat a while my weared limbs to rest
And scann'd the unsuspecting flock around
With anxious care selecting out the best

The prize obtained with slow and heavy step
Pac'd down the steep and narrow winding path
To some smooth vale where chrystal streamlets met
And skillful hands prepared a rich repast
Then hunters jokes and merry humor'd sport
Beguiled the time enlivened every face
The hours flew fast and seemed like moments short
'Til twinkling planets told of midnights pace

But now those scenes of cheerful mirth are done
The horned [herds] are dwindling very fast
The numerous trails so deep by Bison worn
Now teem with weeds or over grown with grass
A few gaunt Wolves now scattered or the place
Where herds since time unknown to man have fed
With lonely howls and sluggish onward pace
Tell their sad fate and where their bones are laid

Ye rugged mounts ye vales ye streams and trees
To you a hunter bids his last farewell
I'm bound for shores of distant western seas
To view far famed Multnomahs fertile vale
I'll leave these regions once famed hunting grounds
Which I perhaps again shall see no more
And follow down led by the setting sun
Or distant sound of proud Columbia's roar

Alfred Jacob Miller, *Bourgeois W——r and his Squaw (Mountain Man Joe Walker)*
(37.1940.78).

Selected Bibliography

† = A source for one or more of the narratives included in *Rendezvous Reader*.
‡ = A twentieth-century mountain-man novel.

Abbott, John S. C. *Christopher Carson, Familiarly Known as Kit Carson.* New York: Dodd, Mead and Co., 1873.

Adams, Percy G. *Travelers and Travel Liars.* Berkeley: University of California Press, 1962.

————. *Travel Literature and the Evolution of the Novel.* Lexington: University Press of Kentucky, 1983.

†Adams, Winona, ed. "An Indian Girl's Story of a Trading Expedition to the Southwest about 1841." *Frontier* (May 1930): 338–67.

Algier, Keith W. *The Crow and the Eagle: A Tribal History from Lewis and Clark to Custer.* Caldwell, ID: Caxton Printers, 1993.

‡Allen, Merritt Parmelee. *The Spirit of the Eagle.* New York: Longmans, Green, and Co., 1947.

‡Allen, T. D. *Doctor in Buckskins.* New York: Harper and Brothers, 1951.

Alter, J. Cecil. *James Bridger: Trapper, Frontiersman, Scout, and Guide, A Historical Narrative.* Salt Lake City: Shepard Book Co., 1925.

Alter, Judy. *Dorothy Johnson.* Boise, ID: Boise State University, 1980.

‡Altrocchi, Julia Cooley. *Wolves Against the Moon.* New York: Macmillan, 1940.

Amsden, Charles Avery. *Navaho Weaving: Its Technic and History.* Chicago: Rio Grande Press, 1964.

†Anderson, William Marshall. *Rocky Mountain Journals of William*

Marshall Anderson: The West in 1834. 1967. Reprint. Lincoln: University of Nebraska Press, 1987.

†Ashley, William H. *The West of William H. Ashley.* Denver: Old West Publishing, 1964.

†Audubon, John James. *Audubon and His Journals.* 1897. Reprint. New York: Dover Publications, 1960.

Ault, Philip H. *The Home Book of Western Humor.* New York: Dodd, Mead, Inc., 1967.

Austin, James C. "Legend, Myth and Symbol in Frederick Manfred's *Lord Grizzly.*" *Critique* 6 (1963–1964): 122–30.

†Averill, Charles E. *Kit Carson, The Prince of the Gold Hunters.* Boston: George H. Williams, 1849.

Baer, George M. *The Natural History of Rabies.* 2 vols. New York: Academic Press, 1975.

†Ball, John. *John Ball: Member of the Wyeth Expedition to the Pacific Northwest, 1832; and Pioneer in the Old Northwest. Autobiography.* Glendale, CA: Arthur H. Clark, 1925.

Barclay, Donald A., James H. Maguire, and Peter Wild, eds. *Into the Wilderness Dream: Exploration Narratives of the American West, 1500–1805.* Salt Lake City: University of Utah Press, 1994.

Barnett, Louise K. *The Ignoble Savage: American Literary Racism, 1790–1890.* Westport, CT: Greenwood Press, 1975.

Barsness, Larry. *Heads, Hides, and Horns: The Compleat Buffalo Book.* Fort Worth: Texas Christian University Press, 1985.

†Beall, Thom J. "Recollections of William Craig." *Lewiston* [Idaho] *Morning Tribune.* 3 March 1918, 8.

†Bennett, Emerson. *The Prairie Flower; Or, Adventures in the Far West.* Cincinnati: J. A. & U. P. James, 1849.

Berry, Don. *A Majority of Scoundrels: An Informal History of the Rocky Mountain Fur Company.* New York: Harper, 1961.

‡———. *Moontrap.* New York: Viking, 1962.

‡———. *Trask.* New York: Viking, 1960.

‡Best, Herbert. *Young'un.* New York: Macmillan, 1944.

‡Birney, Hoffman. *Eagle in the Sun.* New York: G. P. Putnam's Sons, 1935.

†Blackburn, Abner Levi. "Lou Devon's Narrative: A Tale of the Mandans' Lost Years." Edited by Will Bagely. *Montana: The Magazine of Western History* 43 (1993): 34–49.

Blair, Walter, and Hamlin Hill. *America's Humor: From Poor Richard to Doonesbury.* New York: Oxford University Press, 1978.

‡Blake, Forrester. *Johnny Christmas.* New York: Morrow, 1948.

Boardman, Kathleen. "Paper Trail: Diaries, Letters, and Reminiscences of the Overland Journey West." In *Updating the Literary West,* edited by Thomas J. Lyon et al. Fort Worth: Texas Christian University Press, forthcoming.

Bodmer, Karl. *Karl Bodmer's America.* Lincoln: Jocelyn Art Museum and University of Nebraska Press, 1984.

†Bonner, Thomas D. *Life and Adventures of James P. Beckwourth: As Told to Thomas D. Bonner.* 1856. Reprint. Lincoln: University of Nebraska Press, 1972.

Bowden, Mary Weatherspoon. *Washington Irving.* Boston: Twayne, 1981.

‡Brackett, Leigh. *Follow the Free Wind.* New York: Ballantine, 1963.

†Bradbury, John. *Travels in the Interior of America.* 1817. Second Edition. London: Sherwood, Neely, and Jones, 1819.

Brooks, George R. *The Southwest Expedition of Jedediah S. Smith: His Personal Account of the Journey to California, 1826–1827.* 1977. Reprint. Lincoln: University of Nebraska Press, 1989.

Broten, Arthur Ray. "Twentieth-Century Novels of the Rocky Mountain Fur Trade: Toward a Definition of the Form." Ph.D. diss., University of California, Santa Barbara, 1980.

†Brown, David L. *Three Years in the Rocky Mountains.* 1845. Fairfield, WA: Ye Galleon Press, 1975.

†Brown, John. *Mediumistic Experiences of John Brown: The Medium of the Rockies.* Des Moines: Moses Hull & Co., 1887.

Bruce, Chris. *Myth of the West.* New York: Rizzoli, 1990.

Burdett, Charles. *The Life of Kit Carson: The Great Western Hunter and Guide.* 1862. Reprint. New York: A.L. Burt, 1902.

‡Burr, Anna Robeson. *The Golden Quicksand.* New York: D. Appleton-Century Co., 1936.

Burroughs, John Rolfe. *Where the Old West Stayed Young.* New York: Bonanza Books, 1962.

Burt, Maxwell Struthers. *Powder River: Let 'Er Buck.* New York: Farrar & Rinehart, 1938.

‡Butler, Beverly. *The Fur Lodge.* New York: Dodd, Mead, 1959.

†Campbell, Robert. *A Narrative of Colonel Robert Campbell's Experiences in the Rocky Mountain Fur Trade from 1825 to 1830.* Fairfield, WA: Ye Galleon Press, 1991.

†Carson, Kit. *Kit Carson's Autobiography.* 1935. Reprint. Lincoln: University of Nebraska Press, 1966.

Carter, Harvey Lewis. *"Dear Old Kit": The Historical Christopher Carson.* 1926. Reprint. Norman: University of Oklahoma Press, 1968.

Castetter, Edward F., and Willis H. Bell. *Yuman Indian Agriculture: Primitive Subsistence on the Lower Colorado and Gila Rivers.* Albuquerque: University of New Mexico Press, 1951.

†Catlin, George. *North American Indians.* New York: Penguin Books, 1989.

†Chardon, Francois A. *Chardon's Journal at Fort Clark 1834–1839.* Pierre, SD: State of South Dakota, 1932.

Chittenden, Hiram Martin. *The Fur Trade of the Far West.* 2 vols. 1902. Reprint. New York: The Press of the Pioneers, 1935.

‡Clay, Charles. *Fur Trade Apprentice.* New York: Oxford University Press, 1940.

Cleland, Robert Glass. *This Reckless Breed of Men: The Trappers and Fur Traders of the Southwest.* New York: Knopf, 1950.

Clokey, Richard M. *William Ashley: Enterprise and Politics in the Trans-Mississippi West.* Norman: University of Oklahoma Press, 1980.

Cohen, Hennig. *Humor of the Old Southwest.* 1964. Reprint. Athens: University of Georgia Press, 1994.

Collinson, Francis. *The Bagpipe: The History of a Musical Instrument.* Boston: Routledge & Kegan Paul, 1975.

†Conard, Howard L. *"Uncle Dick" Wootton: The Pioneer Frontiersman of the Rocky Mountain Region.* Chicago: W. E. Dibble & Co., 1890.

‡Cooper, Courtney. *The Pioneers.* Boston: Little, Brown and Co., 1938.

†Coyner, David H. *The Lost Trappers: A Collection of Interesting Scenes and Events in the Rocky Mountains.* 1847. Reprint. Glorieta, NM: Rio Grande Press, 1969.

Cracroft, Richard H. *"The Big Sky:* A. B. Guthrie's Use of Historical Sources." *Western American Literature* 6 (1971): 163–76.

———. *Washington Irving: The Western Works.* Boise, ID: Boise State University, 1974.

Craighead, Frank. *Track of the Grizzly.* San Francisco: Sierra Club, 1979.

‡Cranston, Paul. *To Heaven on Horseback.* New York: Julian Messner, 1953.

Cutler, Charles L. *O Brave New Words!: Native American Loanwords in Current English.* Norman: University of Oklahoma Press, 1994.

Dary, David. *The Buffalo Book.* Chicago: Sage Books, 1974.

Deacon, Richard. *Madoc and the Discovery of America: Some New Light on an Old Controversy.* New York: Braziller, 1967.

Deloria, Vine, Jr. *Custer Died for Your Sins: An Indian Manifesto.* New York: Macmillan, 1969.

‡Derleth, August. *Bright Journey.* New York: Scribner's Sons, 1939.

‡———. *Empire of Fur: Trading in the Lake Superior Region.* New York: Aladdin Books, 1953.

De Voto, Bernard. *Across the Wide Missouri.* Boston: Houghton Mifflin, 1947.

Drury, Clifford Merrill. *Henry Harmon Spalding.* Caldwell, ID: Caxton Printers, 1936.

———. *Marcus and Narcissa Whitman, and the Opening of Old Oregon.* Glendale, CA: Arthur H. Clark, 1973.

‡Duffus, R. L. *Jornada.* New York: Covici, Friede, 1935.

†Dye, Job Francis. *Recollections of a Pioneer, 1830–1852.* Los Angeles: G. Dawson, 1951.

†Eells, Myra. "Journal of Myra F. Eells." *Transactions of the Seventeenth Annual Reunion of the Oregon Pioneer Association for 1889.* Portland, OR: Himes Printing Co., 1890.

‡Eggleston, George C. *Long Knives.* Boston: Lothrop, Lee, and Shepard, 1907.

Ehrlich, Paul R. *Extinction: The Causes and Consequences of the Disappearance of Species.* New York: Random House, 1981.

Epstein, Barbara Leslie. *The Politics of Domesticity: Women, Evangelism, and Temperance in Nineteenth-Century America.* Middletown, CT: Wesleyan University Press, 1981.

Etulain, Richard W., and N. Jill Howard, eds. *A Bibliographical Guide to the Study of Western American Literature.* 2nd ed. Albuquerque: University of New Mexico Press, 1995.

‡Evarts, Hal G. *Fur Brigade: A Story of the Trappers of the Early West.* Boston: Little, Brown, and Co., 1928.

‡————. *Fur Sign.* Boston: Little, Brown, and Co., 1922.

Ewers, John C. *The Horse in Blackfoot Indian Culture.* 1955. Reprint. Washington, D.C.: Smithsonian Institution Press, 1980.

————. *Views of a Vanishing Frontier.* Omaha: Center for Western Studies/Joslyn Art Museum, 1984.

†Farnham, Thomas Jefferson. *Travels in the Great Western Prairies.* 2 vols. London: Richard Bently, 1843.

Farrell, James J. *Inventing the American Way of Death, 1830–1920.* Philadelphia: Temple University Press, 1980.

Favour, Alpheus Hoyt. *Old Bill Williams, Mountain Man.* 1936. Reprint. Norman: University of Oklahoma Press, 1962.

Feltskog, Elmer Nathaniel. "Francis Parkman's *The Oregon Trail*: A Textual Edition and Critical Study." Ph.D. diss., University of Illinois, 1966.

‡Fergusson, Harvey. *Grant of Kingdom.* New York: Morrow, 1950.

‡————. *Wolf Song.* New York: Knopf, 1927.

†Ferris, Warren Angus. *Life in the Rocky Mountains: A Diary of Wanderings on the Sources of the Rivers Missouri, Columbia, and Colorado: 1830–1835*. 1843. Reprint. Denver: Old West Publishing Co., 1983.

†Field, Mathew C. *Prairie and Mountain Sketches*. Norman: University of Oklahoma Press, 1957.

Fisher, Vardis. *The Mothers: An American Saga of Courage*. New York: Vanguard, 1943.

‡———. *Mountain Man*. New York: Morrow, 1965.

†Flint, Timothy. *The Shoshonee Valley*. 2 vols. Cincinnati: E. H. Flint, 1830.

Flores, Dan. "Bison Ecology and Bison Diplomacy: The Southern Plains from 1800–1850." *Journal of American History* 78 (1991): 465–85.

Folsom, James K. "Precursors of the Western Novel." In *A Literary History of the American West*, edited by J. Golden Taylor et al. Fort Worth: Texas Christian University Press, 1987.

———. *Timothy Flint*. New York: Twayne, 1965.

‡Footner, Hulbert. *The Fur Bringers: A Story of the Canadian Northwest*. New York: James A. McCann Co., 1920.

Ford, Alice. *John James Audubon: A Biography*. New York: Abbeville Press, 1988.

Foster, Edward Halsey. *Josiah Gregg and Lewis H. Garrard*. Boise, ID: Boise State University, 1977.

†Fowler, Jacob. *The Journal of Jacob Fowler*. 1898. Reprint. Minneapolis: Ross & Haines, 1965.

†Frémont, John C. *Report of the Exploring Expedition to the Rocky Mountains in the Years 1843–'44*. Washington: Blair and Rives, 1845.

‡Gabriel, Gilbert. *I, James Lewis*. Garden City, NY: Doubleday, Doran and Co., 1935.

†Garrard, Lewis H. *Wah-to-Yah and the Taos Trail*. 1850. Glendale, CA: Arthur H. Clark, 1938.

Gaston, Edwin. *The Early Novel of the Southwest.* Albuquerque: University of New Mexico Press, 1961.

Gilbert, Bil. *Westering Man: The Life of Joseph Walker.* New York: Atheneum, 1983.

‡Giles, Janice Holt. *The Great Adventure.* Boston: Houghton Mifflin Co., 1966.

‡————. *Johnny Osage.* Boston: Houghton Mifflin Co., 1960.

Goetzmann, William H. *Exploration and Empire: The Explorer and the Scientist in the Winning of the American West.* New York: Knopf, 1966.

Goetzmann, William H., and William N. Goetzmann. *The West of the Imagination.* New York: Norton, 1986.

Gowans, Fred R. *Rocky Mountain Rendezvous: A History of the Fur Trade Rendezvous, 1825–1840.* Layton, UT: Gibbs Smith, 1985.

†Gray, W. H. *A History of Oregon: 1792–1849.* Portland, OR: Harris & Holman; San Francisco: H. H. Bancroft; New York: American News Co., 1870.

Greenfield, Bruce. *Narrating Discovery: The Romantic Explorer in American Literature, 1790–1855.* New York: Columbia University Press, 1992.

†Gregg, Josiah. *Commerce of the Prairies: Journal of a Santa Fe Trader.* 2 vols. New York: Henry G. Langely, 1844.

Gregory, R. L. "The Confounded Eye." In *Illusion in Nature and Art,* edited by R. L. Gregory and E. H. Gombrich. [London]: Duckworth, 1973.

Grinnell, George Bird. *Beyond the Old Frontier: Adventures of Indian-Fighters, Hunters and Fur-Traders.* 1913. Reprint. Williamstown, MA: Corner House, 1976.

‡Guthrie, A. B., Jr. *The Big Sky.* Boston: Houghton Mifflin, 1947.

‡————. *Fair Land, Fair Land.* Boston: Houghton Mifflin, 1947.

————. "The Historical Novel." *Montana Magazine of History* 4 (1954): 1–8.

‡————. "Mountain Medicine." In *The Big It, and Other Stories.* Boston: Houghton Mifflin, 1960: 132–50.

‡————. *The Way West.* New York: William Sloane, 1949.

Hafen, LeRoy Reuben, ed. *The Mountain Men and the Fur Trade of the Far West.* 10 vols. Glendale, CA: Arthur H. Clark, 1965–1972.

Haig, Bruce. *Paul Kane, Artist.* 1971. Reprint. Calgary: Detselig Enterprises, 1984.

‡Hamele, Ottamar. *When Destiny Called.* San Antonio: Naylor Co., 1948.

†Hamilton, William Thomas. *My Sixty Years on the Plains: Trapping, Trading, and Indian Fighting.* New York: Forest and Stream Publishing Co., 1905.

Hanson, James Austin. *The Mountain Man's Sketch Book.* 1976. Reprint. Chadron, NE: Fur Press, 1982.

Harris, Burton. *John Colter: His Years in the Rockies.* New York: Scribners, 1952.

Herrero, Stephen. *Bear Attacks: Their Causes and Avoidance.* Piscataway, NJ: Winchester Press, 1985.

Holbrook, Stewart. *The Columbia.* New York: Rinehart, 1974.

Horgan, Paul. *Josiah Gregg and His Vision of the Early Far West.* New York: Farrar Straus and Giroux, 1979.

‡Hotchkiss, Bill. *Ammahabas.* New York: Norton, 1983.

‡————. *The Medicine Calf.* New York: Norton, 1981.

‡Hueston, Ethel. *The Man of the Storm.* New York: Bobbs-Merrill Co., 1948.

†Humfreville, J. Lee. *Twenty Years among Our Savage Indians.* 1897. Reprint. Hartford, CT: A. D. Worthington, 1901.

Inge, M. Thomas. *The Frontier Humorists.* Hamden, CT: Archon Books, 1975.

†Irving, Washington. *The Adventures of Captain Bonneville.* 1837. Reprint. Boston: Twayne Publishers, 1977.

†————. *Astoria: Or Anecdotes of an Enterprise Beyond the Rocky Mountains.* 1836. Reprint. Boston: Twayne Publishers, 1976.

————. *A Tour of the Prairies.* Philadelphia: Carey, Lea & Blanchard, 1835.

†James, Thomas. *Three Years Among the Indians and Mexicans.* 1846. Reprint. New York: Citadel Press, 1967.

‡Jennings, John. *River to the West.* Garden City, NY: Doubleday, 1948.

Jones, Daryl. *The Dime Novel Western.* Bowling Green, OH: Popular Press, 1978.

Jones, Howard Mumford. *O Strange New World: American Culture, the Formative Years.* New York: Viking, 1964.

‡Jones, Nard. *Scarlet Petticoat.* New York: Dodd, Mead and Co., 1941.

Josephy, Alvin M. *The Nez Perce Indians and the Opening of the Northwest.* New Haven: Yale University Press, 1965.

†Kane, Paul. *Paul Kane's Frontier: The Wanderings of an Artist Among the Indians of North America.* Austin: University of Texas Press, 1971.

Karolevitz, Robert F. *Doctors of the Old West: A Pictorial History of Medicine on the Frontier.* Seattle: Superior Publishing, 1967.

Kelley, Klara Bonsack, and Harris Francis. *Navajo Sacred Places.* Bloomington: Indiana University Press, 1994.

Kelly, Lawrence C. *Navajo Roundup: Selected Correspondence of Kit Carsons's Expedition Against the Navajo, 1863–1865.* Boulder, CO: Pruett, 1970.

Kent, Kate Peck. *The Story of Navajo Weaving.* Phoenix: Heard Museum of Anthropology and Primitive Arts, 1961.

Kerr, Howard. *Mediums, and Spirit Rappers, and Roaring Radicals: Spiritualism in American Literature, 1850–1900.* Urbana: University of Illinois Press, 1972.

Lamar, Howard R. *The Trader on the American Frontier: Myth's Victim.* College Station: Texas A&M University Press, 1977.

Lamar, Howard R., ed. *The Reader's Encyclopedia of the American West.* New York: Crowell, 1977.

Lambert, Neal. *George Frederick Ruxton.* Boise, ID: Boise State University, 1974.

†Larpenteur, Charles. *Forty Years a Fur Trader on the Upper Missouri: The Personal Narrative of Charles Larpenteur, 1833–1872.* Minneapolis: Ross & Haines, 1962.

Laughlin, Ruth. *The Wind Leaves No Shadow.* New York: McGraw-Hill, 1948.

Lavender, David. *Bent's Fort.* Garden City, NY: Doubleday, 1954.

Lee, Robert Edson. *From West to East: Studies in the Literature of the American West.* Urbana: University of Illinois Press, 1966.

†Leonard, Zenas. *Narrative of the Adventures of Zenas Leonard.* 1839. Reprint. Lincoln: University of Nebraska Press, 1978.

Lewis, Oscar. *The Effects of White Contact upon Blackfoot Culture, with Special Reference to the Role of the Fur Trade.* New York: J.J. Augustin, 1942.

Limerick, Patricia Nelson. *The Legacy of Conquest: The Unbroken Past of the American West.* New York: Norton, 1987.

‡Linderman, Frank Bird. *Beyond Law.* New York: John Day Co., 1933.

‡————. *Morning Light.* New York: Scribners, 1922.

London, Jack. "The Law of Life." *McClure's Magazine* (March 1901): 435–38.

Lopez, Barry. *Of Wolves and Men.* New York: Scribners, 1978.

Luchetti, Cathy. *Under God's Spell: Frontier Evangelists, 1772–1915.* New York: Harcourt, Brace, Jovanovich, 1989.

Lynn, Kenneth S. *Mark Twain and Southwestern Humor.* Westport, CT: Greenwood Press, 1959.

Lyon, Thomas J. *This Incomperable Lande: A Book of American Nature Writing.* Boston: Houghton Mifflin, 1989.

‡Manfred, Frederick. *Lord Grizzly.* New York: McGraw-Hill, 1954.

Martin, Jim. *A Bit of a Blue: The Life and Work of Frances Fuller Victor.* Salem, OR: Deep Well Publishing, 1992.

McCarthy, Patrick. "The Characterization of the Mountain Man as Depicted in Documentary Film." Ph.D. diss., Bowling Green State University, 1986.

McCoy, Genevieve. "Sanctifying the Self and Saving the Savage: The Failure of the ABCFM Oregon Mission and the Conflicted Language of Calvinism." Ph.D. diss., University of Washington, 1991.

‡McGuire, Jerry. *Elijah.* Flagstaff, AZ: Northland Press, 1954.

McLoughlin, Denis. *Wild and Woolly: An Encyclopedia of the Old West.* Garden City, NY: Doubleday, 1975.

‡Millard, Joseph. *Cut-Hand, the Mountain Man.* Philadelphia: Chilton Books, 1964.

Miller, Alfred Jacob. *Braves and Buffalo: Plains Indian Life in 1837.* Toronto: University of Toronto Press, 1973.

†————. *The West of Alfred Jacob Miller.* Norman: University of Oklahoma Press, 1951.

Millichap, Joseph R. *George Catlin.* Boise, ID: Boise State University, 1977.

Milner, Clyde A., Carol A. O'Connor, and Martha A. Sandweiss, eds. *The Oxford History of the American West.* New York: Oxford University Press, 1994.

Milton, John R. "*Lord Grizzly*: Rhythm, Form, and Meaning in the Western Novel." *Western American Literature* 1 (1966): 6–14.

————. *The Novel of the American West.* Lincoln: University of Nebraska Press, 1980.

Moore, Jackson W. *Bent's Old Fort: An Archeological Study.* Denver: State Historical Society of Colorado, 1973.

Morgan, Dale L. *The Humboldt: Highroad of the West.* New York: Farrar & Rinehart, 1943.

————. *Jedediah Smith and the Opening of the West.* 1953. Lincoln: University of Nebraska Press, 1964.

Mumey, Nolie. *James Pierson Beckwourth, 1856–1866.* Denver: Old West Publishing, 1957.

Murray, John A., ed. *The Great Bear: Contemporary Writings on the Grizzly.* Anchorage: Alaska Northwest Books, 1992.

Myers, John. *Pirate, Pawnee, and Mountain Man: The Saga of Hugh Glass.* Boston: Little, Brown, 1963.

Nevin, David. *Dream West.* New York: Putnam, 1983.

†Newell, Robert. *Robert Newell's Memoranda.* Portland, OR: Champoeg Press, 1959.

Newman, Peter Charles. *Company of Adventurers.* New York: Viking, 1985.

Nichols, Claude Andrew. *Moral Education among the North American Indians.* 1930. Reprint. New York: AMS Press, 1972.

†Ogden, Peter Skene. "The Peter Skene Ogden Journals." Edited by T. C. Eliott. *Quarterly of the Oregon Historical Society* 10 (1909): 337–75.

‡O'Hagan, Howard. *Tay John.* 1974. Reprint. Toronto: McClelland and Stewart, 1989.

O'Meara, Walter. *Daughters of the Country: The Women of the Fur Traders and Mountain Men.* New York: Harcourt, Brace, and World, 1968.

†Parker, Samuel. *Journal of an Exploring Tour Beyond the Rocky Mountains.* 1838. Reprint. Minneapolis: Ross & Haines, 1967.

†Parkman, Francis. *The Oregon Trail.* 1849. Reprint. New York: Viking Press, 1991.

‡Parrish, Randall. *The Devil's Own.* New York: A. L. Burt Co., 1917.

‡Pendexter, Hugh. *Kings of the Missouri.* Indianapolis: Bobbs-Merrill, 1920.

Peters, De Witt C. *The Life and Adventures of Kit Carson: The Nestor of the Rocky Mountains, from Facts Narrated by Himself.* New York: W. R. C. Clark & Meeker, 1858.

Phillips, Paul C. *The Fur Trade.* Norman: University of Oklahoma Press, 1961.

Pilkington, William T. "The Southwestern Novels of Harvey Fergusson." *New Mexico Quarterly* 35 (1965–66): 330–43.

Pollard, Juliet Thelma. "The Making of the Metis in the Pacific Northwest; Fur Trade Children: Race, Class, and Gender." Ph.D. diss., University of British Columbia, 1990.

Poulsen, Richard C. *The Mountain Man Vernacular: Its Historical Roots, Its Linguistic Nature, and its Literary Uses.* New York: Peter Lang, 1985.

Reedstrom, Ernest Lisle. *Historic Dress of the Old West.* Poole, UK: Blandford Press, 1986.

†Reid, Mayne. *The Scalp Hunters: Or, Adventures among the Trappers.* New York: Robert M. DeWitt, 1851.

‡Reynolds, Helen Mary Greenwood Campbell. *The Fur Brigade.* New York: Funk and Wagnalls, 1953.

Reynolds, Karen Dewees. *Alfred Jacob Miller: Artist on the Oregon Trail.* Fort Worth: Amon Carter Museum, 1982.

‡Roberts, Richard. *The Gilded Rooster.* New York: G. P. Putnam's Sons, 1947.

Robertson, Frank Chester. *Fort Hall, Gateway to the Oregon Country.* New York: Hastings House, 1963.

Rolle, Andrew F. *John Charles Frémont: Character as Destiny.* Norman: University of Oklahoma Press, 1991.

Ronda, James P. *Astoria and Empire.* Lincoln: University of Nebraska Press, 1990.

†Ross, Alexander. *Adventures of the First Settlers on the Oregon or Columbia River.* London: Smith, Elder, & Co., 1849.

Russell, O. P. *Firearms, Traps, and Tools of the Mountain Man.* New York: Alfred A. Knopf, 1967.

†Russell, Osborne. *Journal of a Trapper, or, Nine Years in the Rocky Mountains, 1834–1843.* 1914. Reprint. Lincoln: University of Nebraska Press, 1965.

†Ruxton, George Frederick. *Adventures in Mexico and the Rocky Mountains.* 1847. Reprint. Glorieta, NM: Rio Grande Press, 1973.

†———. *Life in the Far West.* 1849. Reprint. Norman: University of Oklahoma Press, 1951.

Sabin, Edwin L. *Kit Carson Days: 1809–1868.* Chicago: A. C. McClurg & Co., 1914.

‡———. *White Indian.* New York: A. L. Burt, 1925.

Sacks, Oliver. *The Man Who Mistook His Wife for a Hat and Other Clinical Tales.* New York: Summit Books, 1985.

†Sage, Rufus B. *Scenes in the Rocky Mountains.* Philadelphia: Carey & Hart, 1846.

Saldívar Mendoza, Vicente de. "Account of the Discovery of the Buffalo, 1599 . . ." In *Into the Wilderness Dream*, edited by Donald A. Barclay, James H. Maguire, and Peter Wild. Salt Lake City: University of Utah Press, 1994.

Saum, Lewis O. *The Fur Trader and the Indian.* Seattle: University of Washington Press, 1965.

Schoenberg, Wilfred P. *The Lapwai Mission Press.* Boise: Idaho Center for the Book, 1994.

‡Seifert, Shirley. *Those Who Go Against the Current.* New York: J. B. Lippincott Co., 1943.

Shoemaker, Nancy. *Negotiators of Change: Historical Perspectives on Native American Women.* New York: Routledge, 1995.

Slotkin, Richard. *The Fatal Environment: The Myth of the Frontier in the Age of Industrialization, 1800–1890.* New York: Atheneum, 1985.

———. *Gunfighter Nation: The Myth of the Frontier in Twentieth Century America.* New York: Atheneum, 1992.

———. *Regeneration Through Violence: The Mythology of the American Frontier.* Middletown, CT: Wesleyan University Press, 1973.

Smith, Henry Nash. *Virgin Land: The American West as Symbol and Myth.* Cambridge, MA: Harvard University Press, 1950.

†Smith, Jedediah. *The Travels of Jedediah Smith: A Documentary Outline Including the Journal of the Great American Pathfinder.* 1934. Reprint. Lincoln: University of Nebraska Press, 1992.

†Smith, Sarah Gilbert White. "Diary of Sarah White Smith." In *First White Women over the Rockies.* 3 vols., edited by Clifford Drury. Glendale, CA: Arthur H. Clark, 1966.

Snyder, Gary. *The Practice of the Wild.* San Francisco: North Point Press, 1990.

Southey, Robert. *Madoc.* London: Longman, Hurst, Rees, and Orme, 1807.

Speck, Gordon. *Breeds and Half-Breeds.* New York: Clarkson N. Potter, 1969.

‡Sperry, Armstrong. *No Brighter Glory.* New York: Macmillan Co., 1942.

Statham, Dawn Stram. *Camas and the Northern Shoshone: A Biogeographic and Socioeconomic Analysis.* BSU Archaeological Reports, no. 10. Boise: Boise State University, 1982.

Stearn, E. Wagner. *The Effect of Smallpox on the Destiny of the Amerindian.* Boston: B. Humphries, 1945.

Stenger, Victor J. *Physics and Psychics: The Search for a World beyond the Senses.* Buffalo, NY: Prometheus Books, 1990.

Steele, Joan. *Captain Mayne Reid.* Boston: Twayne, 1978.

Stewart, George R. *Names on the Land.* Boston: Houghton Mifflin, 1958.

―――. *Ordeal by Hunger: The Story of the Donner Party.* Boston: Houghton Mifflin, 1960.

†Stewart, William Drummond. *Edward Warren.* 1854. Reprint. Missoula, MT: Mountain Press Publishing, 1986.

Stouck, David. "The Art of the Mountain Man Novel." *Western American Literature* 20 (1985): 211–22.

Streshinsky, Shirley. *Audubon: Life and Art in the American Wilderness.* New York: Villard Books, 1993.

†Stuart, Robert. *On the Oregon Trail: Robert Stuart's Journal of Discovery.* Norman: University of Oklahoma Press, 1953.

Swagerty, William R. "Marriage and Settlement Patterns of Rocky Mountain Trappers and Traders." *Western Historical Quarterly* 11 (1980): 159–80.

Taylor, J. Golden. "Across the Wide Missouri: The Adventure Narrative from Lewis and Clark to Powell." In *A Literary History of the American West,* edited by J. Golden Taylor et al. Fort Worth: Texas Christian University Press, 1987.

―――. *The Literature of the American West.* Boston: Houghton Mifflin, 1971.

‡Terrell, John Upton. *Plume Rouge.* New York: Viking, 1942.

†Thorp, Raymond W., and Robert Bunker. *Crow Killer: The Saga of Liver-Eating Johnson.* 1958. Reprint. Bloomington: Indiana University Press, 1969.

Thrapp, Dan L. *Encyclopedia of Frontier Biography.* 4 vols. Glendale, CA: Arthur H. Clark, 1988 and 1994.

Todd, Edgeley W. "James Hall and the Hugh Glass Legend." *American Quarterly* 7 (1955): 363–70.

———. "A Note on 'The Mountain Man as Literary Hero.' " *Western American Literature* 1 (1966): 219–21.

———. "Literary Interest in the Fur Trade and Fur Trapper of the Trans-Mississippi West." Ph.D. diss., Northwestern University, 1952.

Todorov, Tzvetan. *The Conquest of America: The Question of the Other.* 1982. Reprint. New York: Harper, 1984.

†Townsend, John Kirk. *Narrative of a Journey across the Rocky Mountains to the Columbia River.* 1839. Reprint. Lincoln: University of Nebraska Press, 1978.

Trimble, Michael K. *An Ethnohistorical Interpretation of the Spread of Smallpox in the Northern Plains Utilizing Concepts of Disease Ecology.* Lincoln: J & L Reprint, 1986.

Trusky, Tom. "Western Poetry, 1850–1950." In *A Literary History of the American West,* edited by J. Golden Taylor et al. Fort Worth: Texas Christian University Press, 1987.

Twain, Mark. *Life on the Mississippi.* Boston, J. R. Osgood, 1883.

‡Van Every, Dale. *The Shining Mountains.* New York: Julian Messner, Inc., 1948.

Van Kirk, Sylvia. *"Many Tender Ties": Women in Fur-Trade Society in Western Canada, 1670–1870.* Winnipeg: Watson and Dwyer, 1980.

‡Vestal, Stanley. *Revolt on the Border.* Boston: Houghton Mifflin Co., 1938.

Victor, Frances Fuller. *Alicia Newcome, Or, The Land Claim: A Tale of the Upper Missouri.* New York: Beadle, 1862.

———. *East and West, Or, The Beauty of Willard's Mill.* New York: Beadle, 1862.

†———. *River of the West: Life and Adventures in the Rocky Mountains and Oregon.* Hartford, CT: R. W. Bliss & Co., 1870.

Victor, Frances Fuller, and Metta Victoria Fuller Victor. *Poems of Sentiment and Imagination.* New York: A. S. Barnes & Co., 1870.

Walker, Don D. "Can the Western Tell What Happens?" *Rendezvous* 7 (1972): 33–47.

———. "The Hollow Men, or, What's Hidden Beneath the Skin Beneath the Buckskin Shirt?" *The Possible Sack* 1 (1970): 1–5.

———. "The Mountain Man as Literary Hero." *Western American Literature* 1 (1966): 15–25.

†Walker, Mary, and Myra Eells. "Mrs. Elkanah Walker and Mrs. Cushing Eells." In *First White Women over the Rockies.* 3 vols., edited by Clifford Drury. Glendale, CA: Arthur H. Clark, 1963.

‡Wallace, Dillon. *The Fur Traders of Kettle Harbor.* Chicago: Fleming H. Revell Co., 1931.

‡———. *The Fur Trail Adventurers.* Chicago: A. C. McClurg and Co., 1915.

Walters, Anna Lee. *Talking Indian: Reflections on Survival and Writing.* Ithaca, NY: Firebrand Books, 1992.

Waters, Frank. *The Colorado.* New York: Rinehart, 1946.

Weber, David J. *The Taos Trappers: The Fur Trade in the Far Southwest, 1540–1846.* Norman: University of Oklahoma Press, 1971.

‡Welch, James. *Fools Crow.* New York: Viking, 1986.

Whelan, Mary K. "Dakota Economics and the Nineteenth-Century Fur Trade." *Ethnohistory* 40 (1993): 246–76.

White, Richard. "Animals and Enterprise." In *The Oxford History of the American West,* edited by Clyde A. Milner, II, Carol A. O'Connor, and Martha A. Sandweiss. New York: Oxford University Press, 1994.

‡White, Stewart Edward. *Folded Hills.* Garden City, NY: Doubleday, Doran, 1934.

‡———. *The Long Rifle.* Garden City, NY: Doubleday, Doran, 1932.

‡———. *Ranchero.* Garden City, NY: Doubleday, Doran, 1933.

†Whitman, Narcissa. "The Coming of the White Women." Edited by H. E. Tobie. *Oregon Historical Quarterly* 38 (1937): 206–23.

Whitman, William. *The Oto.* 1937. Reprint. New York: AMS Press, 1969.

†Wied, Maximilian, Prinz von. *Travels in the Interior of North America.* London: Ackerman and Co., 1863.

Wild, Peter. *The Desert Reader: Descriptions of America's Arid Regions.* Salt Lake City: University of Utah Press, 1991.

Wishart, David J. *The Fur Trade of the American West, 1807–1840: A Geographical Synthesis.* 1979. Reprint. Lincoln: University of Nebraska Press, 1992.

Wolf, Eric Robert. *Europe and the People Without History.* Berkeley: University of California Press, 1982.

Work, James C. *Prose and Poetry of the American West.* Lincoln: University of Nebraska Press, 1991.

†Work, John. *The Snake Country Expedition of 1830–1831: John Work's Field Journal.* Norman: University of Oklahoma Press, 1971.

Wright, Louis B. *Culture on the Moving Frontier.* Bloomington: Indiana University Press, 1955.

†Wyeth, John B. *Oregon: Or a Short History of a Long Journey.* Cambridge, MA: John B. Wyeth, 1833.

†Wyeth, Nathaniel J. *Correspondence and Journals of Captain Nathaniel J. Wyeth, 1831–1836.* Eugene, OR: University of Oregon Press, 1899.

†————. *The Journals of Captain Nathaniel J. Wyeth's Expeditions to the Oregon Country, 1831–1836.* 1899. Reprint. Fairfield, WA: Ye Galleon Press, 1984.

†Yount, George C. *George C. Yount and His Chronicles of the West.* Denver: Old West Publishing, 1966.

Permissions

Gratitude is expressed to the following for permission to reprint extracts from materials copyrighted or controlled by them:

The Bancroft Library, University of California, Berkeley, for *Recollections of a Pioneer,* from Job Francis Dye, "Recollections of California since 1832," dictated to Thomas Savage on 17 July 1877 (BANC MSS C-D 69).

The Arthur H. Clark Company for *John Ball, Member of the Wyeth Expedition to the Pacific Northwest, 1832;* and *Pioneer in the Old Northwest: Autobiography* by John Ball, © 1925; *First White Women over the Rockies: Diaries, letter, and Biographical Sketches of Six Women of the Oregon Mission who made the Overland Journey in 1836 and 1838,* ed. Clifford Merrill Drury, Vol. 2, *Mrs. Elkanah Walker and Mrs. Cushing Eells,* © 1963; *First White Women over the Rockies: Diaries, Letter, and Biographical Sketches of the Six Women of the Oregon Mission who made the Overland Journey in 1936 and 1938,* ed. Clifford Merrill Drury, Vol. 3, *Diary of Sarah White Smith,* © 1966; and *The Southwest Expedition of Jedediah S. Smith: His Personal Account of the Journey to California, 1826–1827,* ed. George R. Brooks, © 1977.

The Huntington Library, San Marino, California, for *The Rocky Mountain Journals of William Marshall Anderson* (1967) by William Henry Anderson (AD 371 (A&B)). Reprinted with Permission.

Montana: The Magazine of Western History for "Lou Devon's Narrative: A Tale of the Mandans' Lost Years," by Will Bagley, vol. 43 (Winter 1993).

The South Dakota State Historical Society for *Chardon's Journal at Fort Clark, 1834–1839,* edited by Annie Heloise Abel, © 1932 by the South Dakota State Historical Society. All Rights Reserved. Reprinted with Permission.

The University of Oklahoma Press for *The West of Alfred Jacob Miller* by Marvin C. Ross, © 1951; *On the Oregon Trail* by Robert Stuart, © 1953; and *The Snake Country Expedition of 1830–1831* by John Work, © 1971.

Gratitude is expressed to The Walters Art Gallery, Baltimore, Maryland, for permission to reproduce the following art by Alfred Jacob Miller: *Trappers Starting for Beaver Hunt* (37.1940.1); *Preparing for a Buffalo Hunt* (37.1940.2); *Hunting Elk among the Black Hills* (37.1940.3); *Camp Fire, Preparing for the Evening Meal* (37.1940.4); *Auguste and his Horse* (37.1940.10); *The Trapper's Bride* (37.1940.12); *Scene on Big Sandy River* (37.1940.20); *The Thirsty Trapper* (37.1940.26); *Trappers* (37.1940.29); *The Grizzly Bear* (37.1940.32); *Roasting the Hump Rib* (37.1940.36); *Laramie's Fort* (37.1940.49); *Caravan "En Route"* (37.1940.51); *Breakfast at Sunrise* (37.1940.52); *Escaping from Blackfeet* (37.1940.67); *Threatened Attack* (37.1940.76); *Bourgeois W———r and his Squaw (Mountain Man Joe Walker)* (37.1940.78); *Large Encampment Near the Cut Rocks* (37.1940.110); *Trapping Beaver* (37.1940.111); *The Grizzly Bear* (37.1940.125); *The Greeting* (37.1940.133); *Moonlight—Camp Scene* (37.1940.135); *The Lost Greenhorn* (37.1940.141); *Interior of Fort Laramie* (37.1940.150); *Free Trappers in Trouble* (37.1940.163); *Attack by Crow Indians* (37.1940.179).

Index